Children living with domestic violence

Towards a framework for assessment and intervention

Martin C. Calder

with

Dr Gordon T. Harold and Emma L. Howarth

RHP

Russell House Publishing

First published in 2004 by:
Russell House Publishing Ltd.
4 St George's House
Uplyme Road
Lyme Regis
Dorset DT7 3LS

Tel: 01297-443948
Fax: 01297-442722
e-mail: help@russellhouse.co.uk
www.russellhouse.co.uk

Reprinted 2005

British Library Cataloguing-in-publication Data:
A catalogue record for this book is available from the British Library.

ISBN: 1-903855-45-4

Typeset by TW Typesetting, Plymouth, Devon
© Front cover design by Stacey Laura Calder
Printed by Bath Press, Bath

Russell House Publishing
is a group of social work, probation, education and youth and community work practitioners and academics working in collaboration with a professional publishing team.
Our aim is to work closely with the field to produce innovative and valuable materials to help managers, trainers, practitioners and students.
We are keen to receive feedback on publications and new ideas for future projects.
For details of our other publications please visit our website or ask us for a catalogue. Contact details are on this page.

Contents

List of Figures

To Janet, Stacey and Emma: for reminding me
that what matters most is what happens at home.

Martin C. Calder

Acknowledgements

To my wife Janet: for supporting me in my writing.

To Kate Rose for her pioneering work in the production of sensible practice guidance in domestic violence.

To Gordon T. Harold and Emma L. Howarth for contributing a chapter of such high quality and impact.

To frontline workers for their dedication to the task in such difficult times.

To Debbie Hulme for her creative imagery on the computer.

Martin C. Calder
January 2004

About the authors

Martin C. Calder MA CQSW is Team Manager of the Child Protection Unit for City of Salford Community and Social Services Directorate. He has published extensively on assessment frameworks in child protection and is driven to produce accessible, informed, credible and evidence-based frameworks for busy frontline staff. Martin also operates as an Independent Social Work Trainer and Consultant and is contactable on *martinccalder@aol.com*

Gordon T. Harold PhD is a Senior Lecturer in the School of Psychology at Cardiff University, Wales. Originally from Dublin, he completed his PhD at Cardiff in 1998, having previously studied and worked as a researcher at the Institute for Social and Behavioural Research, Iowa State University (USA). His research interests focus on the relationship between adaptive and maladaptive family functioning and children's normal and abnormal development, with specific interest in the effects of interparental conflict on children's emotional and behavioural development.

Emma L. Howarth BSc, MSc (Cardiff University) is a doctoral student in the School of Psychology at Cardiff University, Wales. Her research interests relate to child and adolescent development in the context of interparental violence, with a particular focus on the processes that explain the development of children's emotional and behavioural problems.

Chapter One

Introduction

Domestic violence is a criminal problem, a social problem as well as a public health issue. It also represents a violation of human rights and causes far reaching damage to people's lives and development. It is only in recent times that professionals have acknowledged that we cannot protect children and young people from the multiple impacts of domestic violence (directly or indirectly) and that the prognosis for effecting any change is poor (Cleaver et al., 1999). This realisation requires that we as professionals:

- Must challenge myths surrounding domestic violence, such as women/children invite, provoke or deserve violence; or that men who perpetrate violence are somehow different from other men because they are sick or out of control. These are excuses, not causes.
- Must develop a detailed understanding of the impact on the adult and child survivors of domestic violence.
- Unite to produce a system of response that does not replicate their experiences and in fact facilitates their recovery from any trauma.
- Produce local procedures, practice guidance and principles of good practice to guide consistent, effective interventions, enabling survivors to make their own life choices and be free from violence. Unfortunately, child protection systems currently target women and not perpetrators and consequently concentrate on the women's ability to parent and protect rather than focusing on the impact of the man's behaviour on others.
- Must empower the adult survivor, protect the children and challenge the perpetrator.
- Import good practice from associated fields. For example, the practice of seeing mothers of sexually abused children as secondary perpetrators rather than secondary victims has alienated mothers when they offer the best buffer of the effects of child sexual abuse process for their offspring. Such a clear negative outcome has to be challenged and the ways of reversing this articulated and applied. For a detailed discussion of engaging mothers as survivors please refer to Calder, Peake and Rose (2001).

Domestic violence can be harder to deal with than violence on the streets:

- It occurs in relationships, where emotions may be high and loyalties divided.
- Myths and outdated attitudes remain about a form of violence that was historically acceptable.
- Much of the violence takes place behind closed doors.

Shaw et al. (1999) identified some useful goals for intervention with children and their families as being to:

- Provide competent and thorough assessment of the actual violence and its effects on individual family members.
- Heighten the parents' capacity to perceive and respond to their children's needs separately from their own.
- Emphasise that the focus of responsibility for the violence does not rest with the child.
- Help parents make more child-focused decisions.
- Protect children from conflict and ensure safety.
- Break down the intergenerational transmission of violence.
- Focus on more egalitarian relationships.
- Heal and change family relationships.

(p 254)

Burke (1999) argued that child-focused family work with children and families in which there are both domestic violence and child protection concerns prioritise the safety and protection of children. At the same time, the intervention aims to empower and ensure the safety of mothers by placing accountability and responsibility for the violence and its effects with the male perpetrator.

This book attempts to provide some guidance to professionals to help guide them through the points identified above. It endeavours to integrate the best of theory, research and practice wisdom and package it in a coherent and accessible way. It includes practice guidance within a procedural framework, questions to ask, information, checklists, and some pointers to other texts which contains greater detail in certain areas of the process.

The principal focus of the book is on female survivors of male domestic violence and the assessment framework reflects this. There is reference to causal differences and assessment implications for violence between same sex couples and other marginalised groups, but the reader will need to look elsewhere for greater detail. Despite the need to limit the boundaries of content, this book should have broad appeal – both in geographical terms, serving as a useful resource regardless of statute and procedural differences across countries; and across disciplines. All assessments need to be multi-disciplinary in nature to stand any realistic chance of being informed and resourced and they also need to be evidence-based, requiring an integration of causal theories and professional skills (Calder, 2003).

Chapter Two

Contextualising Domestic Violence

This chapter will contextualise domestic violence and child protection by exploring the following issues:

- The evolution of domestic violence in the public conscientiousness.
- The size and scope of the problem.
- The overlap and co-existence of domestic violence and child abuse.
- Definitional issues.
- Causal explanations.
- Marginalised groups.
- Problems with professional intervention involving mothers.
- Towards principles of intervention.
- Importing lessons from the field of child sexual abuse.
- Towards anti-oppressive practice.
- An organising framework at the local level.
- Towards a preventive framework.

The evolution of domestic violence in the public conscientiousness

Domestic violence is not a new phenomenon, but our response to it is. Davidson (1977) has pointed out that domestic violence has long been a part of family life, having been described repeatedly in religious and historical documents for many centuries dating back to the Roman Empire. The comparative invisibility can be explained partly by a patriarchal state controlled by men. Patriarchy claims that the relationships between the sexes are characterised by dominance and subordination in which male rules female and is sustained by both ideological and structural factors. The ideological support stems from a system of socialisation which conditions both men and women to accept male domination as natural. Women are socialised into adopting compliant submissive and passive roles and accepting their essentially subordinate position. Structural constraints reinforce this order. You would therefore expect to find a lower incidence of domestic violence where the inequalities between men and women were less marked and that weaker social bonds gave rise to increased domestic violence. This is expanded upon in the later section on causal explanations.

The Domestic Violence Act 1961 formally acknowledged domestic violence as a crime for the first time and in the 1970s domestic violence became a political issue and the resurgent women's movement rediscovered domestic violence and made it an important public issue. They argued strongly that domestic violence should be classified as a crime and dealt with in this way by the police and the courts. In response, grass-roots organisations, in the form of battered women's shelters, developed to provide immediate safety to battered women and their children. Although the Domestic Violence Act 1961 formally acknowledged domestic violence as a crime for the first time, in practice civil remedies still prevailed until the later Law Commission finding of 1990 which showed that without effective enforcement, injunctions and protection orders were of no use in securing the safety of victims and their children (Dallos and McLaughlin, 1993).

Widespread recognition that women are frequently victims of domestic violence emerged during the 1980s. Since then, a growing body of literature has described the risk factors and the sequelae of women's exposure to domestic violence. In 1992, the American Medical Association issued guidelines that recommended screening every woman for exposure to domestic violence at every portal of entry to the medical care system. However, reports suggest that these guidelines and protocols are infrequently followed, or that some cases of child abuse or domestic violence may be inadvertently linked (Bowen, 2000; Culross, 1999; Sugg and Inui, 1992). Most recently, results from the National Violence against Women Survey conducted from 1995 to 1996 found that lifetime prevalence of women reporting physical assault by a current or former intimate partner was 22% and that 41% of those physically assaulted sustained an injury from the most recent assault (Dube et al., 2002).

During the 1990s there was an acceleration of policy development and the need to support children living with domestic violence was identified. *Messages from Research* (DoH, 1995) found domestic violence may be in the background for up to half of the children experiencing abuse. The draft version of *Working Together* (DoH, 1998) suggested that it was inappropriate to deal with children living with domestic violence as children in need. The revised version (DoH, 1999) went on to indicate the importance of creating clearly defined links between multi-disciplinary domestic violence forums and Area Child Protection Committees. Other government initiatives include audits of local crime and disorder problems (including domestic violence) under the Crime and Disorder Act (1998) and the initiatives arising from the Crime Reduction Strategy. The Government has recognised the need to establish performance indicators which encourage the police not only to take positive action but also to find ways of reducing repeat victimisation of people in this area. The Best Value performance indicators required by the Home Office are:

- Percentage of reported domestic violence incidents where there was a power of arrest, in which an arrest was made relating to the incident.
- Percentage of victims of reported domestic violence incidents who were victims of a reported domestic violence incident in the previous twelve months.

In 1999 the Cabinet Office and the Home Office jointly issued 'Living without Fear' which set out the government's strategic framework in relation to violence against women. The report emphasised the development of effective multi-agency partnerships as the key to good practice and signalled the government's readiness to allocate resources to and support initiative projects under the Crime Reduction Programme to reduce the incidence of domestic violence, rape and sexual assault.

On 21 January 1999 the Government launched a new domestic violence publicity/awareness campaign for England and Wales under the title 'Break the chain'. In Scotland the 'Domestic Violence – there's no excuse' campaign was launched in 1998 and repeated the following year. This followed the campaign in Northern Ireland in 1995–8 featuring television advertising, poster and information leaflets and a 24-hour helpline.

The Secretary of State for the Home Department (2003) reported that 'this year the Government is investing over 61 million pounds on tackling domestic violence, including over 18 million pounds towards additional refuge provision'. In issuing the proposals for domestic violence, he acknowledges that domestic violence has been for too long tolerated or ignored by society and the Government is now determined to prevent domestic violence happening or recurring, as well as protecting and supporting all the victims of domestic violence.

Although there is evidence of domestic violence being a political priority through the guidance requiring continued inter-agency cooperation, research raises some worries in this regard. For example, Abbott and Williamson (1999) in a survey of all health practitioners in one county found that 36.8% of health practitioners believed that social services have principal responsibility for domestic violence, compared with 9.4% who named the police. Systems to replicate those in child protection are needed but there is ironically a move to dismantle the child protection system at a time when it is most needed (Calder, 2004).

The 'invisibility' of children who witness domestic violence is comprehensive and professional and societal attention to these children is relatively recent and sadly inadequate (Fantuzzo, Mohr and Noone, 2000). Children who witness violence in their homes are only the most recent victims to become visible as the evidence that they are harmed by exposure to domestic violence becomes more detailed and persuasive. Much of our information about children's exposure to domestic violence derived from retrospective reports of female victims in shelters, anonymous telephone surveys, or retrospective accounts from adult survivors of inter-parental violence and these each have serious shortcomings. Figure 2.1 offers a visual iceberg representing the universe of exposed children. For example, since we know that refuge or shelter samples represent only the tip of an iceberg, then it is unknown how representative they are of the entire population of battered women and their children. It is equally difficult assessing the impact of the violence on the child when there have been significant changes of circumstances impacting on the child around the same time. For example, being uprooted from their home, being separated from their father, or seeing their mother under conditions of great stress. Fantuzzo et al. (1991) found that children who were living with their mothers in temporary domestic violence shelters evidenced significantly higher levels of psychological distress and different types of distress than carefully matched children who were exposed to the same level and type of violence but were living at home.

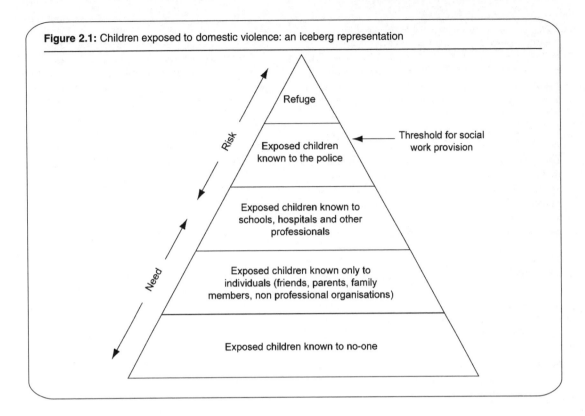

Figure 2.1: Children exposed to domestic violence: an iceberg representation

Although domestic violence is on the agenda, there is still some way to go in our responses. For example, although domestic violence was mentioned in 65% of children's services plans only 26% included plans for actual service provision (Humphreys et al., 2000).

The visibility and naming of domestic violence as a social and political issue has been subject to considerable change over time: appearing and then disappearing from the public view. How workers conceptualise domestic violence and associated child protection issues is both influenced by, and influenced over, its construction as a social problem and developing professional responses. Downs (1972) articulated a cycle of response to social problems that can be usefully applied to domestic violence. He argued that when a social problem is identified, we often respond with a euphoric enthusiasm about our ability to 'solve the problem' or 'do something effective' within a relatively short time. Unfortunately, in the next stage of the cycle there is a realisation of the cost of significant progress. Inevitably, solving the problem would not only take a great deal of money but would also require major sacrifices by large groups of the

population. Downs attributes society's most pressing social problems to a deliberate or unconscious exploitation of one group in society by another or the prevention of one group from enjoying something which others want to keep for themselves. In the penultimate stage of the cycle there is a gradual decline of public interest: some people get discouraged, others feel positively threatened by thinking about the problem, whilst others become bored with the issue. This is coupled with a competing and new issue, which attracts the attention of the public and this leads to a shift of focus.

Davis (1987) analysed 33 articles in the social work literature on domestic violence published between 1976 and 1984, and identified three stages in our understanding of the problem. Initially, domestic violence was seen as a problem affecting large numbers of diverse kinds of women. It was thought to be caused largely by powerful social forces outside the individual, such as sexism and norms permitting men to be physically violent to women, as well as past or current family environments. Little attention was paid to perpetrators at this early stage. The second stage saw domestic violence as just one type of family violence, with some writers beginning to assert that their victims might be playing some role in their own victimisation. The third stage of our understanding of the issue continued the change in focus from women to men, particularly services for men.

The size and scope of the problem

The scope and magnitude of domestic violence is vigorously debated and can overshadow and divert attention from the discussion of the actual problem, its consequences and what can be done to prevent it. Hard data on the incidence and prevalence of domestic violence are in short supply. These two terms mean quite different things although they are often used interchangeably. Prevalence studies attempt to estimate the proportion of a population that have been abused during childhood; while incidence studies seek to estimate the number of new cases occurring in a given period of time, usually a year. Prevalence is thus always lower than incidence as some women are victim's more than once over time. For example, the British Crime Survey of 1992 found that 35% of victims of domestic violence generated 66% of the total number of incidents and of 1996 that 45% experienced repeated violence.

Few of the available figures can be considered reliable and must therefore be treated as rough estimates. Information is based on the findings from various local studies, from self-reported sources and from criminal statistics. That stated, they are the only statistics currently available and therefore should be used but with some preface cautions. Findings are likely to under-estimate rather than exaggerate the scale of domestic violence for the following reasons:

● Domestic violence often (but not exclusively) occurs in the home and thus remains private and rarely reported. It is argued that two-thirds of incidents go unreported (Pryke and Thomas, 1998). On average a woman will be assaulted by her partner or ex-partner 35 times before reporting it to the police (Yearnshire, 1997). Up to one-third of young people who have experienced domestic violence have never told anyone about it (Cleaver et al., 1999). The fact that it remains unreported suggests that it is a problem that is known about but overlooked. People may choose not to disclose their experiences to a

survey, particularly if it is not conducted in private and the presence of others may act as a deterrent. The victims are concerned about the consequences of dealing with it externally with professional agencies. There is often a perceived stigma associated with domestic violence that accompanied with the implication of further violence and society's interpretations and prejudices combine to prevent the victim wanting other people knowing what is happening to them. Despite under reporting, we do know that:
○ One in four women experiences domestic violence in her lifetime.
○ Every week two women in England and Wales are killed by their current or former partners.
○ Domestic violence accounts for a quarter of all violent crime.
○ UK figures suggest that between 40–60% of separated, or divorced, women experienced domestic violence.
○ Women aged 16–29 are at greatest risk of experiencing domestic violence.
○ Domestic violence often starts, or escalates, during pregnancy.
○ The average arrest rate for domestic violence is 12% (Rowsell, 2001).

● The difficulties associated with disclosure and action by the victims of domestic violence. Women may make up to 10 contacts before they get the help they need. Leaving an abusive relationship is often a long process. Whilst most women want to leave in the first year after the violence begins, most only actually leave after 8 years. There are a number of reasons why victims might find it difficult to seek help or disclose abuse:
○ Fear and perceived dangers.
○ They are frightened their partner will find them.
○ They are frightened their partner will kill them.
○ They are frightened their partner will keep the children or harm them.
○ Access to money, housing and other resources.
○ The (anticipated, actual or previous) reactions or responses from agencies they may need to approach.
○ Their own perception of the stigma and blame they may have attributed to themselves.
○ The (anticipated, actual or previous) reactions or responses of the children.

○ The emotional attachment to their partner, despite how irrational this may appear to others.

○ Additional oppressions already experienced or fear of being discriminated against for being:
  – a black person
  – having disabilities
  – physical or mental health issues
  – being an older person or very young person
  – a lesbian women or gay man
  – a person in a travelling community
  – a person working in the sex industry
  – a drug or alcohol user

● Other reasons may include the lack of awareness about or access to available services; concern that agencies will not be sympathetic, sensitive or provide the help that is needed; fear of agencies having different agendas from their own, particularly with regard to their children; and fear of retribution from their perpetrator. Some women approach services but do not necessarily disclose violence as the source of their problems. For example, many women seek medical help and are not asked how their injuries were inflicted, or by whom. Many women do disclose and still fail to get adequate, appropriate responses. If the opportunity for intervention is lost, violence may continue and women and children may be at significant risk.

● When they are reported they may go unrecorded or they are recorded in such a way that they cannot be separately identified. For example, only one incident may be proceeded with, or repeated offences may be taken less seriously and thus be inaccurately recorded.

● Many victims of domestic violence may not perceive themselves in these terms and may justify or explain abusive behaviours.

● Domestic violence is very difficult to research. Most of what we know about the consequences of domestic violence comes from the clinical literature regarding women who request help from professional services as a result of the domestic violence. It follows therefore that these do not offer us a cross section of all the victims of domestic violence, only the most severely abused subgroup. It is thus unhelpful to generalise from these clinical samples to the larger population of abused women with regard to consequences.

● Surveys sometimes focus on particular populations: such as women using a refuge and therefore overlooks women who do not seek help from services (Henwood, 2000). However, such children are often more likely to have witnessed a recent violent event as well as having been moved from their familiar home environments and schools.

● Many other factors have hampered our ability to research this issue: the stigmatising nature of the problem, norms about family privacy, and difficulties in generalising from clinical samples (Carlson, 1991).

● Research on the effects on children of witnessing domestic violence is made difficult by the number of variables which may affect children's behaviour and emotional well-being. For example, if we are measuring the impact of children in a refuge, we have to ensure that there is a control in place to consider other factors which may affect the child, such as the problematic adult relationship and its breakdown; and the displacement to the shelter and often accompanied by a loss of friends, change of school and everything familiar.

● We know from studies that men and women differ in their level of reporting violence (Szinovacz, 1983) and that children report different effects of witnessing violence than do their mothers or fathers (Sternberg et al., 1998).

● The rural figures for domestic violence are hard to identify.

● The belief among some parents that their children are shielded from exposure to the violence, despite the reality that children often provide detailed recollections of the very events they were not supposed to have witnessed. For example, O'Brien et al. (1994) found that 78% of children reported seeing violence used by fathers against mothers when at least one parent reported that no violence occurred or that their children had not seen such events.

● The statistical indicators of need in relation to domestic violence and child abuse represent only the events brought to the attention of agencies within particular definitions of abuse. They do not tell us about the many experiences of children that are not brought to public attention or about the abuse of children which is assessed by professionals as not worthy of investigation.

- It follows therefore that taking a broader definition of domestic violence would increase the number of children and young people reporting they had witnessed domestic violence at home.
- Many researchers have failed to differentiate abused children from those who are not themselves abused but who did not witness domestic violence. Many studies appear to attribute child problems to the effects of witnessing violence, when in fact they may be more strongly associated with having been a direct victim of abuse (see Fantuzzo and Lindquist, 1989 for a detailed critique).

Despite such limitations, there is some important statistical information that deserves to be reported. In order to assist the reader, I have organised the material around countries.

Significant UK findings

Figures from the 1996 British Crime Survey estimated that there were a total of 6.6 million incidents of domestic violence in 1996, of which 2.9 million resulted in injury (Secretary of State for the Home Department, 2003). The British Crime Survey (1999) found that 44% of crimes reported by women were to do with domestic violence. As many as one in three marriages that end in divorce involve domestic violence (Borbowski et al., 1983).

The British Crime Survey (BCS) provides a periodic estimate of the number of incidents of domestic violence. In 1999, the Home Office figures showed that:

- Almost one in four (23%) of women aged 16–59, and around one in seven (15%) of men have been physically assaulted by a current or former partner.
- More than one in four women (26%) and almost one in six men (17%) have experienced physical or non-physical domestic violence from a partner.
- The highest incidence of domestic violence was reported by women aged 20–24, 28% had experienced assault and one third had experienced assault or threats.

Within the past year

- 4.2% of both men and women aged 16–59 said they had been assaulted by a current or a former partner.

- The likelihood of domestic violence appears to decrease with age for both men and women; around 1% of those aged over 45 reported being assaulted in the previous year, compared with 10% of women aged 16 to 19, and 9% of men aged 20 to 24.
- Half of those who had experienced violence from a partner or former partner in the previous year were living with children under 16, and 29% reported that the children had been aware of what was happening. However, where women experienced repeated violence, 45% reported that their children had been aware of the latest incident.
- Women who had separated from a partner are at greatest risk; 29% of separated women had experienced threats of domestic assault from a previous partner in the past year, compared with only 5% of separated males.

Nature of violence

- Pushing, shoving, and grabbing were the most common forms of assault (reported in two-thirds of incidents) and kicking, slapping or punching by the abuser was reported in 47% of the incidents.
- Injuries resulted in 41% of the incidents and women were more likely to be injured than men (47% compared with 31%). Women who experienced a chronic pattern of violence were particularly likely to have been injured in the last incident (58%).
- Emotional distress was reported by 90% of women experiencing chronic domestic violence, and 75% of women whose experience was of intermittent violence reported being very upset. Women were also very fearful: 80% of chronic female victims and 52% of intermittent victims reported being very frightened during the incident (compared with only 11% of chronic male victims and 5% of intermittent male victims).

Domestic violence is the second most common type of violent crime in Britain. In London there were 9,800 domestic violence assaults recorded in 1992. It is suggested that only 2% of such offences ever get reported (Dobash and Dobash, 1980).

Every second in the UK, the police are called to a case of domestic violence. In the next twelve months police services around the country will receive around 600,000 calls about domestic violence, suggesting that on average someone is violently assaulted in their home every 20 seconds (Dobson, 2002).

Pryke and Thomas (1998) reported on the figures for relationship violence in Northern Ireland. In 1991–2 there were 25 homicides (excluding sectarian killings), ten (40%) were as a consequence of domestic violence. The Royal Ulster Constabulary recorded nearly 3,000 domestic disputes: 416 women and their children were re-housed for this reason and a further 1,300 cited domestic violence as a reason for their homelessness.

In Scotland, there were 712 incidents per 100,000 population in 2000 and 330 people experienced serious assault and 17 people were murdered by their partners in the same year (Scottish Executive, 2003).

In 1994, the NCH published a landmark report on children and domestic violence that identified several key points:

- 86% of mothers said they had been slapped or punched, 63% strangled, 61% had been kicked and 61% also said that they had been struck with an object.
- 83% had experienced bruises or black eyes, 50% had been cut, 23% had broken bones and 40% had been to hospital for their injuries.
- 46% said they had been forced to have sex by their violent partner, 23% had been 'raped with threats' and 18% 'raped with violence'.
- 69% of women were regularly imprisoned in their home, actually or with threats, 65% prevented from speaking to other people and 22% had their clothes taken away.
- 73% of the mothers in the survey said that their children had witnessed violent incidents and 67% had seen their mothers beaten.
- 27% said that their violent partners had also physically assaulted their children.
- 10% of the mothers were sexually abused in front of their children.
- 31% said that their children had intervened to protect them and 27% had tried to protect their siblings.
- 23% of the mothers were still living in a violent relationship. Of those who were left 61% had been in the relationship for two years or longer and 35% for five years or more.
- 77% of the mothers no longer lived in the violent relationship – 66% left due to concern about the effects on their children, 49% because they thought their children might be taken into care, 23% because their partner had begun to hit their children and 68% were afraid their partner would kill them.
- 66% of mothers could tell no one about the violence at first. The average time before telling someone was one to two years.
- 70% found it hard to tell professionals about their children's problems caused by the violence.

Of all crimes reported to the British Crime Survey in 2000 more than 1 in 20 were classified as domestic violence.

In England alone, 53,000 women and children use refuges each year and there are over 150,000 calls to Women's Aid for advice and help (Women's Aid, 1997).

Up to one third of children on child protection registers live with domestic violence (Mullender, 2000).

A study by Reder and Duncan (1999) looked at cases in which children died from maltreatment and describes domestic violence as a recurring theme. Although it is never explicitly described as domestic violence, the majority of the caretakers of the children experienced problems with unmet dependency needs or care and control issues. The majority of the children in the study died as a result of violent assault. Research suggested that fatal abuse of children may be preceded by episodes of violence within the home (Reder and Duncan, 1999).

Studies specifically undertaken in child protection have demonstrated a high association between child abuse and domestic violence. Most studies have found that in the vast majority of instances (85–90%) children were present and witnessed the violence and in over 50% of instances it was reported that children were abused during the violent incident (Cleaver, 1999). Gibbons et al. (1995) found that domestic violence was present in 27% of their sample of 1,888 child protection referrals while Farmer and Owen's study (1995) reported that domestic violence was present in 59% of their sample cases who had been brought to initial child protection conference.

Domestic violence imposes significant costs on society: direct financial costs to public agencies and voluntary organisations, emotional costs to victims and those close to them, and indirect financial costs to the economy from lost output. The cost of the one hundred and fifty or so domestic violence murders each year of adult men and women is approximately £60 million in lost output and expense to public services to which should be added a further £105 million in emotional impact. The costs to public services have been estimated as close to £2.25 billion for the UK and when adding the costs of emotional trauma and lost productivity would rise to nearer £4.5 billion per year. In 2001–2 the police recorded 812,594 incidents of domestic crime of which 22% was domestic violence. The average incident of violence against the person costs the police and criminal justice system £2,700 (Secretary of State for the Home Department, 2003).

The Secretary of State for the Home Department (2003) organised some useful statistics:

- One incident of domestic violence is reported to the police every minute.
- Domestic violence has the highest rate of repeat victimisation of any crime.
- On average two women per week are killed by a male partner or former partner; nearly half of all female murder victims are killed by a partner or ex-partner.
- Of all murders of men, about 8% are murders in a domestic context – but some of these may be in self-defence following a history of abuse by their partner.
- People in the LGBT (lesbian, gay, bisexual and transgender) communities experience domestic violence in a similar proportion to the rest of the population (about one in four).
- More than a third of children in a violent home know what is happening. That figure rises to up to half if the violence is repeated. Children may attempt to stop the violence and so put themselves at risk.
- Domestic violence is a major cause of homelessness, accounting for about 16% of homelessness acceptances every year. Over the last seven years, more than 130,000 homeless have been re-housed because of domestic violence.

Significant US findings

What we do know is that the highest rates of violence are experienced by young women. The average annual rate of victimisation is 74.6 per 1,000 for women aged 12–18 and 63.7 per 1,000 for women aged 19–29; in comparison the average annual rate for all women is 36.1 (Bachman and Saltzman, 1995). A recent national random survey in the US estimated that 4.4 million adult women are abused by a partner every year (Plichta, 1996).

National surveys estimate that at least 2 million women each year are battered by an intimate partner and crime data from the FBI record about 1,500 murders of women by husbands or boyfriends each year. Overall, the Bureau of Justice Statistics reports that women sustained about 3.8 million assaults and 500,000 rapes a year in 1992 and 1993; more than 75% of these violent acts were committed by someone known to the victim, and 29% of them were committed by an intimate – a husband, ex-husband, boyfriend or ex-boyfriend (Cromwell and Burgess, 1996).

Depending on the study referred to, from 45–70% of the cases of domestic violence where there are children in the home, the children are also being abused. Conservatively, child abuse is 15 times more likely to occur in households where domestic violence is also present (American Humane Association, 1994). Stark and Flitcraft (1988) found that children whose mothers are abused are more than twice as likely to be physically abused as are the children whose mothers are not abused.

Carlson (1984) estimated that at least 3.3 million children are at risk annually of exposure to parental violence. She also argued that this was likely to be an underestimate because this only embraces those children exposed to serious violence and it assumes that the violence terminates when the adults separate. Jaffe, Wolfe and Wilson (1990) reviewed studies which put the observation rate even higher (68–80%).

Straus, Gelles and Steinmetz (1980) estimated that around three million American households experience at least one incident of domestic violence each year. This study excluded families with children under three years of age. Straus and Gelles (1990) found that 30% of parents who admitted the existence of adult domestic violence in their home reported that their children have witnessed at least one violent incident over the duration of the marriage.

Straus (1992) also estimated that there may be as many as 10 million teenagers exposed to parental violence each year. Straus and Gelles (1990) found that adults in their sample recalled an average of 8.9 violent incidents in their teenage years, with a median of four events.

Research tells us that violence by children is a serious issue. Browne (1993) pointed out that 19 million children in the USA seriously injure their brothers and sisters each year and 6% of parents ring helplines to say that their teenage children are abusing them. 11% of teenagers self-report using abusive behaviour toward their father and 2% to the mother.

Significant Canadian findings

One of the largest surveys of violence directed towards women was conducted by Statistics Canada in 1993. They conducted telephone interviews with 12,300 randomly selected Canadian women aged 18 years and over (Rodgers, 1994). Respondents were asked to report incidents of physical and sexual assault they had experienced since the age of 16 years. They found that:

- 3% of women married or in a de facto relationship at the time of interview reported being subject to physical or sexual assault in the 12 months prior to interview.
- 29% of women currently or previously married (or in a de facto relationship) reported being physically or sexually assaulted by a partner at some time.
- 33% of women who had been assaulted by a partner feared for their lives at some point in the relationship.
- 21% of women who reported partner violence had been assaulted in their pregnancy.
- 45% of partner assaults resulted in injury; medical attention was sought in approximately 40% of cases.

In Canada they found that approximately one-third of married women are estimated to have experienced violence from their current or previous partner (Statistics Canada, 1994). The majority of these women have children, which leads to estimates that 3–5 children in every classroom have witnessed abuse of their mother in their homes (Kincaid, 1985).

Significant Australian findings

The Australian Bureau of Statistics (1998) established that one quarter of assaults Australia-wide related to violence in the family. The majority of victims are under 45 years of age. 77% of victims were female compared to 23% being male. In 73.5% of cases the female victims did not tell the police for various reasons. 64% of victims experienced three or more incidents in

the 12 months prior to the survey, highlighting the repetitious nature of domestic violence.

A national survey by Women's Safety Australia (1996) provided the following information:

- 23% of women who had ever been married or in a de facto relationship had experienced violence by a male partner at some stage during their relationship.
- 1.1 million women experienced violence by a previous partner; this included violence that occurred both during and after the relationship. For 74,700 women violence occurred only after the relationship had ended.
- 11% of men were killed by an intimate partner, with the majority (84%) of these offenders being female.
- 36% of women who had experienced violence by a previous partner and 38% of women experiencing violence from a current partner said they had children who witnessed the violence (believed to be an under-estimate as many children are far more aware of violence in the home than their parents realise).
- 700,000 women were pregnant at some time during a relationship with a previous partner who had been violent. 42% of these women experienced violence during the pregnancy and 20% experienced violence for the first time while they were pregnant.
- Of the women who had experienced violence in the last 20 years, 80% had not sought help from services at all, with only 16% using legal help and 9% accessing crisis support.
- Just 5% experiencing violence from a current partner reported the last incident to the police.
- It is estimated that the Australian Government spends over $200 million annually in direct response to the effects of domestic violence.

Few attempts have been made to research the relationship between domestic violence and child neglect. In Stanley's (1991) assessment of 20 child protection cases however at least 50% of the total sample involved both domestic violence and child neglect.

Goddard (1981) compared the level of domestic violence in 59 cases of child abuse (physical or sexual abuse) admitted to Melbourne Royal Children's Hospital in 1980, with a matched sample of 36 non-abused children. Using mother's reports of physical violence between the child's current caregivers, he reported that physical assaults between the adults had occurred in 12% of the non-abused sample, and in 55% of families where the child had been abused. That is there was a significantly greater level of domestic (physical) violence reported to have occurred in families where a child was hospitalised as a function of being abused, compared with a non-matched non-abused sample. Goddard and Hillier (1993) reported that 40% of identified sexual abuse cases and 55% of identified physical abuse cases where domestic violence was also evident. In summary:

> . . . our collective reluctance to grasp the sheer scale of the problem and its implications is in many ways easy to understand. If we want to resist reality then at this point we can choose to sit back, and relax, we could find other ways to spend our lives. But we may just have noticed something. For many women there is a war going on, not a war that is necessarily ever played out on our TV screens, although sometimes (but rarely) that does happen, this is a war that is private, filled with hate and waged with power and control through force, laws and money. It's that kind of war and it has much to do with the way in which we see ourselves and the society in which we live. Many of us have chosen not to fight that war, many of us were not given that choice. We are on the front line with all rights to leave withdrawn.

> (Rowsell, 2001)

The overlap and co-existence of domestic violence and child abuse

Stark and Flitcraft (1988) explored the association between domestic violence and child abuse by examining the medical records of children in a hospital who were suspected of being abused or neglected. 45% of the mothers of the 116 children seen had medical histories that indicated or were suggestive of domestic violence. The medical records of the women suggested that over their lifetimes they had on average come to the hospital 4.2 times as a result of trauma. This study was replicated by McKibben et al. (1991) and they found that 59.4% of mothers of abused or neglected children had medical records that suggested that they had been assaulted by their partners. This incidence was significantly greater than in a matched sample of mothers of non-abused and non-neglected children. Several population-based studies have reported an overlap between domestic violence with childhood physical abuse of 60% to 75% (Edleson, 1999; Osofsky, 1999).

Bowker et al.'s (1988) study does throw some light on these dynamics. In addition to a high degree of overlap, they found that the severity of abuse to a woman is associated with the severity of abuse to children in the home. That is, the more severely a woman is battered the more severely her child is likely to be abused. They found that child abuse was less severe than woman battering in those families studied. They also found that the more dominant the husband is in the family's decision-making, the more likely a child is to be abused. Finally, the larger the number of children in a family the more likely there is to be child abuse in the home. This only studied children who were biologically related to the abuser. Daly et al. (1993) reported that the presence of children fathered by previous male partners put women at greater risk of being abused.

Humphrey's (1997) found evidence to support the high rates of domestic violence present in child protection cases. In her examination of 32 case files involving children who were the subject of child protection conferences between 1994–1996 she found that domestic violence toward the mother was a feature of the case. Two-thirds of the 32 women in the study had children permanently or temporarily accommodated by the local authority, or had been threatened that their children would be accommodated should separation from their violent partner not occur or be maintained. In many of these cases, the domestic violence was an indirect, rather than a direct cause of child protection concerns. However, in 6 of these cases, reasons given for children continuing to be 'looked after' or where accommodation of the children was threatened or suggested, were that the children had witnessed domestic violence, or that there were concerns for their safety in a household where their mother was being abused, even if they were not being abused themselves. Such findings raise serious questions about how child protection workers intervene in cases where domestic violence occurs and further highlights the demarcation between the way child protection services and more women-centred services may approach women and children in situations of violence. What we need to avoid is that child protection interventions leave the mother feeling doubly victimised by her partner's violence. We need to develop responses that enable and empower the mothers to ensure the mother–child relationship is maintained whilst also maximising the likely reporting of any subsequent incidents or concerns. Fear of professional responses is a powerful barrier to reporting incidents or seeking/accepting help thereafter. It also buys silence for the perpetrator. The challenge is to develop child protection procedures and legislation in such a way that the needs of children at risk of actual or likely significant harm are met, while ensuring that women experiencing domestic violence are neither further victimised, nor adversely affected by the fear that child protection intervention will result in the children's removal (Parkinson and Humphreys, 1998).

Caroline McGee's research (2000) involved interviewing over fifty children regarding their experiences of domestic violence. From this research McGee identified that children are not affected solely by physical violence but by 'ongoing, pervasive abusive behaviour towards women and children'. Children and mothers in the study highlighted the impact of living with fear and intimidation on a daily basis. They reported 'a wide range of effects . . . on the children including powerlessness, depression or sadness, impaired social relations, impacts on identity, extended family relationships and their relationship with their mother'.

Edleson et al. (2003) reported on children's involvement in incidents of adult domestic violence. They found that 52% of the children yelled at least occasionally from another room during abuse to their mother; 53% reported that the children at least occasionally yelled while in the same room, and 21% reported that their children called someone else for help during the abuse at least occasionally. 23% of the children became physically involved during an abusive incident involving the mother at least occasionally. These figures highlight a worrying level of involvement of children in the domestic violence and this has to be considered when intervening into such family situations.

Despite these findings, we currently have a limited picture of the overlap between child abuse and domestic violence against women. Existing studies allow us to state what degree of overlap exists but not much more than this. Part of the problem is that most studies published to date report simple statistics on the percentage of overlapping violence in families based on survey questions or case-record interviews that were carried out for other purposes. The data on the overlap is often mentioned as an aside to the primary findings of a particular study. Whilst we can accept that there is a significant overlap between child abuse and domestic violence against women in the same families, we do not know why these forms of violence co-occur, whether one precedes the other, or what impact their combination has on adult and child victims (Edleson, 1999). Another problem is that many of the samples are drawn primarily from children residing in refuges and as this is a time of severe crisis and dislocation, we are more likely to generate more extreme findings than actually exist.

Whilst more service providers now acknowledge that living with domestic violence is a child abuse issue, there is no consensus about the practice implications of this for service providers. Being able to assess for the presence of domestic violence will not only increase the safety of women victims it will also promote better outcomes for child safety – the mandated responsibility of child protection workers.

Echlin and Osthoff (2000) challenge workers in the respective fields to start working together to end violence against women and children. Given the high rate of co-occurrence of domestic violence and child abuse you would expect there to be a high level of collaboration and co-operation. However, while such efforts are emerging, tensions exist. In fact there has been a long history of hostility and antagonism between the two groups. Schechter and Edleson (1994) report that separate historical developments in child welfare and services to adult victims of domestic violence have been compounded by different philosophies, different professional terminologies, and even the value placed on different outcomes. This has resulted in mistrust and suspicion between the two groups. Beeman and Edleson (2000) identified thematically some of the differences and conflicts between child protection workers and advocates for the victims of domestic violence:

● **Philosophies of practice**: child protection workers adopt a child-centered philosophy (reflecting their belief that they were the only ones looking out for children) compared to the women-centred philosophy of battered women's advocates (working with women to set their own goals). As a result, the same family was often viewed in different ways. For example, while the advocate of the mother may see a mother's decision to leave or stay as her own, a child protection worker may view her decision to stay as a danger to her children.

- **Practice focus**: child protection workers believe that their legal mandate to protect the child often meant they needed to focus case plans on the mothers, even if she herself was a victim of abuse. This often translated into the mother's failure to protect even where a child was physically abused by the father. This occurred more when the worker believed that the mother was repeatedly putting the child at risk. The advocates of the mother objected to the focus on holding mothers rather than the abusers accountable.
- **Lack of communication and co-operation between systems**: characterised by the adversarial working relationship between the two systems.
- **Gender, racial and cultural bias in services**: to all family members.

The same authors went on to suggest some principles of collaboration:

- Best interest of mother and child as common goal.
- Holding the male perpetrator responsible.
- Better collaboration with the courts and other systems with a focus on family safety and accountability for the abuser.

Ultimately it will be the children who judge our response to their needs.

Social services departments should not see domestic violence as just another discrete risk from which they must protect children and other vulnerable people. A holistic approach, including the provision of family support services and other measures to enable all the abused members of the family to make themselves safe may be a more effective intervention. This would include support, where appropriate, after the violence has ended, in terms of helping victims re-build their lives. Departments should also recognise that the involvement of domestic violence experts, such as experienced workers within the voluntary sector, can lead to better decision-making. They can also help ensure a comprehensive assessment of needs, risks and protective steps which can be taken (Home Office, 2000b).

Definitional issues

The issue of definition is not straightforward when considering domestic violence for a number of reasons:

- There are a number of terms used interchangeably in research, theory and practice that need unpicking to look at which should stand alone and for what reason and which may genuinely be integrated.
- The term 'victim' is unhelpful for those women who have experienced domestic violence and many would prefer to be framed as 'survivors'. However, the term victim remains appropriate for children.
- The words domestic violence needs to be seen within a continuum of unacceptable behaviour rather than as a stand alone and discrete term.
- There is a breadth of types of harm that are collectively subsumed under the umbrella of domestic violence.
- Domestic violence also needs to be considered as a process rather than an event.
- There are potential differences between how professionals define domestic violence from those who endure it.
- There is a need to acknowledge a gender difference in how domestic violence is defined.

It is important therefore to unwrap each of these areas to reach some common understanding about the issues that need to be embraced within any definition reached. Before so doing, I will provide an introduction to the areas requiring consideration.

Introductory comments

Definitions are very important: if they are too narrow, they restrict our understanding, figures of incidence and prevalence, as well as our intervention threshold. Conversely, if they are too broad, they are all embracing, invite disbelief and often detract from focusing in on the highest risk cases. Defining what constitutes significant domestic violence is difficult, and Greenblat's 1983 study shows that opinions about what is acceptable between spouses and in society, varies widely. The definition of domestic violence used in studies varies widely, depending on how the relationship and what constitutes violence are measured. The wider the definition of domestic violence, the higher the recorded levels will be. However, estimates of the prevalence of domestic violence is generally high. The British Crime Survey which uses a fairly narrow definition found that 23% of women and 15% of men had been the victims of domestic violence at some time.

In this book, various terms will be used interchangeably and this is in large due to the need to reflect the terminology used in various chapters, books and articles. The main term used is domestic violence since it is used in government documentation and in the absence of any substantially better term. What is important from this section is that the reader goes away with a clear understanding of the breadth of the behaviour of concern.

Domestic violence is a complex and multi-determined problem, which can be viewed from a wide range of perspectives. This is reflected in the number and variance of definitions. Thus, whilst domestic violence falls within the remit of a wide variety of professional groups: social workers, teachers, health service workers, police and legal professionals: they rarely discuss the same phenomenon. There is often more consensus at the severe end of the continuum, whilst there are many differing and often divergent opinions when the consideration relates to hands-off domestic violence. Domestic violence thus tends to be a blanket term for a multitude of vaguely defined acts.

The fact that the problem was brought to our attention by the female victims themselves via the women's movement has been the most important influence on our definitions. From the beginning the issue has largely been defined as a problem in which women are victimised by male partners. The problems were initially labelled wife or woman abuse or battering, with the woman generally being referred to as a battered woman or wife. Many prefer to avoid the use of the word wife, since domestic violence is known to occur at about the same or a higher rate in common-law relationships (Yllo and Straus, 1981). The term spouse abuse or domestic violence is also frequently used, although they tend to shift the focus away from women as the most common victims of abuse. Abuse is also known to occur in both gay male and female couples. Researchers have found the prevalence and types of violence, dynamics, and consequences (except help-seeking) to be more similar to than different from heterosexual couple violence (Brand and Kidd, 1986).

The very fact that domestic violence is an umbrella term used to describe a range of behaviours is often misunderstood, and leads to an over emphasis on physical violence, and the presence of sexual violence, psychological, emotional and financial abuse is often ignored or minimised. The term domestic violence historically and still today for many people, has negative connotations, and brings forth images of passive women asking for a slap because they can't get their lives in order, or don't behave in appropriate ways. How have the two little words 'domestic violence' reached the public and political agenda, and yet they have not managed to convey the pain, distress, damage and injustice that women experience as a result of misogyny. It is safe to say that the words Domestic Violence have become shorthand to describe a whole range of violent and abusive behaviours that we do not want to hear ourselves name (Rowsell, 2001). Naming these behaviours is important for professionals to do as the consequences of not naming them allows us to distance ourselves from the reality, the pain, the suffering, and means that the behaviour stays private, unpunished and sanctioned, and ultimately our refusal to engage with the complexities means that we are guilty of at best indifference and worst collusion. However, a word of caution at this point: women themselves often find violence and abuse very difficult to name, even where they are asked the most sensitive of questions by the most skilled of workers, and particularly difficult is subtler forms of emotional and psychological abuse and sexual violence.

Pryke and Thomas (1998) offered an analysis of the available definitions of domestic violence, noting a preoccupation with three key elements:

- **The nature of the relationship between the people involved**: the intimacy in any relationship, implied by the concept 'domestic' in practice masks considerable variations, from relationships that are of long-standing to those that are only a few weeks only, with corresponding differences in the length of time people may have cohabited.
- **The kinds of violence or coercion involved**: the 'methods of control' used to impose power over women extend much further than mere physical force, although physical coercion may be the ultimate sanction.
- **The place(s) where the violence occurs**: this is not restricted to the 'domestic' situation. Whilst the violence does occur in the complete privacy of the home, it can also occur in public places and in front of witnesses.

There are a number of practical issues relating to definitions, language and terminology:

- Different definitions account for some of the differences in findings of prevalence studies about domestic violence (Mooney, 1993)

- The language and definitions that are used impact upon women's ability to name their experiences. They may remain silent if they feel their experiences are not reflected in dominant understandings or definitions of what constitutes domestic violence (Kelly and Radford, 1991).

A shared definition of exactly what we mean by the term 'violence against women' is of vital importance if we are to be explicit not only about what constitutes violence, but also; the circumstances in which it occurs; whether women define themselves as victims; whether men are named and held to account as the main perpetrators; and ultimately determines who is responsible for deciding what change needs to take place, and in what context that change will occur.

There are a number of terms used interchangeably in research, theory and practice that need unpicking to look at which should stand alone and for what reason and which may genuinely be integrated.

- **Marital violence** and **spouse abuse** presume that partners are married and fail to recognise that violence between partners is overwhelmingly male violence against women.
- The term **battered women** identifies the victim accurately but appears to restrict the violence to physical assault and is ambiguous in that it gives no indication that the violence occurs within the context of private relationships. The term also focuses on the victims rather than the perpetrators of the assault.
- The term **domestic violence** can be misleading. This is because it masks a range of abusive experiences and contexts. The following are some of the reasons it is misleading:
  - ○ The term 'domestic' suggests that it occurs within the home. This masks the extent to which women experience violence and abuse from partners who they do not, or no longer, live with. It is important to be aware of the extent to which women experience continued violence after they have left abusive partners. This constitutes a particularly dangerous time for women.
  - ○ The term 'violence' is misleading because it overemphasises physical violence and masks the broader range of abuse experienced by women. These include, among other things: sexual abuse, economic deprivation such as keeping the woman without food or money, intimidation, threats, emotional abuse through undermining and belittling comments, isolation, humiliation, using or abusing the children to force compliance from the woman, and a myriad of other ways in which dominance and control are enforced to position the women in a role of subservience.
  - ○ The term domestic violence has been criticised for trivialising the problem (e.g. just a domestic) and it also implies some causation from the situation rather than placing the blame firmly on the perpetrators i.e. with men.
  - ○ Although the term has the advantage of covering a range of relationships in which the violence occurs, including between gay and lesbian couples and women's violence against men, the gendered nature of domestic violence is hidden by the term. The term 'domestic violence' masks the issue of gender. The vast majority of situations involve male perpetrators inflicting violence and abuse upon women.
  - ○ The term 'domestic violence' may mask the differences, as well as the overlaps, between this and other forms of abuse such as child abuse and domestic abuse, as well as other forms of sexual violence against women.

- The term **domestic violence** is useful in that it helps to emphasise that it is violence that is being examined, not arguments or minor altercations. It does fall down by not clearly identifying who the victim is and who the perpetrators are (Johnson, 1995). Humphreys (1997) also noted that it names explicitly violence in the home and does not cover up this violence with terms such as relationship conflict. It is also a term in common usage and therefore provides a convenient and well recognised short hand.
- Even **woman abuse** focuses on the victim rather than the perpetrator and places the problem with women rather than where it belongs, with men. The term should be men's abuse of women in intimate relationships.
- The term **'violence against women'** a powerful term for naming patriarchal violence, has been introduced with the

explicit aim of focusing on male physical and sexual assaults on women. By definition, the term excludes violence directed against adult or juvenile males, however, and the violence that may be perpetrated by women against intimate partners or other family members.

- Although the terms family and domestic violence are frequently used interchangeably the term **family violence** is often used purposefully to reflect the range of relationships within which violence can occur.

- The term **perpetrator of domestic violence** implies a homogeneous group of individuals, yet we know that they do not neatly fit into categories, and thus a continuum of behaviours is often a preferred method of definition. There are also as many definitions as there are individuals doing the defining. Many feminists see such offending behaviour along a continuum of 'normal' male behaviour, with such offending representing one of the most extreme consequences of the socialisation of boys and men. It is seen as a means of assuring them of their male identity as well as serving as a method of social control via the maintenance of unequal gender relations. In this book, I will use the terms abuser, perpetrator and batterer interchangeably and this is largely to accommodate the range of terms used in source materials.

- There are important issues to be raised about the concept of **'failure to protect'**. The word failure implies circumstances that are controllable and in the contexts of sexual abuse as well as domestic violence, this suggests that the failure was due to the mother not taking some action that would have protected her children. The concept of failure to protect requires mothers to protect children from fathers who are equally responsible for and available to the children (Magen, 1999). For mothers to avoid allegations of failure to protect requires either leaving the situation and/or taking action against the perpetrator. If they do not, then the problem is defined in terms of what the mother failed to do rather than in terms of the perpetrator's actions. It assumes that leaving is a woman's responsibility; that leaving is a solution to

the abuse, and that leaving is appropriate and available to all women. Those professionals who ask the question 'Why didn't she leave?' continue to reflect victim-blaming attitudes. This is clearly a blaming and fault approach to child protection. It is clearly difficult to work with a mother they perceive as failing to protect yet she herself may continue to be abused by the same man. Child protection remains a no-fault system, which has no room for sympathy, as many workers see inability as damning as the abuse itself. Society needs to expend more effort in protecting abused women and until then, children who remain with their abused mothers may not be safe, but the responsibility and consequences should be for the perpetrator. Berkowitz (1997) calls for a move from the arena of failure to protect to the assignment of culpability and sets out examples of the far-reaching consequences if this doesn't occur. For example, children being removed from the care of both parents, often bringing to fruition the threats of the perpetrator ('if you tell, they will take you away'); or mothers being hesitant to come forward with their concerns as they anticipate the consequences and decide the risk of loss outweighs the benefits from formal intervention.

The term 'victim' is unhelpful for those women who have experienced domestic violence and many would prefer to be framed as 'survivors'. However, the term victim remains appropriate for children.

Terms such as victims of domestic violence, battered women and battered wives are used despite the fact that they negatively label those experiencing violence as victims rather than, more positively, as survivors.

When considering how violence and abuse may have impacted women it is important that a balanced picture is presented. Representing women as merely victims suggests that they have no agency, and are not able to make decisions and choices that are about resisting and surviving violence and abuse. Although anyone who experiences violence or abuse is undoubtedly victimised by their experience, it is important that we view abused girls and women as survivors, instead of merely victims, as this reflects the sheer fact that many do physically survive often against tremendous odds. However, this survival can often be achieved by the use of resistance tactics, and the development of coping strategies, that may not automatically be viewed as rational and logical by society in general, or those around them. And of course some women and children don't survive at all.

The words domestic violence needs to be seen within a continuum of unacceptable behaviour rather than as a stand alone and discrete term.

Straus, Gelles and Steinmetz (1980) defined violence as consisting of aggressive behaviours, such as punching, slapping, or kicking, intentionally used to hurt another person. Abusive violence has been operationally defined as those behaviours likely to injure someone, such as hitting with a fist or beating up. Feminist definitions have focused more on power differentials between the partners and often go beyond aggressive behaviours (Bograd, 1982). Schechter and Gray (1988) define battering as an abuse of power within a relationship, a 'pattern of coercive control that can take four forms: physical, emotional, sexual and economic' (p241). Not all victims will necessarily experience all forms of abuse. However, once physical abuse has been established, the other forms of abuse are typically present, as the perpetrator strives to maintain dominance and reinforce their partner's submission.

Kelly (1988) has argued that conflicts over definition reflect the context of male dominance, in which it is men's interests as a group and as the main perpetrators of domestic and sexual violence, to ensure that the definitions of such violence are as limited as possible. For women and girls to define their own experience as abuse is a difficult and complex process, because of the myths and stereotypes which surround domestic and sexual violence, the coping strategies they adopt of forgetting and minimising, the need to challenge dominant definitions and an absence of a culture of support.

Women experience a wide range of behaviours as male violence. The term violence against women includes not only domestic violence, but, rape, sexual assault, child sexual abuse, sexual harassment, pornography, prostitution and trafficking. The connections between them are not always obvious, and are often easier understood by women than men, but include the fact that: all of them are criminal; they are perpetrated by men against women; they are all about abusing a woman by making the perpetrator feel powerful; and last but not least they are all perpetrated by someone else without explicit consent, and are extremely harmful.

There is a breadth of types of harm that are collectively subsumed under the umbrella of domestic violence.

The term domestic violence is used as an umbrella term to refer to the physical, sexual, psychological, emotional and financial abuse from an adult perpetrator to an adult victim in the context of a current or previously close relationship. This behaviour is used by one person to control and dominate another. Domestic violence involves a range of behaviours and tactics, some of which constitute criminal behaviours. The violence can be actual, attempted or threatened, and includes (but is not exclusive to): slapping; pushing; hitting; biting; burning; choking/strangulation; kicking; pushing; scalding; punching; use of weapons; sleep deprivation; starvation; disability or disfigurement; death; forced sex (anal, vaginal, or oral); sexual assaults involving implements; enforced pregnancy; enforced abortion; enforced prostitution; enforced pornography; constant criticism; isolation from family or friends; extreme jealousy and possessiveness; destroying personal belongings and property; verbal abuse; humiliation and degradation; threats to remove/harm/abuse children; and financial deprivation.

It can also be used to describe murder, stalking, genital mutilation, sexual harassment and pornography. There remains little consensus in this embryonic field on how to define violence against women. This clearly raises an issue about how much better we can define each of the areas within this broad definition. Tara-Chand (1988) identified a range of tactics used in domestic violence including displays of total power, enforcing trivial demands, threats, acts of degradation, enforced isolation, creation of distorted perspectives, creating physical disabilities, exhaustion and manipulation through occasional indulgences.

Straus (1990) defined adult-to-adult domestic violence as 'an act carried out with the intention of causing pain or injury'.

Witnessing a violent event is most commonly defined as being in visual range of the violence and seeing it occur.

Physical assaults typically involve slapping, punching, kicking, biting, hitting with objects, hair pulling etc. The physical injuries that may result from assaults include: bruises, cuts and abrasions, fractured bones, lost teeth, internal injuries and miscarriages. Pregnancy can be a trigger for domestic violence to begin or intensify, and injuries are particularly likely to the breasts, chest and abdomen. Physical violence is most commonly measured by the Conflict Tactic Scales (Straus, 1979) or some modification of it. This list contains nine physical violence items:

- Threw something at you.
- Pushed, grabbed or shoved you.
- Slapped you.
- Kicked, bit, or hit you with a fist.
- Hit or tried to hit you with something.
- Beat you up.
- Choked you.
- Threatened you with a knife or gun.
- Used a knife or fired a gun.

The last six of the list are considered to be 'severe'.

At a minimum, psychological abuse refers to psychological acts that cause psychological harm (McGee and Wolfe, 1991). Many women describe the psychological abuse, especially ridicule, as constituting the most painful abuse they have experienced and it is linked to undermining a woman's self-esteem, self-worth etc and this makes her less able to cope with the physical violence and psychological abuse (Follingstad et al., 1990).

Psychological and emotional abuse can include:

- Constant criticism and belittling comments.
- Verbal abuse and threats (including threats to harm the children).
- Isolation and control of contact with family and friends.
- Restrictions on entry/exit from the home.
- Intimidation.
- Controlling and coercive behaviour.
- Denial of privacy.
- Oppressive control of finances.
- Destruction of personal property and valued possessions.

Follingstad et al. (1990) identified the following categories of behaviour as psychological abuse:

- Verbal attacks such as ridicule, verbal harassment and name calling, designed to make the woman believe she is not worthwhile in order to keep her under the control of the abuser.

- Isolation that separates a woman from her social support networks or denies her access to finances and other resources, thus limiting her independence.
- Extreme jealousy or possessiveness, such as excessive monitoring of her behaviour, repeated accusations of infidelity, and controlling with whom she has contact.
- Verbal threats of abuse, harm, or torture directed at the woman herself or at her family, children or friends.
- Repeated threats of abandonment, divorce or of initiating an affair if the woman does not comply with the abuser's wishes.
- Damage or destruction of the woman's personal property.

Psychological abuse includes activities typically associated with brainwashing: threats of violence (against the victim, others and himself); repeated attacks against self-esteem; coercing victim to do degrading things (e.g. lick a line across the kitchen floor with her tongue); and excessive controlling of the victim's activities (such as access to money, friendships, sleeping and eating habits, holding a job, being an autonomous person). In the destruction of property/pets, even though something else is damaged, the attack is still meant for the victim. It is her clothes that are torn, her pet cat strangled, gifts that he has given her burned etc. The victim of psychological abuse has learned, like prisoners of war, that psychological torment or controlling behaviour can be backed up by physical assault. The power of 'hands-off' abuse in damaging the victim comes in part from the physical or sexual violence that has preceded it (Ganley, 1989). She goes on to differentiate psychological abuse and emotional abuse. With psychological abuse there is always the spoken or unspoken threat and actual occurrence of physical battering. With emotional abuse there is no credible threat of violence since the perpetrator has not been physically or sexually violent in the past. Psychological abuse and emotional abuse may look the same to the observer and they are carried out in the same way and both are damaging to the relationship. However, they occur in different contexts. With emotional abuse there is damage but no immediate threat to life. With psychological abuse, there is always the possibility of physical abuse.

Other actions that may constitute emotional abuse include:

- Entitlement (I have a right to sex).
- Withholding (Why would I want to make love with someone like you?).
- Emotionally misrepresenting (You are just being too sensitive).
- Not taking care of himself (doing drugs, engaging in high-risk behaviours such as driving recklessly).
- Withholding help (financial, with chores, child care).
- Excessive jealousy.
- Threatening to injure or kill himself.
- Threatening to hurt or kill their partner, her friends, family or pets.
- Controlling (being in complete control over where their partner goes).

They offered a separate category of spiritual abuse which is characterised by the trivialisation of ideas opinions, views and desires; discrediting her values as unimportant, silly or unrealistic; or denying their religious beliefs.

Physical abuse and psychological abuse frequently co-exist (Walker, 1979). Indeed, Kilpatrick et al. (1992) found that the actual violence of an attack may be less important in predicting a woman's response than the perceived threat.

However, an important finding from research is that by no means all women who experience violence at the hands of their partner experience negative outcomes: in fact, fewer than half reported elevated levels of psychological symptoms (Gelles and Straus, 1988). Another important finding is that the percentage of those reporting difficulties is directly related to the severity of the violence and abuse experienced: the worse the violence, the worse the symptoms.

Domestic violence also needs to be considered as a process rather than an event.

One problem remains that the focus is often on 'acts' rather than the process. It is probably better to view acts as the accumulation of the abusive process. The process of abuse often starts long before the actual 'hands-on' assault and may continue long after the 'hands-on' assault is over. Domestic violence is thus a pattern of behaviour rather than a series of isolated individual events. They also involve the use of power and control. The goal of the abuser is to ensure that he is in complete control of his partner and of the relationship. His controlling tactics may be subtle and not easily recognised. Within these two

characteristics that are inherent in all abusive relationships, the specific behaviours used by abusers to achieve their goals vary greatly. One form of abuse builds on another and sets the stage for the next violent episode. Domestic violence in its multiple forms constitutes a pattern of control. It may be done intentionally to establish domination or control in a relationship and to inflict suffering. Regardless of the intent, the effects on the victim are the same and are significant.

Trimpey (1989) and Waldo (1987) have identified a three-stage process to explain domestic violence behaviour. The first stage is called the tension-building stage in which unresolved conflict and unexpressed anger collect and there is a sense of walking on eggshells. The tension builds to the second stage, the explosion phase. During this phase, the actual abuse incident occurs, which may involve emotional, verbal and/or physical acts. The stage is followed by the honeymoon period. The abuser seeks forgiveness in a contrite manner, almost as if courting his partner, and promises never to let the abuse occur again. The cycle begins again as the tension builds. Domestic violence tends to increase in severity and frequency each time the cycle is played out unless some intervention is made. Ironically, it is when the woman leaves an abusive relationship to stop the cycle that she is the most vulnerable to extreme acts of violence. When the male realises that his partner intends to abandon him, and his usual methods of control are no longer effective, he is likely to resort to more extreme forms of violence. The abused partner is at risk of being the victim of murder, suicide or rape (Adams, 1990). It is at this point that the woman is also at risk of being the focus of repeated, unwanted attention and harassment from her estranged partner as he tries to win her back. The attention may take many forms: he may send gifts, make phone calls, or approach the former partner at home or at work. The attention may become progressively more violent when these efforts are not successful in reunifying the relationship. Coleman (1997) went on to investigate whether a relationships exists between verbal and physical abuse in dating and marital relationships and subsequent stalking behaviour. His results showed that men who repeatedly stalked their former wives or girlfriends after their relationships ended were more likely to have been verbally and physically abusive during their relationships than were men whose former wives or girlfriends were in the harassed and control groups.

There are potential differences between how professionals define domestic violence from those who endure it.

The effect of the domestic violence on the mother is devastating. They live in constant fear, not knowing when the next attack will take place, although they are certain that it will. They are thus on their guard constantly. They are often isolated from family and friends, often imposed on them by the abuser who may even have their clothes confiscated, or self-inflicted due to shame and a need to conceal what is going on. This reflects the belief that they are to blame for their situation. Such stresses are compounded if they have children as they fear for their safety. Bagshaw and Chung (2000) reported on the experiences of mothers of domestic violence that included:

- Abuse of the mother in front of the children ranging from verbal abuse and 'put downs' through to serious physical violence (some involving weapons) sometimes with children being caught in the fray.
- Torture or killing of children's pets by kicking, strangling, hanging or with weapons such as knives and guns, often in front of the children.
- Obsessive control over what the children eat and when they eat, including locking food in the cupboards – some mothers reported that they and their children were regularly starved of food.
- Unreasonable control over children's outings and friendships and rudeness to visitors to the home.

The parents reported experiences suggested that domestic violence introduced complex tensions into the family that affected the relationships between children and their parents and their siblings.

Ganley and Schechter (1996) identified several ways that children experience domestic violence:

- Hitting or threatening a child while in their mother's arms.
- Taking the child hostage to force the mother's return to the home.
- Using a child as a physical weapon against the victim.
- Forcing the child to watch assaults against the abused.

- Forcing the child to participate in the abuse.
- Using the child as a spy or interrogating them about their mother's activities.
- They are frequently told by abusive fathers that their families would be together were it not for their mother's behaviour, thus attempting to put pressure on the mother through the children to return to him or driving a wedge between the mother and her children.
- Experiencing the aftermath of the violence such as seeing the effects of the violence the following morning in terms of blood, bruises and damage to the house.
- Hearing the violence occurring after they have gone to bed.
- The child may be injured when trying to intervene to protect the mother or the abuse takes place when the mother intervenes to protect her children.
- The child being physically caught up in the violence between the adults.
- They may be killed in the process.

(James, 1994)

Children may be traumatised further from the aftermath of the violence, as a function of having to deal with an injured mother who may require assistance; dealing with a father who alternates from violence and the adoption of a caring role; the involvement of the police and the possible removal of their father from the home, and/or having to leave the family home and possibly moving to a women's refuge or shelter (Tomison, 2000).

For children growing up in violent homes, there are numerous potential lessons that result from regular exposure to family violence:

- Children may learn that it is acceptable to be abusive and that violence is an effective way to get what you want.
- Children may learn that violence is sometimes justified: particularly when you are angry at someone.
- They learn about the traditional power imbalances between men and women.

(Pepler et al., 2000)

Some children may also experience being abused from both parents. O'Keefe (1996) found that 35% of children had been physically abused in the past year: including kicking, biting or hitting with a fist (29.4% by fathers, 11.4% by mothers) and beating the child up (7.6% by fathers, 0.5% by mothers). A high proportion of both mothers and fathers had hit the child with an object (40.2% by fathers, 44% by mothers). Such figures support the co-existence for many children of domestic violence and child abuse. Tomison (1995) identified clearly that the overlap was not restricted to physical abuse (28.3%), finding sexual abuse (16.1%), emotional abuse (56.3%) and neglect (21.5%).

There is a need to acknowledge a gender difference in how domestic violence is defined.
Women define violence much more broadly than men:

- It is estimated that between 12% and 35% of woman visiting emergency rooms with injuries are there because of domestic violence (Abbott et al., 1995).
- Meyer (1992) calculated that the medical costs and lost work productivity of domestic violence at $5 to $10 billion per year.
- Woman becoming homeless as a result of domestic violence range from 27% (Knickman and Weitzman, 1989) to 41% (Bassuk and Rosenberg, 1988) to 63% of all homeless women (D'Ercole and Struening, 1990).

Concluding remarks

Since domestic violence is a multi-disciplinary problem there are a variety of ways to define it. A shared definition or understanding is important amongst agencies working together locally, both to ensure effective operations and to ensure meaningful and comparable data for the assessment of progress and use of resources (Home Office, 2000). The definition of a problem becomes crucial to the development of solutions for that problem. It guides the selection of the goals and the strategies for intervention. Domestic violence is best represented as a typology of behaviours ranging from physical and sexual to emotional harm. It is impossible to gauge with any accuracy which has the most devastating impact on the victim. For example, verbal and psychological abuse may have a more substantial effect over time but there is no specific trigger incident. Since the overwhelming majority of perpetrators are male, definitions need to reflect the gendered dimension in a way that also embraces abuse within same-sex relationships and women who abuse men.

The best definitions recognise the wide-ranging effects of domestic violence and the fact that it may have impacts on children in the family. Within the range of behaviours that comprise domestic violence it is unusual for any one form of violence to occur singly. Violence is rarely restricted to a single incident and it becomes more frequent and severe over time. Workers need to be clear that within such an escalating pattern of behaviour, there is no one level of abuse which is viewed as acceptable or insignificant. The type and combination of the violence deployed by the abuser may well be unpredictable and associated with the mood or situation. The violence may continue over many years. Binney et al. (1981) found that some of the women in their sample had been abused for thirty or even forty years, with the average being seven years.

Dobash and Dobash (1980) analysed the violent event. Two-thirds of the incidents were preceded by an argument, half of them lasting five minutes or less. The men concerned sometimes deliberately provoked arguments as an excuse for violence. Sexual jealousy was the most frequent cause of a violent episode, followed by confrontations about money and complaints about the women's housekeeping, meal preparation and child care. Domestic violence usually escalates in frequency and severity. By the time a woman's injuries are visible, violence may be a long established pattern. On average, a woman will be assaulted by a partner or ex-partner 35 times before actually reporting it to the police. They may be concerned that their children will be taken away from them or they may not want to see their partner prosecuted. They may simply want the abuse to end.

In order to combat the limitations of various definitions, Pryke and Thomas (1998) defined relationship abuse as:

Relationship abuse in essence involves the misuse of power. It includes violence, abuse and intimidation, whether physical, sexual, emotional, mental or economic, against the person or their property, inflicted by a known adult or to another (usually their past or current partner or associated other, within or external to the home of the person experiencing such violence. The perpetrator has a choice (fully recognized or not) whether to exercise their power and control over the other person. Everyone has the right to be free from fear and/or abuse and the potential criminal nature of such offences should be acknowledged.

(page 38)

Causal explanations

A vital part of understanding a social problem is an understanding of what causes it. Research has sought causal factors at various levels of analysis as articulated within the ecological framework (Bronfenbrenner, 1979), which will be used to organise the available information in this section. The dynamics of abusive relationships are complex. Generally, one individual tries to assert domination over other individuals. Domestic violence is an abuse of power and control and the process of repeated victimisation, violence and abuse results in vulnerability. This is particularly pertinent where people who are physically and mentally ill or the elderly are concerned.

Research on violence against women is a relatively young and fragmented field. Having reviewed much of the available literature, we still have significant gaps in understanding the extent and causes of the violence and the impact and effectiveness of preventive and treatment interventions. However, Scourfield (1995) offered a useful overview of the theories as to why domestic violence occurs and how men can change. He identified six main approaches:

- **Biological explanation**: this approach claims that men's violence is natural; we are born that way. We could say that men have a predilection to violence that social construction reinforces. Much violence can thus be avoided through social education and change.
- **Systems theory**: this shifts the emphasis onto the couple or family unit. In times of stress the system will imbalance. Family therapy can help restore equilibrium, without either party being held to blame. Working with the male perpetrator individually perpetuates the symmetrical, adversarial context between man and woman.
- **Psychodynamic approach**: advocates of this approach see the root cause of the violence in the man's past. Here, men replay in their relationships the rage they feel toward an abusive parent. Many believe that change can be achieved by some combination of an acknowledgement of a man's pain, ventilation of his feelings and his gaining insight through psychotherapy into the roots of his violence in childhood experience.
- **Social learning theory:** men learn violence from observing it being modelled by others.

They also learn by trying it out and finding it achieves something, such as ending an argument. As Edleson and Tolman (1992) found, if the police do not come and neighbours do not intervene, men learn they can be violent without sanction. Men also learn distorted thinking which can lead to minimising and justifying their behaviour. Change can be brought about by individually worked-out programmes under the umbrella-label 'cognitive-behavioural'.

- **Social structural theory**: this draws attention to the way social structures define men's roles as dominant. It posits that the inability of some men to fulfil these roles because of structural disadvantage leads to frustration and stress which in turn leads to violence. One target for change might thus be better employment and housing or alternatively re-education about gender roles.
- **Pro-feminist explanation**: this approach claims that violence against women is found across classes and ethnic groups. It would criticise other explanations for being too individualised and gender neutral. Dobash and Dobash (1980) see violence as rooted in patriarchy (the structural and ideological subordination of women). Violence in the home reflects gender inequality in society. It is another way in which men seek to gain and maintain power over women and to control them. Dobash and Dobash's research has found that the conflicts that most often lead to violence are those concerning domestic violence, resources and the man's possessiveness. Pro-feminist agencies tend to offer re-education for men about their understanding of a man's role. This will probably focus heavily on the tactics of power and control he uses in relationships. Some pro-feminist agencies reject anger management as teaching control to men who already use violence as a form of control.

An ecological analysis of domestic violence

Historically, each profession has developed their own theory of the origins of domestic violence and adhered rigidly to it regardless of the presenting circumstances of a case. This is blinkered thinking and has led to a failure to offer a holistic framework within which respective theories could be located. The emergence of an ecological framework has offered the potential for conceptual unity across professions and professionals, although it has not explicitly been adopted or recommended to date. A shared knowledge base, originating from research is essential (Calder, 1992).

Ecology is a science, in which it explores how organisms interact and survive the environment in which they find themselves. It accepts that there are different levels in society where domestic violence can occur – at an individual, family, community and society level. This approach is characterised by its prominent emphasis on the interaction between systems rather than on the properties and processes of any one system.

It allows for the dynamics of domestic violence to be located in a framework which acknowledges that abuse frequently occurs in a socially unhealthy context (Calder, 1991). In my view, this has the potential as a comprehensive framework for organising knowledge of human behaviour as well as highlighting convergence among disciplines and integrating the diversity of theory, as seen in Figure 2.2 below. This is also consistent with the aspiration of the Assessment Framework (DoH, 2000).

I will now explore the relevant theory within each level.

Individual level

The microsystem contains factors that pertain directly to the individuals involved such as personality factors and personal history. Explanations of domestic violence have traditionally focused on the individual level of analysis. Perpetrators have been characterised as sadistic, mentally ill, alcoholic and unable to tolerate intimacy (Rounsaville, 1978), as well as suffering from various psychological problems

Figure 2.2: An ecological framework (adapted from Calder and Waters, 1991).

Ecological levels	Levels of analysis/models
ontogenesis/individual	psychopathology
couple	social interactional
family micro-system	social interactional
community exo-system	socio-situational
cultural macro-system	socio-cultural

such as morbid jealousy (Hilberman and Munson, 1977–8) and compulsive masculinity.

Hart et al. (1993) found a high incidence of psychopathology and personality disorders, most frequently antisocial personality disorder, borderline personality disorder or post-traumatic stress disorder, among men who abuse their wives.

Some psychologist's view men's violence as being to do with their personality and psychological problems. The violence represents an outburst of emotional pain, frustration or confusion. The underlying issues may stem from early childhood rearing that led to fears of intimacy or over-attachment to women. Some men do simply explode or snap but most seem to be dealing with inflated expectations. They feel violated when they do not get their own way. As their expectations or 'entitlements' are lowered, so is their frustration. Moreover, many violent men are clearly deliberate, calculating and outright mean. They are violent toward women because they can be and violence gets results (Gondolf, 2000). Anger management is often mentioned and its appeal lies in the prospect of short-term solutions but it is problematic as it implies that the victim provokes the anger and precipitates the abuse; it fails to account for the premeditating controlling behaviours associated with abuse; and it does not specifically address the social reinforcements for violence against women (Gondolf and Russell, 1986). Indeed, most violent men have more than anger problems.

Physiological explanations include the fact that high testosterone levels may contribute to aggressive behaviour and dominance status. Low levels of serotonin have been correlated with aggressive behaviour, impulsivity and suicidal behaviour. Alcohol has multiple effects, among them physiological and psychological. Alcohol also alters the rules that govern social interaction and it shapes the interpretations of social interaction and of individual behaviour. Dis-inhibition theory suggests that alcohol has a direct and causal relationship to violence because its psycho-physiological properties release violent impulses, tendencies and inhibitions. However, alcohol can have the opposite effect of pacifying, calming and depressing effects. Alcohol use has been reported in between 25–85% of incidents of domestic violence (Kantor and Straus, 1987). It is far more prevalent for men than for female victims. The relationship of alcohol to domestic violence could be spurious, but the relationship of men's drinking to domestic violence remains even after statistically controlling for socio-demographic variables, hostility and marital satisfaction. Alcohol may well interfere with cognitive processes, especially social cognitions. Men who are under the influence of alcohol are more likely to misperceive ambiguous or neutral cues as suggestive of sexual interest and to ignore or misinterpret cues that a woman is unwilling. This distortion increases the probability of escalation to physical violence. In our society, drinking is considered to reduce an individual's responsibility for their actions. As such, drinking can act as a mechanism for neutralising or disavowing the deviance of a family member. Research indicates that drugs are less likely to be an issue in domestic violence attacks than alcohol, but where they are a factor, they are more likely to be related to chronic victimisation – 8% of female victims of chronic domestic violence said their abuser was under the influence of drugs at the time of the last assault, compared with 5% of intermittent victims (Secretary of State for the Home Department, 2003). Certain drugs such as cocaine are more likely to be associated with violent behaviour than others and drug mis-users may be at risk of becoming violent when in a state of withdrawal. There are good reasons to discount that men lose control because of drugs or drink or frustration as some women report that the men would deliberately get drunk before being violent and even threaten violence before taking the substance.

An individual's attitudes, beliefs and gender schemas are important. Where a violence-supportive schema about women has developed, men are more likely to misinterpret ambiguous evidence as confirming their beliefs (Abbey, 1991). Culturally sanctioned beliefs about the rights and privileges of husbands have historically legitimised a man's domination over his partner and warranted the use of violence to control her. Abusers frequently excuse their behaviour: by pointing to their wives 'unwifely' behaviour as justification (Dobash and Dobash, 1979). Values are part of the system that provides a framework for unconscious beliefs about the individual and the world in which they live. Values are imparted by both the individuals who are in constant and close proximity, such as parents, teachers and religious leaders. Values in today's complex and fast-paced world arc also transmitted via electronic media, which bombard

the individual with standards th
not contradict one's beliefs. The cl
up with domestic violence find the
quandary when trying to sort out v
are important, which should be chal
which should be abandoned. Roy (19 J
articulated clearly what children learn about the world around them in such circumstances:

- They learn that might is right. They learn that the bigger and stronger one is, the more control they can exert over another person.
- They learn that there is a hierarchy system: the younger and weaker one is the more vulnerable. Children cannot win in such a situation. They learn to capitulate to the system and very often react to it in maladaptive ways. They learn that when they grow up they will be permitted to use physical force in order to get results. They learn to respect violence and to employ it whenever their own situation gives them the upper hand on the hierarchy.

Domestic violence is motivated by a man's need to dominate the woman. As such he uses the violence to maintain his superiority. Others argue that it may stem from his feelings of powerlessness and inability to accept rejection (Browne and Dutton, 1990).

Social learning theory posits that humans learn social behaviour by observing others' behaviour and the consequences of that behaviour, forming ideas about what behaviours are appropriate and continuing them if the results are positive. This theory does not view aggression as inevitable, but rather sees it as a social behaviour that is learned and shaped by its consequences, continuing if it is reinforced. From this perspective, male violence against women endures in human societies because it is both modelled on individual families and the society more generally and has positive results: it releases tensions, leaves the abuser feeling better, often achieves its ends by cutting off arguments, and is rarely associated with serious punishment for the abuser. Since men may misinterpret social interactions they may respond inappropriately to them. Dutton and Browning (1988) noted that abusers appear to be more likely than non-violent women to attribute negative intentions to their partner's actions and to behave negatively with either anger and/or contempt.

These explanations are not very useful as not all abusive men evidence any form of psychopathology and no consistent patterns have been revealed. This view would indicate that domestic violence of women by men is abnormal yet the statistics would illustrate that this is a normal pattern. The model does not explain why the violence is usually only perpetrated within the home and mainly on women partners rather than in the street or at work.

The modus operandi of male perpetrators

The male perpetrator expresses his dominance and asserts his identity through attempting to control and master every aspect of his partner's life. He uses patterns of coercive and violent behaviour to establish control and power over his partner (Dobash and Dobash, 1980). Through creating an illusion of omnipotence his own feelings of inadequacy and helplessness are temporarily alleviated. Such projective identification is a powerful means of attempting to rid oneself of unacceptable impulses through denying them in oneself and identifying them in another. Their partner becomes the sponge for their feelings of inadequacy and self-contempt. The female often absorbs these feelings, becoming increasingly depressed and he, in turn, loses touch with his own feelings of vulnerability, finding his aggressive and sadistic feelings more acceptable, less frightening to acknowledge. The perpetrator clearly needs the victim to remain alive: the goal is to control and preserve rather than destroy.

Some of the consequences for the perpetrator of the domestic violence include loss of the partner; injury or death at the hands of a partner who decides to retaliate or defend herself, alienation from their children; guilt, shame, and loss of self-esteem; and a range of legal effects, including arrest, trial and incarceration or other penalties.

Like the alcoholic, most perpetrators of domestic violence will not seek help until the situation becomes a crisis and they are mandated to do so (because their partners have taken their children or they have been processed through the criminal justice system).

The Duluth power and control wheel identifies clearly the range of tactics deployed by men who perpetrate domestic violence. (see Figure 2.3)

The adult relationship

The adult relationship, characteristics of the woman and their communication are important considerations. The stage of the relationship

between a man and a woman may partly determine the probability of violence. The assumption here is that domestic violence can sometimes be a two-way street, or part of a communication pattern between two individuals. Practice experience indicated that a man may refrain from violence until a woman has made an emotional commitment to him, such as moving in together, getting engaged or married, or becoming pregnant (Walker, 1979). Once an emotional bond has been formed the man has their sense of entitlement to control his partner's behaviour reinforced. Evidence points to many women being willing to view an initial violent incident as an anomaly and as such are more willing to forgive it. Unfortunately, such a response may reinforce the violent behaviour.

The danger of this area is that we represent domestic violence as a mutual thing that arises out of the relationship.

Goode's (1971) theory of family violence is called resource theory, but it also contains elements of exchange theory. Resource theory views violence as a resource that may be called upon when other resources are deficient; exchange theory views violence as a result of the breakdown in the reciprocal exchange process involved in social interaction. Goode posits that force or its threat is a fundamental part of all social systems (including the family) because it is one way of obtaining compliance from others. He argues that force is a resource that may be called upon by a family member when other resources for obtaining compliance – such as money, prestige, respect or love – are lacking or insufficient. Furthermore, when a family member perceives costs to be outweighing rewards in the social exchange process, and when exiting or submission are undesirable alternatives, they may resort to violence if these other resources are unavailable.

Traumatic bonding is a useful theory that tries to explain why abusive relationships are so powerful. Several factors have been identified that must be present for such a bond to form. First, for traumatic bonding to take place, a relationship must contain an imbalance of power. This often takes the form of the abuser controlling the key aspects to the relationship, making most of the decisions and controlling the finances. The second factor in traumatic bonding is the sporadic nature of the abusive behaviour. In most abusive relationships the bad times are intermingled with the good times. The abuse is

Figure 2.3: The Duluth power and control wheel

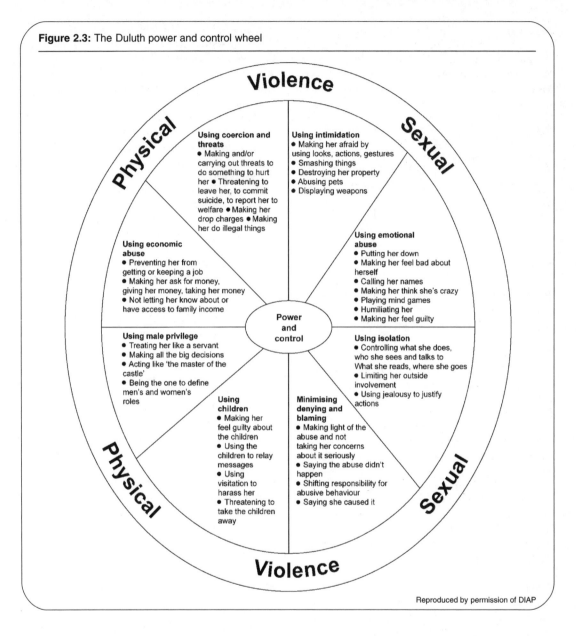

Reproduced by permission of DIAP

usually preceded and followed by very loving, giving periods. This pattern of on-going off-again abuse and affection is the strongest form of reinforcement. The third factor is denial where the victim makes excuses to make the situation seem better than it really was. The final factor involves finding ways to mask the abuse and can include self-medicating with alcohol and/or drugs. These four elements combine to create a traumatic bond with the abuser and once established, become difficult to escape from (Dugan and Hock, 2000).

The Stockholm Syndrome describes how the mother bonds to their captor as a means of surviving a life-threatening situation and this is transferable to domestic violence situations in order to explain the seemingly illogical actions of the victims. Graham and Rawlings (1991) hypothesised that as the abuser traumatises the woman by threatening her physical and/or psychological survival, she comes to see him as a captor. Then, due to her subsequent isolation and her abuser's small kindnesses, she must turn to him alone for nurturance and sustenance. In this closed system, she learns to keep him happy so that he will let her live. However, in doing so, the woman unconsciously takes on his perspective of the world. This includes her denial of the abuse. Like traumatic bonding it assumes four conditions:

- The victim is threatened with death or great physical harm and perceives the perpetrator capable of acting on these threats.
- The victim sees no means of escape and thus perceives that her life depends on her captor.
- The victim feels isolated and holds little hope of outside intervention by family or friends.
- The victimiser offers kindness along with the violence and thus increases the victim's perception of complete helplessness and dependence on him.

Frude (1994) pointed out that the rate of marital abuse has been found to be significantly higher for cohabiting than for married couples. This may be because cohabiting relationships are less well defined, leading to frequent fights over power, rules and roles; they may suffer increased strain and increased social isolation; and may be subject to lower social control than marital relationships. Straus (1974) found that physical violence was more likely to occur in marital relationships in which rational problem-solving strategies were rarely employed, and Lloyd (1990) found that violent couples were less likely to use problem solving, discussion or negotiation and their conflicts were characterised by high levels of anger and verbal attack. Conflicts were typically unresolved and few apologies were given. Marital partners often find each other irritating. They are generally dissatisfied with their relationship. They are generally aware of the kinds of comments that will cause the most distress to the other and use these as ammunition. Since we know that violence is triggered by some verbal behaviour of the victim, this is important. They may nag, criticise or gibe about their poor sexual performance and since it often hits a soft spot, there is an angry response. Conversely, the abuser becomes expert at attacking the victim's weaknesses and when they are angry they go for the jugular and hit below the belt.

Family

One likely repercussion of domestic violence is a general poisoning of the family environment which in turn may indirectly generate the adverse outcomes noted in the children exposed to domestic violence (Barnett et al., 1997). As levels of domestic violence increase, levels of family strengths, marital satisfaction and parental satisfaction decrease (Meredith et al., 1986).

All socialisation begins within the family. Increased risk of adult domestic violence is associated with exposure to violence between their parents while growing up. Widom (1989) argued that one-third of children who have been abused or exposed to parental violence become violent adults. Straus et al. (1980) found that sons of violent parents are more likely to abuse their intimate partners than boys from non-violent homes. They also found that men raised in patriarchal family structures in which traditional gender roles are encouraged are more likely to become violent adults than those raised in more egalitarian homes.

Very little is known about the home environments of families living with domestic violence. This may be due to the focus often being on family processes that occur within these distressed homes. For example, Jaffe et al. (1990) articulated the family disruption hypothesis, which states that domestic violence may impact children indirectly through a number of other events and familial characteristics that are changed or affected by the presence of violence. That is, domestic violence is likely to set into motion a number of other negative processes that either singly or in combination disrupt a child's normal routine and ongoing development. As the authors note, the home environment is often defined by the primary caregiver who is usually the mother. Therefore the family disruption hypothesis would posit that domestic violence may indirectly affect children's adjustment through its negative impact on maternal psychological functioning and maternal parenting capacities. The self-esteem, depression, parenting abilities and stress mediate the impact on children's internalising and externalising problems and trauma symptoms. The family disruption hypothesis also suggests that domestic violence might impact the overall home environment in addition to its impact on mothers specifically. Huth-Bocks et al. (2003) established that domestic violence had an impact on maternal depression, which in turn negatively impacted the home environment. We know that depressed mothers tend to be less verbal, less positive and less responsive to their children (Downey and Coyne, 1990) and as such it should come as no surprise that it impacted to provide a less stimulating home environment for the children. It also affects the mother's capacity to mediate the multiple impacts on the children of the domestic violence.

Motz (2001) argued that:

> *... domestic violence is such an emotive and distressing phenomenon that it is tempting to simplify its dynamics, disregarding its complex nature and the role of each partner in maintaining the destructive interaction. To view the woman as only a passive victim is to deny female agency, but to ignore the social forces which create restricted choices for her is dangerous.*
>
> (page 253)

It is important that we identify the potential contributing factors operating at the family as well as the couple level of analysis (Carlson, 1991).

- The family as a social group has some unique properties that contribute to the likelihood that high levels of conflict will exist. These include norms about privacy; involuntary membership; members of diverse ages, abilities and needs; and expectations of behaviour that are traditionally based on gender at a time when norms for role behaviours are in flux.
- Sex-role norms manifest themselves at the couple level. Most men fully expect to be the dominant partner in a couple relationship and many partners are willing to co-operate, whilst some are not willing to subordinate themselves. Any indications of assertion or autonomy may be perceived as threats to male dominance. This may be especially true when the male lacks the resources (e.g. the education, job prestige or earnings) to justify his superior position.
- Many perpetrators tend to have few close relationships beyond their partners, so that they are isolated and highly dependent, with few resources to support them through difficult times.

The relationship between the perpetrator and the victim of domestic violence is important as it is one where both play an active part. The relationship cannot be established by one person alone. To simply avoid exploring the role of the victim in the violence for fear of blaming her denies her a role and portrays her as always passive. The victim is usually a highly significant person for her partner and she is aware of this.

Initially her partner may have made statements of great love and dependence. However, following the initial violence he expresses profound feelings of remorse and regret, offering to do anything to make up for his behaviour and promises to change. While this may be genuine it is not always easy to enact. The victim is aware that her partner is repentant and has other aspects to his character which are at odds with his destructive and frightening side.

The victim may represent a powerful persecutory mother figure to the violent partner: it is as though her sensitive understanding that her partner's violence stems from his own deprivation prevents her from leaving him. They may be especially alert to the prospect of disappointing their partner replicating earlier rejection.

Overall, the compulsive nature of abusive relationships may be connected with the meeting of unconscious needs and the swapping of roles in that the abuser is actually dependent on his victim, who is at some level, aware of this power. The abusive relationship thus has very strongly entrenched destructive dynamics which makes it very difficult to escape from or be able to leave.

There are some negative consequences worthy of note of the domestic violence for the couple or the family as a system:

- When violence becomes a pattern, a climate of fear, unpredictability, stifled emotions, and dysfunctional roles can be established in a family, affecting everyone.
- For the couple the dependency relationships can become even more extreme and pathological, leading them to bond to each other in a very unhealthy way.
- The couple may become locked in a negative self-perpetuating cycle that feels inevitable for both.
- Reciprocal violence may occur (Carlson, 1991).

Treatment for couples where domestic violence is a feature is available and is premised on the following:

- Violence is a learned behaviour and can thus be unlearned and replaced with less harmful, more effective methods of conflict resolution and anger management.
- The reasons why violence is dysfunctional for families.
- General relationship enhancement (see Weidman, 1986).

Community exo-system issues

This includes policies, procedures and professional groups designed to study, control, and intervene in domestic violence situations. They have the social mandate to operationalise and influence the cultural attitudes discussed below. Social workers may either reflect existing perceptions or shape them through a series of enabling, advocating and direct intervention functions that help identify the needs of the victims of domestic violence and actualise their rights (Peled et al., 2000). Most of the organisations perceive the cessation of violence as a critical measure of their effectiveness and view the separation between perpetrator and victim as a significant means of achieving this goal. The modus operandi of social agencies dealing with domestic violence is guided more often by meaning systems stemming from professional and political values and ideologies than by those of their clients. Meaning systems held by clients that are inconsistent with the organisational needs are often ignored, misinterpreted or acknowledged only minimally and this response may severely interfere with empowerment processes.

Cultural

The cultural social macro-system comprises the set of cultural and social values that pervade and support individual and family lifestyles and community services in today's society. This level is often the invisible layer in theoretical models of domestic violence, yet its influence is increasingly recognised as important in understanding the hidden forces that govern personal and institutional behaviours. Social and cultural factors can foster or mitigate stress in family life and such factors have achieved new importance in emerging models of domestic violence. It is important to note that the wider society does not impact uniformly on individuals, families, and members of ethnic cultural groups.

The socio-cultural system is located within the ideological and institutional patterns of a culture. It serves as a set of broad cultural blue prints, guiding perceptions, interpretations, and actions concerning social phenomena. Culture plays a key role in creating an environment conducive to abusive relationships. Straus (1977–8) identified several certain socio-cultural factors that contribute to both domestic violence and child abuse:

- The cultural acceptance of violence in society and the resultant high level of violence.
- The cultural norms that legitimate certain levels and types of violence within the family unit.
- Sexual inequality and male domination.
- The socialisation of children in violence.
- The high level of conflict that is inherent in the family structure.

Any true ecological analysis needs to embrace the societal context of the presenting problem. Several social and economic factors are related to domestic violence.

- Domestic violence can be found in all educational, economic, religious, and ethnic groups – though not necessarily to an equal extent.
- The most powerful demographic correlate of (and probably contributor to) domestic violence is poverty and the stress it creates. Virtually every study examining the role of social class in family violence has found that low income individuals are significantly more likely to engage in violence and abuse towards family members. This finding has clear social policy implications in that the amelioration of domestic violence is closely linked to the eradication of poverty (Straus, Gelles and Steinmetz, 1980; Gelles and Straus, 1988; Straus and Gelles, 1986).
- Coley and Beckett (1988) examined the correlation between ethnicity and domestic violence and found no consistent pattern when comparing rates of violence between blacks and whites. They concluded that ethnicity does not contribute independently to the incidence of domestic violence when social class is controlled. However, this does not mean that ethnic differences do not exist in the phenomenon or how it is interpreted by the participants (Asbury, 1987). For example, Torres (1987) compared the attitudes of 25 Hispanic and 25 non-Hispanic victims of domestic violence from emergency shelters. She found more similarities than differences in their attitudes, but there were some important differences. The Hispanic women were less likely to label verbal behaviours and hitting as abuse. They were more likely to cite family reasons (e.g. presence of children) for not leaving the relationship. The non-Hispanic women were more likely to say that they loved their abuser or had nowhere else to go.

- Age is another factor associated with domestic violence. Both national surveys have found that younger couples, those under 30 in particular, are more likely to be violent (Gelles and Straus, 1988; Straus, Gelles and Steinmetz, 1980). This might be explained by the developmental stage of family life in which young couples find themselves is more stressful as a result of economic strains or the demands of young children in the home.
- Other societal factors include sexism and sex-role stereotyping (see Calder, 2001 for a review) and our general acceptance of violence of all types. Such tolerance of violence establishes a context for the acceptance of violence in intimate relationships.

Patriarchy

Roy (1988) articulated the cornerstone theory of family violence where the patriarchal right of ownership and children is the primary cause. The theory derives from the historical context of violence against wives and children relying heavily on the similarities of origin, e.g. the belief that wives and children were the property of husbands and fathers, respectively, thus leading to the concomitant societal tolerance and justification for the maltreatment of both groups. The theory assumes that the resultant societal policy and action led to the dehumanisation of women and children and contributed to their common bondage. Wives and children as property devalued their worth as members of the human race and eliminated them from the protection of human rights.

Western societies have endorsed that wives are the property of their male partners. Expectations about dating and intimate relationships are conveyed by culturally transmitted scripts. Scripts support violence when they encourage men to feel superior, entitled, with women as their prey, while holding women responsible for controlling the extent of sexual involvement (White and Koss, 1993). Parents socialise daughters to resist sexual advances and sons to initiate sexual activity (Ross, 1977).

Counts et al. (1992) conducted a review of the cultural differences in the amount of and acceptability of intimate partner violence in 14 different societies. She found that physical violence of wives was tolerated in all the societies and considered necessary in many societies, but the rates and severity of wife beating was found

to range from non-existent to very frequent. These differences seem to be related to negative sanctions for men who overstepped 'acceptable' limits, sanctuaries for woman to escape violence, and a sense of honour based on non-violence or decent treatment of women.

Gil (1970) argued that social factors such as poverty and unemployment contribute to spouse and child abuse as do status inconsistency, size of the family and role reversals. These conditions may create stress, tension and frustration within the family which may erupt into episodes of spouse or child abuse. In addition, factors such as isolation from social support systems (Garbarino, 1977) and a series of life changes for which one is unprepared (Justice and Justice, 1976) may contribute to abuse within the family context. Gelles (1972) argued that the stress produced by these factors and the ability to cope with stress are differentially distributed throughout the social structure.

Where mothers have been sexually abused themselves or witnessed domestic violence in their childhood, they have experienced abuse, powerlessness, helplessness and oppression. This can result in a damaged sense of self, a lack of personal autonomy, and a sense of uncertainty and confusion about adult roles and responsibilities. These responses are in themselves shaped by gender. Boys are more likely to express their distress through externally directed more active behaviour. This may include aggression and violence towards other people. In contrast, girls' responses appear to be more passive and internally directed: their distress may be expressed tearfully, by running away, or in severe cases, by self-mutilation. Gender expectations in our society thus tend to steer boys towards an abusive victimising role and girls into a perpetuation of the victim role. Women need to be taught that they have a right to assert their wishes, or at the very least that they have a right to say 'no'. They need to know that they can have non-abusive relationships or realise that such relationships exist. Otherwise they too may carry the consequences of abuse into adult life. This may result in an inability or fear of hugging or touching their child/ren, as they fear it will be perceived as abuse. Some mothers may actually remain afraid that they may actually abuse their own children. In contrast, other women who have suppressed their abusive experiences may, as adults, miss or deny the symptoms of abuse in their own family or household. Those who have continued in a passive victim role may in their adult life, be targeted by abusing men and replicate risky situations based on submission to dominant men. Their capacity to recognise and resist both their continuing experiences of oppression is thus severely impaired.

While the patriarchal right no longer exists in the extreme physical form, modern societies around the globe are still strongly influenced by this legacy, but are in most cases unaware of the critical importance that it continues to have on the complicated inter-relationships within the family of the 20th century. Whilst a great deal has been done in improving the status of women and the position of children, much remains to be done.

Khan (2000) in Figure 2.4 provided a useful framework to organise the factors that perpetuate domestic violence.

Multi-factorial models

Since violence can be conceptualised in many ways, there seems to be an acceptance that we need to move toward an integrative, meta-theoretical model that considers multiple variables operating at different times. Dutton (1985) developed an ecologically nested theory of domestic violence. He proposed that whether or not a man will assault his wife is influenced by an intricate network of variables within each of the four nested layers of environmental experience – an ontogenic core of individual experience within a micro-systemic layer of nuclear and extended family members within an exo-systemic layer of occupation, religious and social affiliations and neighbourhoods within a macro-systemic layer of society's formal rules and informal norms. Figure 2.5 illustrates the structure of the model and gives some examples at each layer of experiences that have been clinically and/or empirically associated with perpetrators of domestic violence.

Roy (1988) provided us with a useful visual listing of the most common causes of child abuse and domestic violence within a broad ecological framework (see Figure 2.6 overleaf).

Figure 2.4: Factors that perpetuate domestic violence (Khan, 2000)

Cultural	● Gender-specific socialisation ● Cultural definitions of appropriate sex roles ● Expectations of roles within relationships ● Belief in the inherent superiority of males ● Values that give men propriety rights over women and girls ● Notion of the family as the private sphere and under male control ● Customs of marriage (bride price/dowry) ● Acceptability of violence as a means to resolve conflict
Economic	● Women's economic dependence on men ● Limited access to cash and credit ● Discriminatory laws regarding inheritance, property rights, use of communal lands, and maintenance after divorce or widowhood ● Limited access to employment in formal and informal sectors ● Limited access to education and training for women
Legal	● Lesser legal status of women either by written law or practice ● Laws regarding divorce, child custody, maintenance and inheritance ● Legal definitions of rape and domestic violence ● Low levels of legal literacy among women ● Insensitive treatment of women and girls by police and judiciary
Political	● Under-representation of women in power, politics, the media and in the legal and medical professionals ● Domestic violence not taken seriously ● Notions of family being private and beyond the control of the state ● Risk of challenge to status quo/religious laws ● Limited organisation of women as a political force ● Limited participation of women in organised political system

Figure 2.5: An ecologically nested model of male violence toward female intimates (adapted ... 1985)

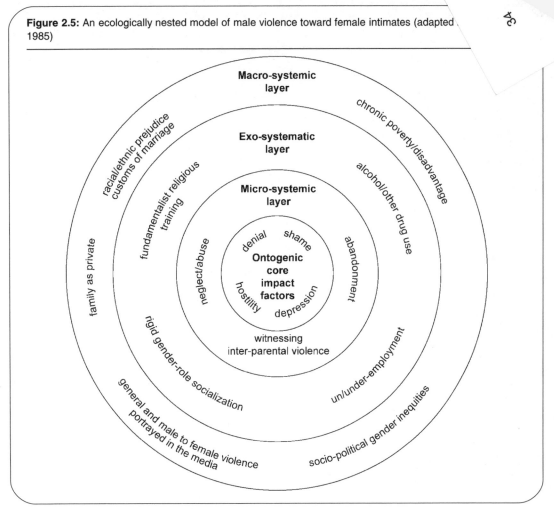

The cycle of domestic violence

Walker (1979) has described a cycle of events which exist periodically in an abusive relationship (see Figure 2.7). This graphically depicts the cyclic pattern of violence observed by Walker in her interviews with 120 battered women. This cycle is made up of three phases: a tension-building phase, a period of acute violence and a state of reconciliation. Each of these phases varies in time and intensity for the same couple and for different couples. In the tension-building phase the abuser uses one or more of the control tactics. Minor physical assaults were described during this phase but differed from the acute battering incident in the intensity of the attack and in the sense of the control the women reported feeling they still had over the violence.

Denial, anger, fear of the anticipated beating, and rationalisation for the abuse were common elements in the women's descriptions of this phase. This phase tended to last from several months to several years. The acute battering incident was described by the women as a psychologically and physically paralysing event where the futility of escape prevailed. This phase can last from two hours to two days or more. After the attack many of the partners became extremely contrite and loving, tearfully apologised, and promised never to be violent again. A honeymoon-like period followed but inevitably drifted back into a new tension-building phase. Over time, the battering incidents tended to increase in severity and frequency and the honeymoon period shortened and then disappeared.

Figure 2.6: Common causes of domestic violence and child abuse (Roy, 1988)

Child Abuse	Domestic Violence
1. Psychiatric Disorders	
Hysteria	Masochism in wife
Schizoid personality traits	Paranoid schizophrenia
Character neurosis	Primary substance abuse
Depression	Depression
Narcissism	Obsessive-compulsive neurosis
Sado-masochism	Personality disorder
Poor self-image	Poor self-image
Dementia	Dementia
	Catathymic crisis
	Episodic discontrol
2. Psychosocial	
History of family violence	Abuser's parental violence history
Poverty	Poverty/financial dependence of wife
Burdens of child care	Sex-role stereotyping
Early and unwanted pregnancy	Marriage on impulse due to pregnancy
External stress	External stress
Media violence	Media violence
Isolation/mobile society	Isolation/mobile society
3. Sociopolitical	
Children as chattel	Women as husband's property
Customary extremes in discipline	Husband's right of chastisement
Rights of parents over children	Women as children/patriarchal authority
Inequity of minor status	Sexual inequality

This cycle mirrors that created by Frude (1980; 1989) in relation to child abuse. Frude suggested that the first stage is the presence of a stressful situation, followed by the perception of the situation as threatening and then as escalation of anger and emotional distress as a response to the situation. This then leads to a lack of inhibition with regard to violent expression in response to a trigger, such as an argument, culminating in the individual exhibiting aggression and performing a violent act on their partner. After an act of violence, the abusive spouse may continue with his hostile attitude or show a long period of sullen silence. Frequently the abuser expresses regret, apologising and promising no more attacks. This has been linked to the 'Jeckyll and Hyde personality' (Bernard and Bernard, 1984). Despite this, it often results in reconciliation and hope for the victim.

Browne and Herbert (1987) combined the ideas proposed by Frude and Walker to construct a battering cycle which maintains violent interactions within a relationship (see Figure 2.8).

Typologies

Johnston and Cambell (1993) developed a five-fold typology of inter-parental violence:

- **Ongoing and episodic male battering**: is characterised by terrifying and severe violence to women, perpetrated by possessive, domineering men who minimise and deny their violence, blaming the woman, and who become even more dangerous at separation. These men experienced enormous internal tension and exercised little or no restraint.
- **Female-initiated violence**: these women also experienced intolerable internal tension, fed by a perception that the man was holding back. Violence tended to be relatively minor with the possibility of escalation. The men were generally passive, attempting to contain the

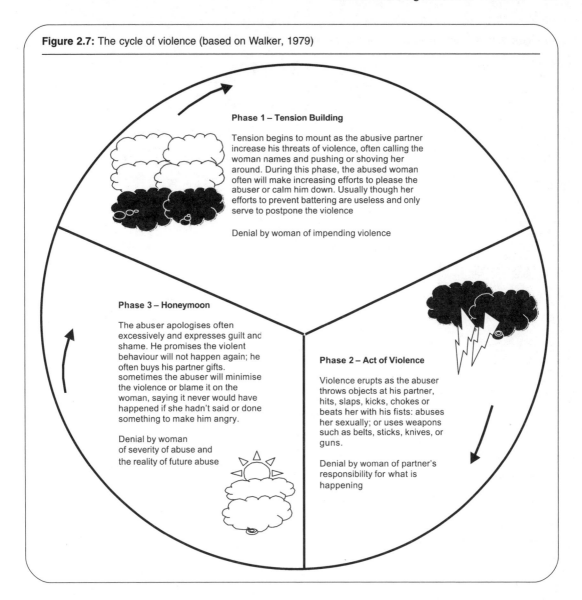

Figure 2.7: The cycle of violence (based on Walker, 1979)

Phase 1 – Tension Building

Tension begins to mount as the abusive partner increase his threats of violence, often calling the woman names and pushing or shoving her around. During this phase, the abused woman often will make increasing efforts to please the abuser or calm him down. Usually though her efforts to prevent battering are useless and only serve to postpone the violence

Denial by woman of impending violence

Phase 3 – Honeymoon

The abuser apologises often excessively and expresses guilt and shame. He promises the violent behaviour will not happen again; he often buys his partner gifts. sometimes the abuser will minimise the violence or blame it on the woman, saying it never would have happened if she hadn't said or done something to make him angry.

Denial by woman of severity of abuse and the reality of future abuse

Phase 2 – Act of Violence

Violence erupts as the abuser throws objects at his partner, hits, slaps, kicks, chokes or beats her with his fists: abuses her sexually; or uses weapons such as belts, sticks, knives, or guns.

Denial by woman of partner's responsibility for what is happening

---

assaults but also capable of retaliating. Women admitted their actions although they projected blame.

- **Male-controlled interactive violence**: was often consequent upon an argument, with the man characteristically responding by seeking to control and dominate his partner. Men and women were abusive of each other, with the severity of the violence being consequent, in part, upon the level of resistance offered. Mutual blaming and 'just desserts' rationalising were common.
- **Separation-endangered trauma**: involved uncharacteristic violent acts during difficult separations/divorces and were either male- or female-initiated. Victims were shocked and frightened by the out-of-character, generally limited violence in their partner, who was remorseful and ashamed.
- **Psychotic and paranoid reactions**: involved both women and men as perpetrators, acting in an unpredictable, sometimes seriously and restrained abusive manner. They were driven by disordered mental processes perceiving outside threats or plots against them which justified their defensive attack. Victims were traumatised and intimidated.

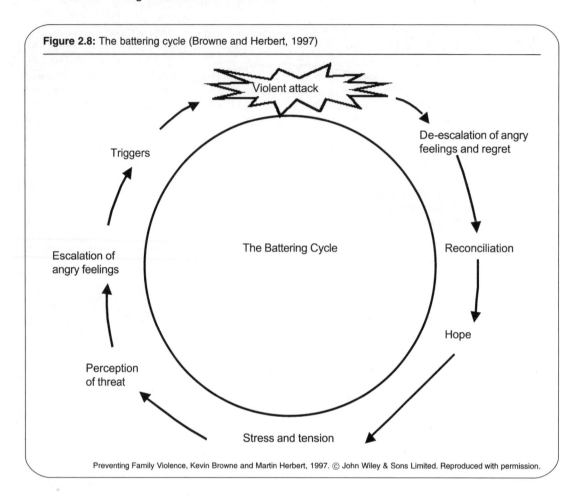

Figure 2.8: The battering cycle (Browne and Herbert, 1997)

Violent attack

De-escalation of angry feelings and regret

Triggers

The Battering Cycle

Reconciliation

Escalation of angry feelings

Hope

Perception of threat

Stress and tension

Preventing Family Violence, Kevin Browne and Martin Herbert, 1997. © John Wiley & Sons Limited. Reproduced with permission.

Saunders (1995) suggested that perpetrators of domestic violence can be divided into three main groups to reflect the fact they are not a homogeneous group:

- **Family-only batterers**: these are the least severely violent spousal abusers and abuse only in their own homes. They report little abuse in childhood and tend not to abuse alcohol. They are described as having more liberal sex role attitudes and have compulsive and conforming personalities.
- **Emotionally volatile batterers**: this group is the least psychologically abusive to their partners. They display high levels of anger, jealousy and depression and are at higher risk of suicide. They are sometimes violent outside their homes.
- **Generally violent batterer**: these spouse abusers are the most severely violent. They are most likely to have been severely abused in

childhood and tend to be violent outside of the home as well. They are more likely to abuse alcohol and drugs than the other groups of domestic violence offenders. They often have rigid sex-role attitudes and high levels of anger, depression, jealousy and anti-social attitudes.

Marginalised groups

Domestic violence within gay relationships

Little is known about the prevalence of domestic violence in gay relationships as crime surveys have tended to ignore this issue. Whilst it is important to acknowledge that it does take place it is also important to note that it does not simply mirror the abuse found in heterosexual relationships. The availability of services and the difficulties gap people face as a result of discrimination presents specific problems. Disclosing an experience of violence from a partner frequently means the victim will also have to disclose their sexuality and thus face the risk of a homophobic reaction from the service provider. Perpetrators may also use 'homophobic control' over his partner by threatening to disclose his sexuality to his family and/or employer. For men the fear of AIDS or suffering from AIDS can limit the man's capacity to leave an abusive partner (Morgan, 1998).

Vaughan (2000) noted that domestic violence within same-sex relationships is considered to be an exception to the rule and then goes on to explore the issue as a remedial strategy. Estimates of the extent of domestic violence within gay male relationships are anecdotal in nature. Island and Letellier (1991) believe that the figure is disproportionately double to that of heterosexual instances of violence. Many gay couples are isolated from friends and family as a result of intolerance and homophobia and this often leads to the couple becoming more dependent on each other. Since the precursors of violence within relationships are stresses and social isolation, this is significant in the origins of violence within gay relationships.

One of the unique characteristics of gay domestic violence is that many are unable to see that they are victims simply because they are men. As a result, they may not take the necessary emotional or practical steps to deal with the situation. If they do, then the next obstacle lies in the belief that seeking help may reinforce their sense of failure which they experience not only as a partner in a violent relationship but also as a man. Many victims felt that they deserve their injuries because they are gay. They may perceive themselves as defective and this can be linked to difficulties in maintaining feelings of self-worth and dignity. The resulting low self-esteem from this may contribute to a poor ability to develop committed and trusted relationships. Further effects of this can be that the gay man turns the feelings of worthlessness into a hatred of those parts of himself and others. The process of internalising the oppression against gay men can become acted out in horizontal hostility, an expression of self-hatred felt owing to one's own membership of a minority group. Instead of showing hostility toward the oppressing force it is safer to direct this against other people.

Many men feel traumatised and feel ashamed because they have not been able to stop the

violence and they are reluctant to approach the police because they feel they will not be believed. Wellard (2003) reported on a recent national survey that found that only 18% of gay men and 13% of lesbians who experienced domestic violence had reported this to the police. Only 5% of men and 4% of women had reported incidents more than once.

Research shows that women and men from violent backgrounds are three times more likely to be violent to their partner. One in three women admits they grab, shove, push or slap their partner during rows. One in seven admits they bite, hit, scratch or throw dangerous objects. One in 30 women admits they use knives or threaten to attack their partner. And one in five casualty admissions resulting from domestic violence are of men attacked by women (Bell, 2002).

Violence within all same-sex relationships differs from male to female domestic violence in all or some of the following respects:

- They are not similarly supported by conventional power structures.
- They will not be experienced as the same by the persons involved (in the same sense as racist violence does not constitute the same experience for perpetrator or victim as violence between persons of the same ethnicity).
- There may be different access for victims to social networks of support.
- There may be different institutional responses to the different institutional resources available for both perpetrators and victims (*www.ahimsa.org.uk*, 11.10.02).

Violence against men

It is known that husbands and male partners can also be physically abused by their wives or female partners, and reciprocal violence is also known to be quite common (Straus, Gelles and Steinmetz, 1980). However, the problem of husband abuse is much less common insofar that women are much less likely than men to have the superior power in a heterosexual relationship necessary to abuse someone physically/and or emotionally (Pagelow, 1984). Although women do behave violently this violence within an adult relationship is often defensive in intent.

Motz (2001) explored battered women who kill. She argued that women who have disturbed early experiences may be more likely to enact violence than others because of the difficulties which they have experienced in integrating their murderous feelings; first, their aggression is projected onto others, their violent partners, and, when this becomes unbearable, they retaliate through violent action themselves. Importantly, however, Browne (1987) stresses that the background of the violent partners who are killed is a more significant predictive factor than the background of the women who kill, emphasising the role of the dynamics between the abused women and her violent partner.

To what extent can it be said that a woman who 'chooses' a violent partner is aware of her actions and to what degree does she contribute to the violence? Does she have the option to leave earlier in the relationship or is she making a conscious choice to stay in a high-risk relationship? Is she implicitly condoning the violence through her apparent decision to stay? These questions relate to the extent to which women in violent relationships lose their capacity to make real choices or exercise their autonomy. There are important social and economic factors which are highly relevant to the continued dependence of some women on partners who may be violent and emotionally abusive.

In situations where the female partner responds with violence and sometimes murder, represents a moment of rebellion: of challenging the polarised and distorted roles which may have been imposed. Browne (1987) identified several key factors that were present in situations when victims of domestic violence went on to kill that were not present in those cases where they did not go on to kill. These included the abuser's threats to kill, the abuser's alcohol abuse, the presence of a firearm or weapon in the house, and the women's perception of experiencing severe psychological abuse. These seemed more important than the escalation and severity of violent incidents. This lends support to the notion that what is most important in determining what makes women kill their abusive partners is their own perception of the situation and their subjective experience of humiliation, degradation, isolation and terror imposed on them by their partners.

In her study, Browne found that the factors which best predicted which women would kill their abusive partners were the severity of the woman's injuries, the man's alcohol or drug use, the frequency with which abusive incidents occurred, the man's threats to kill and the

woman's suicide attempts. In a separate study, Cambell (1986) established that the factors relevant in determining whether the battered women would become a victim or perpetrator of homicide included: threats to kill, a gun present in the home, drug or alcohol abuse by the perpetrator, sexual abuse, suicide threats or attempts by the women, and the degree of control of the woman's life by the abuser. Foster et al. (1989) established that the woman's perceived psychological abuse in the form of enforced isolation, humiliation and degradation to be more devastating than the physical abuse. Other factors which were present but which the woman themselves perceived as less important reasons for taking lethal action, included an escalation in the severity and frequency of violence, the occurrence of sexual abuse and the women's threats of suicide.

Surveys conducted in the US during the 1970s and the 1980s that examined the incidence of physical aggression in heterosexual relationships showed that men and women perpetrated violence at roughly the same rate. However, when researchers measure only physically violent acts and do not examine contextual factors, they are assuming that they are engaging in comparable behaviour. What is often not taken in to account is the use of the other forms of violence (rape, financial deprivation etc); the degree of severity of the violence; the effect of violence on the victim; and the different motivations of men and women in perpetrating violence. While men's violence in the home towards women appears to occur at the same rate as men's violence outside the home (e.g. robbery, rape), women's violence is relatively non-existent in the wider community. When examining this more closely, it becomes apparent that women's violence is not equivalent to men's violence in the following ways:

- Men's violence is more severe.
- Women's violence is often a response to frustration and stress, whereas men's violence is most often an attempt to dominate and control.
- Women's violence is more likely to occur in self-defence.
- Women's violence is often a reflection of dependence, whereas men's violence is a reflection of dominance (James, 1999).

Women's violence toward her partner often places her at greater risk. Indeed, studies have shown that the men's violence increases in intensity and severity when the woman uses violence in self-defence (Saunders, 1988). Goldner et al. (1994) emphasises the importance of assisting women to take responsibility for their own safety and in doing so need to desist from retaliation. This may be difficult to achieve if they are losing their only form of protest and retribution.

Women do need to be held accountable for their behaviour. A woman's violence may victimise and oppress her partner even if in other respects he is in a more advantageous position. No matter how understandable her violence may seem it can never be condoned. In confronting the woman's violence her level of stress, frustration and distress needs to be explored and acknowledged (James, 1999).

Violence within lesbian relationships

Gelles and Cornell (1985) explored the lesbian violence within a social exchange/social control framework. Here the key assumption is that a partner in a committed relationship will be violent toward the other partner because she can, and because social control mechanisms (e.g. victim hitting back) do not serve to increase the cost to the batterer. The batterer must feel that she is entitled to control her partner and that it's her partner's obligation to acquiesce in this practice. They must also believe that violence is permissive, and must be able to live with herself as an ethical and moral person even if she chooses to use violence against her partner. She must believe that violence will produce the desired effect or minimise a more negative occurrence. They must also feel that neither partner will sustain physical harm or suffer legal, emotional or personal consequences that will outweigh the benefits to be achieved through her use of violence.

Renzetti (1992) reported that of the 100 victims of lesbian battering in her study, more than half of the respondents (54%) experienced more than 10 abusive incidents. Brand and Kidd (1986) studied the extent of physical aggression experienced by 75 heterosexual women and 55 lesbians to determine whether men or women were more abusive in their intimate relationships. The results of their study indicated that men (6%) were more abusive against their female partners more often than were females (51%) in their lesbian relationships. They also found that

physical abuse occurred more frequently in heterosexual relationships than in lesbian relationships. Of the 55 lesbians in their study, 25% reported physical abuse in their committed relationships, whereas 27% of the heterosexual women stated that they had been physically abused by their male partners. Many battered lesbians have reported that the emotional abuse encountered along with, or separate from, the physical battering and diminished self-esteem is more painful and difficult to endure than the physical injuries (Hart, 1986). Hart also found that lesbians perceive a power imbalance to exist when one partner has greater resources (i.e. more education and a higher income) than the other. It may also lower the weaker partner's sense of satisfaction with the relationship. Whilst a power imbalance does not generally signal violence, it is over-represented in lesbian relationships (Renzetti, 1992).

There are some commonalities in the experience of all children living with domestic violence, however, where abuse occurs in a lesbian relationship, there are some particular complications for children:

- **The abuse is hidden:** the hidden nature of the abuse when a parent has not 'come out' means that the children are silenced, or feel unable to acknowledge the impact of the abuse on them for fear of publicly compromising their birth parent's relationship;
- **Homophobic attitudes**: even when the parent is open about their lesbian relationship, children are aware of the possible negative reactions from teachers, friends or the parents of their friends;
- **Limited access to extended family**: children can be cut off from potential support from their extended families because their mother has been alienated. This serves to compound their difficulties.
- **No public or legal recognition of the consequences of separation**: children also have to cope with the social attitudes about lesbianism should their parent's relationship end.
- **Parenting issues**: a common occurrence within lesbian relationships is that the birth parent is not automatically the primary caregiver of the child. In those cases where the abuse is from the birth parent to the primary caregiver children also lose a sense of safety and security when they lose the primary

care-giver and are left with the abuser (Bagshaw and Chung, 2000).

There has been no Home Office research on domestic violence among the lesbian, gay, bisexual and transgender communities (LGBT). Sigma Research undertook research on behalf of FLAME TV to discover the prevalence of domestic violence among lesbians and gay men. Among those surveyed, nearly a quarter of women (22%) and 29% of men had suffered domestic violence/domestic abuse. There was significant under-reporting: 86.9% of women and 81.2% of men failed to report incidents to the police (The Secretary of State for the Home Department, 2003).

Violence against ethnic minority women

Government statistics do not mention ethnic minority women. This is unfortunate since 40% of the women in refuges come from ethnic minority communities. Services for ethnic minority women are known to be patchy, inconsistent and often dependent on individuals or one particular organisation. For women whose immigration status was not settled, between 2000 and 2002 there were 119 cases of alleged domestic violence brought by women. Of these settlement was granted in 72 cases; 24 within the terms of an immigration concession and 48 outside. In terms of refuges, there were approximately 3,700 household spaces in England. There are 20 bed spaces for gay men and 25 refuges specifically for black and Asian women.

Women from ethnic minority communities face particular difficulties which include racism, language barriers, and worries about what will happen to their immigration status if they attempt to leave their violent partner. They may fear deportation if they leave a violent partner within 12 months of coming to the UK. Many may be hesitant in contacting professional agencies for fear of racism and discrimination. Difficulties of communication are also apparent where few or no language facilities exist. Some are ostracised for having shamed her family honour and betraying their community by challenging the violence. Many will be subjected to pressure from their extended families to stay because of the stigma attached to the breakdown of family structures.

Suicide and self-harm among Asian women is associated with pressure to conform to strong traditional roles. They may be also subject to abusive and oppressive practices within the family, including domestic violence which may embrace forced marriage; abduction and imprisonment in the home; restrictions placed on lifestyle and freedom of movement, dress and association; denial of education and career choices; and other controlling or belittling behaviour, such as constant criticism undermining their independence and sense of self-worth (Siddiqui, 2003).

Mama (1989) conducted the first major study of violence against black women in the home. She found that it demonstrates the full meaning of triple oppression along the dimensions of race, class and gender. That being said, there is much stronger evidence that domestic violence is not the preserve of any one social class (Walker, 1979).

Fernandez (1997) reported on the domestic violence perpetrated by the extended family members in India. She found that mothers-in-law and sometimes sisters-in-law contribute to the violence perpetrated by men. Unlike the nuclear family residence of the West, in a modern Indian family a young daughter-in-law is subordinate not only to the men but to older women as well. Generally, the mother-in-law lives with the couple either permanently or intermittently. There are two ways in which the mother-in-law may collude or assist in the violence: either directly abusing the daughter-in-law (oppressor) or goading her son to abuse his wife (instigator). The oppression may be physical or verbal – such as regularly shouting at them for not bringing in dowry or gifts, not working fast enough or being childless or not bearing sons. The abuse may be less direct, such as overworking the daughter-in-law, demeaning her, neglecting her, or denying her basic necessities. They may also deny her food. Whilst there is evidence of her mother and father monitoring her situation and intervening when the abuse becomes severe, they also often facilitate her return home usually when the abuser promises that things would get better. This suggests that women's experiences of violence may not be universal.

Women's experiences of violence can also vary within cultures as well. Indian women's experiences with oppression vary by their generation or life-cycle stage, social class, caste, and region of the country (Miller, 1992). Some women go from being victims when they are young daughters-in-law to becoming batterers when they become mothers-in-law. As contributors to violence, older women align themselves against, rather than with, younger women who marry into their families.

As is typical of domestic violence cross culturally, husbands use violence to dominate and control their wives. Any incident (e.g. allegations of unfaithfulness, lack of sexual co-operation) is provocation enough for the husband to punish his wife with physical violence. They may be supported by their father-in-laws as direct or indirect abusers.

It is sometimes claimed by abusers that their religious beliefs or community values support the violence but this is not the case (Home Office, 2000). However, Pryke and Thomas (1998) pointed out that world religions have been influential in maintaining the 'natural order' of the male head of household and subservient women and children. In many religions, marriage requires the total subjugation of the women by the male partner and male children are favoured over any female members of the family, including their mother and other female elders.

Poor practice persists and stems from a misconceived commitment to anti-racist practice; assumptions about the need to 'respect' the supposed disciplinarian behaviour of Afro-Caribbean men, or of assuming that Asian communities prefer to look for their own problems – leading to women not being offered effective help (Pryke and Thomas, 1998).

Harris Hendrick et al. (1993) in their study of wife killing found that there was a five-fold increase in the incidence in Asian immigrant families compared with the indigenous ones. Although factors common to all immigrants (poverty, housing problems) play a part in this increase, factors pertaining to the role of women in Asian families are also relevant, particularly the belief that adulterous wives are deserving of death.

Winchester (2002) reported on evidence to suggest that between 20 and 30% of all woman, from all cultures, will be attacked by a partner at some point in their life.

In Jewish communities, there is great resistance to the idea that domestic violence ever happens. There are a powerful set of standards and beliefs around the culture about how great it is to be part of that community and how important families are. That has a silencing effect on people. Those women who do disclose abuse often find themselves isolated from the only support network they ever had. Being sent to a refuge a long way away helps prevent women being

found but it increased their sense of iso[...] When in refuges, many Orthodox women[...] sharing a kitchen with non-Jewish people[...] intolerable because of the need to keep kosher[...] Observance of holy days can be impossible in a mixed refuge. Racism and ridicule from other residents may exist.

Workers need to ensure that they are not immobilised by race anxiety which prevents them from acting decisively in domestic violence cases. They suggest that there is a nervousness about being seen to be interfering in a different culture's practices and beliefs.

Women from ethnic minority groups (especially those for whom English is not their first language) may find it much more difficult to get protection from domestic violence, because of poor accessibility of refuges, legal and welfare services. Stereotypical beliefs about 'passive' Asian women or about endemic domestic violence in some communities may underlie the responses of some service providers. Feelings that the police may not give a helpful response and fears of deportation resulting from insecure immigration status have a significant impact upon the levels of reporting domestic violence among black women. Notions of family honour ('izzat') and shame ('sharam') play an important part in Asian families and can severely constrain an abused woman's ability to contact the police or social services or separate from a violent partner. Women who have strong religious identities may find it difficult to cope without the support of their family and local community, especially if they have children. The problems some women face in separating from the abuser are compounded if his family is abusive as well. The poor accessibility of services for Asian women is frustrated further by the gatekeeping practices of some members of the police and social services who are reluctant to intervene because they feel that such matters are best dealt with by the community. Women from ethnic minority groups are consequently more likely to suffer domestic violence for longer because there are fewer alternatives available to them (Morgan, 1998).

Violence against women with disabilities

Many disabled women may be at additional risk because of their enhanced dependency and isolation, making departure more difficult, especially if they fear being unable to cope alone. The abuser may be the sole carer and extended

see through the
…use.
aged 16–29 reported
…lence in 1995,
…n-disabled children
…). In a snapshot
…ion for disabled women
…2001) reported that 48% did not have
wheelchair access and 29.6% could not offer a
disabled woman a place in their refuge. There is
also a difference in social power between disabled
and non-disabled people and between women
and men that acts as a double whammy for
disabled women in intimate relationships.
Disabled women are unable to defend themselves
and they cannot leave the situation. Their abusers
are often their paid carers or their intimate
partners. Disabled women often stay with their
abusive partners as they fear they will not find
suitable accommodation or another partner.
Abusing partners are often seen as saintly
because they are caring for a disabled woman.
They can fool agencies as well as the women
themselves. Disabled women are also vulnerable
to abuse because the services they live with
condition them to say 'yes'. At this stage, the
Home Office do not have a formal policy for
dealing with domestic violence against disabled
women.

Problems with professional intervention involving mothers

Davies and Krane (1996) have noted that social
work practice in the child welfare arena is
pervaded by mother blame. Although in theory
the focus is on the needs and interests of children,
the bulk of the activity actually entails the
evaluation of women-as-mothers and mothering
functions or capacities. The public scrutiny is
more likely if mothers are poor, people of colour,
on welfare or single parents. The assumptions
which inform social workers' assessments of
mothering do not take place in a vacuum, but
instead reflect the problematic way mothers and
mothering are constructed more broadly in
contemporary western society. One cannot help
notice just how little professional perceptions of a
mother's culpability have changed, despite the
emergence of a much expanded child sexual
abuse and domestic violence literature. Insidious
forms of mother blame need to be made visible
and challenged by workers. Social workers need
to accept that many mothers do take steps to

protect their children. Blaming mothers for
somehow having failed when the domestic
violence and the sexual abuse occurs, is not only
hurtful but is counterproductive in the context of
an intervention model based on the centrality of
the mother in the protection process. Expectations
that mothers ought to be able to cope on their
own following disclosure and investigation are
unrealistic.

We are waking up to the fact that social work
intervention into families where domestic violence
is a feature reinforces the established cultural
socialisation process (see causal section for further
details). Women continue to be seen as
disproportionately responsible by social workers
for the wellbeing of their children. What is often
missing is the contribution of men to the
originating problem (Caplan, 1985), and worse
still, the mothers can be portrayed as being to
blame for their partner's actions, for not
controlling him or for 'provoking' him. Domestic
violence destroys women, it destroys children,
and it destroys communities. Women may often
keep silent about the extent and severity of their
situations in order to minimise the level and speed
of this destruction. Women do not leave for all
sorts of reasons, and in some cases women do not
leave initially because they genuinely want to save
the relationship, but they do want the violence and
abuse to end. Attempts to seek help are mostly met
by inadequate and inappropriate responses, and
in my experience most women stay in or return to
a violent relationship because of the inertia that
they meet along the way, and the fear that leaving
may put them in increased danger. This is a very
rational fear because research tells us that the most
dangerous time for a woman is at the point of
leaving or after she has left, and simple solutions
put forward by all agencies fail to grasp the
dangerousness of her situation (Rowsell, 2001).

The aggregate effect of women and children
not receiving appropriate responses to help
seeking behaviour, or appropriate and consistent
support to end the abuse, is that they may be left
with little or no option than to choose
progressively more negative, or risky, coping
strategies in order to escape the violence and
survive. Use of these often may lead to women
being in contact with (and often at odds with)
child protection agencies, and/or mental health
services, and/or the criminal justice system, and
mean that they are not only coping with the
reality and effects of violence and abuse, but are
also dealing with the repercussions of the very

actions that were designed to get them through the violence and abuse in the first place.

There is little doubt that where a woman's or child's family, friends, agencies and community all respond with sensitivity, speed and consistency to domestic violence and deliver seamless services, the potential for a positive outcome is increased dramatically. Given the complex needs of women and children no one agency alone can meet their needs, and this means more than ever that agencies must work together in partnership, sharing understanding, definitions, and information. Practitioners have a responsibility to check out a woman's history with other agencies, although no information collected will not mean abuse hasn't happened, it just hasn't been adequately recorded (Rowsell, 2003).

Farmer and Owen (1998) explored in some detail gender-based social work interventions and identified some important indicators for improving practice in cases of sexual abuse and domestic violence. They pointed out that mothers have tended to be under-represented in relation to offers of service and over-included in respect of agencies' efforts to control them. They also highlighted from research that there is a significant gender bias at each stage of the child protection process. They found that 27% of mothers in their sample had actively sought help and initiated action from the child protection agencies, yet this is an unused fact in determining subsequent responses. The mothers actively turned to the child protection agencies in the hope that they will receive assistance either in dealing with their own problems or in regulating the actions of the men with whom they were living. Unfortunately, rather than being treated as allies in the protection of their children, they were treated with suspicion. This often led to them rejecting subsequent offers of help in the guise of child protection plans. The exclusion of the mother from any investigation can leave them feeling very angry, vulnerable and very distrustful about the agencies, and this then clearly impacted upon the direction a case developed. In nearly 80% of cases of sexual abuse, the child was interviewed without the mother being informed, never mind involved. This was more acutely distressing where they had initiated the process. Thus, the mothers who were struggling to assimilate the notion that their partners had sexually abused their children found that the children had been encouraged to talk about the abuse to professionals, whilst they had been excluded. The investigation had thus marginalised them, whilst also replicating their experience of discovering that their children had been abused without their knowledge.

Once the non-abusing parent was brought into the investigation, they also became the subjects of scrutiny. Judgements were made against mothers who were in a state of shock. If they did not react as the workers expected, they were sometimes held to be unable to protect their children. When an allegation of sexual abuse was made against a male partner, there was an expectation that the mother would immediately sever her relationship with the alleged perpetrator to ensure her child's safety. Professionals do not consider mothers able to protect the children if the perpetrator remains in the house. The difficulty of the mother's position and the complexity of her emotions were rarely acknowledged. If they were uncertain whether or not they believed their children's allegations (a situation more likely to occur when the mother had not been present to hear the evidence given by the child during the investigation), or were thought to have retained their attachment to the perpetrator, the possibility of removing the children was given active consideration. When alleged perpetrators protested their innocence, the mother was torn between their child and their partner, caught in a position where believing one meant losing the other. Mothers like these need help in dealing with their feelings about what had happened. Women who believe the child often experience a change in the power balance in the relationship with the perpetrator, as he needs her to believe him. However, an exclusive focus on mothers as secondary perpetrators rather than secondary victims of the abuse of their children often left the workers to judge them as 'non-protective' mothers. There was a need for a woman's feelings of shock, self-blame and loss to be understood and for support to be offered at this time. When such support was not forthcoming, this in turn made it more difficult for mothers to provide the understanding needed by their abused children. It can also affect how she perceives the role of professionals, as fighting rather than supporting.

What is needed is consideration at the outset of an investigation of how best to intervene strategically in order to strengthen the support given to the child, particularly since sexual abuse distorts the relationship between the victim and the mother in any case. This will often mean strengthening the alliance between the non-abusing mother and the child, particularly since research has shown that children have the best prognosis for recovery when they are believed by a parent (Conte and Schuerman, 1987). Women who do not immediately reject an abusing partner may still be able to sort out their painful and conflicted feelings, with appropriate help, and succeed in protecting their children (Macleod and Saraga, 1988).

When it came to the initial child protection conference, the mother attended in 80% of the cases. They found the experience very stressful, feeling that they were blamed and that their moral fitness as parents was being judged. The researchers found that there was a tendency to shift the focus from the allegations to the mother, often because the professionals had more information on the mother, and also because of assumptions that mothers were responsible for their children's welfare. Indeed, the mother often assumed some responsibility for the abuse on the grounds that they should not have allowed it to happen in the first place. In 60% of cases, the conference considered the mother's ability to protect, compared to only 19% in cases where the father was in a parallel role. Overall, attendance at conferences often served to make women feel that their views had been discounted and to underline their position of powerlessness (Farmer, 1993). This is worse when the risk of domestic violence is overlooked by the professionals. In Farmer and Owens sample (1998), they found that domestic violence co-existed in 20% of the sexual abuse cases, increasing to 40% post-conference. The principal reason for this is that many women conceal the facts, fearing that revealing it would worsen their position and might lead to losing their children (see Mullender, 1997). This is very important, as professionals should never expect women to protect children when they struggle to protect themselves. It is sadly only a small step from the mother's actions and attitudes being assessed, to seeing her as the principal risk. This allows the abuser to opt out.

There is a very clear negative impact on the mother of child protection registration: feeling blamed and stigmatised, while assuming an even greater burden of the practical childcare. They were treated as possibly having known about or 'colluded' with the abuse, and as if they were guilty until proved innocent (Driver, 1989). They were harshly judged in relation to their reaction

to the discovery of the abuse, and even those who made arrangements to ensure their children's protection were considered suspect if they continued to feel affection for their former partners. Those women who were thought to harbour a continuing allegiance to the perpetrator, or whose parenting were seen as deficient, were viewed as partially culpable and found themselves subject to regulatory visits, even when the abuser was securely off the scene.

However, when women were able to demonstrate that they had taken steps to protect their children from their partners, generally because they had separated from them, their cases were usually quickly closed, leaving them with the full responsibility of coping with the aftermath of the abuse and its consequences for them and their children. Some 20 months later, the researchers found a high number of women still expressing deep feelings of anger and pain at their child's abuse which they had been unable to resolve. Without outside help, these women had been unable to move on emotionally. This was most noticeable where they were victims of sexual abuse themselves, and the process had rekindled painful memories from the past.

Overall, Farmer and Owen (1998) found that 'a kind of blame by association meant that non-abusing mothers were censured and regulated if they did not meet the exacting expectations of professional agencies about how they should protect their children . . .' (p553). Farmer and Owen (1995) have also pointed out how often mothers are restricted to a particular maternal identity in child protection work. As the focus of attention, they are expected to take prime responsibility for child care and child protection. This has continued to occur despite the existence of feminist involvement on social work training courses.

It is one thing acknowledging what needs to change but quite another thing changing practice. Workers need to understand, accept and work with the fact that it takes most mothers many months to open up, share themselves, and to relate their individual experiences. They fear judgement, blame and criticism. They fear being disloyal to the perpetrator and the victim by exposing the family secret. They fear touching their pain. They fear the workings of the response systems. There is fear of failing to cope with practical issues such as housing or money. They may fear they are 'bad' for allowing the violence to happen, and fear that something else unexpected may occur again at any time. They fear intensely, without knowing all the reasons why. This fear can be immobilising. Mothers need a safe place to explore the presenting situation, one where they will not be judged and where they can begin to understand themselves and the domestic violence and often associated sexual abuse. Many feel the need to educate social workers about the issues they face and the negative experiences many have experienced at the hands of the helping professionals. It should not come as a surprise that mothers, due to their own trauma, respond inappropriately and insensitively to their own children before and after disclosure. They should be helped to understand this and to accept any part of the responsibility for the abuse – for not seeing, for excusing, enabling, or even tolerating. Even when the mother begins to accept the abuse intellectually, they often stay disconnected from the emotional impact.

Cammaert (1988) argued that rather than viewing the mother as a secondary perpetrator, it is important to conceptualise that she has strengths. Many mothers struggle to keep the family together; the children are fed, clothed and disciplined. Part of the package of survival skills includes a need to be compliant and to please the powerful male in order to avoid confrontation. Workers thus need to acknowledge that some mothers may not have any resources left to relate emotionally to anyone – after attending to the basic survival needs of the family. It is important that workers build on her survival skills and enlarge her skill repertoire to include the ability to increase her self-worth and independence for herself and skills to heal the mother–daughter relationship. For a detailed discussion on how to conduct strengths-based assessments, the reader is referred to Calder (1999) and Calder, Peake and Rose (2001).

Towards principles of intervention

Rabenstein and Lehmann (2000) set out several useful principles for professionals approaching intervention work in domestic violence situations that if adopted may unite professional responses:

- All women and men are equal and that it is wrong for women to be subordinate.
- Each individual in the family is responsible for their behaviour.
- All family members have a right to personal safety.

There are a numbe[r]
working with fami[l]

- Recognise the po[wer]
  and maintain do[minance]
- Support women e[ ]
  and form alliance[s]
  their children whe[ ]
- Be aware of the la[ ]
- Communicate dire[ctly] ... with the
  mother present if desired. If the male
  perpetrator is present evidence suggests little
  if any disclosure will occur.
- Challenge the behaviour of violent and
  abusive men.
- Incorporate anti-discriminatory principles into
  work with children and families.
- Acknowledge dangers to staff and make
  arrangements for protecting them wherever
  possible.
- Ensure inter-agency networks include
  appropriate links between the statutory and
  voluntary sectors, and between the local
  domestic violence fora and Area Child
  Protection Committee. Such links need to be
  based on mutual understanding and respect
  between statutory child protection agencies
  and voluntary organisations with knowledge
  of domestic abuse.

The Home Office set out clearly for all agencies basic points that they should consider when dealing with situations involving domestic violence:

- All agencies must be fully aware of the level
  and nature of domestic violence, of the need
  for their policies and practices to address it,
  and of its possible presence in cases in which
  they have to deal. Importantly this includes
  those cases which originally come to the
  attention for other purposes.
- Domestic violence training is important for
  staff at all levels.
- When dealing with individual cases, the
  priority for agencies must be the client's safety.
  They should themselves undertake such
  emergency action as they can take.
- As employers, agencies should develop
  appropriate responses to members of staff who
  may be experiencing or perpetrating domestic
  violence.
- Agencies should ensure that information about
  both statutory and voluntary domestic
  violence services is available to staff and the
  public in an accessible format.

...n with local inter-agency domestic
...fora is desirable where such fora exist,
...ust be seen as a means to an end, not an
...d in themselves.

Agencies should work to create a safe and
supportive environment which encourages
people to report domestic violence.

- Services may be fully accessible to all. Agencies
  must be aware of the needs of women from
  ethnic minorities, those with disabilities,
  elderly people, those with drug or alcohol
  dependency, people with mental health
  problems and those in same sex relationships.
- The success of any initiative to reduce
  domestic violence depends on a careful
  implementation strategy and needs to be
  confirmed by thorough evaluation and
  monitoring.
- Agencies should consider the importance of
  information sharing (section 115 of the Crime
  and Disorder Act 1998) as a valuable part in
  the co-ordination of their client-based services
  (Home Office, 2000b).
- Workers need a model for working with
  domestic violence that is grounded in treating
  people with integrity and respect.
- We need to understand their world without
  imposing our judgements on them.
- We need to ensure any work is client-centred,
  flexible and able to acknowledge different
  forms of violence.
- Survivors of domestic violence need to be
  engaged in work through informed choice.
- We need to validate their expressed needs,
  experiences and beliefs without colluding with
  and/or justifying violent and abusive
  practices.
- Transparency of work is essential coupled
  with actively involving the survivors in the
  decision-making as much as possible.
- Workers should remain accountable to the
  women as well as to the system.

When working with the perpetrators of domestic
violence all intervention must be underpinned by
a clear philosophy and principles which might
include:

- Domestic violence is unacceptable and must be
  challenged at all times.
- Men's violence to partners and ex-partners is
  largely about the misuse of power and control
  in the context of male dominance.
- Violence within same-sex relationships or
  from women to men is neither the same as –

nor symmetrically opposite to – men's
violence to women.

- Men are responsible for their use of violence.
- Men can change.
- There needs to be a community response that
  is consistent and integrated at all levels.
- Everyone affected by domestic violence should
  have access to support services which address
  their needs.
- Promoting positive relationships.
- Workers should apply these principles to their
  own lives (*www.ahimsa.org.uk*, 11.10.02).

Importing lessons from the field of child sexual abuse

Hooper (1992) highlighted clearly the
inter-connections between woman abuse and
child sexual abuse, suggesting that ongoing
violence and abuse directed towards women
provides the context for men to sexually abuse
their children. Moreover, the sexual abuse of
children is often intended as a further abuse of
mothers. The forced sex aspect of domestic
violence is often neglected. Approximately
40–45% of all battered women are forced into sex
by their male partners (Cambell, 1998). Forced sex
can range from unwanted roughness, painful or
particular sexual acts, through threatened
violence if sexual demands are not met to actual
beatings prior to, during or after sex and/or sex
with objects (Cambell and Alford, 1989). Browne
(1993) reported some similarities between those
who physically and sexually abuse their children
and those who abuse their wives: a misperception
of the victim, low self-esteem, sense of
incompetence, social isolation, a lack of support
and help, lack of empathy, marital difficulties,
depression, poor self-control, and a history of
abuse and neglect as a child.

Calder (2003b) provided a framework within
which the accumulated knowledge of working
with sexual abuse could be exported to help us in
our intervention battle with domestic violence.

Towards anti-oppressive practice

At the heart of oppression is difference where
'those regarded as different are ignored,
devalued, blamed, dehumanised, with their
difference being used to 'justify' the 'reaction'
(Preston Shoot, 1995: 15). Empowerment is
therefore a key theme in anti-oppressive practice
and involves the practitioner engaging with the

client to reduce the impact of stereotyping, stigmatising and pathologisation of a person. As such, 'an empowerment perspective which assumes that issues of power and powerlessness are integral to the experience of the service user enables us to move away from pathologising individuals to increasing personal, interpersonal or political power, so that individuals can take action to improve their life situations' (Dalrymple and Burke, 1995: 52). Furthermore, anti-oppressive practice 'identifies, therefore, with a radical value base which emphasises *user control* rather than participation in welfare agencies' agendas, *equality* rather than equal opportunity, *rights* not needs, and *citizenship* more than respect for persons' (Preston Shoot, 1995: 16).

Oppression is concerned with power relationships and the abuse of power at both the individual and at the structural level. It is a process by which life chances are constructed and maintained to work in favour of some groups and to the disadvantage of others. There are several clearly identifiable components of oppression: inequality, social justice, domination, stereotyping, discrimination and accessibility to services (Phillipson, 1992). Whilst oppression can be specific to any one of these components, they frequently interconnect. Anti-oppressive practice – seeks to achieve a fundamental realignment of these power differentials, values and relationships, starting with the acknowledgement that structural inequalities exist and impact heavily on both groups as well as individuals.

Thompson (1996) argued that anti-oppressive practice means that professionals must achieve three different objectives:

- recognise the impact of discrimination and oppression on people's lives
- avoid the pitfall of reinforcing or exacerbating such discrimination and oppression
- challenge and undermine the oppressive structures, attitudes and actions that disadvantage certain groups in society.

(p153)

Hackett (2000) set out the following questions as an integral part of an anti-oppressive response for workers engaging in assessment and intervention with mothers:

- What have you done to critically examine your own values and perceptions regarding mothers, with specific regard to those from minority groups?
- How does your assessment make a distinction between the person's possible control of personal problems and external constraints beyond their control?
- Are you restricting your assessment because you think that there are no suitable resources for this particular person as a result of their difference or minority status?
- Is your assessment of the person's behaviour located within a clear child protection framework, where the needs of victims are the paramount concern?
- Is your assessment sensitive to the cultural implications, expectations and aspirations of the person without collusion on the basis of these cultural issues?
- Have you challenged and included critical assessment of racist and oppressive practice and procedures of other institutions and professionals involved?
- What steps have you taken to check whether your assessment is influenced by oppressive pathological or oppressive liberal approaches?

Preparing for anti-oppressive practice: a multi-levelled approach for the practitioner

Hackett (2000) highlighted some of these key steps for individuals wishing to developing anti-oppressive responses in sexual abuse work which one can easily export to the domestic violence arena (see Fig. 2.9).

An organising framework at the local level

In order to survive domestic violence women are likely to need a range of services, which cannot ever be provided by one agency alone.

- Information and advice.
- Emotional support and advocacy.
- Medical treatment/psychiatric treatment/ support to overcome substance dependency.
- Counselling.
- Legal protection and justice under both the criminal and civil laws.
- Safe, suitable accommodation.
- Safe arrangements for the care, education and health needs of their children.
- Financial and practical support.

Figure 2.9: Developing anti-oppressive responses: a multi-layered approach (Hackett, 2000)

Level One: The Intra-personal (The self)

- Personal acknowledgement of the existence of power imbalances within one's relationships with others.
- A readiness to focus on how one's own personal and professional power is used and experienced.
- Ownership of one's own personal power.
- An ability to maintain critical openness with respect to individual mothers and their families, etc.
- Recognition of others' difference and a willingness to validate and value this in contact with others.
- Scrutiny of personal values and behaviour; with specific regard to sex, sexuality, gender and race.

Level Two: The Organisational (Self-Organisation)

- An organisational framework which promotes partnership and values difference in all interactions with people who abuse and their families.
- Written aims and objectives to services for mothers and an explicit philosophy, agreed at organisational level, to underpin practice.
- A clear and unambiguous policy on exchange of information and the limited nature of confidentiality.
- An anti-oppressive statement, which has as its core prevention and protection of actual and potential victims, but which defines service users' rights.
- An agreed organisational risk management policy in respect of sexual abuse work.
- Power issues centre stage when planning services and when allocating resources within the organisation.

Level Three: The Interpersonal (Self-Other)

- An interpersonal approach which builds upon people's (and their family's) experiences to consolidate their strengths.
- A belief in the possibility of change and a desire to be a vehicle of change for the person who has abused.
- Practice which acknowledges and values the diversity of individual people's experiences of power, abuse and discrimination.
- A willingness to hear and embrace people's wider experiences, rather than a focus solely upon 'the offence'.
- Practice models which seek to understand the complex connections between people's experiences, context and abusive behaviour (reproduced by kind permission of Simon Hackett).

- Help to reach long term independence, support to access training, education and work opportunities.

It is clear that women cannot always access appropriate supportive, responsive services, nor do they always receive adequate support when they do so. Currently most agencies individually and collectively are working to a model based on exclusion, entrapment and escalation of violence and abuse. Why is this and what can be done to redress this unfortunate state of affairs?

The Children's Act 1989 does not recognise the disrupting impact of domestic violence on the lives of children. It does not refer to domestic violence nor offers any guidance and regulations. The omissions of the Act have been partly remedied through the recently issued guidance on child protection procedures and in good practice guidance for working with children in need. 'Working Together to Safeguard Children (DoH, 1999) as well as in the Framework For Assessing Children and Families in Need (DoH, 2000) raise the expectation that social workers and other professionals will consider the impact of domestic violence on children. 'Safeguarding children' (DoH, 1999) says the following about domestic violence:

- Everyone working with women and children should be alert to the frequent inter-relationship between domestic violence and the abuse and neglect of children. Domestic Violence Forums as well as Area Child Protection Committees (ACPCs) should have clearly identified links and should contribute to an assessment of the incidence of children caught up in domestic violence, their needs, the adequacy of local arrangements to meet those needs, and its implications for local services.

- Where there is evidence of domestic violence, the implications for any children in the household should be considered, including the possibility that the children may themselves be subject to violence or other harm. Conversely, where it is believed that a child is being abused those involved with the child and family should be alert to the possibility of domestic violence within the family.
- When responding to incidents of violence, the police should find out whether there are any children living in the household. It is good practice for the police to notify the social services department when they have responded to an incident of domestic violence and it is known that a child is a member of the household.
- If the police have specific concerns about the safety or welfare of a child, they should make a referral to the social services department citing the basis for their concerns. It is also important that there is clarity about whether the family is aware that the referral is being made. Any response by social services should be discrete, in terms of making contact with women in ways which will not further endanger them or their children.
- Normally, one serious incident or several lesser incidents where there is a child in the household would indicate that the social services department should carry out an initial assessment of the child and family.
- Whilst children may benefit from a range of support and services, supporting the non-violent parent is likely to be the most effective way of promoting the child's welfare.

Whilst this points us to develop local procedures there is no guidance on 'how'. That remains the territory of each area, allowing multiple responses and unnecessary duplication at a time of diminished capacity to respond. If we look to the new assessment framework (DoH, 2000) for direction, then we will be disappointed. There has been a singular failure to address domestic violence within the framework, expecting workers to generate their own evidence-base and assessment structure (Rowsell, 2003).

Calder (1999b) developed a useful model for Area Child Protection Committees to use when developing local responses to nationally identified problems (see Figure 2.10) which has been applied to domestic violence.

Aims and purpose

There has to be a local explicit agreement and a shared understanding between workers and agencies about the aims and purpose of work with cases involving domestic violence. If individuals and agencies are working with different aims, they will interpret their roles and responsibilities in different ways. This is especially true with the advent of Domestic Violence Forums alongside ACPCs in addressing the issue of domestic violence in their area. In many cases, both will issue procedures to guide agencies in their responses and there is a potential for conflict and role confusion.

No one agency on its own can address the full range of problems created by domestic violence. There has therefore to be an initial recognition of the need to collaborate, a belief that it cannot be tackled by agencies working alone, and a perception that the benefits far outweigh the costs of so doing. The ongoing focus on working together is based on a belief that it has the potential for achieving more than the sum of the collaborating parts operating individually.

There must be detailed consensus between agencies on what constitutes domestic violence and what the impact on children will be and we must enter into a process of enhancing public perception and knowledge about domestic violence.

Mandate, standards, structures and resources

Domestic violence is not in itself a criminal offence although it is seen as a serious problem because it represents a continued threat to an abused person's safety. It is clearly a major social, economic and public health problem. The Crime and Disorder Act (1998) places a statutory duty on local authorities and the police to develop local partnerships to reduce crime and disorder. The government drive to reduce social exclusion applies to domestic violence when we consider the social, economic and criminal costs. Those experiencing abuse can face social exclusion by being unable to work or play an active part in the community; by being isolated from friends or family; being physically and emotionally unfit for work; health, education and homelessness can have an impact on parents and their children. Lack of employment, independent resources and access to information may make it more difficult for a victim to leave a violent relationship if they want to.

In order to effectively respond, there needs to be a clear mandate. This is especially so given the

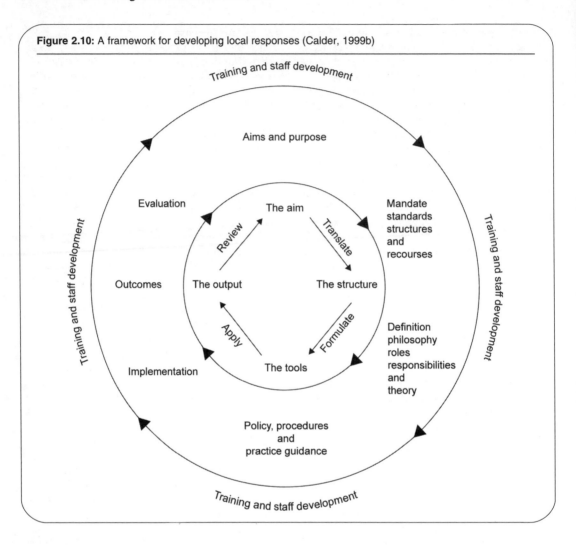

Figure 2.10: A framework for developing local responses (Calder, 1999b)

climate where social services are introducing explicit thresholds for the provision of a social work service that is often at a child protection level and which demands other agencies construct referrals that cross the defined threshold (see Calder, 2003 for a detailed discussion on this point). Once a common aim and purpose has been agreed among senior managers, this needs to be enshrined in some local mandate to ensure that each agency cannot deny their roles and responsibilities. This is essential when the obstacles to working together professionally grow steadily (see Calder, 1999b and 2003 for a review). There has to be a mandate for, and meaning of, collaboration. This means different things to different people in different situations. Collaborative structures and leadership are then needed. This means that

ACPCs have to go beyond 'Working Together' to develop a sense of shared meaning, vision, belonging, and inter-dependence. This can be achieved by developmental work which looks at building confidence, understanding and trust in each other' roles, sharing anxieties and feelings, trouble shooting tensions and conflicts early on, and identifying local needs and resources. ACPCs have to manage changes and anxieties affecting working together.

Alongside mandate is best value: a government initiative to make public services more accountable and ensure that they provide a high quality service. It has been estimated that the public cost of not tackling domestic violence is as high as £278 million per annum in Greater London alone (Stanko et al., 1998).

Standards offer the baseline for quality

assurance, audit and inspection, and provide a benchmark against which both agency and professional performance can be measured. They should be constructed with reference to the available resources and thus have to be both realistic and attainable. They should not be seen as a benchmark against which workers constantly fall short. Any standards produced require cross-agency support. A failure to provide such standards ignores the emotional aspects of the job and the impact upon the workers. It also leaves managers 'high and dry' when managing the work as there is no agreed baseline from which to work.

Structures would clearly be needed in all of the agencies that have responsibility for dealing with this problem. Once individual agencies have their own infrastructure in place, the ACPC can use these as the platform from which to construct a corporate framework for responding to this problem. Workers then need to understand the formal structures of the agencies involved. This includes their geographical boundaries, duties, and the legislation and guidance within which they work. It also requires an understanding of the informal systems operating within them. Agencies working together can operate more or less closely and have links at different layers of their structure.

Resources are a big issue when we don't have many. There is a question mark about how realistic it is to expect ACPCs to be in a position to respond to this new problem. Many have set off with the right intention, but have then struggled to translate vision into reality. It is unfair to ask workers to address domestic violence in the absence of the necessary resources.

Definition, philosophy, roles and responsibilities, and theory: offering a corporate baseline

It is essential that we strive to define the philosophical base for what we do as well as offering a clear definition of the problem to be tackled. Domestic violence cuts across all boundaries of class, ethnicity, disability, sexuality, religion and age. It can begin at any time in a relationship, go on for many years and continue once the relationship has ended. It can happen to anyone, although it is recognised that in the majority of cases, women are the victims and men the perpetrators. It involves the misuse of power and the exercise of control in a

relationship and is usually a pattern of abuse and intimidation which becomes more severe over time. It is often expressed in a number of ways and it is very common for there to be more than one form of abuse happening at the same time and it is likely to have been going on for some time. It can have physical, psychological and social consequences, which in turn may impact on a parent's ability to offer care for their children (see later discussion around this point). The earlier section on definition sets out the breadth of behaviour that comprises domestic violence and the aim is for a universally accepted definition to inform practice. Common factors include:

- Physical injuries
- Sexual violence
- Verbal abuse
- Withholding financial support
- Controlling independence and choice
- Denial of physical freedom
- Threats of being returned to country of origin or deportation
- Threats that the children will be removed
- Threats of referral to mental health services
- Blaming the person for everything that is 'wrong'
- A process of being humiliated and undermined both individually and as a parent
- Isolation from family, friends and community
- Using pregnancy as a means of control

Based on a shared philosophy, each agency next needs to identify its particular roles and responsibilities in relation to this group. The following represent some of the essential ingredients of a service procedure and philosophy:

- Provide a domestic violence policy and procedures in which abusers are held accountable and strategies for improving victim and children's safety is enhanced.
- Develop data sharing protocols on exchange of information and case management.
- Ensure that crisis support is adequate and provided (there is no use having a statement of philosophy and/or a procedure and no resources to implement it).
- Record all incidents of domestic violence in families where children are present, assess risk and take action where necessary.
- Record and document all injuries incurred due to domestic violence.

- Undertake safety plans with the parent and children experiencing domestic violence.
- Ensure safety measures are in place in any child contact decisions and arrangements.
- Look to providing a holistic support package to families experiencing domestic violence.
- Ensure that the safety and well-being of children is paramount.
- Ensure there is accessible information (posters, leaflets) available in prominent positions and ensure services are accessible to all victims in the community.

Theory is an essential foundation upon which practice and procedures are built. Domestic violence is usually committed in the context of an abusive environment within the home. There are likely to be high levels of punishment, the misuse of power and authority by the perpetrator and a failure of appropriate self-control. This mirrors our understanding of sexual abuse perpetrators and we know that the cycle of anger features centrally in the development, maintenance and timing of sexually abusive behaviour and domestic violence. The Duluth power and control wheel offers an excellent theoretical framework upon which to pin our responses (see causal section earlier).

Policies, procedures and practice guidance: plugging the gap
It is unfair to ask workers to deal with domestic violence if they have not been equipped with the appropriate tools to do so.

Horwath and Calder (1999) argued that policies, procedures and practice guidance together provide a useful framework to guide actions and clarify individual roles and responsibilities. They need to reflect the desired standards for practice. They differentiated between the three terms as follows: policies are the principles or recommended course of action based on the mandate and standards agreed by senior managers. They focus on contextualising the task. Procedures offer the structural framework for practice based on policies. They focus on the process. Practice guidance provides a mechanism for converting the policy and procedures into an operational working tool.

Clearly defined policies, procedures and practice guidance, supported by senior representatives of each agency provide front-line practitioners and managers with a clear remit providing a framework to guide action and

clarify individual roles and responsibilities. They should be clear, credible, congruent, resourced and monitored, and reflect local conditions (e.g. formal/informal networks and the local collaborative culture) (see Morrison, 1996).

Inter-agency procedures should always compliment internal agency policies, enabling workers to appreciate not only what is expected of themselves, but of other professionals. Good practice should ensure that the ramifications of changed policies in one agency are clearly planned for and negotiated with the other agencies involved.

Procedures can be a double-edged sword. Firstly, they can help workers by providing a structure for the work, in clarifying professional roles and in resolving any inter-agency difficulties. However, they can constrain practice if they are perceived by workers as an added burden, leading to a rigid and unresponsive service. Many workers tend to utilise procedures as a guide to action so, where none exist, they may hesitate taking any action, fuelled in a belief that the work is of low priority.

We should always remember that procedures are no substitute for good practice and, once constructed, are not inviolate. Procedures should never be regarded as set in stone; rather they represent a distillation of what is believed to be best practice at a given point in time. As the knowledge base expands, so it becomes necessary to re-evaluate established policies and practices in order to ensure that they continue to be relevant and appropriate and make best use of available resources. An over-emphasis on procedure can also mask a lack of exploration about philosophy, values and outcomes. Horwath and Calder (1999) also argued that they should be embedded in the real world, with an acknowledgement of the pressures that are being placed on individual agencies and their employees. Practice guidance is an essential partnership document to policy and procedures, attending to the micro-level detail. In the absence of this document, workers tend to end up working in isolation from each other, and practice develops in a fragmented, ad hoc, and unco-ordinated fashion. Good practice can emerge, but cannot be sustained in such an environment.

Implementation
Whilst careful consideration needs to be given to the choice of workers, it needs to be built on a

departmental package of support and procedural guidance. Effective supervision needs to look at the triad of feelings, tasks and thinking, and needs to be accompanied by consultation from someone knowledgeable in this area of work. A failure to pair workers together can lead to isolation, stress and secrecy which mirror the dynamics of the abusers themselves, and leads to unsafe decisions and premature burn-out. It is important that the work takes place in an environment which supports the sharing of knowledge and responsibility, whilst also prohibiting scapegoating and secrecy. It is important that opt-out mechanisms are in place for workers involved and these may be time-limited or permanent.

Practitioners in each agency need to be provided with structured opportunities to reflect on practice, the exercise of professional judgements, feelings and prejudices – either through supervision or consultation – if procedures are not to be used as checklists and families processed through the system without adapting them to the individual circumstances of each case. Senior managers do have a duty to identify ways in which their staff will be provided with opportunities to reflect on and develop their practice. They also need to promote staff care as they remain our most valuable resource.

Outcomes

Outcome measures are important so that workers can become aware of the impact of their actions and decisions on others. There needs to be a very clear differentiation between different kinds of outcome: professionals themselves need to develop outcomes so that they have clear expectations about what they are trying to achieve and also about what change has come about. But we also need to explore the introduction of performance indicators, linked to practice standards. This provides a framework enabling the worker to appreciate exactly what is expected and a measure to determine whether this has been achieved. These should reflect policy and procedures.

Evaluation: keeping your eye on the ball

There is a need to set out explicit criteria in terms of methods of evaluation so that the goalposts are not moved, and so we begin to get a better feel of what works with child victims of domestic violence.

Everitt and Hardiker (1996) have noted that 'evaluation involves processes of dialogue and practice and policy change. The structures and processes through which apparently objective facts and subjective experiences are generated and filtered need to be interrogated. Furthermore, the purpose of evaluation is not merely to provide better or more realistic accounts of phenomena, but to place a value on them and to change situations, practice and people's circumstances accordingly'.

To enable this to take place, the following should be part of the evaluation:

● Do the aims reflect the purpose of practice in light of national guidance and local policies, e.g. children's service plan?
● Are the standards realistic in terms of mandate and resources?
● Do inter-agency policies compliment individual agency policies?
● Is accountability clear?
● What has been achieved in terms of services provided?
● What has been achieved in terms of outcomes?
● What are the opinions of service users regarding policies, procedures and their implementation in practice?

This is a difficult and costly exercise for ACPCs. Gone are the days when a set of procedures could be developed and implemented and the ACPC was able to move on to the next task. Policies, procedures and practice need to be regularly monitored and adjusted to accommodate both local and national changes.

Training and staff development

Training may emphasise the need to follow guidelines and procedures but it is ineffective if professionals do not know how to access them or if training is seen as a vehicle to compensate for any lack of procedures. Training is only effective if it is used as part of a wider strategy to promote and develop practice. This broader strategy should include a framework of policies and procedures together with resources and support to enable professionals to work within the framework. Training also has a key role to play in the management of change. In a world of fragmenting structures and relationships, training can offer staff a group experience, which is safe and directed at meeting their needs. This can help participants feel a sense of belonging and self-efficacy: both which are major determinants of successful change and a buffer to burn out. Training is a key for promoting and modelling inter-professional work, desirable inter-professional behaviour and collective responsibility. It also improves attitudes to inter-agency co-operation and enables participants to gain clarity regarding the roles and responsibilities of other professionals. Those who attend inter-agency training often express fewer concerns about occupational rivalries and power struggles. We have to do a lot more than bringing together a mixed audience in one room: we have to enhance mutual understanding of clarity and of roles and responsibilities. Effective practice requires a workforce with appropriate knowledge, values (especially around discrimination, perceptions and conflict resolution) and skills. Training is pivotal in developing these areas and in promoting effective working relationships, modelling what is expected in practice. A strategic approach to training is required that focuses not only on practitioners, but senior front-line managers as well: 'Training should help policy makers and practitioners critically evaluate the developing body of knowledge and implement relevant changes. It should contribute to their knowledge of good policy and practice'.

Training is an encompassing structure as it influences every part of the framework. It can become the vehicle whereby senior managers are given an opportunity to consider the aims of intervening in situations of domestic violence and discuss their mandate and desired standards for practice. Policies and procedures can then follow. Once these are in place, training can help prepare first-line and middle managers to supervise staff involved in this work. These managers need to have knowledge of policy, standards and their role in terms of promoting high quality practice. It is only when these managers have been trained that it is appropriate to train practitioners.

Towards a preventive framework

Mullender (2000) identified three levels of prevention when addressing domestic violence:

- **Primary prevention**: working to prevent domestic violence from happening at all.
- **Secondary prevention**: stopping domestic violence as soon as the agency learns it is happening and preventing its occurrence.
- **Tertiary prevention**: reducing the harm to those who have already experienced domestic violence.

Any early intervention programme for domestic violence has to:

1. At the individual level:
   ○ Reduce the child's isolation and blame,
   ○ Encourage children to assume responsibility for their own behaviour,
   ○ Encourage an understanding of the effects of domestic violence,
   ○ Increase children's ability to identify and express their feelings,

2. At the family level:
   ○ Give a clear message that this is not acceptable behaviour.
   ○ Encourage understanding of the effects of domestic violence on children and encourage effective parenting strategies.
   ○ Model strategies for staying safe.
   ○ Monitor child development and child safety issues.
   ○ Work to raise the self-esteem of victims.
   ○ Promote responsibility in the perpetrator.
   ○ Encourage women to identify and move towards their personal goals.
   ○ Reduce isolation and self-blame.

3. At a societal level:
   ○ Empower those in low status.
   ○ Act as agents of change for clients and society.
   ○ Model in our own relationships with client's fair use of power and responsible power relationships.

The costs of failing to move toward a preventive framework are enormous. Buvinic et al. (1999) provided a useful typology of the socio-economic costs of violence (see Figure 2.11):

Figure 2.11: The socio-economic costs of violence: A typology (Buvinic et al., 1999)

Direct costs: value of goods and services used in treating or preventing violence	• Medical • Police • Criminal justice system • Housing • Social services
Non-monetary costs: pain and suffering	• Increased morbidity • Increased mortality via homicide and suicide • Abuse of alcohol and drugs • Depressive disorders
Economic multiplier effects: macro-economic, labour market, inter-generational productivity impacts	• Decreased labour market participation • Reduced productivity on the job • Lower earnings • Increased absenteeism • Intergenerational impacts via grade repetition and lower educational attainment of children • Decreased investment and saving • Capital flight
Social multiplier effects: impact on interpersonal relations and quality of life	• Intergenerational transmission of violence • Reduced quality of life • Erosion of social capital • Reduced participation in democratic process.

Chapter Three

How Marital Conflict and Violence Affects Children: Theory, Research and Future Directions

Gordon T. Harold and Emma L. Howarth, School of Psychology Cardiff University

Conflict across the spectrum: setting the stage

The impact of domestic violence and conflict on children constitutes a problem of significant social concern. According to recent estimates, more than 10 million children living in the United States are exposed to violence between their parents each year (Straus, 1992), with more than 34,000 children in England and Wales passing through domestic violence refuges annually (Shankleman, Brooks and Webb, 2000). In addition, rates of intimate partner violence are highest among women and men in their 20s, suggesting that young children are at a particularly high risk of exposure (Koenen, Moffit and Caspi, 2003); a proposal recently supported by the finding that over 40% of all households where intimate partner violence occurs contain children under the age of 12 (Fantuzzo, Boruch, Beriana, Atkins and Marcus, 1997; O'Leary, Barling, Arias and Rosenbaum, 1989).

In a recent review of research focusing on the effects of domestic violence on children, Holden et al. (1998) suggest that about 40% of children from families characterised as domestically violent exhibit clinically significant behavioural problems (in comparison to 10% of children whose families are not characterised as domestically violent). Other research substantiates the finding that children exposed to the conditions of domestic violence exhibit a variety of adverse emotional and behavioural problems, including increased internalising symptoms (Adamson and Thompson, 1998), externalising problems (Singer, Miller, Guo, Slovak, and Frierson, 1998), decreased cognitive functioning, including IQ deficits (Koenen et al., 2003) social competence (Parker and Asher, 1987; McCloskey and Stuweg, 2001; McCloskey and Lichter, 2003) as well as an elevated risk of post-traumatic stress disorder (Graham-Berman and Levendosky, 1998a). Yet, while there is a large and established body of research focusing on the specific outcomes associated with

children's exposure to domestic violence, there is a dearth of research highlighting the underlying processes that explain why some children appear resilient to the trauma of exposure to violence while others go on to develop long-term, clinically significant emotional and behavioural problems. Conversely, in the context of non-violent, interparental conflict there is not only a long and established literature highlighting the link between conflict in the couple relationship and children's psychological development (Towle, 1931; Baruch and Wilcox, 1944; Gassner and Murray, 1969; Porter and O'Leary, 1980; Emery, 1982), there is also an expansive body of research highlighting the processes through which interparental conflict affects children. This body of research explicitly aims to explain *why* some children show little or no signs of psychological distress in the context of such conflict while others go on to develop long-term emotional and behavioural problems (see Harold, Pryor and Reynolds, 2001).

This chapter will provide a comprehensive review of research findings highlighting the link between interparental conflict and children's psychological development.

In reviewing the processes that are proposed to explain children's psychological responses to discordant, but non-violent interparental conflict, light will also be shed on the possible processes that underlie the psychological responses seen in children exposed to the conditions of domestic violence.

The effects of marital conflict on children

While the aim of this chapter is to review research relating to the effects of interparental conflict on children, it should be noted at the outset that most children are exposed to conflict between their parents at some point, with the vast majority of children showing little or no evidence of adverse effects (Cummings and Davies, 1994). However, children differ in the type of conflict they experience at home and the perceived implications of such conflict (Harold, Pryor and Reynolds, 2001). Children exposed to conflict that is frequent, intense, poorly resolved and child-related have been shown to respond more negatively than children exposed to conflict that is expressed without animosity, concerns a topic unrelated to the child and is successfully resolved (Grych, Seid and Fincham, 1992). When children are exposed to negative marital emotion or when the degree of expressed marital quality is so low that partners fail to communicate any positive emotion, children have been shown to be at increased risk for internalising symptoms (e.g., depression and anxiety), externalising problems (e.g., aggression and hostility), academic underachievement, low social competence (e.g., negative peer relations), as well as decreases in general health and well being (e.g., alcohol and tobacco use; eating disorders).

Internalising symptoms

Children's symptoms of depression, anxiety, dysphoria and withdrawal have been shown to be adversely affected by exposure to interparental conflict (Emery, 1982; Harold, Fincham, Osborne and Conger, 1997; Dadds, Atkinson, Turner, Blums and Lendich, 1999). Until recently, however, the assessment of depressive symptoms in childhood has received little attention. This may best be explained by the tendency to view such symptoms as incidental and non-problematic until they attain a level of clinical significance or 'disorder'. Recently, however focus has been directed to the role of children's emotional problems in their own right with the proposal that symptoms should be assessed along a continuum rather than being seen as a simple present or absent dichotomy (Cummings, Davies, and Campbell, 2000).

Family factors have been identified as a primary determinant of depressive symptoms in children. Behavioural geneticists have suggested that there is a heritable association between the occurrence of a depressive episode in marital partners, typically mothers, and the observation of symptoms in children (for a review see Downey and Coyne, 1990; Rice, Harold and Thapar, 2002). However, the activation of any genetic potential is facilitated by exposure to the right kind of environment. That is, a predisposed depressive tendency may not be expressed in a warm and loving family environment but it may

well, on the other hand emerge within the con. of a family environment marked by conflict or violence. As Downey and Coyne (1990) note, problems in the marital relationship, particularly marital conflict, most likely account for the emergence of child symptoms above and beyond any potential genetic predisposition for such symptoms. However, Grych and Fincham (1990) in their review of the marital conflict – child adjustment literature conclude that research findings suggest that there is a moderate relationship at best between marital conflict and children's internalising symptoms. In answer to this, Cummings and Davies (1994) suggest the finding may actually be an artefact of underreporting by those typically relied on to provide information on children's symptoms – parents and teachers. However, these adults may not be the best observers of the subtle behaviours typically associated with children's internalising symptoms (Compas et al., 1991). In the context of interparental conflict, parents distracted by their own marital problems may be less likely to accurately appraise, or indeed notice, covert child responses in comparison to more overt, acting out type responses. Similarly, teachers who are not familiar with the circumstance behind a child's individual symptoms may be less likely to see such symptoms as a particular problem for that child (e.g., viewing the child as a quiet child rather than a depressed child). Equally, a teacher who is familiar with a child's family background may be more likely to report a child's behaviour as being symptomatic of family background, irrespective of the presence of depressed, anxious, withdrawn or dysphoric behaviour (e.g., a depressed child rather than a quiet child). A growing body of literature therefore appropriately highlights the importance of assessing children's reports of their own internalised states in response to negative marital and family conflict (Achenbach, 1991a), and indeed, a convincing volume of literature exists linking children's experience of negative marital emotion to their self-reported symptoms of internalising; depression (Peterson and Zill, 1986); anxiety (Wierson, Forehand and McCombs, 1988); withdrawal (Jouriles, Barling, and O'Leary, 1987) and dysphoria (Harold et al., 1997).

Externalising problems

Externalising behaviours such as aggression, hostility, anti-social and non-compliant behaviour

ncy and vandalism in the
st frequently cited
ital and family disruption
d adolescents (Buehler, 1995).
eral longitudinal studies
indicates that aggressive tendencies emerge
during childhood and are relatively stable across
time (e.g., Farrington, 2000). Other studies have
also reported continuity of aggressive and
anti-social behaviour across generations within
the same families (e.g., Thornberry et al., 2003).
These findings have led researchers to suggest
that such behaviours are rooted, at least in part,
in family process. Increases in externalising
behaviour as a product of negative marital
emotion can occur through one of three possible
mechanisms. First, it has been suggested that
children who are exposed to heightened levels of
marital hostility learn to imitate and utilise
similar behaviours when resolving their own
interpersonal difficulties (e.g., Straus, 1990).
Second, researchers have pointed to the link
between lax, inconsistent parenting in the context
of marital difficulties and child behaviour
problems. Failure to monitor children's behaviour
adequately and consistently may inadvertently
reinforce aggression in children (Patterson, Reid
and Dishion, 1992). Third, recent research
suggests that children's externalising behaviour,
particularly aggression, is the result of biased
attributions and beliefs concerning the intentions
of others and the potential consequences of
parental expressed hostility (Dodge, 1980; Dodge,
1986; Crick and Dodge, 1996).

Understanding specific family level conditions
that may amplify or ameliorate the likelihood of
aggressive behaviours emerging in childhood is
of critical importance to researchers, practitioners
and other mental health professionals. As with
internalising symptoms, the expression of
externalising behaviours lies along a continuum
of expressed severity ranging from mild
demonstrations of frustration and temper
tantrums to instances of extreme or explosive
violence. The developmental pathways that lie
behind a child's progression from agitated to
anti-social behaviour appear to be located in a
complex matrix of family and peer influences
(Loeber and Hay, 1997). Indeed, as Kazdin (1995)
points out, children with diagnosed conduct and,
more recently, attention deficit disorder are often
exposed to family conditions marked by a highly
negative emotional climate. In particular,
disturbances in both the marital and parent–child

relationships accentuate behavioural difficulties
among clinically referred children. However,
while questions remain as to the possible
direction of effects with respect to understanding
the impact of parent behaviour on child
behaviour, most available evidence converges to
suggest that negative behaviours in the marital
and parent–child relationship lead to increases in
negative child behaviour rather than the
converse. The case for marital problems, in
particular, as a causative agent in the emergence
of children's behaviour problems has been
strengthened by demonstrations of relations
between inter-adult anger and children's negative
behaviour under controlled laboratory conditions
(Cummings and colleagues, 1989; 1991).

Academic achievement

An emerging body of research suggests that a
link exists between family factors, school
behaviour and academic achievement (e.g.,
Forehand and Wierson, 1993). To date, most
research focusing on family influences on school
outcomes has focused on the specific impact of
divorce. Amato and Keith (1991b) found a
significant difference between children whose
parents had divorced compared to those children
whose parents had not divorced and their
respective levels of academic achievement.
However, as Amato and Keith (1991a) point out,
when levels of pre-divorce conflict are also
considered in relation to children's adjustment,
conflict may actually be a better predictor of
adjustment than divorce. Although the statistical
significance of effects between family factors such
as marital conflict and divorce on children's
academic achievement is moderate at best, the
practical significance of this link is becoming
increasingly apparent. Those children exposed to
positive family experiences tend to respond well
with respect to academic achievement and school
behaviour, whereas those exposed to negative
marital and family conditions tend to respond
negatively with respect to teacher and peer
interactions as well as underachieve academically
(Forehand, Neighbors, Devine and Armistead,
1994). In order to promote school competence, it
is becoming increasingly apparent that the family
setting must provide a basic foundation for
learning and achievement. Indeed, future
attempts to design and implement effective
intervention strategies for disruptive or
underachieving school children that fail to

consider the impact of marital and family influences on child behaviour will be limited in their potential success.

Social development

A considerable amount of research attention has been devoted to investigating the link between children's experiences at home and their ability to function effectively in other social contexts (e.g., peer and school settings; Ladd, 1992; Russell and Finnie, 1990). This research concludes that the lessons learned by children through the quality of relations they experience with their parents influences their ability to successfully engage, negotiate and manage interactions with their siblings, peers, romantic partners and other adults (e.g., a teacher). Parent–child relations marked by positive parental affect (e.g., warmth, support, effective problem solving) have been linked to children's prosocial behaviour (Eberly and Montemayor, 1998), whereas negative parental affect (e.g., anger and hostility, parent-to-child ridicule, low problem solving skills) has been linked to negative social behaviour among children (Paley, Conger and Harold, 2000; Gottman and Katz, 1989; Kahen, Katz and Gottman, 1994). Although most research in this area supports the notion that the general quality of the parent–child relationship strongly influences children's social development, researchers have increasingly emphasised the importance of identifying the specific processes that underlie this link (e.g., Elicker, Englund and Sroufe, 1992). Two important theoretical frameworks-attachment theory and social information processing theory – have proved useful in understanding the linkages between positive and negative parent–child relationships and children's social development (Paley, Conger and Harold, 2000).

Attachment Theory: Most research focusing on the influence of family experience on children's social development has been guided by Bowlby's model of attachment theory (1973; 1980). This perspective suggests that, in the context of their early primary care-giving experiences, children develop internal representations or working models of how sensitively and reliably their caregivers can be expected to respond to their emotional needs, and how worthy the child feels they are of such responses. These representations or models are thought, in turn, to generalise to other close relationships, guiding the

child/adolescent/early adult's appraisals and behaviour during social and interpersonal exchanges throughout life. As Parke, Cassidy, Burks, Carson and Boyum (1992) have noted 'the working model acquired in the family acts as a template to apply to new social settings'. The acquisition of functional working models derived from the observation of family interaction therefore appears critical to children's successful social development. Studies using attachment theory as a guiding theoretical framework have found that primary and secondary school children with histories of insecure attachment exhibit less empathy towards their peers (Sroufe, 1983), are less well-liked by peers (LaFreniere and Sroufe, 1985), have less positive and co-ordinated interactions with peers and friends (Kerns, 1994), as well as being rated as less socially skilled by adults (Shulman, Elicker and Sroufe, 1994) than children with secure attachment histories.

A central element of attachment theory is the role that children's internal representations, or 'understanding and expectations' associated with parent behaviour, plays in mediating (explaining) the link between such behaviour and children's social development. Greater emphasis is placed on the qualitative nature of the care-giving relationship, however, than on children's own understanding of specific aspects of this relationship. Research in the area of social cognition, on the other hand, directly focuses on the role of children's understanding and expectation as a filter through which family experiences affect their social development.

Social Cognitive Theory: Social cognitive theory (how we understand the interplay between ourselves and specific social contexts) has emphasised the role of perceptions, appraisals and understanding of parent behaviour as central to any understanding of children's experiences of, and responses to, aspects of family life, including marital and parent–child behaviour. Essentially, this theoretical perspective suggests that the way children learn to mentally process exchanges between themselves and adult figures early in life has implications for their long-term social development. Indeed, the development of maladaptive social cognition in childhood (e.g., always expecting others to act in a hostile or aggressive manner) has been likened to the process of rolling a rock down the side of a hill. Although early attempts to descend from top to bottom may appear gradual because of the need to navigate past initial obstacles encountered en route, repeated descents will eventuate in an indelible path, thereby allowing a more rapid descent from top to bottom. In the future, this route more than any other will be chosen and indeed cemented in increasingly accelerated fashion. Children's responses to parents, teachers, other adults, siblings, and peers may be similarly understood in that such responses may become a product of tried and tested strategies derived from the cartography of early family experience.

Evidence is increasingly emerging that the way parents express and manage conflict in their own relationship serves as a primary context through which children acquire understanding and expectations of how their parents are likely to behave toward them. Furthermore, it has been proposed that lessons learnt from children's exposure to conflict between and with their parents become 'tools of the trade' in directing children's interpretation of and responses to the actions of other individuals in different social settings (e.g., peer and school contexts). Studies support the proposal that the roots of maladaptive social cognition in childhood may lie, at least in part, in negative family interactions. Dodge and colleagues (1984; 1987; 1993) have found that children across primary and early secondary school age who demonstrate aggressive tendencies were less accurate in interpreting the intentions of others and were generally more biased in attributing hostility toward others. More recently, Dodge, Petit, Bates and Valente (1995) found that physically abused children were more vigilant in their interpretation of hostile social cues and more likely to interpret ambiguous stimuli as hostile than non-abused children. These findings support the proposal, therefore, that aggressive and rejected children are more likely to attribute hostile and aggressive intentions to their peers than their non-aggressive and non-rejected counterparts (see Crick and Dodge, 1994). The emergence of maladaptive social cognitions such as these has, in turn, implications for children's long-term positive social development.

Physical health

Some research has concluded that a link exists between family events and smoking, drinking, substance use and disordered eating behaviour among children and adolescents. The link between smoking and family factors has received a considerable amount of attention in previous

research (see Glenndinning, Shucksmith and Hendry, 1997). However, links have most often been understood as stemming from socio-economic factors, parents' smoking behaviours and family structure (for example see Tucker, Ellickson and Klein, 2002; Goddard, 1992). A small body of research has linked other family factors such as general family climate and the quality of relations between parents and children to increased smoking and alcohol use during adolescence. In a recent review conducted by Foxcroft and Lowe (1991) 'family support' and 'family control' were identified as particularly important in the socialisation of adolescent alcohol use. In a more recent study, these authors also examined associations between adolescent perceptions of family life and self-reported health behaviours, including smoking and alcohol use. Generally, their findings suggest that children from 'authoritarian' and 'neglecting' families versus 'supportive' families are more likely to indulge in alcohol and smoking related behaviours (Foxcrofte and Lowe, 1995, 1997). In a separate study, Melby, Conger, Conger and Lorenz (1993) observed that in a sample of early adolescent boys, harsh/inconsistent parenting styles were associated with increased tobacco use, whereas nurturant/involved parenting styles were associated with decreased tobacco use.

Parenting behaviour has also been implicated as a factor in the onset of negative eating behaviours among children, primarily girls. For example, the families of anorexic girls have been found to lean toward overprotection and perfectionism, characteristics of authoritarian parenting.

Research aimed at identifying specific links between *marital* behaviour and children's risky health behaviour has received little direct attention. However, the relationship between marital conflict, parenting behaviour and negative behavioural outcomes for children has received considerable attention (see Erel and Burman, 1995). The effects of discord between parents on children's risky health related behaviours may, therefore, occur *as a result* of maritally induced disturbances in effective parenting behaviour. Indeed, this proposal has received support as a possible mechanism through which conflict exerts effects on each index of child maladjustment considered in this section.

While identifying 'what' symptoms children experience when exposed to discordant marital behaviour is an important area of enquiry, identifying the particular mechanisms that explain 'why, when and how' children are adversely affected by exposure to marital conflict is an area of equal, if not greater, importance if we are to improve our understanding of what may be done to alleviate negative effects on children.

'How' marital conflict affects children

Most of the explanations advanced to explain the relationship between marital conflict and children's adjustment have presumed that negative marital behaviour affects children more so than the converse. This is a reasonable conclusion given that although children's behaviour is also likely to influence spouse behaviour (Bell, 1979) this association is unlikely to reflect child influences alone (e.g., financial difficulties or parents psychological distress may lead to marital problems). In support of this proposal, O'Leary and Emery (1984) report that the probability of having a problem child given the existence of marital distress is greater than the probability of experiencing marital distress given the presence of a problem child. At what point, however, marital conflict becomes a problem for child development is a question that remains relatively unclear, other than to conclude that children exposed to negative examples of marital and parent–child interaction tend to manifest increased emotional and behavioural problems in comparison to children exposed to more positive examples of marital and parent–child behaviour (Cummings and Davies, 1994). What *is* known however, is that when handled effectively, conflict in the marital relationship can provide the basis for general family harmony as well as provide children with powerful and positive models of dealing with interpersonal difficulties in their own lives. Children who are exposed to models of well-managed conflict between their parents can learn constructive problem solving skills and strategies (Cummings, 1994) and are more likely to be well functioning emotionally and behaviourally in the face of subsequent marital conflict (Cummings, Goeke-Morey, and Papp, 2003). When conflict between parents is unresolved and poorly managed, its effects can be damaging to general family well being as well as disruptive to children's immediate and long term emotional and behavioural development (Harold et al., 1997). Not only can poorly resolved

problems between parents undermine overall marital quality, it can also be very upsetting to children who are exposed and often involved in their parent's marital disputes. Notwithstanding this observation, advances in both theory and research during the past decade have significantly improved understanding as to why conflict between parents may have a negative impact on children (see Harold et al., 2001; Davies et al., 2002). Indeed, by reviewing research that highlights the underlying processes, or mechanisms, through which children are affected by exposure to discordant, but non-violent conflict between parents, greater understanding of the processes that underlie children's responses to domestic violence may be provided.

Direct versus Indirect Effects Hypotheses: Researchers working in the area of marital conflict and children's adjustment have typically relied on two primary theoretical proposals to explain why conflict between parents may lead to maladaptive emotional and behavioural responses by children. First, researchers have proposed that conflict in and of itself is distressing because of one, the negative feelings it elicits in children and two, the models of behaviour that parents embroiled in a hostile and distressed marital relationship provide for their children. This perspective, therefore, proposes that children are *directly* affected by exposure to interparental conflict. An alternative perspective suggests that marital conflict acts as a catalyst for changes in other family relationships, primarily the parent–child relationship, and it is disruption in this relationship that adversely affects children. In other words, marital conflict *indirectly* affects children's symptoms of psychological distress by altering the quality of relations children experience with their parents.

Proponents of a direct effects hypothesis highlight that early studies in this area have facilitated the conclusion that children show significantly more distress in reaction to behaviour between parents marked by conflict and discord than to parental behaviour not marked by discordant exchanges (Kitzmann, 2000). Furthermore, distressed responses among children have been shown to be stronger as a result of exposure to conflicts that concern the child (Grych, Seid and Fincham, 1992), end with hostility (Davies, Myers and Cummings, 1996) are unresolved (El-Sheikh and Cummings, 1995) and involve children's actual parents rather than other adults (Giacoletti, 1990). Researchers

...se parents act as such powerful ...iour for children, children's ...be heavily influenced not only by ...ney have with their parents but by ...they observe occurring between their pare... ...ummings and Davies, 1994). Through imitation, reinforcement and the acquisition of behavioural 'scripts' (general strategies for behaviour derived from observing the behaviour of others Bandura, 1986), children may acquire maladaptive models of problem solving or conflict resolution as a result of exposure to interparental conflict. These models may then be employed by children during similar instances in their own lives (Grych and Fincham, 1990). Children who intervene or act out, by crying or becoming disruptive, in response to expressions of conflict between parents may also have these behaviours maintained through a process of negative reinforcement (Patterson, Reid and Dishion, 1982; Cummings and Davies, 1994). For example, children may interrupt interparental conflicts by misbehaving in an attempt to distract their parents from the conflict or reduce its negative effects and potential implications for them. Such strategies may be adaptive in the short term because they distract parents from the original source of the marital argument. However, in the event that these behaviours are rewarded by the fact that parents *are* actually distracted from their argument by a temporary disruption of parental quarrelling, the likelihood of the child repeating the behaviour on subsequent occasions is increased. As the negative reinforcement is repeated again and again, the child may show increasingly strong and persistent behaviour in response to conflict at home and other social settings (e.g., school), contributing to risk for the development of a broad pattern of behaviour problems (Cummings and Davies, 1994). Indeed, observing angry parents may reduce children's inhibitions about hostile behaviour in general. If the parents as authority figures engage in aggressive behaviours, children become less inhibited about employing such behaviour because they assume its use is acceptable (Cummings and Davies, 1994). Johnson and O'Leary (1987) have provided some support for the modelling hypothesis. These authors found that the mothers of girls who were conduct disordered were more hostile and the fathers more aggressive than the mothers and fathers of girls who were not conduct disordered. This study, however, has received

criticism in that it fails to provide any information specific to boys' behaviour. At the very least, some evidence is provided for a similarity in the behaviour of parents and their children (see Figure 3.1, Panel A). Critics of the direct effects proposal, however, highlight that conflict between parents is unlikely to occur in isolation of effects on other family relationships.

Proponents of an indirect effects hypothesis recognise the role that conflict between parents plays as a starting point to understanding how negative effects are transmitted to children. According to researchers in this area, an alternative mechanism through which marital conflict affects children is through a 'spillover' of tension and hostility emanating from the marital relationship into the parent–child relationship, which, in turn, leads to an increase in children's symptoms of psychological distress (see Figure 3.1, Panel B). This hypothesis suggests that parents who have more satisfying marital relationships are more likely to have satisfying relationships with their children, as well as being more emotionally available and sensitive to the needs of their children. On the other hand, parents who have less satisfying marriages are more likely to be less satisfied with their children as well as less sensitive and emotionally responsive to their children's needs, thereby increasing the potential for the development of children's maladaptive behaviours. The proposal that parents engaged in a hostile marital relationship may become less attentive and emotionally sensitive to their children and their needs has received considerable attention in previous research (see Erel and Burman, 1995). Researchers interested in accounting for the association between marital conflict, parent–child conflict and children's adjustment have suggested that conflict in the marital relationship may be transferred into the parent–child relationship via four possible transmission processes:

Modelling: Parents involved in a relationship marked by marital distress engage in, and thus model, negative interactions that are lacking in warmth and care. Conversely, parents experiencing positive marital relations model more functional interactions that are marked by greater warmth and care than hostility (Burman, Margolin, and John, 1993). The suggestion that the quality of the marital relationship as witnessed by children determines the quality of the parent–child relationship is underpinned by the theoretical foundations of social learning

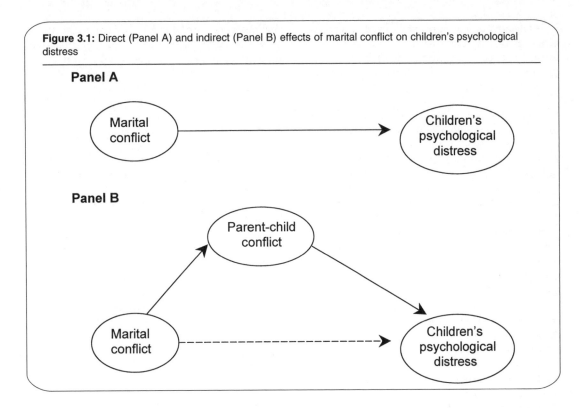

Figure 3.1: Direct (Panel A) and indirect (Panel B) effects of marital conflict on children's psychological distress

theory. Social learning theorists suggest that children's behaviour can be greatly influenced by learning as a result of observing behaviour modelled by parents (Grusec, 1992). This hypothesis can be linked to the role of modelling discussed earlier with regard to the direct effects of marital conflict on children. However, in this instance, the modelling process is specific to interaction observed and then expressed within the *parent–child* relationship. This aspect of a social learning approach to understanding parent and parent–child interaction is consistent with a spillover hypothesis in its prediction that conflicted behaviours that occur in the context of the marital relationship will also be observed in the parent–child relationship.

Socialisation: The socialisation hypothesis suggests that parents experiencing marital problems tend to use 'less consistent discipline practices' and 'less optimal parenting techniques' than parents involved in non-discordant marital relations (Erel and Burman, 1995). However, inconsistencies in parents' discipline practices may stem from more than one source. Parents involved in a discordant marital relationship may fail to communicate with each other regarding appropriate disciplinary practices. Such

discrepancy may lead to differential parenting practices, thereby increasing the likelihood for conflict to occur in either the mother–child or father–child relationships. Rather than co-operating in the task of effective co-parenting, parents embroiled in marital difficulties tend to be hostile and competitive with respect to marital and child-related issues, be ineffective as a team in helping their children deal with general problem solving and express inconsistent and discrepant expectations for their children (see Kitzmann, 2000).

Scapegoating: This perspective is one of the least investigated theoretical proposals aimed at explaining the relationship between marital and parent–child conflict. Essentially, the scapegoating hypothesis, derived from a family systems perspective (Minuchin, 1988), suggests that parents engaged in marital conflicts focus their attention on child related problems in order to distract their attention from the initial source of the conflict – their own relationship (Vogel and Bell, 1960). This strategy reduces strain on the marital relationship by redirecting attention toward the child, but leads to an increase in rejecting behaviour by the parent toward the child (Fauber, Forehand, Thomas and Wierson., 1990).

Family Stress: The fourth spillover mechanism is also primarily derived from family systems traditions and is really a combination of the previous three mechanisms proposed. In a well-functioning family system, family members form a cohesive group. Under stress, however, the balance in any set of family relationships (husband–wife, mother–son, father–daughter etc.) may be adversely affected (Kitzmann, 2000). According to this perspective, therefore, discordance in the marital and parent–child relationships are reciprocally linked; in other words, stress occurring in the context of one relationship affects the other, and vice versa. Reciprocity of affect is a central concept in both family systems and social learning approaches to understanding the propensity for increased negativity between spouses, and between spouses and their children.

In contrast to research that highlights how negative emotion in the marital relationship may spill over in to the parent–child relationship; this process has been set against what has become known as a 'compensatory' process. Essentially the hypothesis proposes that individuals seek out more satisfactory experiences in a particular relationship in order to compensate for deficiencies experienced in other relationships (Erel and Burman, 1995). This hypothesis specifically proposes a negative association between satisfying marital relations and the quality of the parent–child relationship (e.g., Brody, Pellegrini, and Sigel, 1986; Goldberg and Easterbrooks, 1984). For example, the compensatory hypothesis makes the claim that a parent who does not fulfil their personal needs for intimacy, love, and warmth in the marital relationship seeks to satisfy these needs in the parent–child relationship (Erel and Burman, 1995) and vice versa. A stronger investment in the child, therefore, is likely to occur when parents experience deficits in their perceived levels of marital quality (Engfer, 1988). It is, of course, possible that more complex associations may develop via a compensatory process. For example, it may be the case that a positive association exists between the quality of the marital relationship and the quality of the parent–child relationship with one child, while a negative relationship exists between marital quality and the parent–child relationship with another child.

A central proposition inherent to either a spill over or compensation approach to understanding the impact of marital conflict on child adjustment is that children experience adjustment difficulties *because of* changes to the quality of relations they experience with their parents as a result of conflict occurring between their parents. As Fauber and Long (1991) conclude 'it is at the site of parenting practices that conflict has its effect on children'. However, if children are only affected through changes in the quality of the parent – child relationship, then children need not actually be present or directly exposed to marital conflict in order to experience its effects. If conflict in the marriage affects children's well being solely through changes in the quality of the parent–child relationship, children should be equally affected irrespective of whether they actually witness the conflict or not. Research findings, however, do not support this proposal.

Children who are exposed to overt marital conflict, conflict that occurs in their presence, respond more negatively than children who experience so-called covert conflict, conflict that occurs in their absence. Why? Recent research suggests that children's *perceptions* of conflict may actually be a more important predictor of their maladjustment than the actual occurrence of conflict per se. As Harold et al. (2004) point out, children actively interpret and respond to their environment, and closer attention to children's thoughts and feelings (cognitions and emotions) in the context of interparental conflict is crucial to providing a better understanding of how conflict affects children's psychological development.

The role of children's perceptions of interparental conflict

Emery (1982) in a seminal review of the marital conflict – child adjustment literature, initially drew attention to the importance of assessing children's perceptions of conflict in order to explain why conflict may adversely affect children. How a child interprets conflict in terms of its meaning and implications for both themselves and for the general well being of the family may explain 'why' some children exposed to conflict seem relatively unaffected while others go on to develop long-term psychological problems (Harold et al., 2001). Three recent theoretical perspectives stand out in terms of expanding this initial proposal, one, the cognitive-contextual framework (Grych and Fincham, 1990), two, the emotional-security hypothesis (Davies and Cummings, 1994) and three, the family wide model (Harold and colleagues, 1997; 1999).

A Cognitive-Contextual Framework: Grych and Fincham (1990) provide a theoretical framework proposing that children's responses to interparental conflict occurs through their mental (cognitive) processing of the conflict. According to this perspective, the impact of interparental conflict on children depends both on how the conflict is expressed and how children interpret its meaning and potential implications for their well being. These authors propose two stages of cognitive processing underlying the link between children's exposure to interparental conflict and their interpretation of its meaning. The first of these, primary processing, is a stage where the child first becomes aware that conflict is occurring and experiences an initial level of arousal. Specific characteristics of the conflict episode such as its frequency, intensity or resolution properties, as well as contextual factors, such as the quality of parent–child relations, are proposed to influence this initial stage of appraisal. This 'primary' stage of processing may then lead to a more elaborate stage of processing, known as secondary processing, during which the child attempts to understand why the conflict is occurring and what they should do in response. Secondary processing involves making an attribution for the cause of the event, ascribing responsibility and blame as well as generating efficacy expectations relating to the child's ability to cope with the conflict. Children who view conflict as threatening or feel unable to cope effectively are hypothesised to experience more anxiety and helplessness when conflict occurs, and those who blame themselves for parental disagreements or feel responsible for helping to end them are proposed to experience guilt, shame, and sadness. If conflict is frequent, these appraisals are believed to increase children's risk for internalising problems (Grych and Fincham, 1990; Grych, Fincham, Jouriles and McDonald, 2000). Conflicts that are frequent, hostile, poorly resolved, and child-oriented are predicted to be more likely to be perceived as threatening and elicit self-blame, but the types of appraisals that children make are also thought to be influenced by contextual factors, such as their age and prior exposure to conflict (see Figure 3.2).

Many of the hypotheses drawn from the cognitive-contextual framework have been supported in research. Links have been documented between particular dimensions of conflict and children's appraisals (e.g., Grych, 1998; Grych and Fincham, 1993) between appraisals and children's immediate responses to conflict (Grych and Fincham, 1993), and between appraisals and child adjustment (Cummings,

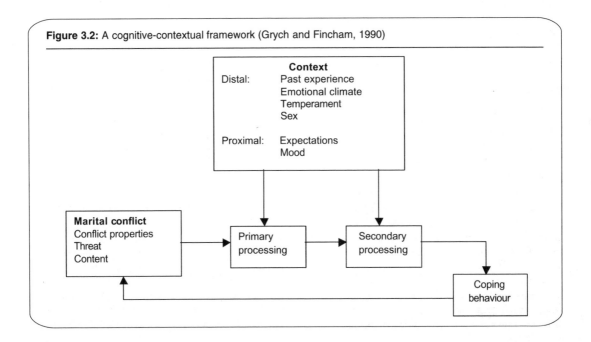

Figure 3.2: A cognitive-contextual framework (Grych and Fincham, 1990)

Davies and Simpson, 1994; Grych and Fincham, 1992; Kerig, 1998b). Further, studies with American, Australian, Canadian and British samples have shown that appraisals mediate, or explain, the association between conflict and adjustment problems, suggesting that the effects of conflict operate through the kinds of appraisals children make in the context of interparental conflict (Dadds, et al., 1999; Grych et al, 2000; Kerig, 1998a; Grych, Harold and Miles, 2003). Furthermore, Grych, Harold and Miles (2003) have recently shown that children's appraisals of threat are consistently related to their internalising symptoms, whereas appraisals of blame are more consistently linked to their externalising problems. These results underscore the specific role of appraisals as a determining feature of children's symptoms of psychological distress as a result of exposure to interparental conflict – when they perceive direct threat, children may manifest symptoms of anxiety, depression and withdrawal, when they perceive they are at fault for or blame themselves for their parents arguments, they are more likely to act out in a hostile and aggressive manner. Acquiring 'mental models' of properties typically associated with parent's marital conflicts, such as frequency, intensity and resolution potential, as well as feelings of threat and self-blame generated by perceptions of these properties may, therefore, explain the negative effects conflict has on children's development.

An Emotional-Security Hypothesis: A complementary perspective, the emotional security hypothesis (Davies and Cummings, 1994) proposes that children's emotional security about interparental conflict is reflected by three interrelated, yet conceptually distinct, components. When children are exposed to the conditions of marital conflict, effects are determined through:

(1) *Emotional regulation*: Children may be activated to feel anger, sadness, fear, relief, or happiness depending on how conflict between parents is expressed and managed. The implications for children's functioning is determined by how much a child feels sad or angry or other emotional reactions, and how well the child can regulate the activation of such emotions.

(2) *Cognitive representations*: Children assess how much of a problem a given conflict expression constitutes and its potential to adversely influence other family relations.

Children from high conflict homes, therefore, would be expected to be more prone to developing insecure internal representations of family relations than others.

(3) *Behavioural regulation*: What children do in response to the conflict behaviour demonstrated by parents. For example, children might attempt to regulate exposure to marital conflict by actively intervening, or, alternatively, withdrawing from or otherwise avoiding a destructive conflict setting (see Figure 3.3).

According to the emotional security hypothesis, therefore, exposure to negative forms of marital conflict compromises children's sense of emotional well being. Indeed, when exposed to models of negatively expressed and managed marital events, children are motivated to preserve and promote their own sense of emotional regulation, cognitive representations and behavioural regulation in the context of broad family relations. Marital conflict, it is proposed, has its effects on children not so much through the simple occurrence of conflict *per se* but rather through the ways conflictual issues are expressed and managed by parents. Destructively managed issues reduce children's sense of emotional security, mediating effects on children's adjustment (Davies and Cummings, 1998).

In initial tests of this perspective, Davies and Cummings (1998) found that exposure to marital conflict led to differences in children's emotional security, and that these differences accounted for, or mediated, initial effects of conflict on children's internalising and externalising symptoms. Specifically, children's emotional reactivity and their internal representations of family relations were most closely linked with marital relations and child adjustment, especially with regard to internalising symptoms. More recently, Harold, Shelton, Goeke-Morey and Cummings (2002) assessed the impact of interparental conflict on children's long-term adjustment through their appraisals of threat, self-blame *and* emotional insecurity. Findings suggest those children's appraisals of threat and feelings of self-blame generated from exposure to marital conflict adversely affect feelings of emotional insecurity, which, in turn, affects their symptoms of psychological distress. These results represent the most advanced articulation of the complimentary role of children's cognitions and emotions as intermediate elements in the link between marital conflict and children's symptoms of psychological distress. Because initial symptom

Figure 3.3: An emotional security hypothesis (Davies and Cummings, 1994)

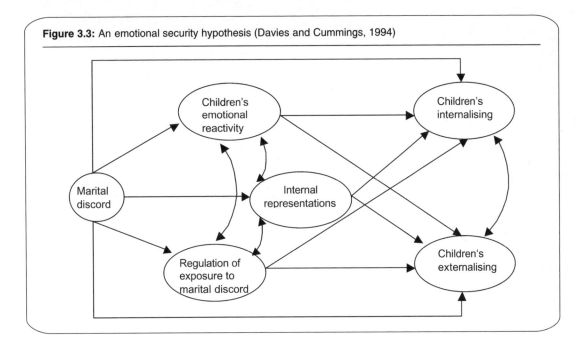

levels are considered in the statistical analyses conducted in this study, they are also among the very first set of findings to implicate marital conflict as a causative agent in the development of emotional and behavioural problems during childhood and adolescence (see also Harold and Conger, 1997; Harold et al., 1997).

Cognition versus emotion – A brief review: The cognitive-contextual and emotional security hypotheses are grounded, respectively, in information-processing theory and attachment theory. While information-processing theory proposes a sequence of 'mental' steps or stages that describe how children's reactions to certain stimuli, including conflict, are perceived, interpreted and acted upon (Dodge, 1993; Grych and Cardoza-Fernandez, 2001), attachment theory locates the impact of family experience on child development in the provision of a positive 'secure-base' or infant-caregiver relationship during early childhood (Bowlby, 1958; Waters and Cummings, 2000). Both offer plausible perspectives in accounting for children's disrupted development as a function of exposure to conflicted family relationships. However, it is unlikely that children's thinking (cognition) or attachment (emotional security) solely determine children's maladaptive responses to interparental conflict. From a review of earlier literature, we know that parent's marital conflicts and conflicts

with their children are interlinked ('spill over' hypotheses). We also know that children are astute observers of parent behaviour and that their perceptions of interparental conflict affects their psychological responses. The question is, what role does marital conflict play in determining the broad orchestra of family effects on children? Does conflict represent nothing more than one of many players, contributing to children's psychological distress only in the presence of other factors, or does it on the other hand have a lead part to play in generating effects on children, even when other family factors are simultaneously considered? If so, how? Harold and colleagues (1997; 1999) have recently developed a theoretical model that goes some way to addressing these questions.

A familywide model (Harold, Fincham, Osborne and Conger, 1997)

Harold and colleagues (1997; 1999) have extended the proposals offered by Grych and Fincham (1990) and Davies and Cummings (1994), as well as those researchers proposing that children are adversely affected by marital conflict due to disruptions in parenting behaviour (see Erel and Burman, 1995). These authors propose a model (see Figure 3.4) whereby marital conflict and parent–child hostility respectively affect

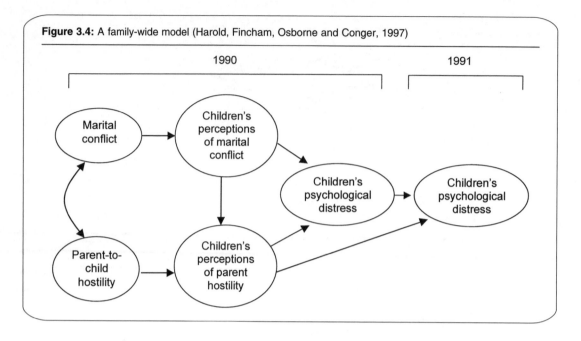

Figure 3.4: A family-wide model (Harold, Fincham, Osborne and Conger, 1997)

children's perceptions of conflict both *between* and *with* their parents. Children's perceptions of marital conflict and parent–child hostility, in turn, are hypothesised to affect their concurrent, or immediate, and longer-term symptoms of psychological distress. While conflict between parents and between parents and children is proposed to affect 'how' children see these respective relationships, the arrow linking perceptions of marital conflict to children's perceptions of parent hostility suggests that children's appraisals of how parents behave toward each other determines how children expect their parents to behave toward them. These perceptions then jointly activate children's immediate symptoms of internalising and externalising, respectively, and go on to influence their longer-term symptoms of psychological distress (see Figure 3.4).

Results from initial tests of this model supported the hypothesis that marital conflict is associated with a 'spill over' of emotion in the form of increased hostility directed toward the child. They also showed that parent and independently observed reports of interparental conflict and parent–child hostility were positively associated with the level of marital conflict and parental hostility *perceived* by the child. Moreover, the adverse influence of marital conflict and parental hostility on current and future

symptoms of psychological distress was completely accounted for by children's perceptions of negative parental behaviour (see Harold et al., 1997).

The theoretical perspectives offered by Grych and Fincham (1990), Davies and Cummings (1994) and Harold et al. (1997) offer insight into the psychological processes that underlie children's reactions to interparental conflict and go some way to explaining what may happen *within* children when they are exposed to discordant exchanges between parents. However, children do not experience or react to conflict between their parents in isolation of other family factors or their experience of other family influences. In order to put the effects of conflict on children into perspective, consideration must be given to the role of both individual characteristics within the child and to factors within the broader family climate that affect children's interpretation and reactions to interparental conflict. While conflict between parents is generally accepted as a stressor that adversely affects children's psychological development, other factors such as the child's individual temperament and ability to 'cope' with conflict, as well as additional familial factors such as parent psychological health and parent conflict management styles may serve to increase or reduce the effects of conflict on children.

The role of child and family characteristics

Child Temperament: Children with 'difficult' temperaments are less sensitive to positive aspects and more susceptible to negative aspects of their social environment. Children with 'easy' temperaments, on the other hand, are more sensitive to positive aspects and less sensitive to negative aspects of their environment. Children with difficult temperaments, therefore, may be more reactive to negative family climate and less responsive to positive aspects of family life. Chess and Thomas (1984) identified that children with a more stable temperament adapted more easily and were less over-emotional when exposed to conditions of social stress, including family conflict, than children who were generally reactive and had problems dealing with change. Research into the relative interplay, however, between child temperament and family environment is an area that is under researched, particularly in relation to how child temperament affects the propensity for increased interparental conflict or how the effects of interparental conflict are exacerbated in temperamentally difficult children.

Child Coping: Children's individual or personal coping strategies have been shown to be a particularly important moderator, or 'buffer', of relations between marital discord and child outcomes (Cummings and Cummings, 1988). Indeed, recent research concludes that the 'strategies children use to cope with their parents marital conflict . . . are powerful predictors of adjustment' (O'Brien, Margolin and John, 1995). A fundamental distinction exists in the literature suggesting that children may activate one of two primary coping strategies – problem focused or emotion focused coping (Folkman and Lazarus, 1980). The former occurs at a behavioural level and involves the child's efforts to act directly on the source of stress and attempt to change it. The latter involves the child's cognitive or mental attempts to regulate their emotional state. Studies aimed at explaining why some children appear more resilient to the effects of family and marital stress have led researchers to conclude that these children may employ more adaptive appraisals and coping strategies and thus experience better emotional and behavioural functioning than their counterparts who employ more ineffective strategies and acquire more problematic beliefs. Understanding the role of coping as a potential risk factor in the context of interparental conflict has important implications for the development and implementation of effective intervention strategies.

Parent Psychological Health and Family Economic Pressure: It is possible that any links between marital problems and children's adjustment reflect the effects of other family variables rather than representing any unique effects of conflict alone. For example, parent psychopathology (e.g., depression) and family stresses such as socio-economic pressure have been implicated in the onset and maintenance of both marital problems and child behaviour problems (Downey and Coyne, 1990; Conger, Conger, Elder, Lorenz, Simons and Whitbeck., 1992). According to these authors, having a depressed parent probabilistically increases children's risk for a wide range of psychological problems, including depression and conduct problems. However, most children who grow up in the company of a depressed parent, usually the mother, develop without any interruption to their psychological development (Cummings and Davies, 1994). Given that conflict is usually higher in the marriages of depressed persons, what role might marital conflict play in the company of depressed parental affect? In a study by Hops, Sherman and Biglan (1990) comparisons of family interactions were made between maritally concordant (well functioning) and discordant families that included a depressed mother. Children of depressed mothers in maritally distressed families were more irritable than children in non-maritally distressed families. Marital difficulties may therefore play a part in accounting for the effects of parent psychopathology on children. Downey and Coyne (1990) suggest, however, that effects may vary depending on the type of adjustment considered – marital conflict may be more closely associated with children's risk for externalising, whereas parent depression may exert greater effects on children's internalising.

The economic conditions within which children are raised have been shown to indirectly influence their internalising symptoms (Conger, Conger, Elder, Lorenz, Simons and Whitbeck, 1993), externalising problems (Skinner, Elder and Conger, 1992), delinquency (Conger and Conger, 1995), academic underachievement (Melby and Conger, 1997), and levels of social competence (Paley, Conger and Harold, 2000). Working from a family systems perspective, Conger and colleagues (1990; 1994; 1999) have suggested that economic pressures affect children through negative influences on parent's psychological functioning, exposure to marital discord and disrupted parent–child relations. When parents struggle to meet basic economic needs as a result of direct economic hardship, or as a result of increased time commitments at work, their ability to provide the type of home environment necessary for children's long-term well-being is at risk. Therefore according to this perspective, children are adversely affected through the impact such pressure has on the parents marital relationship, parent–child relations and, in turn, children's psychological functioning. In developing this theoretical model, however, little attention has been paid to the child's perspective on family relationships – a factor that has been shown to have significant implications for their psychological development. Parent's psychological functioning and general family stress, however, may serve as important contextual factors in determining the propensity for conflict to occur in families and must be considered in any attempt to understand the effects of conflict on children.

Parent Gender – Different Processes: Aside from the general finding that there appears to be an association between conflict in the marital and parent–child relationships, there are a number of inconsistencies in reported findings when the respective behaviours of mothers and fathers in the context of conflict are considered separately. Recent evidence suggests that negativity in the marital relationship has more negative effects on the father than on the mother in terms of their role as parents (Belsky and Rovine, 1990; Fincham, Beach, Harold and Osborne, 1997). Yet, most studies have tended to focus on the impact of negative mother–child relations on children's emotional and behavioural development. In a noteworthy study by Osborne and Fincham (1996), these authors' highlighted two very important findings relating to differential effects of marital conflict on mother–child and father–child relationships in accounting for children's externalising and internalising problems. First, children who witness their parents fighting do not form a global perception of negative parent–child relations. Rather, such conflict is perceived in relation to both father–child and mother–child interactions. Results from this study, suggest that exposure to interparental conflict has a detrimental impact on

father–child relations above and beyond that noted for the mother–child relationship. Indeed, this effect was noted for both boys and girls in the analyses conducted by Osborne and Fincham (1996). Second, marital conflict was found to have a differential impact on the parent–child relationship depending on the gender of the parent and the gender of the child. Conflict was more strongly related to mother–son relationships than father–son relationships in the case of internalising symptoms. Whereas, for girls, exposure to marital conflict was more strongly related to negativity in the father–daughter relationship than the mother–daughter relationship when externalising behaviour was the outcome measure considered. These results are consistent with what is known as the opposite gender spillover hypothesis (Howes and Markman, 1989). According to this proposal, interparental conflict may have a greater influence on parents' behaviour toward the opposite sex child. Osborne and Fincham (1996) explain that this effect may be because mothers or fathers are more likely to react to their opposite sex child because that child is reminiscent of their spouse.

Two recent reports provide further evidence for the proposal that conflict between parents differentially impacts on mothers and fathers with regard to their behaviours in the parent–child relationship. A study conducted by Brody et al. (1986) noted that fathers used less positive feedback and were more intrusive with regard to their child's behaviour when they were unhappy in their marriage. Mothers who were experiencing marital distress became more facilitative, asking more questions of their children, than did mothers in non-distressed marriages. Similar results using a longitudinal design were reported by Belsky, Youngblade, Rovine and Volling (1991). These authors noted that deterioration in marital quality across time was associated with increased paternal related intrusive behaviour and maternal related facilitative behaviour. Collectively, these results are consistent with parenting theory in that discordant marital relations may lead mothers to compensate for their poor spousal relations by becoming more involved with their children, whereas such discordance may lead fathers to withdraw from the paternal role (Gable, Belsky and Crnic, 1992). These authors also note one other interesting possibility relating to differential parent–child interactions in response to marital discord. A mother's increased involvement with her children may reflect a desire to compensate for possible aversive experiences that the children are having with their fathers which in some way 'makes up' or 'compensates' for the inadequate support she herself is receiving from her spouse (Gable et al., 1992). Whatever differences may exist in terms of mother–child and father–child interactions, little doubt exists regarding the association between marital disharmony, changes in the parent–child relationship and child adjustment.

Studies focusing on the possibility that complex parent–child cross-gender interactions may occur in the context of negative marital behaviour have also revealed some interesting findings. O'Leary (1984) first proposed that negative emotion in the parent–child relationship in the context of interparental conflict might be more likely to influence an opposite sex child. Osborne and Fincham (1996) provided support for this observation by showing that marital conflict had more negative effects on the mother–son relationship than the father–son relationship and that the impact of conflict on the mother–son relationship was stronger than that observed for mother–daughter relations. For father–child relations, girls who witnessed marital conflict were more likely to perceive the relationship with their fathers as more negative than they were to perceive their relationship with their mothers. With respect to father–daughter relations, McHale (1994) found that marital conflict was associated with increased paternal withdrawal only in the case of daughters. Increased hostility directed toward sons by mothers and increased withdrawal from daughters by fathers is consistent with evidence focusing on spouse responses to marital distress. In the context of marital discord, women may be more likely to respond with direct attempts to confront their husbands, regarding specific behaviour or issues relevant to the source of the discord. Conversely, husbands may be more likely to withdraw or attempt to withdraw from conflict that might cause them to 'lose their cool' (Gottman, 1994). Osborne and Fincham (1996) propose that the way in which spouses respond to problems in their marriage determines their responses to their opposite sex child because that child is reminiscent of the spouse. These results highlight the possibility that subtle differences in how parents respond during interactions with their children in the context of marital conflict

may have important implications for children's development. Indeed, findings suggest that boys and girls may experience the impact of conflict differentially as a function of their gender.

Child Gender – Different Outcomes: Findings are mixed with respect to the possible implications of child gender in accounting for differences in children's responses to marital and parent–child conflict. For example, Emery and O'Leary (1982) suggested that family relationships have more negative consequences for boys than for girls. Cummings, Davies and Simpson (1994) went a step further by proposing two hypotheses related to this difference: one, boys are more reactive to family conflict than girls and two, boys are less shielded from family conflict than girls. These authors concluded that very little support has been provided for the former hypothesis, but there is evidence to support the latter hypothesis (Harold et al., 1997; Grych and Fincham, 1990). Harold et al. (1997) showed that boys' but not girls' perceptions of marital conflict directly affected their concurrent internalising symptoms. For boys and girls, perceptions of marital conflict indirectly affected concurrent and long-term internalising through children's respective perceptions of parents' hostility. When externalising symptoms were assessed, neither boys' nor girls' perceptions of marital conflict affected their concurrent symptoms. Only indirect effects from children's perceptions of marital conflict through perceptions of parental hostility influenced children's long-term externalising behaviours. Interestingly, however, an indirect effect from perceptions of marital conflict through parent–child hostility to long-term externalising was apparent for girls but not boys when the effects of initial (concurrent) symptom levels were also considered. This is consistent with emerging evidence that girls' behavioural adjustment is primarily influenced through disruptions in the affective quality of the parent–child relationship.

Using a sample of parents and children living in the United Kingdom, Harold (1999) further demonstrated differences in boys' and girls' responses to marital conflict and parent–child hostility. For boys, parent reported marital conflict influenced internalising symptoms through two primary mechanisms, one, directly from their perceptions of marital conflict and two, indirectly from their perceptions of marital conflict through their perceptions of negative mother–child and father–child relations. For girls, all effects appeared indirect through disturbances in mother–child and father–child relationship quality. These and related results (e.g., Davies and Windle, 1997; Owen and Cox, 1997) suggest that subtle differences in children's responses to interparental conflict may be apparent and indeed that these differences may vary as a function of child gender. Furthermore, the impact of marital conflict on children may have greater implications for boys' emotional well-being and girls' behavioural well-being than has previously been considered.

Parents' Conflict Management Style: Parents' conflict management style has been shown to be a particularly important predictor of children's symptoms of distress during negative family interactions. Indeed, discriminations between parents' negative and positive marital conflict styles have been shown to be an important determinant of children's psychological responses. Previous studies with younger children suggest that it is important to examine the contributions of both positive *and* negative parental affect during instances of marital and family discord (Parke et al., 1992) as it remains unclear whether they play comparable roles in shaping children's psychological responses. Some studies suggest that positive parental affect is more predictive of children's peer functioning than negative parental affect (Hammen, Burge and Adrian, 1991; Putallaz, 1987), whereas others have found that higher levels of negative, rather than positive, parental affect are predictive of children's social maladjustment (Kahen et al., 1994; Parke, Burks, Carson, Neville, and Boyum, 1994).

One explanation for the lack of consistent findings in this area is that it may be the *balance* between positive and negative behaviours expressed by parents during instances of family discord that is most predictive of children's psychological adjustment. Thus, children who interact with parents who are predominantly hostile may develop representations of relationships that are largely or uniformly negative and learn maladaptive ways of interacting with and responding to others. Conversely, children who are exposed to negative parental affect that is tempered by some positive behaviour may develop representations of relationships that are at least somewhat positive and, indeed, may have positive implications for their development. The role of constructive versus destructive marital behaviour has received very recent attention, and findings already

suggest that distinguishing conflict behaviours along positive and negative dimensions has important implications for understanding child effects (Goeke-Morey and Cummings, 2000).

Constructive versus Destructive Marital Behaviour: The emerging picture from research suggests that the effect that marital conflict has on children depends upon the manner in which it is expressed, managed and resolved, as well as the extent to which the conflict concerns, involves, threatens or blames the child more so than its simple occurrence (Cummings and Davies, 1994; Grych and Fincham, 1990). Recent evidence suggests that distinguishing between constructive and destructive conflict management styles may have implications for children's adaptive and maladaptive responses. Destructive conflict behaviours such as violence (Holden and Richie, 1991) aggression (Jouriles, Norwood, McDonald, Vincent and Mahoney, 1996) non-verbal conflict or the silent treatment (Cummings, Vogel, Cummings and El-Sheikh, 1989), intense conflicts and conflicts about child related matters (Grych and Fincham, 1993) are linked with increased distress or risk for adjustment problems in children. By contrast, constructive conflict expression and management such as mutually respectful, emotionally modulated conflicts (Easterbrooks, Cummings and Emde, 1994), conflict resolutions and explanations of unresolved conflicts (Cummings et al., 1989; 1991) are linked with a lowered risk for child distress and an increased potential for improved social competence and general well being. Resolution of conflict, in particular, has been shown to be a powerful factor in reducing the negative effects of discord on children. Indeed children have been shown to respond to subtle variations along the continuum of possible conflict resolution. For example, in a study reported by Cummings et al. (1991) children exposed to a condition of unresolved conflict (continued fighting, silent treatment etc.) responded more negatively than children who were exposed to partially resolved conflicts (changing topic or submission), who in turn responded more negatively than children who were exposed to resolved conflicts (apology, compromise).

The early message derived from research considering the role of constructive versus destructive conflict behaviour is that children of all ages, 2–16 years, are astute observers of conflict and are well able to infer potentially negative implications of parent conflict for themselves and other family members both during and after the conflict episode. When parents provide positive models of conflict negotiation and resolution, children learn very valuable lessons that they may then employ in their own lives. When parents handle conflicts in a destructive and unresolved fashion, long-term disturbances in children's emotional, behavioural and social well-being may result.

General summary

Conflict between parents is regarded by many as a natural and normal part of family life. Violence is not. This chapter reviews literature focusing on the effects of interparental conflict on children and shows that conflict ranging from non-verbal and low-level exchanges to overt aggression can adversely affect children depending on one, how conflicts are expressed and managed by parents and two, how children interpret and understand the cause, content and consequences of conflict between their parents. Conflicts that are frequent, intense, poorly resolved and child related are more distressing to children of all ages than conflicts expressed without animosity, concern a topic unrelated to the child and are successfully resolved. The processes that explain these effects involve children's underlying feelings of threat, self-blame, emotional insecurity as well as their

expectations that conflict occurring *between* parents will adversely affect their relationships *with* parents. These underlying components of 'mental processing' have, in turn, been linked to a variety of negative responses in children including increased internalising symptoms, externalising problems, low social competence, academic underachievement, as well as anti-social behaviour and delinquency in the extreme.

While the effects of marital violence on children has received considerable attention in previous research, little attention has been paid to the underlying processes that explain 'how, why and when' marital violence exerts effects on children. Emphasis to date has been placed on the outcomes associated with living in a domestically violent home rather than on the processes that explain why some children appear resilient to the trauma associated with such violence while others go on to develop long-term, clinically significant emotional and behavioural problems. Consideration of the marital conflict – child adjustment literature provides a 'road-map' for future research in this area as well as guidelines for the development of more effective intervention programmes aimed at mental health professionals, policy makers and, of course, those parents and children who live with the everyday realities of domestic violence.

Chapter Four

Parenting and Domestic Violence

Introduction

While the rhetoric of domestic violence is one of responsibility and accountability of those who perpetrate domestic violence, in practice, women are often blamed and held accountable. We need to be wary about zooming in on women's parenting deficits and ignoring men's accountability. Where issues of women's parenting arise, we need to make transparent the impact of men's violence on women's beliefs about their parenting. However, as Edleson (1999) points out:

- Many child protection agencies continue to hold battered women solely accountable for their children's safety.
- These actions are based on the belief that separating from the abuser will always be the safest path for the woman and her child.
- Yet holding the violent abuser responsible for ending the use of violence is the path that leads to safety for these children and their abused mothers.

This chapter will address the following areas:

- Parenting by abusive fathers.
- The impact of domestic violence on mothers.
- Coping mechanisms/strategies.
- The effects of stress on parental functioning.
- Parenting behaviours and beliefs of survivors.
- The impact of domestic violence on mother–child relationships.
- The identification of the mother's needs.
- The support required.
- Recovery.
- The potential for change and intervention options.
- Messages for professionals.
- Concluding remarks.

Parenting by abusive fathers

Domestic violence can compromise both the battered woman's and the perpetrator's ability to parent. A perpetrator is clearly not providing good parenting when he physically attacks the child's mother. Abuse can also compromise a woman's ability to parent. The physical demands of parenting can overwhelm mothers who are injured or have been kept up all night by a beating. The emotional demands of parenting can be similarly daunting to abused women suffering from trauma, damaged self-confidence, and other emotional scars caused by years of abuse. An additional problem occurs when the abuser undermines her parenting as a means of control.

Hester and Radford (1996) in their study of child contact found that men had little interest or concern for the care of the children. There has been little work documenting the parenting skills of violent and abusive fathers. However, Holden and Ritchie (1991) found that men are less involved with their children and their irritability spills over into fathering.

Impact of domestic violence on mothers

Two possible outcomes of domestic violence on parenting are hypothesised by Levendosky and Graham-Bermann (2000).

- The first is that there is no apparent change in parenting functioning. Here, it may be that some victims step up their attentional focus in order to compensate for the deficits experienced in such chronic and traumatic circumstances. The mother may be able to achieve consistency in parenting despite the trauma in her life, although there is some question as to whether this can be sustained over long periods. We have to remember that parenting for battered women includes making up for and attempting to correct the mal-parenting of the abuser.
- The second possible outcome is that the psychological and physiological reactions of alternating states of hyper-arousal and numbing associated with trauma could serve to diminish the mother's ability to maintain adequate functioning, including her parenting capacities. This means that some victims of domestic violence may have parenting that oscillates between periods of being disengaged or withdrawn, angry, warm and loving, as they attempt to respond to the violence, their

internalised traumatic state, and to the externalised demands of parenting. Their undermined trust in friends, family etc may cause them to withdraw, compounding their social isolation, or to be over-protective and hyper-vigilant about their children, restricting their normal growth towards independence. In either situation their parenting is compromised.

The problem is often that abused mothers may have few resources to bring to the task of parenting. Given the myriad of additional stressors it is not surprising that some mothers fall short in providing the nurturance and support necessary for the optimal development of their children.

Society still has, despite years of campaigning by women, expectations of mothers that are very different from those of men who are fathers. Women are expected to be the homemakers, carers, nurturers, and protectors, whilst men are expected to be the head of the family, the disciplinarians, the main breadwinners and in control. Mothering is a tiring and exhausting business at the best of times, and most women will have the ideal text book definition of motherhood as their primary aim. An abused woman may have chosen to have her children to compensate for the abuse she has experienced, and she may well throw herself 100% into being the best mother possible. However, her ability to mother and care for her children may well be significantly affected by her physical, mental and emotional state and at times achieving effective mothering will be almost impossible, which may well increase her feelings of failure as a mother.

Clearly living with a violent man has considerable impacts on a woman's whole life and, for some women, the physical and psychological effects of living with a violent and abusive partner may make mothering very difficult to achieve in a way which would hold up to the scrutiny of child protection professionals. Given this it is important that professionals, when assessing the woman's parenting capacity, include all of the following inter-related factors: the type of violence and abuse the woman is experiencing; how long she has been in a violent relationship and whether she has experienced violence and abuse at any other time in her life; the severity and frequency of the violence and abuse that is perpetrated against her by the man and how she makes sense of this; the level of

control that the man imposes upon her relationship with her children; how she perceives herself as a mother; the extent to which her physical, emotional and mental health are affected by the violence and how this subsequently impacts upon her ability to mother; and how the children individually and collectively make sense of and respond to the abuse (Rowsell, 2003).

To live with a violent man takes courage, strength and resolve, especially where agencies have failed to respond appropriately. It will deplete a woman's energy levels greatly, as her whole life is controlled by the need to ensure that both she and her children can survive. To take herself out of this situation may take additional energy that she cannot summon up without consistent, co-ordinated and unconditional support over a period of time that may not fit in with child protection time-scales. However, many abused women will try to minimise their pain and suffering by developing coping strategies. It is important to note that where women have themselves also been abused as children, the range of coping strategies used are generally greater, and self-destructive strategies, are more than twice as likely to be used.

A woman's mothering style may change significantly when the man is at home, and this can create a great deal of confusion for her children. She may well use abuse herself to pre-empt even worse abuse that could be perpetrated by her partner if she fails to keep the children in check or under his rules of control. Some abused women believe that they can protect their children from being directly abused by the man by keeping them quiet, out of his way, or by not challenging his behaviour in front of them. For the vast majority of abused women, caring for, and protection of, their children are their primary concern. However, many women underestimate both the impacts of witnessing or overhearing violence upon their children, and the man's opportunities to directly abuse children without their knowledge. Women will sometimes believe that they have genuinely protected their children from the abuse, and may well be shocked later on to find out from professionals (or indeed their children) that their children were aware of the abuse, and the fact that they may have been directly abused themselves.

Professionals need to be alive to the fact that some men will deliberately set out to prevent women from parenting effectively, and women

...orced to choose between their
... caring for their children. Life
...comes a series of unwanted compromises, and abusive men will use her ineffective parenting against her, by threatening to expose her to child protection intervention agencies, or by threatening to remove her children from her care.

Women who experience domestic violence are not a homogeneous group. They range from women with great strength and coping capacity to women who experience a wide range of mental health difficulties. Given the stress associated with a violent household, abusive behaviours by mothers are likely to emerge from those at risk of such reactions. In the context of domestic violence, the battered women may view themselves as being more in control of their anger and the level of punishment of the children than their partner. In reality, their frustration with their situation combines with the stress of parenthood to set the stage for physical abuse of the children. Finally the mother may be so fearful of her partner's response to the children that they over-discipline them in an effort to control their behaviour and protect them from what they perceive as even greater abuse.

Gayle (2002) identified the ways in which domestic violence could impact on a mother's parenting:

- If she is living from day to day trying to keep the peace, to keep the children out of the way and to conceal her emotions from the children, she will find it difficult to give them a sense of stability and well-being.
- Some mothers are so run down that they cannot cope with everyday tasks like cleaning and washing, because they have been constantly criticised or assaulted for not doing everything perfectly.
- Others cannot cope with finance, because they have never been allowed to have any control over money.
- A woman who has been injured may not be able to get up in the morning and take her children to school.
- Sometimes women cannot talk to their children or play with them, because they have never been allowed to have a close relationship with their children. A man who feels that he should be the sole focus of his partner's attention may complain that she is spending far too much time with the child and order her to leave the child alone.

- Some fathers rule their children with an iron rod, and the mother may feel forced into a disciplinarian role (page 97).

Theory, research and practice experience indicates clearly that most victims of domestic violence are traumatised by the abuse that they experience. In addition to the factors associated with PTSD (post-traumatic stress disorder), they also experience depression, idealisation of the abuser and dissociation. Many will have endured deprivation of sleep, food and shelter by the abuser, greatly diminishing their capacity to be proactive whilst also rendering them emotionally numb. Studies have shown that infants are incredibly sensitive to their surroundings including their caregiver's depressed or anxious mood or any outright display of anger. Recorded effects of infants exposed to violence over time include poor general health, poor sleeping habits, excessive screaming and distorted emotional development as they mirror responses of significant carers.

Levendosky and Graham-Bermann (2000) examined the theoretical perspectives on the effects of domestic violence on parenting. They noted that little attention has been paid to the effects of violence on women's ability to parent and especially the effects of the mother's mental health on her parenting. What little research exists shows that physical and psychological abuse of the mother affects parenting stress and parenting behaviours. Maternal stress comprised of maternal physical and emotional health, negative life events and socio-demographic variables (Wolfe et al., 1985).

The mental health issues associated with domestic violence are often under-played. Research by Stark et al. (1979) showed one in four women experiencing violence from known men were in receipt of tranquillisers, while Stark (1984) reported that 25% of women admitted for emergency psychiatric care have experienced domestic violence.

The primary mental health response of women to being battered in an ongoing relationship is depression. Cambell and Soeken (1999) established that for African women, the depressive effects of abuse lasted beyond the end of the violence whilst for non-African women the end of the abusive relationship resulted in a dramatic improvement in depression.

McHugh and Hewitt (1998) detailed the personality changes that some women go through after being the victim of domestic violence. They coin this 'the thought reform' of battered women. Lifton (1961) said that the thought reform process is equivalent to a death and re-birth experience as all the individual is, and has been, disappears, and she re-emerges in the mould of her reformers. They then applied this to the women who are brainwashed by their abuser – that is their beliefs and attitudes about themselves and their world become their abuser's view of reality. The psychological steps they go through are:

Assault upon identity: This assault usually occurs when abusers unjustly criticise and question their actions, beliefs and opinions. Everything comes under attack: including their strengths, abilities, intelligence, physical appearance, their relatives, their career and other interests. As a result, they question their sense of identity, their own judgement and they fall more and more under the control of the abuser.

The establishment of guilt: occurs when the mother is told that all the problems in their relationship are her fault. When they start to question themselves and their behaviour, they often conclude that they are to blame.

Self-betrayal: their guilt is broadened when they are led to betray a vital core of themselves by renouncing others in favour of their abuser. Self-betrayal also occurs when women are forced to behave in ways that violate their own strongly held views or values. It also contributes to their social and emotional isolation and binds them to their abusers.

Total conflict, basic fear: as the abuse continues, women become afraid of the violence and begin to fear that they may be seriously injured or killed. Their physical and emotional integration begins to break down and they seek assistance for a range of physical and emotional signs of distress.

Leniency and opportunity: Most women experience a period of leniency following battering incidents, either when the abuser apologises for their actions or when there is an absence of tension in the relationship between violent incidents. Leniency allows the women to believe that they can have the happy relationship they desire, if only they changed their behaviour.

The compulsion to confess: abusers often make accusations against the women that have no foundation. This may include suspicions of affairs and they can sometimes interrogate the women about these alleged infidelities for hours to the point that they confess as a self-protection measure. In making such false confessions, they begin to take on the guilty role, believing that they have been wrong and deserve to be punished.

Channeling of guilt: once the woman feels guilty, abusers channel this guilt into precisely those areas that they believe they ought to feel guilty about. As a consequence, the women come to see ordinary actions as having been destructive or wrong.

Re-education: women are expected to learn and accept their abusers' ideas, beliefs, and opinions which are generally grounded in patriarchal values, as a guide against which to judge themselves. It serves to expand the woman's self-condemnation and their positive identity can be replaced with a negative one.

Progress and harmony: during the periods when the tension in the adult relationship is reduced, women can feel a sense of harmony with their environment. The feeling that they have made progress toward attaining the happy relationship they want can appeal to many women.

The final confession: abused women's self-accusations are made with conviction as their abuser's judgement of them has been integrated into their own belief system.

Re-birth: The thought reform process is complete when women identify with their abusers and accept their reality as their own.

Release and transition: those women that do leave their abuser face a struggle to re-establish a new positive sense of identity and they must undergo a new identity crisis in order to recover from the effects of this process.

Mothers in violent relationships commonly have their psychological energy absorbed by feelings of guilt, depression, low self-esteem or fear for their own safety (Sato and Heiby, 1992). In addition to these typical victimisation effects, women living in these circumstances also report feeling much less able to cope with the ordinary demands of parenting than non-victimised mothers. Holden and Ritchie (1991) compared abused and non-abused mothers reports and established significant differences in parenting styles (parental inconsistencies) between mothers and fathers and in the mothers' changes or modifications in parenting (e.g. become more lenient or harsher in the presence of the father).

Levendosky et al. (2000b) attempted to capture the richness and complexity of woman abuse on the woman's parenting. Their findings are reported around three key areas:

- Women's perceptions of the influence of their partner's violence on their parenting.
- Times when parenting is difficult.
- Parenting without violence.

Women's perceptions of the influence of their partner's violence on their parenting

Numerous ways in which their parenting had been influenced were identified:

- **No influence on parenting:** these women did not see the battering as a major problem in their family.
- **Negative effects on parenting:** this included the reduced amount of emotional energy or time they had to devote to their children as well as the increased anger they felt toward their children.
- **Positive effects on parenting:** this included an increased empathy and caring toward their children; avoidance of negative strategies with the children; and increased protectiveness. These examples illustrated that rather than passively accepting the effects of the violence they were developing strategies to ensure that their children suffered the fewest effects possible.
- **Wish to avoid repetition of the violence:** mothers wished their sons to avoid repeating the violent behaviour they saw in her partner whilst she was concerned that her daughters might be abused by partners as adults.
- **Effects on the child:** most women were clearly aware of the destructive pattern of violence on their children's well-being and many seemed to be actively working to compensate for the negative effects of the violence on their children.
- **General comments:** some of the women appeared to strengthen their defences by increasing their sense of competency through parenting and focusing on parenting. Thus, the mothers' responses reflect their ability to perceive and intervene in the impact of violence in a way that is not often recognised by societal interventions where women are often pathologised simply because they are in a violent relationship.

Times when parenting is difficult

Numerous ways in which parenting was made more difficult were identified:

- **No difficult times:** some women felt that the abuse had not affected their parenting whereas some felt that it had changed their parenting behaviour but had not made it more difficult.
- **Financial or work-related difficulties:** the principal difficulty they experienced was financial: many of them referred to not being able to buy what their children needed or wanted or not being able to do activities with their children. For others, this was compounded when having worked all day they were left with no energy to engage in parenting.
- **Physical health problems:** often made parenting more difficult, often due to broken bones, pain and tendon or ligament injuries.
- **Emotional challenges:** women described being upset, depressed, overwhelmed, unhappy, distracted, or frustrated as interfering with their ability to parent. These reflect the higher rates of depression, anxiety and general psychological distress among battered women.
- **Problems with partners:** the romantic relationship was affected and their authority with the children was undermined by their partner's lack of respect for them, which in turn made it more difficult for them to feel effective as parents.
- **Difficulties of single parenting:** characterised by the lack of help they receive when making decisions or providing support to their children.
- **Difficulties of disciplining:** they described children not complying with requests or their concern about their children's understanding of why limits are set. Some felt limited in their ability to establish and maintain limits with their children, whereas others reported that their children disregarded their directives.
- **Difficult times in parenting as a result of children's worries, feelings and behaviours:** they described a variety of concerns regarding the children, ranging from them crying or being injured, to asking questions of family events, academic difficulties, stealing and fighting. The women's attention to their children's emotions and behaviours suggest that many of these mothers have concerns about parenting that are more similar to than different from other parents' concerns and worries. Some described their children's behaviour or feelings following contact with their father (see Chapter 6) as making their parenting task much more difficult.

Parenting without violence

Some women do not feel that their parenting would be different if they did not have a violent partner. However, many described a positive emotional change in themselves, a general improvement in the family, or a positive change in their method of parenting in the absence of violence.

Various researchers (e.g. Jaffe et al., 1990; Walker, 1979) have argued that in addition to becoming more aggressive, parenting is likely to become more disrupted and diminished as a consequence of living in a violent relationship. Indeed, it is very difficult to imagine that mothering is not affected in some way by living in such a hostile environment. Violence between parents is likely to be distracting at the very least; more likely it is consuming and debilitating. Attention and energy must be devoted to monitoring and assessing the partner's mood and propensity for violence, engaging in frequent verbal combat, and defending oneself and one's children against verbal and physical attacks. These mothers undoubtedly fear for their own physical safety. It is suspected that living in such a context makes women preoccupied with their own needs. For one or all of these reasons it is commonly thought that these mothers have difficulty being warm, emotionally available, consistent, and responsive to their children. Consequently, mothers who experience marital violence are likely to exhibit deteriorations in the quality of their parenting.

Kelly (1994) found that there can be contradictory consequences and outcomes for women hiding the domestic violence from their children. It makes it more difficult for the children to voice their experience and feelings. For some women, bearing and caring for their children is so connected to their own abuse that it is extremely difficult if not impossible to disconnect them. For example:

- Where children were conceived as consequence of rape.
- Where continual pregnancies have been used by the abusive man as a control strategy.
- When children have been encouraged, or have chosen to side with the abusive man.
- Where children have been drawn into the abuse of their mother and, in the case of some boys, have chosen to replicate aspects of their

father's role or behaviour after their mother has decided to leave.

In each of these situations, the child and/or the child's behaviour is a continual reminder or extension of the woman's abuse. In such circumstances she may understand and experience her mothering responsibilities as an un-chosen imposition.

Kelly goes on to list other impacts of domestic violence on mothering:

- Women being forced to sacrifice children or a child in order to protect themselves and/or other children.
- Women choosing to have children as the only source of positive feeling and/or identity in their lives can backfire when they become the only source of company, support and nurturance.
- Women using violence themselves – either to pre-empt harsher treatment from their partner or as an expression of their own frustration and distress.
- Women losing confidence in their ability and/or their emotional resources to care for their children as a result of repeated degradation.
- Women making inconsistent responses in relation to rules, boundaries or discipline – either as a result of their fear or their children turning out like their father or to compensate for what they have to endure.

Holden and Ritchie (1991) found that mothers might be inconsistent in their parenting due to the abuse they were experiencing from their partners. In some cases, the abuse prevented them from maintaining standards of care or led them to perceive child care as more stressful than those women not experiencing violence. Some mothers were also found to act in a more punitive way towards the children in the presence of a violent man.

Some mothers describe losing their self-confidence as mothers, being emotionally drained with little to give to their children, taking out their frustrations on the children, and experiencing an emotional distance between themselves and their children. The mothers pointed out how these effects could be compounded by the difficult behaviour of the children at a time when they too could be trying to come to terms with the violence they were witnessing and experiencing.

Coping mechanisms and strategies

The most common strategy used by women is to withdraw or switch off from the world around them. Given that many abusive men use isolating tactics to control women, and keep them away from their family and friends, and that some women report that the violence they experience leads to depression, this seems a logical response to the situation that they are in. For child protection practitioners this withdrawal may be viewed at best as unhelpful, at worst as non-compliance with the system, and she may experience more punitive responses than other women may. In these instances women find themselves drifting through the child protection system seemingly cut off from the process, and practitioners need to find a way of breaking through the woman's isolation that has become her survival jacket.

Some women may use alcohol, prescribed or non-prescribed drugs to block out or cope with the abuse that they suffer. Where this usage becomes visible and problematic, or women develop profound mental health problems that mean they are struggling (or failing) to care for their children effectively, at this point women may come to the attention of child protection agencies. Intervention at this stage will often focus on the symptoms, with little or no attempt to make the connections to abuse, and fail to have the desired effect.

Mohr et al. (2001) examined the strategies women used to cope with violence in the home:

- **Withdrawing to endure:** when we encounter situations that present threats to our integrity, safety or values, most of us tend to engage in some form of avoidance as a self-protective strategy. Women described withdrawal as a way of trying to maintain peace in the home. This meant they had to restrict the range of activities and the safest way of doing this was to focus only on their own circumstances.
- **Turning against myself to make a point:** at the same time that they acted in a way so as to protect their children, some women turn to self-harming behaviour as a means of control that were not in her or the children's interests. However, such behaviour is perceived as self-sacrificial action that they had to take on behalf of their children.
- **Putting him on notice**: some women give their violent partners very clear statements of consequences if the domestic violence recurs. They serve as a sort of a moral invisible hand.
- **Fighting back:** some women respond by means of outright rebellion. They pull on some deep strength to declare war and fight back. This going on the offensive might take the form of counter-aggression and can offer an alternative to leaving the abusive relationship.

The effects of stress on parental functioning

There are well-documented effects of stress on parental functioning:

- Physical: message your body gives you that you may be suffering from stress.
- Emotional: feelings you experience.
- Intellectual: changes to your thinking/ability to process thoughts and information.
- Social: changes in your social/behavioural self.
- Spiritual: changes to belief in your work/what you do.

If someone affected by stress is caring for children, it is likely that their ability to perform these duties will be eroded. For example, the woman may become depressed as a result of domestic violence, leading to feelings of disempowerment, resulting in irrational thoughts. She may become isolated and unable to cope. If stress is not recognised and addressed, for example at the 'physical stage', then inevitably the cumulative effects will put children at risk.

For some women, therefore, the physical and emotional effects of domestic violence can have a detrimental impact on their mothering and relationships with their children. Mothers may therefore appear to professionals as inadequate or as unable to cope. It has to be recognised, however, that this is likely to be a direct effect of the domestic violence and that with support, and in particular help to be safe, mothers can resume parenting of their children. The shift to a functional cycle is the desired outcome of any professional intervention. In this cycle, the women who fear not coping seek help or support when they recognise they need it. They then develop coping strategies that they endeavour to maintain and in so doing gain insight and awareness that helps them sustain any changes they have effected.

Figure 4.1 sets out the range of effects of stress on parental functioning in a range of impact areas.

Figure 4.1: The multiple effects of stress on parental functioning

Physical
neck and shoulder tension
lower back pain/tension
stomach problems
diarrhoea
heartburn
headaches
lethargy/tiredness
high blood pressure
sleep disturbance
lower resistance

Intellectual
lack of concentration
inability to make decisions
inability to prioritise
inability to focus on task
memory problems
loss of perspective
questioning own intellectual abilities

Spiritual
questioning things and feeling
guilty about questioning them
questioning your belief in your own abilities
having feelings of personal confusion, of being lost
losing sight of the difference you can make
loss of belief in your vision
(why you came into this work in the first place)

Emotional
irritability
anxiety
depression
anger
tearfulness
resentment
paranoia
mood swings

Social
eating, drinking, smoking too much
(over-reliance)
withdrawing from social life
using social life as a debriefing for work
   issues (work intrudes)
becoming intolerant of friends/
   acquaintances, linked with developing
   rituals – cleaning, getting ready,
moving/straightening furniture (getting
   control)
becoming superstitious

Parenting behaviours and beliefs of survivors

Holden et al. (1998) examined the parenting abilities of mothers living in maritally violent homes. They found:

- That almost all of the battered women engaged in violence toward their children compared to just half of the comparison mothers.
- Battered women reported high levels of parenting stress and such stress was positively correlated with mother-to-child aggression.
- There was no evidence of diminished parenting in the battered women as compared to the matched community mothers.
- That some aspects of maternal behaviour change when they have left the abusive partner. The most important finding was the significant reduction in the percentage of mothers who continued to aggress toward their children. More generally, most mothers

appeared to be functioning considerably better only six months after leaving a shelter. Their level of parenting stress and their depressive symptoms were down. The children were also reported as showing significantly fewer behaviour problems and this was correlated with improved interactions over time. The mothers reported no change in their disciplinary practices or their reliance on corporal punishment.

- Overall they found no evidence to indicate that battered mothers were less affectionate, less protective, less likely to provide structure for the child, or more punitive. This suggests that the view of abused mothers as deficient in parenting and highly aggressive may be misguided and needs to be modified significantly to one that recognises and documents the strengths and coping strategies of these women. We need to look at identifying the proactive, strategic, adaptive, and compensatory behaviours that many of these mothers engage in to protect or even save their children from the detrimental effects of being reared in a martially violent home.

DeVoe and Smith (2002) discussed with mothers the challenges of being a mother in the context of domestic violence. Women identified general stresses associated with parenting very young children, such as having limited time, feeling exhausted, losing patience, and feeling overwhelmed at times but also described several added dimensions of their parenting strategies that seemed quite unique to the circumstances of domestic violence. For most mothers, there was a sense of trying to compensate for children's exposure to domestic violence and for the lack of positive father figures. And whereas mothers generally endorsed a zero tolerance stance against violence in all relationships, there were two areas of parenting in which they practiced a continuum of beliefs and practices. Some mothers specifically tailored their parenting to the gender of children so as to break the cycle of violence by telling boys that they could not use violence in their interpersonal interactions. However, where they were being bullied in the playground, they encouraged them in fighting back.

The impact of domestic violence on mother–child relationships

Children whose mothers are abused are sometimes abused by their mother as well. Mothers are much more likely to neglect or abuse their children while they are in an abusive relationship. Straus, Gelles and Steinmetz (1980) found that women were eight times more likely to hurt their children while they themselves were being battered than after they left the abusive relationship. Sometimes mothers abuse their children in an effort to protect themselves and their children – for example, a mother may slap her children when the abuser threatens to set fire to the house if the children are not quiet. Other seemingly neglectful behaviours on the part of the mother may be a direct result of the battering. For example, an abuser may prevent his partner from taking the children to school because the child has injuries that would reveal their abusiveness. Or, in an effort to protect her children, a mother may tell them to go outside during an attack on her, even though the temperature is below freezing or it is the middle of the night. These examples indicate that

children cannot be adequately protected unless the presence of domestic violence in their families is investigated and if identified appropriately addressed. Often the most effective way to protect children is to protect their mothers.

We need to explore whether the harm is a result of an over-stressed mother or a serious manifestation of an emerging pattern of abusive behaviour.

Holden et al. (1998) reported on a longitudinal study of parenting in 50 battered women over six months after leaving their abusive partners. They found a marked decrease in maternal aggression towards the child after six months. Conversely, increased trauma symptoms are associated with decreased warmth, control and effectiveness.

Blanchard (1999) notes that mothers may be reluctant to discipline their children because they associate control with the domestic violence. They may also be concerned that they contributed to this by remaining with the abuser. Work clearly needs to be done on developing some family rules which are fair to everyone.

Child neglect may result from the non-offending caregiver (usually the mother) giving less attention to her children's needs as a result of her need to focus attention on her violent partner in an attempt to appease him and hopefully, control the level of violence. In addition, the need to attend to her own needs (including treating physical injuries) and at times personal survival will reduce the resources available to her to care for her children (Tomison, 2000). According to Sykes and Symons-Moulton (1990) children who are neglected may show physical signs including failure to thrive, developmental delay, and listlessness. Behavioural problems may include begging or stealing food and eating inappropriate objects; erratic school attendance; poor social relationships with peers; and delinquent acts such as vandalism, drug use and drinking.

At the other extreme, some victims of domestic violence are so fearful of the abusive partner's focusing their anger on the children that they over-discipline them in an effort to control the children's behaviour and protect them from what they perceive as greater abuse.

Roy (1988) found that whilst the father was the principal disciplinarian in the home during the period that the family was intact (90%) when the mother left the abusive home, she became the primary disciplinarian and tended in 85% of the cases to become abusive both verbally and physically and was described by many children as impatient and a 'screamer'. A significant number of the female children assumed a parental role by taking care of the household when the mother's coping mechanism dysfunctioned. They cooked, shopped, bathed younger siblings, did the laundry and assumed the everyday responsibilities of the parent. In addition to this, they became victim-orientated, silent, withdrawn and fearful of becoming the direct object of physical abuse. Those who were sexually abused submitted to their victimisation out of fear of reprisals. A significant number of the boys opted for the role of the abuser, joining their fathers in victimising their mothers. This is seen as identifying with the aggressor, guaranteeing them a way out of being a hostage.

Mothers who are victims of domestic violence are often less able to offer emotional support to their children than mothers who have experienced violence outside of their homes. These mothers are frequently afraid of their lives. They are preoccupied with basic survival and are unable to attend to their children's psychological needs. If one parent is the terrified victim and the other is the perpetrator of the violence, what choice does the child have? For women who live with domestic violence, there exists a constant tension and fear about the next violent explosion. Women may focus on making sure that things in the home are orderly and quiet in order to avoid another violent outburst from their partner. However, their preoccupation interferes with their ability to be responsive to children's needs and to assess their children's emotional turmoil (Groves and Zuckerman, 1997).

Women who live with domestic violence may suffer from symptoms of post-traumatic stress disorder where one of its manifestations may be becoming desensitised to violence in the home and as such their threshold of acceptance of violence is lowered. This desensitisation may make it difficult for them to be available emotionally for the children whilst also interfering with their judgement of what is appropriate for their children to see and hear. As a result, they may allow them to occasionally watch inappropriate television and movies that are further upsetting for them.

Parents whose children have witnessed domestic violence or been victims of violence often do not know how to talk to their children about the violence. It is difficult to know how to offer explanations for the violence and many

avoid the issue as a result. The consequence of avoidance is that it communicates to the child that it is an issue that is too scary and big to mention. Some children then go on to blame themselves as they misattribute the cause of the violence.

Mullender et al. (2002) reported on the influence of domestic violence on the relationships between children and their mothers. They identified six themes:

- **The desperate straits women found themselves in and how domestic violence altered the contours of mothering:** children's needs for reassurance, attention and support are accentuated in situations of domestic violence at the same time as the resources of the mother are taxed to the limit and invariably depleted. Mother's were constantly on their guard, leaving them exhausted and limiting the energy left to devote to the children.

- **The extent to which children were deliberately used by abusive men to hurt and control women:** fell into two broad categories – implicating and involving the children in their mother's abuse; and controlling women through threats towards and mistreatment of the children. The most common way in which children had been made parties to the abuse involved men systematically and deliberately forcing them to witness the abuse and/or compelling them to listen to accusations about, and the demeaning of, their mothers. The deliberate attempts to destroy or damage the connections between the mother and the children had major impacts.

- **Children's complex thinking in assessing who was at fault and why their mothers had not left the violence sooner:** many mothers make considerable efforts to protect their children, both from the knowledge of the abuse and by trying to minimise the amount of violence that occurred. It often comes as a surprise to them when they learn from the children the extent of their awareness. Children attributed the responsibility firmly with the abuser. They suspected that their mothers had been trying to look after their best interests and had seen how depressed and hurt they were, so had chosen not to say anything, whilst their mothers thought they were leaving the children in happy ignorance.

- **The ways children affected the women's decisions to stay or leave:** children sometimes interpreted the mother's refusal to be subservient as meaning that she too had some responsibility for the incidents. They were often clearer about responsibility for the abuse than about whose fault it was that the situation had continued. Older children whose lives had been disrupted on more than one occasion did tend to see their mothers as carrying some responsibility for staying or returning, even when they placed the blame for violence squarely in their fathers.

- **How protective actions could create unhelpful silences:** it is widely recognised that women remain in violent relationships for the sake of the children. The silences between women and children are a direct outcome of the dynamics of domestic violence, coupled with cultural constructions of motherhood and childhood. Both women and children's coping strategies and their desire to protect each other militate against openness.
- **Conflicting needs and perceptions between some mothers and their children:** whilst there are many shared interests of women and children, there are also some needs and perceptions that are incompatible. An example of this is often where the women chooses to prioritise a new partner over her children and investing everything in making it work. This can result in the children living with violence for longer or spending longer periods of time away from their mother because of her choices, e.g. being in the care system. Despite this, women and children have, through honesty and openness, learned to support each other. This shows that despite everything, she often has a good relationship with her children that can be built on.

The identification of the mother's needs

Mothers as victims of domestic violence have a variety of needs related to their life circumstances: and these will be unique to each one. As a group, the following kinds of services have been identified:

- Crisis intervention.
- Temporary emergency shelter.
- Concrete services such as temporary financial assistance, food and clothing.
- Acceptance and understanding, validation that they are not crazy and the abuse is not their fault.

- Assurance that there are non-violent alternatives and information about what those alternatives are.
- Information about how to secure protection from the police and courts for themselves and their children.
- Supportive services and programmes that facilitate their independence, such as long-term housing, educational counselling and job training.
- Counselling if they desire it to address the consequences of being abused (Lynch and Norris, 1977–78).

To date, however, many victims of domestic violence do not seek assistance from professional agencies, preferring informal sources such as family members and friends. Workers do need to be alert, therefore, to the need to work especially hard at establishing a trusting relationship. This is imperative when the mother has made previous, unsuccessful attempts to seek help from the professional network.

Recognition by a mother that she has her own needs and priorities is very important for a child's development. If the child is to develop a sense of themselves as a person in their own right, the mother must offer the child the experience of engaging with another autonomous being. This is because a child cannot experience recognition by someone whom they control. Not only should mothers have their own needs, but it is actually very good for their children if they do.

The mother's safety is linked to their potential to parent and protect. There has been some recognition that parental needs, where unmet, potentially contribute to child abuse. This then requires workers to re-mother needy clients so they could then go on to care for their children. This was compromised with the introduction of parental responsibility where intervention was designed to locate mothers as responsible for meeting their children's needs.

A list of needs experienced by mothers might include:

- Someone to talk to: to express trust and belief in them, often for weeks or months afterwards.
- Someone to counsel them about the domestic and possibly sexual violence perpetrated upon them.
- To know they weren't the first mother this had happened to: so they are not alone, and can possibly meet and learn from shared feelings.

- To have a break from the perpetrator in order to gain a perspective, consider their feelings about the relationship, etc.
- To be treated as a person: to have their feelings listened to seriously, to feel respected, to be acknowledged when they are present, etc.
- To regain control of their lives and minds: particularly resuming control over the day-to-day events and their personal thoughts.
- To obtain basic information on survival: to embrace new aspects of their life, such as courts, police, treatment, etc.
- To understand how domestic violence and sexual abuse were related: and to understand they are separate issues that need to be addressed.
- To make basic life decisions: to move away, separate or divorce their husband, tell people, etc.
- To know options regarding contact and custody: both in relation to their partner, but also if the child has been removed from home by the local authority.
- To know how the children will react: as everyone will be affected to some degree by the trauma.
- To ensure this will not happen again: taking steps to safeguard the child from continued abuse is important, such as no contact or supervised contact.

The needs of non-abusing parents can be neglected as professional responses focus on the children. In this sense, the professional response system is insensitive to the needs of women. However, both for the women's emotional survival and growth and so that they can provide appropriate parenting for their children, thereby reducing the need for their children to be removed from their care, or remain there long-term, these women need the therapeutic opportunity to deal with their feelings about what has happened and to adjust to the major change that has taken place in their lives.

The support required

Mothers require a diversity of support in recovering from their abuse and the services they require could potentially include individual counselling, sheltered living arrangements, respite care of their children, counselling for their children, housing, legal aid, and financial aid. Since many women may have experienced the early responses from professionals as treating them as secondary abusers, then there may well be an additional challenge of engaging them.

Many women benefit from meeting and mixing with people who have experienced similar violence. This can allow them some breathing space and offer them an opportunity to reflect on their own needs and share experiences with other survivors. This contributes toward them regaining their self-esteem, self-confidence and the financial, material and emotional resources to control their own lives rather than living under the influence or control of a violent man.

Recovery

Bilinkoff (1995) suggests that there are four issues mothers need to resolve before they are able to develop a parenting style of their own which will fulfil their and their children's needs. These are using power and control, making up for the absent father, using the child as confidants or allies and dealing with their perception of the children's similarity to their father.

Lebowitz et al. (1993) set out a stage by stage model of recovery from sexual trauma that is transferable to victims of domestic violence. Underlying this model is the assumption that central to the experience of interpersonal trauma is helplessness, meaninglessness, and disconnection from oneself and others. The recovery process is thus based on the empowerment of the victim and the creation of new contexts and new meanings:

- **Safety:** the first stage of recovery is safety and nothing else should be attempted until this goal has been achieved. The focus of safety begins with control of the body and moves outward to issues of control of the environment. Issues of bodily integrity including attention to basic health needs, regulation of bodily functions such as sleep, eating and exercise and the control of self-destructive behaviours and the symptoms of post-traumatic stress disorder. Environmental issues include the establishment of a safe living situation with adequate attention to survival needs (work and money) and a carefully considered plan for self-protection. The work of this stage is complicated in proportion to the intensity, duration and age of onset of the violence and in relation to poverty and other forms of oppression.

- **Remembrance, integration and mourning:** in the second stage of recovery, the focus of the work shifts to an active and in-depth exploration of the traumatic experiences. This should not be attempted until the basic safety of the woman has been reliably established. Exploratory work involves careful attention to previously dissociated or regressed aspects of memory, cognition, and affect. Pacing and timing will need to be adjusted to the survivor's tolerance so that the work represents a mastery experience rather than a symbolic re-enactment of the trauma. However, the risk of precipitating a depressive episode at this point is particularly high.
- **Reconnecting with others:** the third stage of recovery involves the active pursuit of social re-connection. In the process of establishing mutual, non-exploitative peer relationships, the survivor will re-assess and re-negotiate long-standing relationships with friends, lovers and spouses. Where these relationships have been abusive, issues of boundaries, limits and secrecy may be addressed explicitly for the first time. With the family of origin, the recovering person may wish to disclose the abuse that has been kept secret or to confront the abuser. This stage also includes a new level of meaning-making and a transformation of the traumatic experiences, sometimes taking the form of a survivor mission.

The potential for change and intervention options

Hendricks-Matthews (1982) suggested evaluating the woman's cognitive functioning to assess her readiness for change. In order to do this, the worker should ask:

- To what extent does the client suffer from learned helplessness?
- Have these feelings of powerlessness generalised so that she feels her situation is hopeless?
- Is she using a great deal of denial, rationalisation, and minimisation about being abused?
- Does she feel she has any control over what happens to her?
- Does she believe she has any control over her partner's violence?

It is important that we help her identify both internal and external factors that inhibit her or

which can be mobilised on her behalf (Carmen, 1981). These include:

- Her personal strengths and resources.
- Her social network.
- The lethality of the situation (how frequent and severe the violence has been, how longstanding, the presence of weapons in the home, and histories of injuries).
- Her perceptions and interpretations of the abuse (why it occurs and its consequences).
- Her mental status or psychological state.
- Her use of alcohol or drugs.
- Her physical condition, especially the presence of injuries necessitating medical attention.
- Her need for concrete services.
- What she is seeking help with at this time.

Depending on the woman's readiness for change, several intervention options exist:

- **Immediate intervention:** should include her personal safety and that of her children through the creation of a safety or protection plan (to enhance a sense of personal control); identifying her strengths and resources; determining how she perceives the violence and what information she may need to end any denial; obtaining essential services such as shelter and food; and identifying future options.
- **Shorter-term intervention:** where the woman appears ready to examine their own behaviour and to begin to explore changes in themselves, numerous proximal goals can be undertaken, and which may involve participation in a support group to help them tackle feelings of stigma and self-blame, social isolation and the development of trust. The workers aims to support and nurture; reinforcing her strengths; and helping her to develop some insight into her problems.
- **Longer-term intervention:** may involve a return to the relationship if it has become violence free or relinquishing it where this has not occurred.

Messages for professionals

Many professionals find it hard to accept and understand why a battered mother becomes physically or emotionally abusive or neglectful of her own children. This may be because the mother has given the abuser their full-time attention to control the level of violence or because she has retreated to protect herself and in so doing withdraws from the children also.

Bograd (1990) argued that it is thus impossible to assess a mother's true capacity to care for her children while she is being battered or experiencing post-traumatic stress from the abuse. Unless the children are in imminent danger from the mother, offering a mother and her children safety together first and prolonging the assessment process would allow the worker to get a clearer understanding of the mother's capacities. In addition, removing the children may endanger the woman's life.

A review of the literature on child protection indicates that workers fail to recognise the simultaneous abuse of the mother and the children and this leads to intervention strategies that rely on the mother protecting her child from the same partner who is abusing both of them (Brown, 1991).

Workers need to place the responsibility for the violence with the abuser. Without this, the mother all too often is labelled a poor parent and becomes the sole focus of attention. Mandating her attendance at parenting skills groups or counselling reinforces the notion that she is to blame for the violence in her family and that her partner bears no responsibility.

Whilst women will need help with their health problems, these interventions will fail to deliver unless the women has opportunities to disclose her abuse and be appropriately supported through the resulting issues. It is not surprising that abused women are far more likely to attempt or commit suicide than those who are not abused, and often these women are already in contact with health services. Given this point, it is important to note that appropriate support services available to women with the most complex of needs are still sadly lacking, and there is an urgent need for the development of women centred services and practice.

Radford and Hester (2001) in a review of the research findings on the harm and injuries suffered from violent partners found it is likely to have an impact, temporary or lasting, on a mother's capacity to provide physical and emotional care for children. What we need to guard against however is the focus exclusively on the deficiencies in mothering and explore more the steps that they take to compensate their children for living with domestic violence. The polarisation of mothers into 'abusive' and 'non-abusive' is also profoundly unhelpful to

workers since it encourages the belief that if the husband as the perpetrator is removed, the mother and the children will be safe and secure and no longer need any support. If resources and support are removed quickly and the mother has to cope with issues such as child contact, then they are left to muddle through by themselves.

A mother's inability to protect her children from witnessing further domestic violence is often classified as a 'failure to protect' children (Magen, 1999). However, such a classification raises a number of issues: is it appropriate to expect a battered woman to be able to protect both herself and her children? Is it appropriate to put the onus on the mother solely to protect her children? Is it appropriate to 'punish' her by taking statutory protective action if she fails to protect? Clearly the responsibility for exposing the children to violence should first and foremost lie with the violent partner. Yet a gender bias has been identified in that the child protection focus is frequently on the mother as the assumed primary caregiver. It is from the field of sexual abuse where some exception can be drawn in that the male perpetrator is often held accountable for his behaviour (Calder, 1999c; Calder, Peake and Rose, 2001). The over-reliance on the mother could easily be construed as abusive as it draws the responsibility away from the male abuser and places often inappropriate demands on the mother (McLeod and Saraga, 1988). This can have a further negative effect in that it deters mothers from seeking professional help when the threat to their children becomes a reality. As Burke (1999) articulates clearly, 'how to intervene without reinforcing the woman's sense of guilt, self-blame and failure as a mother; (and how to) avoid placing even more responsibility for protecting children onto women who are often powerless to act because of their own victimisation' (p257).

Humphreys (1997) found that in her sample of cases that went to child protection conference a number of themes emerged:

- There was a general failure of men to take responsibility for the alcohol abuse.
- Within the context of child protection issues, it appeared easier for conference to name and tackle the man's alcohol abuse rather than the domestic violence.
- The ability to gain some leverage in the situation.

A number of patterns emerged in relation to the mother and alcohol abuse:

- The focus of the child protection inquiry became the mother's alcohol abuse and the significant relationship between alcohol abuse by women and the domestic violence they were suffering was not recognised.
- By the time that some of these families came to the notice of social services, domestic violence had occurred over many years and the key problem within the family was now named as the mother's abuse of alcohol,
- At times there appeared to be an overly optimistic approach to managing the problems of alcohol abuse.

Humphreys (2000) argued that women who experience domestic violence will benefit from social workers acting as their advocates not adversaries, provided that this is done in an empowering way. Blaming a woman for the abuse, accusing her of failing to protect her children from the abuser when she may be in fear of her own life, expecting her to leave instead of tackling the abuser, and reproaching the woman for staying in the abusive relationship can discourage her from disclosing what is happening, and leave her in greater danger than before the intervention. The social work role should be to help the woman, as well as the children, to be safe.

The overwhelming message from research is that the best place for most children most of the time is with their mother and that woman protection is frequently the most effective form of child protection.

Concluding remarks

It is easy to understand that parenting is undermined if women are:

- Being physically abused and emotionally abused.
- Having to cope with repeated crises.
- Experiencing major economic and social dislocations when leaving the abusive relationship.
- Subjected to continued harassment and conflict after the separation.

Mothers living with domestic violence will frequently have their availability and ability to parent reduced due to the time and energy she must devote to dealing with her own psychological and physical trauma and in ensuring the safety of her children. Many women who are abused experience full blown depression, which may further impair their energy to parent.

Domestic violence provides an adverse context for bringing up children (Kelly, 1994). Domestic violence is likely to have a cumulative effect on women. Domestic violence and women's identity and definitions of themselves are inextricably bound together.

While empowering and protecting women who are abused is overall the most effective way to protect children who witness abuse, there are some extreme cases where they need to be removed from their family due to the level of risk identified. Such high risk often occurs when multiple risk factors are identified.

Chapter Five

Towards A Framework for Assessment and Intervention

Introduction

This is the backbone chapter of this book and is designed to provide some guidance on what to look for and why at each stage of the assessment and intervention process, as well as some of the essential worker characteristics. The framework provided is holistic and comprehensive and represents an optimally desirable structure for workers. The framework is designed to offer some flesh to the skeletal structure of the assessment framework and its limitations. The assessment framework triangle is flawed in that whilst it makes some reference to the different role played by mothers and fathers (father figures), it actually lumps them both together when looking at parental capacity, and we may find ourselves talking about 'family violence' rather than 'domestic violence'. The problem with this is that we start from the premise that there is a dual level of responsibility, that each parent is able to contribute equally to the child protection process, and in many cases the judgement concentrates on the capacity of the women to parent and protect rather than on the effect of the man's violence on the woman and her child/ren. All too often the focus of child protection assessments are on women, and this means that we are asking women to sort out the problem and operate as our agent, rather than including men and assisting them to take responsibility for the violence. It may well be worth child protection agencies assigning different practitioners to each parent (and then co-working) in order to ensure that the needs of women and children are more accurately identified, and to ensure that men are given an opportunity to talk about the violence. In this way the professional can achieve a far more accurate child protection assessment. There are obvious issues of safety here, particularly for female workers, and issues of men working with men where collusion may be sought and entered into. Both of these issues need careful thought and planning by child protection managers and practitioners (Rowsell, 2003).

Guidance within the assessment and intervention process

Indicators of domestic violence

Figure 5.1 sets out some useful indicators:

Heath (2003) sets out the following list that should help staff considering the possibility of domestic violence:

- The mother reports past or present abuse.
- They present with unexplained bruises, whiplash injuries consistent with shaking, areas of erythema consistent with slap injuries, lacerations, burns, or multiple injuries in various stages of healing.
- They have injuries to areas hidden by clothing which may be found inadvertently while doing something like a cervical smear.
- They have injuries to their head, face, neck, chest, breast or abdomen.
- They have symptoms suggestive of sexual trauma.
- The extent of the injury does not seem to match the explanation given.
- There is a substantial delay between the time of the injury and the presentation for treatment.
- They describe the áccident' in a hesitant, embarrassed or evasive manner
- There is recorded evidence of repeated presentations with áccidental' injuries.
- They repeatedly present with physical symptoms for which no explanation can be found.
- They are accompanied by their partner who is reluctant to allow her to speak for herself.
- They are pregnant.
- They have a history of miscarriage.
- They have a history of psychiatric illness or alcohol or drug dependence.
- They have attempted suicide.
- They have a history of depression, anxiety, feeling unable to cope, social withdrawal or an underlying sense of helplessness.
- There is a history of behaviour problems or unexplained injuries to children.

Figure 5.1: Indicators of domestic violence in mothers

Physical and emotional	Behavioural	Pregnancy
• The woman reports chronic pain or there is pain due to diffused trauma, without physical evidence. Bruising may be present where the explanation does not fit with the description of the injury • Repeated or chronic injuries. Injuries that are untended and of several different ages, especially to the heads, neck, breasts, abdomen and genitals • The woman minimises injuries or repeatedly gives the same explanation • The women exhibits physical symptoms related to stress, other anxiety disorders or depression, such as panic attacks, feelings of isolation and inability to cope, suicide attempts or gestures of deliberate self-harm • There is frequent use of prescribed tranquilisers anti-depressants or pain medications • There are gynaecological problems such as frequent vaginal or urinary tract infections • There is evidence of rape or assault, such as injury to genitals • Dental emergencies • There is evidence of alcohol problems or substance misuse	• The woman misses appointments or does not comply with treatment regimes • There are frequent admissions/appointments for apparently minor complaints e.g. backache • The woman appears unable to communicate independently. The partner may accompany the woman at all times, and insist on staying close and answering all questions directed to her. He may undermine, mock or belittle her. She may appear frightened, ashamed, evasive, embarrassed or be reluctant to speak or disagree in front of her partner • The woman reports, or the partner expresses, intense irrational jealousy or possessiveness or conversely may appear overly concerned • The woman or her partner denies or minimises abuse. The woman exhibits an exaggerated sense of personal responsibility for the relationship, including self-blame for her partner's violence	• Late booking • Unplanned or unwanted pregnancy • General unhappiness about the birth of the baby • Frequent visits with vague complaints or symptoms of an unknown clinical cause and without evidence of physiological abnormality • Recurring admissions usually for foetal movements/abdominal pain/investigation of UTI • A high incidence of still birth, miscarriage and termination of pregnancies • Foetal injury and foetal deaths • Intrauterine growth retardation/low birth weight • Pre-term labour or prematurity • Evidence, or history of, postnatal depression • Post-natally removal of perineal sutures (constructed from Scottish Executive, 2003).

Workers should be alert to the recognition areas in children of domestic violence. Whilst most children exhibit some of these signs at various times in their development, workers need to be aware that if a child manifests several of these behaviours for an extended period of time and they continue to increase in intensity, it is possible that they may be experiencing domestic violence.

Harris Hendriks et al. (1993) established that children are most likely to disclose at a time of crisis such as a police intervention or after a traumatic event such as a mother's killing. Interviewing techniques need to be appropriate with arrangements in place to provide or refer for ongoing support. There may be adverse consequences if no help is offered at the point of disclosure. Children may provide a disclosure that is inadvertent, spontaneous or in reaction to classroom material or discussions or more indirectly through play or drawings (Black and Newman, 1996).

Identification of domestic violence

Domestic violence is a crime cloaked in secrecy and kept from view. Unsurprisingly, few victims want to admit their partner hits or emotionally abuses them and few perpetrators own up to taking their frustrations out on their partner.

Women and children who have experienced abuse may not disclose what has happened to them because:

Figure 5.2: Indicators of domestic violence in children

Signs	Children
Physical	Unexplained injuries Injuries attributable to the domestic violence
Emotional	Panic attacks Frozen watchfulness
Behavioural	Angry behaviour

- They may not perceive what is happening to them as abuse.
- They may be ashamed and embarrassed about what has happened to them.
- They fear reprisals and serious escalation of abuse from their partner if outsiders become involved.
- They think they may receive an unsympathetic response or not be believed, particularly if the abuse is psychological or there are no physical symptoms.
- They fear that their children will be taken into care.
- They do not know what help might be obtained from professionals.
- They are afraid of the police and other authorities, and fear deportation if a refugee, asylum seeker, or woman who has entered the country to get married.
- They may feel trapped, degraded or humiliated; lacking self-esteem.
- They may be depressed and unable to make even basic decisions.
- They fear if insecurity, including financial.
- They do not realise that abuse is something that they should not have to tolerate.
- Children fear that their mother will be blamed.
- Of emotional dependence.
- Of stigma of being without a partner.
- Of lack of support from family and friends.
- They hope that their partner's behaviour will change

(Scottish Executive, 2003)

The National Strategy on violence against women (1993) estimated the cost of intentionally inflicted injuries identified in the hospital system at around $286 million per annum. The professional failure to identify cases of domestic violence is often compounded when they do it through blaming the mother's behaviour.

Screening issues

Hess et al. (1992) found that in 56% of the cases in their sample, domestic violence had either not been identified by professionals serving the family or adequate services had not been provided to address the domestic violence.

Pahl (1995) concluded from her research with health professionals that they routinely fail to identify physical abuse in women and that this reflects both the reluctance of health professionals to probe and the reluctance of women to disclose how their injuries have been caused.

Workers may be reluctant to confront a woman about the possibility of domestic violence for fear of being too intrusive or causing offence; concern that they do not have sufficient time to deal with the issue; fear of not knowing what to do next; fear of making things worse; and fear of opening a can of worms. However, screening, investigating and assessing domestic violence are essential ingredients for an effective child protection response. Screening procedures should include routine, direct inquiry with clients regarding whether they have ever been hurt by their partner, as well as the identification of indicators that suggest the presence of domestic violence. Such screening should occur in an ongoing manner during all phases of working with a family, since violence could begin at any point during the child abuse investigation, assessment or intervention. It should only occur in the absence of the alleged perpetrator.

There are significant benefits for child protection agencies in the blanket screening of all women in contact with their services, and monitoring and recording the abuse that they and their children experience. There is evidence to suggest that when agencies introduce blanket screening conducted in a sensitive and meaningful way that the disclosure rate of domestic violence will increase from about one third to two thirds of women. Screening should occur at the initial visit and on every subsequent occasion, to maximise women's opportunities to tell us about their abuse. Being asked the questions does not necessarily lead to disclosure by women. Research (Rowsell, 2000) suggests that women, even when blanket screening is in place, will fail to disclose for a range of reasons including: the fear of not being believed; the gender of worker; a perceived lack of follow up support; previously poor experiences when disclosing, or being placed on a referral circuit that means women feel out of control and over-loaded by agency roles and responsibilities; some women are simply not ready (hence the importance of keeping asking the questions); the blocking of the abuse out of their minds as a way of coping; issues of mistrust and the poor quality of relationship between women and workers; and being worried about confidentiality and partners being informed about the disclosure.

Given that contact with the child protection agencies is stressful for women, and they may be asked for a great deal of information in a short period of time by practitioners, whether these questions are heard when asked, and subsequently responded to, may be dependent on a number of factors, including how the question is asked, in what context, and by whom. Abused women are skilled at assessing body language, dissecting oral messages, and making predictions on what another person will do next – after all they have had to become skilled at these to survive. Research with women consistently suggests that being honest, and open, and asking questions in a direct work is more likely to result in her being enabled to disclose. Therefore, it is important that the right practitioners are chosen to undertake this work, and are equipped with the awareness, knowledge and tools in order to do this sensitively, consistently and in a way that will empower and enable women to disclose. It is also important that practitioners understand that a differential approach must be taken to confidentiality in relation to women and their partners, and from a sheer safety point of view there cannot be the same rule applied to abused women and the men who perpetrate violence against them.

Workers need to be aware that women often do not name their experiences as violence. Workers also need to be aware that women may only disclose over time and when they can trust. This is a good pointer to the need to keep asking. The following guidance is worthy of consideration:

- In all situations, single interviews should be offered as a matter of course.
- Workers should be familiar with local resources and procedures, location of refuges and how to contact them. What is the DSS policy on women in refuges, bed and breakfast, safe taxi forms, sympathetic police officers, access to trained interpreters.
- Leaflets and posters should be available amongst others offering help and making it clear that it is confidential. Helpline numbers should be visible and readable across a room.
- Women should be listened to. It takes courage to seek out help: the response the women get will determine whether or not she seeks help again in the future. Women are usually a good judge of how much danger they are in.
- Let her control the discussion: talking about things may be difficult so allow her to go at her own pace.
- Confidentiality is important. Soundproof interview rooms or rooms away from the general waiting area. Women should wherever possible be seen without their children as they may not want them to be party to the full details.
- Clear records are important and they may be needed at a later point as evidence. It is thus important to record what she says rather than an interpretation of them. Let the woman decide for herself. Do not penalise her for returning or assume because she returned last time she is not worth helping. Records should include details of any concerns about the woman, child and family; details of any contact or involvement with the family and any other agencies; the findings of any assessment; any decisions made about the case; a statement that the woman has been asked about sharing information and has given or withheld consent.
- Help her identify her own support networks if she can use them without risk.
- Believe her if she discloses any abuse and say so.
- Affirm her strengths and acknowledge her experiences.
- Beware that children who are referred for behavioural problems may be experiencing domestic violence.

There are a number of environmental factors that could influence a woman's ability to disclose domestic violence. These could include the size and appearance of the waiting area; privacy in the waiting room; the triage situation and the consulting area; and the long wait for service. Time constraints on the service providers and their attitude could also prevent the woman from discussing their problem. Other problems include the discontinuity of service provider. Conversely, the provision of information; a protocol for response; and follow-up services are seen as important. An attitude of compassion, support and understanding by the service provider is more important for many women than their gender and staff training on the appropriate questions to ask is essential.

A useful checklist for conducting a screening assessment with women is outlined in Figure 5.3.

The following screening questions are merely for guidance (and others may be more appropriate to use in specific situations with women):

- Do you get support at home, who from and how often?

Figure 5.3: Screening assessment checklist (Rowsell, 2003)

Element of assessment	Considerations, benefits, potential outcomes
All women should be routinely asked questions about domestic violence, and told that this is routine. This should be done calmly as practitioner anxiety or being in an emotional state can put the woman off disclosing.	Need to create a safe place that can meet her needs, with a high degree of privacy, and away from the man. Will reduce tension felt by woman who may well suspect that the practitioner knows something. Will give positive messages to woman that DV is common and on the agenda for all. Will not only create space for every woman to disclose, but will increase practitioner's skills in asking the questions and responding to disclosure effectively.
It should be made clear that the purpose of asking these questions is to ensure that she and her children are safe.	Will reduce resistance and encourage disclosure if the woman believes that the practitioner will not just hear the disclosure but will be able to support her to be safe. It also will raise the issue of the potential impact upon her children, and means that she has to consider their safety alongside her own.
Explain agency confidentiality issues and that any information she shares with you will not be disclosed to the man unless she agrees with this and has a safety plan to accommodate it, the boundaries and exceptions to confidentiality.	Will ensure that women know that information they share with workers is confidential, and will not be told to the man. Ensures that women know that some information cannot be kept confidential and must be shared within and across agencies.
Workers should ask questions gently, and in a non-blaming way.	A range of questions needs to be asked, and there is some issue about who asks the questions, how and when. Whilst some woman may feel comfortable in disclosing to a male others won't, and this should be openly discussed between professionals and strategies be in place to accommodate this.
It should be made clear that if women choose to disclose that this will not result in her children being removed from her care unless the risk to the children is serious.	Telling women the truth, will allay their fears and will counteract any threats the man may have made to her previously in relation to her children. Ensures she understands agency agendas.
Where women do not disclose at this stage, it should be made clear that they can come back to the worker at any time in the future should this become an issue.	It is important to leave the door wide open, to send signals that tell women whilst they are not yet ready to disclose that they may be, and can do so, in the future.
If disclosure occurs it is important to remember that she may only tell the bare minimum. One way of finding out more is to ask about the first incident, the last incident and the worst incident of violence.	Gives the practitioner an opportunity to explore the spectrum of abuse, the severity and the time span. Gives the woman an opportunity to snapshot without having to think about the whole at the first disclosure – this may be too much for her to bear. Prevents probing for too much detail, in the first instance.

Figure 5.3: *Continued*

Element of assessment	Considerations, benefits, potential outcomes
Use the Duluth Power and Control wheel (see Chapter 2 for details) to explore with women the type and range of abuses they may have experienced.	This will mean that women have an opportunity to engage with the range of abuses they may have experienced, will help them share practitioner's definition of abuse, and will tell them that abuse is common and they are not alone.
Document what the woman tells you, in her words, ensuring that you have her explicit consent to do so. Make sure that she knows that some things are not negotiable.	Will provide evidence for assessment, and evidence for future criminal/civil action if required.
With her permission photograph, date, sign (both you and the woman) any visible injuries, or arrange for this to be done by health/police. Ensure that she is able to access medical attention, and is encouraged to report her injuries to the police.	Will provide evidence for future criminal/civil action if required. Will ensure that health risks are minimised.
Document fully all disclosures, and add any concerns that you may have to her notes factually and accurately. This is very important if the woman's explanation of the situation/injuries is not consistent with worker findings.	Will ensure that all information is recorded, and that workers and subsequent workers can track the case appropriately.
Discuss options available to her. Women should be given a package with information about all these services, and engaged in a discussion about where they can keep this information so that the man cannot find it.	Practitioners need to be fully aware of all available services, systems of referral and access points and thresholds (if any).
If she isn't ready to leave/doesn't want to leave conduct an assessment of safety, and agree a safety plan with her if appropriate.	Some women will have a safety plan but formalising it with her will check that it is in place, is viable, that she knows she has options, gives her a degree of control, and demonstrates that she is thinking about her safety and forward planning. In some circumstances the level of risk may be so great that practitioners are left with no option but to remove children if the women refuses to engage with the reality of the situation.

- How does your partner help you?
- Is everything all right at home between you and your partner?
- We all have rows occasionally, tell me do you ever argue or row with your partner?
- What happens when you argue or row?
- Does your partner get jealous, and if so how does he behave when he is jealous?
- Have you ever been in a relationship with anyone who ever hurt you?
- Has anyone ever hit, punched, kicked, or done anything that has hurt you physically?
- Does your partner ever make you feel frightened or scared by his behaviour?
- Does he call you names, or shout, or threaten you in any way?
- Where are your children when your partner behaves like this?
- Does his behaviour frighten them?
- Have they ever got hurt when he has been hurting you?
- Many women tell me that their partners are not always nice to them, and can be cruel either physically or emotionally – does this ever happen to you?
- You have a nasty looking bruise/cut/scratch/burn, can you tell me how they happened and when?

- Your partner seems very concerned about you and your injuries, sometimes men behave like that when they have hurt a woman and she has injuries, did he do anything to you?
- Has your partner ever destroyed your possessions, or things that he knows are important to you?
- Has your partner ever followed you, checked up on you, does he ring you constantly?
- Does your partner withhold sex or reject you sexually in a way which makes you feel punished, or rejected?
- Does your partner ever persuade or coerce you to have sex when you really don't want to?
- Does your partner make you do things sexually that you really don't like, don't enjoy or hurt you?
- Does your partner threaten to, or abuse your children?
- Does your partner ever drink, or take drugs? What happens when he takes them, how does he behave around you, your children?
- Tell me about the first time your partner abused you, the last time, the worst time?

(Rowsell, 2003)

Investigation of domestic violence

It is likely that other agencies such as the police will be involved in the investigation of domestic violence incidents in the first instance. Police officers have been provided with the following guidance. They should ensure that all the available evidence is collated in order that an informed decision can be made as to whether a prosecution should be made. Such actions include:

- Obtaining a full statement from the victim. The statement should include details of the family composition, the history of the relationship and any other previous incidents, the actual incident, the victim's injuries (physical and emotional), whether a weapon was used, whether any threats have been made since the attack, whether any children were present and, if so, the effect on them and the victim's view of the future of the relationship. If a victim asks to speak to a female officer, every effort should be made to obtain the services of such an officer.
- Obtaining the 999 tape.
- Speaking to neighbours.
- Speaking with any other potential witnesses.

- Considering interviewing children in the household who may have witnessed the incident. The Memorandum of Good Practice should be complied with at all times. The welfare interests of the child should remain paramount; checking children to see if they have been harmed.
- Police officers providing comprehensive statements including the condition of the house and any comments made by the alleged offender or the victim.
- Making use of a call recording/intelligence/crime recording systems to establish whether this is a repeat incident.
- Taking a witness impact statement just before the court appearance if there has been any delay.
- Arranging support through the victim support agencies.
- Considering the use of Section 23 of the Criminal Justice Act 1988, which allows the CPS to use the victim's statement as evidence without calling the victim to court.

(Home Office, 2000)

In addition, Accident and Emergency records as well as GP surgeries may offer valuable sources of information, especially in pointing to or verifying a pattern of historical abuse and injuries sustained. They should establish whether or not any legal order in existence has been breached, such as an injunction or a prohibited steps order.

If the woman's first language is not English, the services of an interpreter will be needed. The following then need to be considered:

- Wherever possible, use a female interpreter. Be sensitive to the fact that for some woman the use of a male interpreter may preclude any discussion about the circumstances of the violence.
- **Never** use children as an interpreter.
- Try not to use an interpreter from the community she associates with. If in doubt, ask.
- Ensure confidentiality statements are agreed and signed.
- Ensure that the interpreter has had training in domestic violence and that they do not have judgmental opinions regarding marriage and external community influences.
- Ensure that you have a working understanding to how such an interview should be conducted. Appreciating roles, guidelines, timing, and how to address the

ghout the interview; i.e. to
k to her and not the interpreter.

ssional has identified the presence
lence, there is a need to deal with
the issues, and these will vary according to her
capacity to accept help at that point and also the
presence of children in the home. When workers
are referred to a family where domestic violence
occurs, this may be the primary concern, or one of
several issues.

The child protection system in domestic violence cases

It is difficult to establish with any clarity how
children affected by domestic violence are
processed through the child protection system.
Some systems will adopt an approach of holding
the mother accountable for her 'failure to protect'
if they do not leave their abusive partner, often
because the system has some leverage of the
mother; whilst others will argue that the children
have endured actual emotional abuse or likely
physical injury.

If research guides us to recognise domestic
violence as a significant indicator of risk of harm
to children, it is equally important to recognise
the research that indicates children are best cared
for in their own families where this can be made
safe. The nature and impact of domestic violence
demands a co-ordinated multi-agency approach
to ensure that women and children are protected
and supported. In all cases of domestic violence,
assessment for family support under the wider
remit of 'Families in Need' should be made in
partnership with the woman. In a majority of
cases need and support can be planned with the
women via family support interventions on a
multi-disciplinary basis. However, there will be
instances where the threshold of harm to the
child demands that the focus of intervention
requires direct protection of the child.

There is a need for adequate communication
between the police and social services with clear
criteria in place for referrals involving incidents
where a child is in the household where a
domestic violence incident has occurred. At the
present time, practices vary considerably and
may include:

- Automatic referral to social services of all
  incidents where there was a child at the
  address.
- Referral of 'selected' incidents only.

- Referral only if it was thought the children
  might be harmed physically.
- No referral if the children were asleep when
  the incident occurred.
- Informing social services of a single serious
  incident or three less serious incidents in a
  short period of time.
- Asking the police child protection unit to refer
  where there is a second incident, and
- Leaving the decision to child protection
  officers on whether to refer to social services.
  (Plotnikoff and Woolfson, 1998)

There is a concern that a referral about a family
with children involving domestic violence is still
unlikely to trigger a child protection
investigation: possibly because people are
ignorant of the effects on children; that they are
wary of the possibility of violence from the
abuser; or that they are unclear about the
threshold for initiating action concerning
domestic violence (Pryke and Thomas, 1998).

It is important to acknowledge that in living
with violence the situation will be fluid. It is
likely that the risks will change over time and
may therefore require different responses. It is
important to acknowledge that black and ethnic
minority families face additional hurdles in
obtaining a service, and that research suggests
that disabled children are more vulnerable to
abuse. Wherever possible, the child should
participate in the process of identifying need and
shaping responses.

Some issues for initial consideration
irrespective of whether the work is being done by
a social worker or someone else are:

- Individual work to agree the safety of the
  woman and child with the man being asked to
  devise his own safety plan to minimise the
  possibility for further violence.
- Identify any minimisation or denial of
  responsibility for the violence, examination of
  excuses, reasons for the violence.
- Identifying other controlling/abusive
  behaviour patterns.
- Men keeping a 'control log' to facilitate more
  acceptable behaviour.
- Use of video exercises to illustrate controlling
  behaviours.

Assessing a child's safety would need to include:

- When was the most recent incidence of
  violence/abuse?

- Ask the child to give details about what happened during this incident (cognitive interview techniques may facilitate this).
- Were any weapons used or threatened to be used?
- Have any weapons been used or threatened to be used in the past?
- Was their mum locked in a room, or prevented from leaving the house?
- Has either of these things happened in the past?
- Was there any substance abuse involved?
- Might the child be returning to a potentially violent situation? For example is the child concerned about what might happen today, tonight, tomorrow?
- How often do the violent incidents/abuse occur?
- Have the police ever come to your house? What happened?
- What does the child do when the violence is happening? Does the child try to intervene? What happens?
- Where are the child's siblings during the violence?
- Has the child been hurt during incidents of domestic violence?
- Links to non violent support.
- Emotional presentation of the child.
- Mum's awareness of the impact on the child.
- Has the mum explained injuries/bruises to the child/professionals?
- Sibling relationships with each other.
- Ability of the child to identify and express own feelings in the household.
- The positives for the child.
- Degree of distortion in the child's relationships with mother-violent partner; others.
- Material consequences for the mother.
- Parenting capacity of the mother.
- Routines already established to increase safety.
- Safe places and child's access to them.

(Mullender and Morley, 1994: 324)

On some occasions this threshold is reached early on in the intervention and forms the basis for a child protection investigation. More commonly, workers are placed in a situation where they are managing the issues in co-operation with the woman over a longer period of time. On these occasions it can be difficult for workers to judge at which point the threshold into child protection has been reached, particularly when a good working relationship has been established. It is important therefore to be clear about the risks outlined in the assessment, the changes expected including how this will be monitored and evaluated, together with the support available.

The first step is to create an initial 'place of safety' for the woman so that she can have the space to gather her thoughts and to make initial decisions. If the perpetrator has accompanied her or is thought to be in the vicinity, arrangements should be made to see him separately or put physical distance between him and the woman concerned or to ask the police for the man to be restrained. An early assessment of risk is a priority as are initial safety arrangements for the children. It should be determined whether the children are in any kind of danger, their whereabouts and who needs to be contacted to ensure safety – such as the police, schools, grandparents, neighbours or friends (Pryke and Thomas, 1998). It is also important to identify sources of immediate support and, by implication, assessing what she is able to do for herself and where she clearly needs assistance. The importance of community groups for abused women cannot be underestimated as they can be helped by other women who are at varying stages of the healing process.

Where women indicate that they are not yet ready to leave then the practitioner has to decide whether trying to coerce or force a woman, by threatening to remove her children will be counterproductive in the longer term. Without a doubt this means that the practitioner will have to make an assessment of risk. It is important that in order to make a thorough assessment of risk to children, the practitioner asks themselves the following:

- Is the woman accepting that she is abused/disclosing the abuse?
- Does the woman recognise the scale and impact of the abuse that is being perpetrated against her?
- Is the abuse getting worse, increasing in frequency and severity?
- How does she cope on a daily basis – what coping strategies does she use, and how risky or successful are these to her, her children?
- Does she have any mental health problems and if so is she in contact with appropriate support agencies?
- Has she made previous attempts to leave, how successful have these been and what have been the problems, have there been barriers to leaving?

- What involvement has there been from other agencies and how does she feel this has impacted upon her life (positive or negative)?
- Which agencies does she trust and could these agencies be brought in to increase her safety?
- What does she believe has been the impact upon her children, is the likely future impact upon her children, and how can she take action that will minimise risk of harm to her children?
- Has she previously raised concerns about her children, and have these been met with useful interventions?
- To what degree does the woman seem to be compliant with the child protection process (the practitioner needs to be able to work out whether disinterest, anger or non-compliance is as a result of her abuse and previous experiences or a genuine refusal to take seriously the concerns that may be held)?

Where the practitioner decides with the woman that risk is acceptable, then they will often need to assist a woman to formulate safety plans. These should include as a bare minimum:

- Identifying with her what she will do if an incident of violence occurs, how will she ensure her own safety.
- Identifying ways of trying to minimise the risk to her children, getting them out of the room, sending them to get help etc.
- Her being able to identify somewhere safe that she and her children can go to in an emergency.
- Always carrying a list of important/ emergency numbers.
- Packing a bag which contains a spare set of clothes for herself and the children, important documents, important photographs, a spare set of keys for the house/car, a bit of money if possible, and if possible get the bag out and store it with a trusted friend.
- Ensuring that she is in touch with key support agencies i.e. Women's Aid, Rape Crisis, Police Domestic Violence Unit etc., and calls them when needed, particularly if a crisis occurs.
- Being able to access a good solicitor who will be able to explain legal options, panic will be reduced if she knows her rights.
- Getting a trusted friend to ring/check on her at least once a day: using key words that will identify to her friend whether she is safe or needs help is very important.

It is often helpful to agree the safety plan with the woman, and formally record it. This should then become an integral part of the work that the practitioner undertakes to evaluate whether the woman's situation improves or deteriorates over an agreed time period. In this way the practitioner can assist the woman to review her situation on an on going basis, and ensure that their own assessment is updated and appropriate decisions made as necessary. Where the level of risk assessed relates to parenting issues, then it is of vital importance that the practitioner is realistic in what a woman can achieve if she is living with violence and abuse, or the threat of it from a previous partner. However, the attempts a woman may make to comply with, and achieve child protection goals may be deliberately undermined or thwarted by the perpetrator, and practitioners need to find a way of establishing whether the woman won't or can't co-operate.

Abused women deserve honesty and openness, and the system needs to become transparent so that women understand their own role and responsibility within the child protection process, and are clear about the consequences of non-compliance. It is the practitioner's responsibility to ensure that this happens.

Safety planning (Rose, 2001)

Building up a safety plan can help women and children take control, increase their options and ensure a greater degree of safety than previously experienced. If she's not ready to leave then this is one of the most important tasks that anyone can do. Find and give her contact numbers for all local support networks (friends, community groups, woman's aid, helpline numbers etc), she will need practical information and advice (housing, money, legal, children), assure her of confidentiality, check if she wants an injunction or him to leave, can she come back at any time to speak to you again.

Documentation

1. Seek the woman's explicit consent for documentation of disclosure prior to writing; inform her of any professional obligations to do so.
2. Explain the benefits associated with documenting in detail the disclosure, particularly for legal proceedings she may wish to pursue e.g. Injunctions, criminal proceedings, or at least to be taken seriously

by other agencies in future, such as the police in responding to a domestic violence emergency.

3. Document **fully** all disclosures, including your own suspicions and intuitions on file. Where there is only conjecture or suspicion, record that the woman's explanation of her injuries is not consistent with your findings.

4. Use the woman's words wherever possible, such as 'woman states. . . .'

5. Document emotional signs, behaviours and symptoms as well as physical injuries; this can be crucial for court evidence.

6. Record previous violence if disclosed.

7. Record any previous disclosures to other individuals or agencies or other witnesses or evidence, such as photographs.

8. Record previous attempts to stop or contain the violence; record also if she wants to save the relationship.

9. Document where the woman may be contacted safely; **check this out** with her, her safety must not be compromised further.

10. Record all information regarding children; how many; how old; their gender, their schools or nurseries.

11. Record where children were when incidents took place and how the woman thinks they were affected as well as your own impressions. Record any child protection inputs.

12. Check if the man is dangerous; is he threatening her, stalking her, using sexual violence, using weapons, choking her, threatening abduction of or violence towards her family or children etc?

13. If there is any risk of the perpetrator accessing the written record, do not give her a copy of any statement that she has made, but inform her where she can obtain this should she wish to later.

Safety Plan – information to give to women

Domestic violence is a crime. You have a right to be safe. There are some ideas as to what you can do to re-gain some control over your situation. The plan will differ depending on whether the mother intends to remain in the home or leave. The following suggest what should be considered in such situations.

Safety whilst living with violence

- If possible try to get to a room or area you can exit – **not** a bathroom or kitchen.

- Have an extra set of keys and bag packed ready – maybe kept at the home of a safe friend/relative if you have to leave.
- If possible identify a neighbour you can tell about the violence and who will call the police if they hear a disturbance.
- Have a plan for where you will go if you need to leave home.
- Ensure you discuss with your children a safety plan for what needs to happen during an incident.
- Practice ways you and your children can leave your home safely, and in the dark.
- Don't run to where your children are as your partner may harm them as well.
- Make sure your children's school/nursery know who is authorised to pick them up.
- If you work make sure someone at work knows your situation.
- Keep a copy of any Court Order with you.
- Use your own instincts and judgement.
- Teach your children:
  - what to do during an incident.
  - how to call the police/safe family member/friend.
  - violence is never right.
- Take legal advice about your situation.
- Learn defensive tactics. Learn how to position your body to reduce damage – dive into a corner, curl into a ball, protect your face with your arms each side of your head, fingers intertwined.
- Do whatever you need to, to buy time/space to diffuse the situation, or to protect yourself and your children.
- If you can get a mobile phone, programme it for emergency calls, and have a code-word that triggers help.
- If possible open an account in your name and pay small amounts in.
- Keep a record of incidents/or tell someone who will keep a record, including; date, time, what happened, witnessed, names and numbers of police officers/photographs.
- Remind yourself of your worth, positive coping strategies, strengths.
- Decide who you can talk openly with and who you need for support.
- Frequently review your safety plan.

Figure 5.5 offers a template for a suggested safety plan.

Figure 5.4: On making the decision to leave (Rose, 2001)

	Tick when done
What to take with you:	
● Identification, birth certificates (for you and your children)	☐
● National Insurance card, passport etc.	☐
● Health records – NHS card, school immunisation records etc.	☐
Money – including details of accounts.	☐
Medication.	☐
Legal orders.	☐
Agreements about your home – rent books etc.	☐
Insurance papers.	☐
Jewellery.	☐
Address book.	☐
Clothes, nappies, formula.	☐
Toys.	☐
Sentimental items.	☐
Before you resume a potentially abusive relationship, discuss alternatives with someone you trust.	☐

Figure 5.5: Proforma safety plan (Rose, 2001)

This information held is agreed by _____ and _____

Date: _____

I and my child/ren have a right to be safe.

1. If I decide to leave, I will practice how to get out safely.
2. I have taught my children what to do during an incident, and important phone numbers.
3. I can tell _____ about the violence and request they call the police if they receive the code-word or hear a disruption coming from my house.
4. I will use _____ as my code for my friends and children to call for help.
5. I can leave extra money, clothes, documents with _____
6. If I have to leave my home I will go to _____
7. When I expect an argument I will move to an area with access to an outside door _____
8. I can keep my purse and keys ready and put them in _____ in order to leave quickly.
9. I will rehearse my escape plan and, as appropriate, practice it with my children.
10. I will keep my mobile phone/change for the phone on me at all times.
11. I will use my judgement and intuition. If the situation is serious I can give my partner what they want to calm them down. I have to protect myself until I/we are out of danger.
12. When I leave I will have (refer to list on information leaflet) _____
13. If I have injuries I will have them treated by _____
14. I will talk to _____ about what has happened.
15. I will give my children permission to speak to _____ about their experiences.
16. If my children are hurt I will tell _____
17. I will tell the following people who has permission to pick my children up _____
18. If I feel low I can _____
19. To protect my children I can _____
20. To feel stronger I can _____
21. The formal support I have is (i.e. family centre attendance) _____
22. My informal support is (i.e. women's centre, friends) _____
23. I will review this safety plan with _____ on _____
24. I can be safely contacted at _____

This safety plan is given to _____

signed _____

signed _____ (worker)

(adapted from 'A Guide to Domestic Violence'
www.mpolice.com/safety.htm)

A framework for conducting a core assessment

Organisational considerations

Assessing the process, not the event

If the problem of domestic violence can take so many differing forms, services need to be devised to cope with the diversity and the complexity of such cases. Similarly, since violence is a process rather than an event (Calder, 2003b) – an interaction between individual characteristics and situations or circumstances, then we need to try and construct an assessment framework that accommodates for this process and the situations it involves (Gondolf, 2000). Unfortunately, attempts to construct a framework for predicting repeat violence has been poor.

Acknowledging worker risks

Domestic violence situations are difficult to assess because of the complexities of the domestic violence situation which often involve multiple risks. This potentially includes risks to the worker and so we should construct a worker safety plan. The use of mobile phones, working in pairs and applying risk assessment procedures are some examples of how to achieve this. Stanley and Goddard (1997) suggest that the consistency with which minimisation of violence occurs in the files of social workers suggest that the dynamics of survival when under severe threat, which affect women who experience violence from known men, may also be affecting workers. It seems logical therefore to conclude that unless workers are much better protected that it will be unlikely that the practices which collude with, or minimise male violence will change (Humphreys, 1997).

Worker selection

In selecting the workers, we should seek staff with good interpersonal skills (empathy, compassion, and being a good listener); communication skills; and the ability to work in a multi-agency setting. They need to be able to work unsupervised, prioritise, cope with stress, frustrations of the role and grief-ridden work; and be able to challenge the system (Plotnikoff and Woolfson, 1998). Supervision is essential for the staff and should cover the following areas:

- Exploring the personal impact of the work.
- Looking at how workers' own issues impact on their practice.

- Exploring relationship between co-workers.
- Ensuring worker accountability and adherence to minimum standards and principles.
- Supporting workers in critically examining their interactions with clients and to explore group process and dynamics.
- Supporting workers in dealing effectively with diversity and the consequent power issues.
- Ensuring workers develop further skills and identify training needs.

(*www.ahimsa.org.uk*, 11.10.02)

Every effort should be made to meet all these goals. However, where no interventions exist, which will meet all of the goals simultaneously then the protection of the child should take precedence over all the other goals. In domestic violence cases, a safety plan should be developed for both the child and the adult victim. They should be developed with the party concerned and in the case of the child with the child and the non-abusing parent.

Criteria for a core assessment

A core assessment may be completed in two slightly differing scenarios:

- Where it is judged that the level of violence experienced by the woman is likely to have a direct/indirect impact on the children, or the level of violence may be affecting the woman's capacity to care for the children or protect them, a more detailed assessment is required to ascertain how the woman might be enabled to protect their child. This will require longer-term involvement and will include other supporting agencies who may be involved with the family.
- Where informal agreements have broken down, placing the children at risk, or where the woman is unable to accept the impact the violence has on the children. It is also possible that the impact on the woman prevents her parenting her children adequately. It may therefore be necessary to take the matter to a child protection conference or consider legal intervention. In this scenario, the emphasis changes from the child being in need to questions of suffering or likely to suffer significant harm. In some situations where the children cannot be made safe by leaving them with their mother, consideration will need to be given to removing the children.

Scope of the core assessment

These assessments are often conducted in relatively brief time frames, typically with less than co-operative respondents. A greater responsibility is thus imposed on mothers to protect the child. Compounding this difficulty is the fact that the mother's own safety is typically not assessed (Magen et al., 2001). Many risk assessment tools do not screen patients for the presence of domestic violence. If we want to remedy this situation then we need to ensure that the knowledge is accompanied by the necessary skills and approaches otherwise we could, in the process of identifying domestic violence, cause greater harm to women and children. For example, the mother or her children may be mandated to have contact with her abusive partner. She may not leave her partner if she is more fearful of the abuser than the child protection mandate held by professionals.

Once domestic violence has been identified, workers should conduct a core assessment of three factors affecting the child's safety:

● Danger posed to the children and the mother from the domestic violence perpetrator.
● Physical, emotional and developmental impact of the domestic violence on the children, and
● Strategies that the abused mother has used in the past to successfully protect the children that can be reinforced to help her protect herself and the children in the future.

The worker's interactions and interventions with the family members should attempt to meet three goals in domestic violence cases. These are:

● To protect the child.
● To help the abused mother protect herself and her children, using non-coercive, supportive and empowering interventions whenever possible.
● To hold the domestic violence perpetrator, not the adult victim, responsible for stopping the abusive behaviour.

Worker understanding of trauma

There are a number of dimensions that should be considered in assessing the impact of trauma on children, including characteristics of the child, the social environment and the traumatic experience itself (Koverola, 1995). All these factors interact with one another to shape specific outcomes for individual children, and each can provide either a source of protection, or increased risk for the

development of psychopathology in children exposed to domestic violence (Foy et al., 1996).

There are a number of feminist writers who have criticised the responses of helping professionals: especially in their confusion of effect with cause (Bograd, 1982; Schechter and Gray, 1988). Here, workers may have assumed that the effects of being a victim of domestic violence are seen as the reason why the abuse occurs, rather than seeing it as the consequence of the abuse.

Components of a core assessment

Listed below are some essential elements of any assessment where there are concerns about domestic abuse:

● the perpetrator
● the mother
● the mother–perpetrator relationship
● the child
● the mother–child relationship
● the child–perpetrator relationship
● the siblings
● the extended family/community

This framework for assessment can be used as a specific tool within the assessment framework (DoH, 2000). It fits into the areas of parental capacity, parent's perspectives and wider family, community and environmental factors. However, because of the dynamics of an abusive relationship, the use of dominance, power and control by one partner over the other, it is more likely that it will be used with the non-abusing partner (usually the woman), as in families where there is domestic violence it is the woman who is the responsible parent and with whom social services aim to intervene and attempt to support. The perpetrator often does not engage with social services unless child protection and/or court action is being considered.

The key task of the engagement of the victim and the perpetrator in the assessment process is problematic as in many families the perpetrator does not co-operate with the assessment. Very often it is the non-abusing parent, the woman, that the social worker engages with and attends case discussions and child protection case conferences. Therefore, it is crucial that the social worker's primary intervention is to protect the children and this can best be achieved by protecting and supporting the non-abusing parent.

However, in some families where domestic abuse occurs the woman is not proactive in protecting herself and her children. In these situations, the social worker needs to assess the woman's ability and her decision-making regarding the violence. The woman could have issues regarding historical abuse in childhood, limited parenting skills, and be in a powerless situation due to the perpetrator's dominance and power over her. Social workers need to identify the barriers that are preventing her from making safe decisions about herself and her children. Very often it is only when the woman finally has to address risks with social workers that she can make safe decisions.

Educating the non-abusive partner on the complex issues and dynamics of an abusive relationship is an effective tool in enabling her to make informed decisions in terms of safety and changes in the family situation.

There are special tools which social workers can use to undertake this educative role with the non-abusive parent – safety planning and educative materials (however be careful about what written materials you give to a woman as it could risk her safety if the perpetrator finds them).

Myths about the cause of violence are all too common and allow us to collude with and condone male violence as a society:

- The myth that somehow women and children enjoy, invite and desire male violence.
- They ask for it, provoke it or in some way deserve it.
- That it only happens in certain types of families, cultures or neighbourhoods.
- That women and children lie or exaggerate.
- That if women and children resisted male violence they could prevent it.
- That the men who perpetrate violence are somehow different to other men because they are sick, out of control, have poor communication skills, are under stress, abuse alcohol or drugs, or have childhood experiences that have led them to act out violently.

None of these are causes or reasons, they are excuses:

- Premeditated, secret, frequent, violent, child sexual abuse. There is no excuse.
- Whoever, wherever, whenever, sexual assault. There is no excuse.

- Blame the woman, blame the drink, blame the weather. There is no excuse.
- Drunk or sober. There is no excuse.
- What's love got to do with it – violence against women and children.

There is never an excuse. Holding onto the myths clouds why the violence happens, and who is responsible for it. It clouds our perspective and makes it difficult for us individually and collectively to challenge the root cause of male violence and its many repercussions (Rowsell, 2001).

The key message for intervention must be:
- Empower the mother.
- Protect the children.
- Challenge the perpetrator.

It is with the perpetrator that we must start. Browne and Herbert (1997) provided us with the following characteristics associated with violent partners:

- Feelings of low self-esteem and inadequacy.
- Feelings of isolation and lack of social support.
- Lack of social skills and assertive behaviour.
- History of psychiatric disorder such as anxiety and depression.
- History of alcohol and/or drug abuse.
- Poor impulse control and antisocial behaviour problems.
- Possessiveness, jealousy and fear of abandonment.
- Externalisation of blame, escalation of arguments and showing aggression and violence when provoked.
- Lack of empathy for over-dependent victim, possibly due to poor physical or mental health, sexual problems or difficulties arising during pregnancy or childbirth.
- Displacement of anger at job dissatisfaction, stress at work or recent aversive life event (e.g. separation from spouse or death of a parent or child).
- Socio-economic problems such as unemployment, poor housing or financial difficulties.
- Exposure to violence as a child.
- Current history of violence, threatening behaviour or use of weapons.

The perpetrator

Aims of the work

The primary aim in working with perpetrators of domestic violence is to increase the safety of women and children. Secondary aims include holding men accountable for their violence towards women, promoting respectful, egalitarian relationships, and working with others to improve the community's response to domestic violence.

The aim of any intervention should seek to have an admission from the perpetrator to the following:

- The full extent of his abuse.
- The significance and seriousness of his abuse.
- His culpability.
- The consequences of his actions.
- The impact and effect on his partner, children and others.
- The ability to change his thoughts, feelings and behaviour belongs with him.
- His use of the abuse in the context of power and control.
- Reason and acceptance that the violence/abuse must stop.

Principles of the intervention

Caesar and Hamberger (1989) set out the following principles and observations:

- Abusers do not enjoy being abusive: the most typical abuser is often unhappy with his life and his behaviour.
- Violence has harmful immediate and long-term effects on every member of the family.
- Abusers often have negative attitudes toward women, which contributes to the occurrence of aggression in marital relationships.
- Abusers generally lack non-violent alternatives for expressing themselves or for achieving desired goals within their marital relationships.
- Abusers are frequently saddled with traditional, patriarchal notions that men are expected to be dominant and infallible.
- Marital aggression is an individual's problems, most commonly the man's. Marital discord is a couple's problem.
- Abusers have often learned their abusive behaviours from their parental role models.
- Abusers must take responsibility for their aggressive behaviour.

To this we can add:

- Do not 'psychologise' violent or abusive behaviour within the context of domestic violence.

- It is not an inevitable system of psychological illness, interactional provocation, or developmental or social stress.
- Violence does not necessarily breed violence – a perpetrator is seven times more likely to come from a non-violent home.
- The act of violence and responsibility for it rests solely with the perpetrator. Unless this is accepted, a change in behaviour and attitude can not occur.
- Men will deny their behaviour, by using denial strategies such as justification, minimising, victim blaming or accusing a higher authority (society, parents, etc).
- The abuse must have ceased, and the safety of the woman and children ensured before any form of mediation, conciliation, conflict resolution or 'couple work' is attempted.
- Work with the perpetrator in anger management can be helpful but this will never be sufficient to address the changes in attitudes, beliefs and actions that he will be required to demonstrate.
- Instead of asking the question, 'why has the woman not left?' try asking the question 'why the man stays?'

Workers need to promote an alternative, positive and constructive model of human relationships based on respect for the autonomy and self-determination of all individuals; belief in the fundamental equality of all human beings; willingness to negotiate and compromise; acceptance of power as a shared and negotiated commodity; determination to seek and apply non-violent ways of relating; and a refusal to accept, tolerate or practice beliefs or behaviours which breach these principles (*www.ahimsa.org.uk*, 11.10.02).

Engagement issues for workers

Most abusers do not come forward and ask for help until they have to. This most frequently is when they are arrested for domestic violence. Arrest is a useful strategy and it is correlated with lower rates of violence in the future. It clearly serves a deterrent effect.

Men have become good at avoiding intervention and we have become good at allowing this to happen. However, the process of engaging with men is complex and needs to be thought through by child protection agencies. Social workers are not taught how to engage with men, and often lack the skills needed to do so and therefore often consciously or unconsciously exclude them from the process. Any intervention needs to be undertaken by a skilled practitioner who has an excellent understanding of domestic violence and men who perpetrate it. Men need to be working on not only understanding how and why their behaviour occurs, but also how they can develop their own plan of safety that will keep their partners and children safe. Practitioners need then to actively include men as a matter of urgency, because unless they do so how can they truly assess the level of risk posed, or work out a long term effective intervention strategy.

Men employ various tactics to keep workers at a distance: they may absent themselves from the process in a practical sense by being unavailable; they may minimise, deny and blame the woman thereby convincing the practitioner that there is no problem, or that the problem is the woman; and they may intimidate practitioners and use the process as a way of silencing woman and children. However, there is some evidence that when practitioners refuse to allow men off the hook, and actively seek to engage them in the process, that they will and do talk about violence and abuse, even if this is only in a very piecemeal way to begin with.

Practitioners working with men on men's re-education programmes report that the most effective way to engage with men is to ask them general questions to begin with, followed by very specific questions that demonstrate that the practitioner knows that violence and abuse is present, and is presuming that the man should and will take responsibility for its perpetration. It is vital that the language used by practitioners is not that of the counselling or therapy, as research suggests that men have learnt how to avoid these kinds of techniques, or use them to their own advantage e.g. to assume victim status. Therefore practitioners need to ask questions of men directly, that tell them quite clearly that we know abuse is present, and allow them to assess against the following:

1. How willing is the man to co-operate and comply with the child protection process?
2. How does the man's version of events/his relationship compare with the woman's?
3. Does he have a history of violent behaviour, particularly against other women/children?
4. If so, what has been the outcome of this behaviour?

5. To what degree does he minimise his abuse, deny the abuse, or blame the woman?
6. How aware is he of the impact of his behaviour on the women and the children?
7. To what degree does he accept responsibility for his behaviour?
8. To what degree does he seem likely to respond to intervention?
9. How willing is he to leave the relationship if this is necessary for child protection reasons?
10. Are there currently any charges being laid against him, and what are his bail conditions?
11. Does he have any alcohol or drug misuse?
12. Does he have any mental health issues?
13. To what degree does the practitioner feel confident that they can work with the man, and how far will their own safety be compromised? (Rowsell, 2003)

The ability to engage men in a manner and discourse with which they can relate must avoid minimising the impact of their violent behaviour as well as avoiding colluding in their avoidance of taking responsibility for these behaviours. Research has shown that engaging men to reflect on their violent and abusive behaviour can face a number of obstacles:

- Opposition and resentment because you are perceived as representing authority and criticism.
- Anger and resentment at you interfering in his family's 'private affairs'.
- Refusal to talk (e.g. 'It is none of your business').
- Denial that anything happened (e.g. 'do you really think that I could do something like that?').
- Blaming someone other than himself (e.g. 'She provoked me, it's her that has the problem').
- Make it seem that he could not help himself (e.g. 'I just snapped').
- Underplay the extent and impact of his violence (e.g. 'It wasn't really that bad').
- Trying to get you to side with him and accept that what he has done is OK (e.g. 'You know what it's like').
- Men may not fully understand what male family violence is nor its impact.
- Men may blame external factors such as alcohol/substance abuse and poor anger management skills.
- Many men believe they are persecuted and unfairly blamed for all family violence.
- Many men believe violence is understandable in certain circumstances (e.g. nagging).

- Men may see themselves as a victim as well as a perpetrator of violence.

Conversely there are a number of motivators that can help men to commence and remain with the change process:

- This is a chance to take time out, to stop and think about what they have done and its impact.
- The potential/real end of this relationship.
- The man's desires not to repeat these behaviours in future relationships.
- Regret for hurting – the man may care for his family and does not want the incident to recur.
- The detrimental effect on their children.
- The potential or real loss of contact with their children.
- The men want to prevent their children growing up and behaving in a similar manner.
- The criminal and legal consequences of their actions.
- The recognition that they can change and help is available.

Men can change their attitudes and behaviour and learn positive, equal and non-violent ways of relating. Although men who do use violence do so to assert and maintain power and control with damaging effects on others, they also report a negative range of effects on themselves. These include shame, guilt, hating themselves for what they do and frustration at not having the kind of relationships with their partners and families they would like to have. They may also feel powerless themselves and use violence to try and increase their sense of power (*www.ahimsa.org.uk*, 11.10.02).

Assessing motivation to undertake the work

In making an assessment as to whether it is possible to work with the man, workers need to consider whether:

- He believes he needs to make changes, not just his partner or children.
- He wants a relationship with his partner, not just his role as father to his child or children.
- He is prepared to make a commitment to not using violence in the future.
- He agrees to attend for assessment – treatment and to co-operate with what is asked of him or his partner by child protection workers (Burke, 1999). If he agrees to this then a responsibility plan should be devised to demonstrate his

intentions and actions to prevent further violence and abuse.

It is useful to establish several factors at the start of any assessment process:

- **Motive:** is he trying to win her back or gain access to the children?
- **Lethality:** how dangerous is he?
- **Amenability:** are the chances of change realistic at this time?
- **Responsibility:** who does he blame for the violence?
- **Risk:** is his violence likely to continue? (*www.ahimsa.ord.uk*, 11.10.02).

Denial: excuses, excuses, excuses

Jukes (1999) identified a useful four-part model of denial exhibited in perpetrators of domestic violence:

- **Denial of abusiveness:** this is where the abuser completely denies that they are abusive in any way and that they wish to be dominant in the relationship. In the extreme form it will involve the abuser forgetting abusive incidents or behaviour.
- **Denial of responsibility:** this is where the abuser is able to acknowledge that they are abusive but insists that their behaviour is caused by factors outside their control. This could include drugs and alcohol, provocation or a loss of control.
- **Denial of frequency, intensity and severity – minimisation:** this is when the abuser lies to themselves and probably to their partner about how abusive they know they are. They tell her that they did not hit her that hard or so often and they also tell themselves the same things. They tell her that they did not mean it and try to convince her that her experience of his behaviour is false and even crazy.
- **Denial of consequences:** this is when the abuser refuses to see the effect of their behaviour on their partner or her children. They refuse to see their partner's increased confusion, fear and incompetence as being caused by their abusiveness or that she fears him. The abuser may hate the woman for her increasing dependency and uses this as a justification for further abuse (page 63).

Domestic violence is inexcusable but the following represent some of the excuses offered by abusers:

- When I get angry I just lose control.
- I didn't really hit her, she moved and she bruises easily.
- I just get fed up with all the arguments.
- She never listens to me or does anything I say.
- I have a short temper and always have had.
- She doesn't seem to realise that I am a man and I have needs and my frustration builds and builds if I do not have sex.
- She should not lead me on and make promises.
- I am the only one who can sort out the money and pay the bills (*www.ahimsa.org.uk*, 11.10.02).

Areas of assessment

Does the perpetrator have a:

- history of abusive behaviour?
- willingness to leave/co-operate/comply?
- honesty/openness about abuse (minimisation/re-framing/victim blaming)?
- awareness of impact on victims?
- acceptance of responsibility?
- likely response to intervention (including worker safety)?
- alcohol/drug misuse?
- mental health issue?

Any assessment should include:

- An understanding of what constitutes violent behaviour.
- The degree of responsibility accepted by the abuser for their behaviour and actions.
- The choices the abuser has made when perpetrating domestic violence.
- The functions that the behaviour serves for the abuser.
- Identifying and challenging any denial of their behaviour.
- Their understanding of the motives underlying their behaviour and especially the misuse of power and control over their partners.
- Helping the man understand the impact of the violence on the partner and the children both in the long and the short term.
- To explore any victim experiences they may have (without allowing them to shift the focus from their responsibility as a perpetrator).

More specifically, there are a number of assessment areas to isolate particular kinds of risks and to quantify them. Bell and McGovern (2003) identified the following areas:

Assess the nature of the domestic violence

- Severity of the incidences.
- Pattern, frequency and duration of violent incidences.
- Perpetrator's use of the children/children caught up in the abuse.
- Escalation and use of isolation.
- Sexual violence/abuse.

Assess the risks to the children posed by perpetrators

- They may physically abuse children.
- They may sexually abuse children.
- They may endanger children through neglect.
- The perpetrator may focus so much attention on controlling and abusing his adult partner that he ignores and neglects children.
- They may also prevent the woman from caring for her children resulting in neglect.
- They may harm children by coercing them into abusing their mothers.
- They may endanger children emotionally and physically by creating environments in which children witness assaults against their mothers.
- They may endanger children by undermining the ability of social services, women's aid and other community agencies to intervene and protect children.

Assessing risk of lethality and danger

- Perpetrator's access to the woman.
- Pattern of the perpetrator's abuse.
- Perpetrator's state of mind.
- Significant factors – lifestyle of perpetrator.
- Criminal record of perpetrator.
- Substance abuse.

Questions that need asking:

- Establishing with them what actions they consider to be abusive and which actions or attitudes constitute domestic violence.
- Ask them if they have ever slapped, punched, kicked, pushed, shoved, threatened or thrown things at her? Have they called her names, smashed or damaged property, isolated her from family or friends or made her afraid of him? Do they feel that she deserves it/provoked it/? Do they think that every man has a right to control his partner?
- Ask them which of their actions (past and present) fit within their own definitions.
- What controlling behaviours do they exhibit?

- In what ways do they deny their abusive behaviour?
- What defences do they use most frequently?
- What makes it difficult for them to hold themselves accountable for their thoughts, actions and feelings?
- Who is responsible for what in the adult relationship? (Money, housework, birth control, drinking, holidays, etc.)
- Get them to identify situations which frequently result in arguments (e.g. money, housework, social activities, sexual activities, discipline of the children, other women/men etc).
- Who usually has the last word in the argument?
- Has the argument ever turned into a physical fight?
- Has there ever been a fight during a pregnancy?
- Have you ever threatened to hurt your partner?
- Have you ever threatened to hurt the children?
- Have you ever threatened to hurt yourself?
- What is the frequency and intensity of their behaviour and the arguments?
- Get them to consider any non-violent alternatives to resolve the argument.
- Have they ever used drugs and alcohol? Do they feature in the violence?
- Have you ever forced sex on your partner?
- Get them to list any consequences they have experienced for their controlling and abusive behaviour.
- Do these consequences motivate them to change?
- Have they ever asked for or accepted help previously? With what outcome?
- In what ways do they think that their violence has impacted on the children?
- In general where are the children when the arguments/fights take place?
- How do the children react when this takes place?
- Get them to describe their responsibilities and tasks as a parent.
- What is his experience of family life? How did his father treat his mother? What elements of his father's parenting style has he adopted? What elements of his mother's parenting style has he adopted?
- How was he disciplined as a child? What did he learn as a child from this discipline? How does he discipline his own children?

Following on from the framework advocated in Bell and McGovern (2003) they identify a series of questions within each of the required areas of assessment as follows:

Perpetrator's access to the woman:

- Frequency of contacts.
- Perpetrator has collusive friends/allies who have contacted the woman.
- Perpetrator has legal rights to visit children.
- Perpetrator has custody.
- Frequency of phone calls/writing.
- Perpetrator has breached 'no contact' order in the past.

Pattern of perpetrator's abuse:

- Frequency/severity of the abuse in current, concurrent, past relationships. Specific information relating to the type of violent and abusive behaviour used by the perpetrator, the duration of violent incidences, the perpetrator's use of weapons, details of the types of threats used by the perpetrator.
- Has taken family members hostage.
- Has forced the woman to leave without the children.
- Has prevented the woman seeing to the needs of her children during and following a violent incident.
- Having been abusive towards the woman he has failed to take into consideration the emotional well-being of the children in the family.
- Has locked the woman and children out with nowhere to go.
- Has access to weapons.
- Threatens to kill.
- Harms or kills animals.
- Exhibits stalking behaviour.

Perpetrator's state of mind:

- Demonstrates obsession with the woman; jealousy.
- Ignores negative consequences of his violence.
- Experiences depression/desperation.
- Has suicidal thoughts or plans.
- Makes comments about reuniting after death.
- Has thoughts or makes comments about hurting the woman by harming or killing the children.
- Makes comments about not being able to live without the woman.
- Makes comments related to religious/cultural sanctioning of brutality and rights to control women and children.

Individual factors that reduce perpetrator's own control over behaviour:

- Substance abuse.
- Certain medications.
- Psychosis or mental illness.
- Brain damage.

Additional factors that can contribute to potential for lethality:

- Victim has recently separated from the abuser.
- Victim has autonomy (separation/activities/work/school/friends).
- Perpetrator wants to reconcile with woman.
- Woman uses physical force in self-defence.
- Children use violence.
- Woman has begun relationship with new partner.
- Perpetrator has past criminal record.
- Perpetrator will soon be released from jail/prison.
- The woman and children have moved to a more isolated community (with or without the perpetrator).
- Pattern of inappropriate system response.
- An adult victim being unable to care for the child as a result of trauma from an assault.

Perpetrator's pattern of assault and coercion:

- Methods of resolving conflict.
- Physical assaults.
- Sexual assaults.
- Emotional and psychological assaults.
- Economic coercion.
- Use of children to control partner.

Assessing the perpetrator's pattern of assault and coercion:

- Methods of resolving conflict.
- Physical assaults.
- Sexual assaults.
- Emotional and psychological assaults.
- Economic coercion.
- Use of children to control partner.

For excellent workbooks for working with men who perpetrate domestic violence, crammed with lots of useful worksheets and exercises, the reader is referred to Fall et al. (1999) and Heery (2001).

Treatment issues

Treatment programmes for perpetrators of domestic violence are increasingly requested for both voluntary and mandatory candidates.

However, some questions about their usefulness remain and have been usefully summarised by Scott and Wolfe (2000) as including:

- High drop-out rates (20–80%) are problematic even where the perpetrator is mandated to attend. Hamberger and Hastings (1986) found that only 16% of batterers who were offered free voluntary treatment took up the offer.
- Major methodological problems exist ranging from small sample sizes through to lack of control groups and short or incomplete follow-ups.
- Up to one-third of those who attended the programme continued to be physically abusive (Gondolf, 1998).
- There is no evidence of greater effectiveness based on the use of a particular theoretical approach, treatment modality, treatment length or intervention intensity (Gondolf, 1998).
- The probability of re-assault is greater for men with prior convictions for assaults against their partners or other and men with drug or alcohol addiction (Shepard, 1992).

The mother

Introductory comments

I have already explored in some detail in Chapter 4 the impact of domestic violence on parenting. In this assessment area I am exploring the impact of domestic violence on the mother and her ability to make the appropriate choices when considering her own safety and that of her children.

Living with a violent partner can have far reaching short and long term impacts upon women physically, socially, emotionally and psychologically (Cambell et al., 1994; Hoff, 1990), although it will vary greatly for each individual woman and the circumstances that she finds herself in. Apart from the obvious physical harm that women may suffer, domestic violence can include women experiencing: sleep deprivation, isolation, depression, loss of confidence, self-harm, and an increased tendency to commit suicide; miscarriage, stillbirth and foetal abnormalities; difficulties in mothering and caring for their children; in homelessness and in some instances being deported; being prevented from gaining employment and/or training opportunities; increased sick leave from employment or being forced to give up employment; the development of coping strategies such as alcohol or drug abuse; forced or unwanted sex can result in pelvic problems; and can also result in a woman experiencing severe menstrual problems, sexually transmitted diseases or any kind of urine infection, vaginal or anal tearing, and of course unintended pregnancy; in some instances women may commit minor criminal offences to survive on a day-to-day practical basis, or serious criminal offences (such as killing a partner) as a strategy of self-preservation. There is little doubt that living with domestic violence has a hugely negative impact on the lives of women.

McHugh and Hewitt (1998) remind us that where women are brainwashed in their relationship then they can act to satisfy the needs of the abuser rather than of their children. How can we expect a mother to protect her children when they judge everything in terms of how it affects their abuser? This view has major implications as to the way workers may choose to intervene. Rather than seeing them as the main protector of their children, they may question how she can attain this when the thought change process (described earlier) ensures that she acts against her own best interests. Workers may be better placed by assuming control for the woman and then equipping her to counter the power and control of the abuser. This can offer an empowerment option for the mother but there is a question as to the timing of when it is operationalised and the context within which the handover is made from the professionals to the mother.

Assumptions when approaching the mother

There are a number of useful assumptions we should remember when dealing with victims of domestic violence:

- They may have been experiencing the abuse over a long period of time.
- The violence may be a mixture of physical, sexual and emotional abuse.
- They may have been limited in their movements.
- They may have had no access to their own money or have been excluded from dealing with finances.
- They will probably have done a whole range of different things already to stop or manage the violence.

- You may have been the first person they have spoken to or the twentieth.
- They will want to stop or escape the violence, but they may also want to try and save the relationship.
- It is likely that they will blame themselves for the violence, be lacking in confidence and be sensitive to your views.
- They may be frightened of the perpetrator and possibly you.
- Women are most at risk of life-threatening or fatal violence when they try to attempt to leave or have recently left the violent partner.
- It may not be easy for a person to make a decision to leave a relationship and your response could be crucial as to how they respond next.

Rules of engagement

When interviewing mothers workers are advised to:

- Prepare: be alert to what is available locally and consult with a domestic violence worker.
- Ask abuse screening questions: to assess whether or not abuse is occurring. If in doubt, ask directly.
- Reassure: without offering false confidentiality if children are involved.
- State that abuse is wrong and not acceptable: it is the first time many will have heard it and even so they will be faced with making a choice with immense consequences for them.
- Assess immediate safety: short-term and longer-term safety plan proforma do exist to guide workers in this task.
- Acknowledge and validate: victims often need to hear that they are doing something right. They may feel ashamed or embarrassed and like a hopeless failure that the abuse is happening.
- Challenge excuses for the abuse: victims are more likely to minimise abuse done to them (and their children) than to overstate it. They may feel disloyal to their partner and may want to make excuses for their behaviour. They may have made the victim responsible for their abusive behaviour. Victims can play down the abuse as a coping mechanism.
- Refer and follow up: help define options and alternatives; avoid ultimatums but encourage decisions; try to inform the victim and empower them to make safe plans. If we tell them what to do, then we mirror the

behaviour of the abuser, who is an expert at ordering them around.

Aims of the work

There need to be clear and explicit aims of our work with mothers, namely:

- To increase the physical safety and emotional and mental well-being of women and children who have experienced domestic violence.
- To promote realistic expectations with women with regard to the future and the outcome attainable from any assessment and intervention work with the abuser.
- To provide the services to the mother in an accessible and non-discriminatory way that corresponds with the individual needs of the mother.

High quality practice has been identified as including lifting the blame and helping women name domestic violence; belief in the woman's accounts; a non-judgemental approach; and providing adequate time, support and understanding (Humphreys and Thiara, 2002).

First and foremost it is important that the woman herself is able to recognise that she is being abused and is encouraged to name the behaviour that is being perpetrated against her. This is often very difficult for many reasons, including: not wanting to acknowledge the seriousness of the situation; not wanting to own the problem; being frightened of being pushed into making decisions; being scared of the agendas of other people and agencies. Very often women will reframe their experiences and find other ways of dealing with/or legitimising the situation they are in, and the behaviour they are experiencing. Many women will blame themselves; will be told its their fault and many believe it; will make excuses for the behaviour; and will change their own behaviour to try and counteract or prevent violence occurring in their relationship. In the majority of cases none of these strategies are likely to work in the long term because it is the man who needs to change and to take responsibility.

Women often seek informal support, often from family and friends before they will formally themselves approach an outside agency. Sometimes women will directly name the abuse, sometimes family and friends will ask themselves. However, research suggests that unless a woman is believed, not judged, taken seriously and informed of all options available to them, that this is unlikely to be helpful in the longer term. Very often family and friends want to 'rescue' women and many withdraw support if she doesn't behave in a way that they think is rational. Some women may seek support and advice within their communities, or from professionals that are seen as being able to offer a confidential, listening ear, such as GP's, health visitors, or religious leaders etc. Again unless communities are aware of the options then women are unlikely to find that this prevents future or a reoccurrence of the violence. Sometimes women are forced to go public and contact more formal agencies, or someone else makes contact on their behalf (with or without her permission).

If a woman has not gone through previous stages then contact with formal agencies may be very difficult, unless personnel are adequately trained and equipped to deal with her presenting issues, or their own limitations. Going public is a difficult thing for many women to do and is often an indication that the violence is spiralling out of control, that she needs help to renegotiate her situation, that she now believes that she has no option but to try and reassess the situation and her circumstances, and that she can't do this safely alone.

Mothers require information about the modus operandi of domestic violence abusers and clear messages about men's violence. Shaw et al. (1999) identified a number of issues that should be addressed with the mother:

- Providing information about violence and safety is important in helping the mother make their own decision without pressure for any one outcome to occur.
- Ensuring the women are clear that the violence is not their fault: allowing them to unpack the years of abuse and brainwashing takes time. Allowing them to tell their story is important and it can be very important that they are believed.
- Unpacking the emotional bond/attachment: workers need to help the mother acknowledge and explore the positive as well as the negative aspects of the relationship.
- Working through the effects of the abuse: and sometimes helping them understand the breadth of the abuse they have endured. Many parts of the relationship which they accepted as normal are now seen to be oppressive. The

need to talk openly about the abuse to avert any sense of shame is important.

- Exploring the possibility of a temporary or permanent separation: is often very difficult for the mother to consider. Staying in the relationship often seems like the exclusive way of ensuring her needs are met. Some may choose to remain in the relationship but aim to have the violence cease. This goal can be used as leverage with the male to get them into treatment. We have to concede that some men are capable of change and this can benefit women and children in the end.

Reviewing the safety plan

In preparing and reviewing the safety plan with the mother we need to:

- Be aware of any weapons in the house.
- Make a plan about what to do and where to go if they are in danger. Tell the children the plan if they are old enough to understand and follow directions.
- Make sure she has easy access to a telephone – keep change handy.
- Hide/carry a survivor's card/list of telephone numbers that she may need in an emergency.
- Always keep some money hidden to help her get away.
- Try to keep safe any essential legal documents, benefit books, medical cards, bank books, cheque books, marriage and birth certificates, passports, injunctions or court orders, driving licence, rent book, divorce papers. Also any sentimental items e.g. photographs.
- Keep the car in good repair and make sure they have petrol.
- Keep extra sets of keys (house and car) in a hiding place.
- Try to keep keys, a crisis fund, medicines, children's clothes and favourite toys and a set of their own clothes in an 'emergency bag' so that she can get away quickly if she needs to.
- Get her to leave her 'emergency bag' with a trusted friend or in a hiding place where her partner will not find it.
- Make sure the children have enough essential medication.
- Work out a code word with someone she trusts that can be used if she is in danger.
- Have a signal (put on a light, hang something out of the window, have curtains half open etc) that can be seen by a neighbour or friend.

- Identify a place of hiding she can go to.
- Remind her to call people in advance to tell them that she is coming so they can watch out for her.
- Try and leave when the abuser is not around.

(available from
www.domesticviolence.biz/safety.html)

When the mother gets to her new home or is living alone:

- Change the locks.
- Install a security system, smoke alarm and security lighting.
- Programme emergency numbers on the telephone, including 999.
- Show the abusers photograph to neighbours, tell them of any injunctions etc and ask them to notify the police if they see him around.
- Tell those who look after her children and make sure they know who is permitted to collect the children.
- Get her to report any breach of injunctions, however minor.
- Get them to talk to a trusted friend or family member about what support they need.
- Keep contact numbers for different support agencies.

(available from
www.domesticviolence.biz/safety.html)

If there is a risk that the children may be abducted women should be advised to:

- Keep the child's passport, birth certificate and NHS card in a safe place.
- If the child does not have a passport, lodge an objection with the passport office.
- Not to agree to the child being taken abroad.
- Not to leave the child unaccompanied.
- Warn anyone caring for the child to maintain and keep to agreed arrangement details.
- Alert the police.

Areas to cover in the assessment

The purpose of a domestic violence assessment is to identify factors within the mother and in her environment that will either assist in her attempts to free herself from violence and abuse or serve as barriers to achieving this goal. The first step should be whether the mother is currently in crisis as a result of a recent violent or abusive incident. If so, crisis intervention may be necessary to stabilise her.

Ensuring her personal safety and that of her children is the primary consideration at this point. If the mother is stable, a major focus of the assessment should be the history of physical violence and emotional abuse in the current relationship. This should include the hands-off abuse such as name calling and other attempts to humiliate the person, threats to harm her or her possessions, and attempts to control her behaviour or other aspects of her life such as whom she spends time with. The type and extent of any physical violence as well as how long it has occurred for should be assessed.

Although the main attention should be on the here and now, attention to past victimisation in childhood, either in the family of origin or in institutions, as well as in previous romantic relationships may be appropriate, depending upon the circumstances. This information may be helpful in determining whether the client perceives the abuse experiences to be normal or expected in close relationships. Attention should also be paid to client strengths as well as limitations. Access to physical and material resources also needs to be assessed. Their income, living situation, social network, employment etc needs to be established. We should never overlook the need to identify with the mother what she wants from the assessment and intervention package: immediate protection, information, support, advocacy etc (Carlson, 1997).

Workers need to establish whether the mother:

- Acknowledges the abuse/threats used/level of minimisation of abuse.
- Sees the violence escalating.
- Recognises the impact of the abuse on her.
- Recognises the impact on each of the children.
- Has help seeking and survival strategies already employed.
- Is misusing alcohol/drugs.
- Has mental health problems/personality disorder.
- Has medical/health problems requiring treatment.
- Has access to appropriate support and coping strategies.
- Is responsive to intervention/support.
- Will provide details about the frequency/intensity/duration/forms of abuse.
- Has made any previous attempts to leave.
- Has taken any action to minimise impact on children – positive and negative.

Questions to ask

Magen et al. (2000) set out some useful questions to raise with the mother:

- How often do you and your partner argue about things?
- What do you argue about (money, housekeeping, sex, the children, pregnancy, etc)?
- Who usually has the last word in the arguments?
- Has the argument ever turned into a physical fight?
- In general, how afraid are you of your partner?
- Has your partner ever threatened you/himself/the children?
- Have you ever left your partner, or tried to leave, because of domestic violence?
- In general, where are the children when the violence takes place?
- How do they react to the violence?
- Does he ever prevent you from leaving home, using the telephone, seeking family/friends or otherwise control your activities?
- Does he destroy your possessions or hurt things you value, including pets?
- Is he ever under the influence of drugs and/or alcohol when he abuses you?
- Has he ever forced you to have sex?
- Has he ever threatened or used a weapon against you?
- Have you ever contacted the police because of domestic violence?
- Have you ever gone to a doctor or a hospital due to injuries caused by your partner?
- Have you ever asked for help to stop the abuse before?
- Would you like help with safety planning for you and your children?
- How can we help you in dealing with the domestic violence and the impact of this for you and the children?
- How has living with the domestic violence impacted on your thoughts and feelings as a mother?
- What is the effect of your partner's control of the money and decisions made to provide for the child's needs?
- What has living with violence encouraged in your child's behaviours and interactions with you and others?

Within the Northern Ireland model for assessing domestic violence (2001), the following areas are identified:

- How does conflict between you usually get resolved?
- What happens when you and your partner disagree and your partner wants to get his/her way?
- How are things at home?
- How are arguments settled?
- How are decisions reached?
- What happens when you argue/disagree?
- Do you feel/have you ever felt frightened by your partner?
- Do you feel/have you ever felt threatened/ intimidated by your partner?
- What happens when your partner gets angry?
- Does your partner shout at you? Call you names?, Put you down?
- Has your partner ever physically hurt you? How, what happened?
- Has your partner ever thrown things?
- Has your partner ever destroyed things you care about?
- Has your partner ever forced you to have sex or engage in any sexual activities against your will?
- What do the children do when (any of the above) is happening?
- How do the children feel when (any of the above) is happening?

Physical assaults
Has your partner:

- Ever used physical force against you?
- Pushed, slapped, shoved, kicked, shaken or grabbed you?
- Restrained you, blocked your way, pinned you down?
- Hit you? Open hand? Closed hand? Struck you with an object?
- Assaulted you physically in any other way?
- Lifted a hand as if to hit you?
- Implied that he had 'connections' that could be used against you?

Sexual assaults
Has your partner:

- Pressured you for sex when you did not want it? If so, describe how.
- Manipulated or coerced you into sex at a time or in a way that you did not want?
- Injured you sexually? Forced you to have unsafe sex? Prevented you from using birth control?
- Humiliated you in a sexual manner?

Emotional and psychological assaults

Has your partner:

- Threatened violence against you, the children, other, themselves?
- Used violence against the children, family, friends, or others?
- Attacked property or pets, stalked, harassed or intimidated you in any other way?
- Humiliated you? What names or putdowns does your partner use against you?
- Attempted to isolate you, attempted to control your time, activities and friends? Does he follow you, listen to telephone calls, or open mail?
- Kept you away from your family, friends or neighbours?
- Prevented you from going somewhere you wanted to go?
- Threatened to hurt someone you love?
- Threatened to make you lose your job?
- Threatened to have you committed to a mental institution?
- Threatened to 'out' you as a lesbian to your work, family, other?
- Threatened suicide if you did not comply with something?

Economic coercion
Has your partner:

- Tried to control you through money? How?
- Prevented you from getting a job?
- Spent joint assets without consultation?
- Intentionally not contributed to supporting the family?
- Taken your money or pay cheque?
- Who makes the financial decisions? How are the finances handled?
- Have you been kept from access to money?

Use of children to control partner
Has your partner:

- Threatened or used violence against the children in order to make you comply?
- Used the children against you? How?
- Used your children to keep track of what you are doing when he is away?
- Used the children to relay messages, needs and demands to you?
- Threatened to harm the children? Interfered with the care of the children?
- Made the children watch or participate in you being abused? Made the children spy on you?
- Threatened to report you to social services? Have you reported your partner?

- Does your partner sabotage your parenting? Obstruct visitation?

Assessing the impact of the abuse on the woman

- physical health impact
- emotional impact
- degree of perpetrator's control
- barriers to leaving

Assess the impact of the abuse on parenting

- How does the violence affect the woman's parenting of the children?
- How does the perpetrator's violent behaviour and abuse affect their parenting role?
- Areas of concern regarding parenting skills of perpetrators.

Assessing the results of the woman's past help-seeking

- extended family
- supports outside the family
- police
- court
- leaving
- counselling or medical intervention
- social services
- women's aid
- counselling for perpetrator

(Bell and McGovern, 2003)

An alternative framework of questions was developed by *www.ddvf.org/training/cascade.htm (8.10.02)*.

The questions below are not in any specific order. They are categorised in order to provide patterns and connections of the abusive behaviour. They all relate to the Duluth Model. Workers need to bear in mind that the mother may well deny, minimise, justify or blame others for the abuse. Many of the questions are presumptive stances, which often enables and gives the woman permission to speak up if you have made the assumption that violence/abuse is occurring and what's more you are not shocked or surprised. This allows the interview to be conducted with an air of normality and provides the mother with immediate validation and support.

Using emotional abuse and isolation:

- What sort of mind games does your partner play?
- How does he make you feel when with your friends/family etc.?
- Does he ever try to humiliate you or put you down?

- Do you think you're going crazy?
- What sort of a wife/mother are you?
- How often do you go out with your friends? Do you ever go out alone?
- Is he jealous of you? If so how do you know? What does he say to you about how you behave with his friends, strangers or other men?
- Does he tell you what to say, where to go, who to see and what to read?
- Has he ever called you stupid and if so how often?

Minimising, denying and blaming her for the abuse

- Does he ever play down what happened?
- Does he talk about the violence/incident?
- Does he tell you that you nag him, ignore him etc. and therefore that is why he got 'upset' with you?
- If he ever hurts you, does he help you afterwards, perhaps taking you to the hospital/GP? What does he tell you to say?
- What does he tell you to say to your friends and family?

Using children

- How does he make you feel about the children?
- What is his relationship with them?
- When do the children talk to him?
- Does he take the children out to play? If so do you go with them?
- If there is an argument, where are the children?
- What do you tell the children after an incident?
- How does he behave, what does he say and think after an incident?
- Do the children like him? If so, when? Does he ever scare them? If so how?

Using male privilege

- What does he expect you to do in the house?
- Does he ever get upset if you have not done the housework?
- How often does he help out in the house?
- Who makes the Big Decisions in the relationship?
- What happens when you disagree?
- Do you feel you have to obey him?
- Does he ever change his mind and accept your opinion?
- Has he got very fixed ideas about the roles of men and women?

- What is his attitude to women? – To his mother – sister other family members –
- Does he enjoy/read/watch pornography?
- What does he tell his children about male and female responsibilities?

Using economic abuse

- Do you work? If so what does he think about it?
- Who controls the finances?
- Who buys the groceries?
- Do you know what he spends his money on?
- Does he know what you buy and what it costs?
- Do you ever have to use the children to ease the situation?

Using coercion and threats

- Does he ever threaten to hurt you?
- Does he do this in front of others?
- Has he ever threatened to leave you?
- Has he ever threatened to commit suicide?
- Has he talked about going to the Social Services and having the children taken into care?
- After a violent incident has he ever convinced you to drop charges?
- Has he ever made you do anything against your will?
- Have you ever had to do anything illegal because he asked you?
- Do you believe that his threats to hurt you are real?

Using intimidation

- What body language does he use to let you know he is unhappy/upset with you?
- Which gesture does he use when you are out with friends?
- Does he smash things up and destroy property in the house? If so what does he attack?
- Has he ever used a weapon or something like a weapon (table lamp, cricket bat, telephone cable, cigarettes, tv) to threaten to hurt you?
- Does he ever tell you that you are ugly and unattractive?
- What does he say about your relationship and its future?
- What does he ask you about your previous relationships?

Using animals to intimidate and threaten

- If you have pets, what are they, and how long have you had them? Have you had many pets? Find out their ages and history.

- How does he treat his pets?
- Has he ever hurt an animal? If so how and what happened afterwards?
- What is he like with the children's pets?
- How do you feel about the pets?

Using physical abuse or violence

- Has he ever slapped you on the face?
- Has he ever punched you? If so, which part of your body?
- Where did the first assault take place and when?
- How often does he scream and shout at you?
- What is he like when he hurts you? Cool, calm, excited, loud?
- Do you ever know when he's going to hurt you? What are the signs?
- What do you do, when you think/know he's going to be violent? i.e. Do you go to bed, go into the children's room, lock yourself in the bathroom, go outside, try and calm him down, etc?
- Has he ever hurt you so much that you had to go to hospital?
- Has he ever used a weapon? If so what?
- What is his pattern of hurting you? Or does it seem completely random?
- Where are the children and what do they do when he's hurting you?
- Can you put up with his violence on a regular basis?
- Is it better between you both after the violence has occurred?

Using sexual violence

- Has he ever demanded to have sex with you when you did not want to?
- What do you feel about sex and your intimate relationship with your partner?
- Has he encouraged you to watch pornography and act out what you see, but you did not really want to?
- Has he ever used anything to hurt you when having sex?
- Can you talk to friends or family? Do they know what's going on?
- Has he ever mentioned your sex life in front of his friends or family?
- Has he ever made you do anything in front of his friends that you did not want to do?
- Has he ever scared you when you were having sex?
- Has it always been like this?

The mother-perpetrator relationship

Aims of the intervention

The belief that women who do not leave the relationship renders them unable to protect themselves or the children is unfair and insensitive. Our intervention must thus be directed at enabling the mother to retake control of her life, to offer her realistic choices while accepting the decisions are hers alone and are always valid in her particular situation. No woman should be condemned for her decision to return to the abuser. It can take a very long time for a woman to acquire the confidence to choose a different life for herself and her children. Even if the mother returns to the violent situation, she is unlikely to forget the information and care given and over time may help her to escape the violence.

Workers need to consider how to maintain the children at home with their mother. To this end, we should be considering ways of excluding the abuser from the home and making the woman safe. This may involve the use of Section 17 money to change locks, getting a telephone, or paying the fares to and from a refuge.

The key question: 'should I stay or should I go?'

The majority of the literature concentrates almost exclusively on the question for the mother: 'should I stay or should I go?' This important question is central to how professionals view the mother and her ability to protect herself and the children. Indeed, there appears to have been a sea change over the years. In the 1980s there was evidence that workers persuaded women to remain with their violent partners for the sake of the children, even threatening to remove the children if they left. In the 1990s this was replaced with an equally rigid attitude that the women must get rid of the man, without any recognition of how difficult this might be.

The emphasis on asking why women leave or stay in violent relationships also reveals the extent to which such action is framed in terms of individual choice and agency rather than as a product of social forces and the unequal distribution of power. It would be far more acceptable to ask the abuser to leave rather than social care agencies mirroring the expectation that the women themselves should leave and will be judged if they do not.

We need to guard against the belief that leaving the abusive partner is the best and only safety plan. We know of the relentless retaliation from the abuser after separation and research confirms that the domestic violence tends to escalate when women leave the relationship (Campbell, 1992). For the children of abused women, separation does not end the violence and uncertainty with which they lived.

Despite the impact of domestic violence professionals still find it difficult to understand why women do not leave violent partners, or why they return to a violent relationship once they have left. Women are faced with complex issues and choices when they are making decisions about their relationships and whether to leave violent partners. For each woman these decisions are dependent on her own particular circumstances and needs, and the particular circumstances and needs of her children, such as:

- Fear and perceived dangers (she is frightened he'll find her; she's frightened he'll kill her; she's frightened he'll keep the children/harm the children etc.).
- Access to money, housing and other resources.
- The (anticipated, actual or previous) reactions or responses of family and friends.
- The (anticipated, actual or previous) reactions or responses from the agencies she may need to approach.
- Her own perception of the stigma, and blame she may have attributed to herself.
- The (anticipated, actual or previous) reactions or responses of her children.
- The emotional attachment to her partner, despite how irrational this may appear to others.
- Additional oppressions she may already experience or be frightened of: being discriminated as a result of being a black woman; woman with disabilities (physical, hearing or mental health issues); being an older woman or a very young woman; being a woman who is lesbian; a woman who is a part of a travelling community; or being a woman who is working in the sex industry; drug user or alcohol user.

The process of seeking help is fraught with difficulties and workers need to bear in mind that on average women will be physically assaulted 35 times before they seek help and contact at least 10 agencies before they receive an appropriate, supportive response.

Choice and Lamke (1997) suggested that the stay/leave decisions revolve around two central questions:

1. Will I be better off (outside of this relationship)? She will consider the level of relationship satisfaction, her perception of irretrievable investments and her quality of alternatives. If she thinks that her quality of life will be better outside the relationship then she can proceed to the second question:
2. Can I do it (exit successfully)? This often relates to the personal resources and barriers for the woman and inevitably relate to feelings of self-concept and feelings of control.

Obstacles to departure

There are a number of important reasons why women do not, or cannot, leave their violent partners:

- **Practical difficulties in effecting separation:** the process of leaving an abusive relationship typically involves numerous stressors, such as relocation, economic instability, legal actions, child custody issues, disruption of social networks, and possibly difficulties involved in terminating the emotional connection with the abuser. Many are concerned that their children will suffer in a more tangible way if they leave, because women leaving this way often face equal or increased poverty. They have to weigh up the financial options against the health and housing needs of the family and the security of the protection which they can offer to their children and themselves (Pryke and Thomas, 1998). If the woman either inaccurately perceives or minimises the difficulties that she may experience throughout this process, she is more likely to be unprepared for the feelings that may arise during these struggles and may be more vulnerable to making a sudden decision to return to the abuser. This can include the fact that most friends and relations are well known to the violent partner and this can make escape more difficult. It is difficult to cut oneself off from those whose support you would be reliant on. The violent partner is often very jealous and possessive and may well be aware of potential refuges that she would seek in a crisis. Even access to Women's Aid refuges is problematic both from an access point of view as well as the increasing difficulties of

retaining their location secretive. The impact on the children of such a move is a critical consideration for many mothers: disrupting their peer group, schooling, daily routines and similar considerations. This has to be balanced against the child protection issues involved. The victim may also be struggling with feelings of selfishness and self-blame for the situation. The difficulties involved in custody battles often follow especially if there have been no prior concerns about the perpetrator's relationship with the children. Women are petrified about professional intervention especially if there are concerns about actual or likely harm to the children. Sadly professional intervention frequently relegates the mother's needs to secondary, often disrupting the most important person for the children (Calder, Peake and Rose, 2001).

- **Fear of retaliation:** this is a significant factor in preventing victims of domestic violence from leaving violent relationships. Their partners have threatened to kill them and their children if they leave. The perpetrator may even have threatened to commit suicide if they leave. This emotional blackmail taps into the women's overriding sense of responsibility for her partner's mental state and frightens her. The fear of escalating violence following separation is grounded in fact and that there is evidence that the most dangerous time for an abused women follows attempted separation or its discussion (Glass, 1995). If a woman has left, taking her children with her, and she is found by her partner, she believes that they will all be at greater risk of harm than previously, which thought terrifies her. In Browne's (1987) study, 98% of the homicide group and 90% of the comparison group believed that their abuser could and would kill them, and were convinced that leaving would not prevent this. Some women feel they can mitigate their children's safety far more effectively by staying in their relationship. Abuse of children is far more likely when the marriage is dissolving, the couple has separated and the abuser is highly committed to continued dominance and control of the mother and children. Women are often terrorised by threats to abduct their children and this is driven by a desire to hurt the mother.
- **The effects of severe abuse on the victim:** Finn (1985) reported that battered women are

more likely to use passive coping strategies and avoid situations rather than confront them and some withdraw into social isolation. They lose control over their lives and this increases stress and so a cycle develops with a gradual decrease in personal coping ability and self-esteem. In many cases of domestic violence, the victim becomes dependent on the abuser and develops a state of learned helplessness with her violent situation. The main effect of severe abuse is to heighten the victim's level of perceived helplessness. The vulnerability factors of some of the women, who formed relationships with men who became abusive, will still be present when those relationships became worse. While their vulnerability in terms of their background or lack of family or social support does not cause them to be abused, and cannot be held responsible for their partner's violence, it does play a role in increasing the likelihood that they will be victimised and also makes it more likely that they will be disadvantaged in terms of escape routes. If anything, their lack of self-esteem and feelings of helplessness will have been increased by their experience of violence in a relationship and they will feel even less able than previously to take effective action and leave. Many women report that the abusers often give them hope that they can change. Social pressure from family/friends/church to stay together further challenges women who are also taught to take the major responsibility for the success or failure of the relationships. For those women who had strong social and family support the experience of trying to placate and subdue a jealous partner will often have meant weakening those links, becoming socially isolated and estranged from the family, resulting in a loss of confidence and increasing dependence on the violent partner, who demands that he is the main, if not the sole, recipient of devotion and attention. The dynamics of abuse create a vicious cycle in which the victim becomes increasingly more passive and frightened and the abuser more able to control and terrorise; the more she gives up her external sources of support, the easier it becomes for the abuser to dominate her (Motz, 2001).

- **Rule of optimism:** Martin et al. (2000) established that battered women's perceptions of personal risk for returning to the abuser were biased by unrealistic optimism; specifically personal risk was estimated as significantly lower than the risk of most battered women and was not correlated with actual risk factors. Furthermore, the magnitude of the optimistic bias was significantly greater among women expressing high certainty about their decision to leave than among women who expressed less certainty. Violent relationship unfolds over time and is only with glorious hindsight that a pattern can be seen. Often the first incident takes place after some commitment has been made to the relationship, women are shocked and want to forget and men plead forgiveness. It is not usually a clear signal that the relationship should end. They may have feelings for their partner who aren't easily changed by a one-off incident or they may cope by minimising the abuse. Some women may choose to stay and attempt to change the situation. Many care for their abuser when he is not being abusive. Hoff (1990) noted that many women stay because of embedded social norms about women, violence, marriage and the family. Many love the abuser and simply want the violence to stop and thus they cling to a belief that they can change. This can lead to them giving the abuser the benefit of the doubt that it will not recur. Hope that the violence will stop probably explains the usually extended time which elapses between the start of the violence and the woman seeking help. An additional obstacle lies in the loss of familiarity if they leave: changing houses, jobs, schools, friends etc. They thus pay a potentially high price of extricating themselves from the abusive situation. The mother may still love or have feelings for the abuser and the violent relationship may be the only intimate relationship she has and this is a lot to lose. It is because of this that this type of violence is so unique. Many will have been threatened with death if they leave. In these circumstances, staying may seem the only way to protect herself from something worse.

Ferraro and Johnson (1983) describe the process of victimisation as experienced by the women. Within this they identified six categories of rationalisation:

- **The appeal to the salvation truth:** this is grounded in a woman's desires to be of service to others. Abused husbands are viewed as deeply troubled, perhaps sick, individuals dependent upon their wives nurturance for survival. Battered women place their own safety and happiness below their commitment to saving their man from whatever malady they perceive as the source of his problems.

- **The denial of the victimiser:** women perceive battering as an event beyond the control of both spouses, and blame it on an external force. The violence is judged situational and temporary, because it is linked to unusual circumstances or a sickness which can be cured. Pressures at work, the loss of a job or legal problems are all situations which battered women assume as the causes of their partner's violence.

- **The denial of injury:** is often associated with no requirement to seek medical treatment, allowing routines to return to normal quickly. The denial of the injury does not mean that the woman does not feel any pain. They know they are hurt, but define it as tolerable or normal.

- **The denial of victimisation:** victims often blame themselves for the violence, thereby neutralising the responsibility of the spouse.

- **The denial of options:** comprises two options: practical options and emotional options. Practical options such as alternative housing, source of income, and protection from the abuser are clearly limited for many mothers and there is a variance as to how these obstacles are overcome. The denial of emotional options imposes still further restrictions. Battered women may feel that no-one else can provide intimacy and companionship. While physical beatings are painful and dangerous, the prospect of a lonely, celibate existence is often too frightening to risk. It is not uncommon for the women to express their belief that their abuser is the only man they could love, thus severely limiting their opportunities to discover new, more supportive relationships.

- **The appeal to higher loyalties:** involves enduring battering for the sake of some higher commitment, such as religious. They may feel that any marriage is better than no marriage as far as her children are concerned.

Ferraro and Johnson (1983) then went on to identify a series of catalysts for redefining the abuse:

- **A change in the level of violence:** the severity of the abuse is linked to the women's decision to leave. What is important is the sudden change in the relative level of violence.

- **A change in resources:** the availability of shelters and new legislation produce new resources for women.

- **A change in the relationship:** Walker (1979) in discussing the series of stages of a battering relationship, notes that violent incidents are usually followed by periods of remorse and solitude. Such phases deepen the emotional bonds and make rejection of the abuser more difficult. But as battering progresses, periods of remorse may shorten, or disappear, eliminating the basis for maintaining a positive outlook on the marriage. After a number of episodes of violence, a man may realise that his victim will not retaliate or escape and thus feel no need to express remorse. Extended periods devoid of kindness or love may alter a woman's feelings toward her partner so much so that she eventually begins to define herself as a victim of abuse.

- **Despair:** changes in the relationship may result in a loss of hope that things will get better, When hope is destroyed and replaced by despair, rationalisations of violence may give way to the recognition of victimisation.

- **A change in the visibility of violence:** battering in private is degrading, but battering in public is humiliating for it is a statement of subordination and powerlessness. Having others witness abuse may create intolerable feelings of shame which undermine prior rationalisations.

- **External definitions of the relationship:** a change in visibility is usually accomplished by the interjection of external definitions of abuse – either professionals, family or friends. When they respond with unqualified support for the victim and condemnation of the abuser, their definitions can provide a powerful catalyst toward victimisation.

The decision to leave: a framework for analysis

Rothery et al. (1999) developed an ecological framework for considering the decision-making processes of women facing the tough choice about whether to stay or whether to go. In doing so, they noted that pressure to make quick, clear decisions to leave an abusive relationship is frequently present because the safety and well-being of women and their children are at stake. The need for urgent decisions is inconsistent with the model of change which acknowledges that change takes time.

Demand factors: the effects of demands depend on their severity balanced against other factors. Sometimes demand factors motivate action, while under other conditions they are disorganising or debilitating. Being treated violently is debilitating, immobilising and traumatising. It can include an emotional and psychological 'numbing' as well as a desire to avoid confronting the experience of having been assaulted and its implications (Herman, 1992). Violence contributes to depression, low self-esteem and lowered sense of personal control – impacts that would also impede effective decision-making.

Resource factors: there are different types of support.

- *Concrete/instrumental resources:* it is clear that finances and housing are critical factors affecting the ability to become independent. Employment and child care are other examples. Gondolf and Fisher (1998) found that women were more likely to live independently if they were economically self-sufficient. If women are unable to afford housing, they may return to an abusive relationship out of economic desperation. The type of abuse women experienced is significant in predicting the choice they made.
- *Informational/emotional resources:* are critical as they provide validation of a cognitive position comprising three beliefs: the abuse is real; the abuse is not acceptable; and something can be done about it. Resources such as counselling, education about abuse, and books can support women and affect how they perceive or evaluate their experience. Professionals can also help by offering insight into relationship dynamics, especially difficult boundary issues with the perpetrator.

Mediating factors: as important as demands and resources are, a woman's perception and interpretation of those realities are also powerful in shaping how she responds to them. Whilst many wonder why the obvious decision to leave eludes many women, there is a considerable interest in the role of beliefs affecting readiness to change. Readiness is a function of empowerment and clarifying values. It is important to view the decision to leave as a process rather than an event. Change is seldom linear and tidy. It is often characterised by uncertain progress and frequent re-acquaintance with old problems before a clear sense of direction is acquired and new options firmly established. Thus, when women appear to vacillate regarding their relationship to abusive partners, they are engaged in a normal change process. There are a number of indicators around their readiness to change: labelling the abuse accurately and recognising the seriousness of what they have been subjected to; accepting that their partner is unlikely to change; challenging the socialising belief that the women must sacrifice their own needs and keep the family unit together; stop blaming themselves for the violence; clarifying their own rights for safety and respect; and embracing their own strengths, competence and resources.

What the research tells us

- Scott-Gliba et al. (1995) reported on the experience of being victimised along with the coping strategies and the psychological and social consequences of such violence. Few women left their partner after the first episode of violence; most women remained with their partner although they described feeling hurt, angry and confused by the incident. Psychological mechanisms that allowed the woman to remain in the relationship after the first incident included justifying and excusing the behaviour or denying the experience and carrying on without referring to the incident again. As the violence progressed, half of women repeatedly threatened to leave. Most women continued to rationalise the violence by denying the abuser personal responsibility for his actions. Most women felt pity for them and saw them as pathetic in spite of their attempts to terrorise them. Most of the women felt controlled by their partners in all aspects of their daily lives and thus they found it impossible to make decisions which ran counter to the wishes of their partner's. As a result of the repeated violence and abuse the women lacked the assertiveness or sense of personal efficacy to enable them to break away. Frequently the increased recognition of the danger they and their children faced led to their decision to leave, often coupled with a concern that their behaviour was spiralling out of control. Nearly half of the women in the sample has remained in the abusive relationship for up to 10 years before escaping to the refuge. They cited a number of reasons why they could not have left earlier: economic dependence on their partner; unable to take risks with their children's future; the lack of an identifiable safe place to go; fear of retaliation by the partner; a belief that the partner would track them down and a sense of loyalty in which the women felt responsible for protecting and shielding her partner.

- Hilbert and Hilbert (1984) suggested that about half of all women who leave an abusive relationship ultimately re-unite with the abuser. The reasons reported for this have largely focused on social and demographical variables, such as having limited economic resources or a long-standing relationship with the abuser. It may also be because women are at considerably higher risk of further violence if she stays away. What Martin et al. (2000) found was that women appeared to underestimate their vulnerability to returning to an abusive relationship. Whilst many victims of domestic violence are relatively knowledgeable about the prevalence of repetitive abuse dynamics in the general population, they struggle to apply that information to their own situation.
- Griffing et al. (2002) reported on the self-identified reasons why survivors of domestic violence return to abusive relationships. A significant percentage of women (73.3%) reported that emotional attachment played an influential role in their decision to do so. This was especially true if they were leaving for the first time. It is likely that workers need to forewarn women that these feelings may emerge as a mechanism for reducing feelings of shame and secrecy as well as giving permission for them to express them.

Studies have shown that from 43% (Okun, 1988) to 70.5% (Strube and Barbour, 1984) of battered women eventually end their relationships with violent partners. These women and their children often flee a residence shared by a violent husband and must reconstruct their life for their family as single parents.

McGibbon et al. (1989) reported that women consistently say that they want the abuse to cease and having a group of professionals who at the very least have more power than her in relation to the man could give the women greater support, resources and leverage than she has when trying to act alone. However, many women report that the cavalier attitude of social workers leads to responses experienced by the mother as punitive and alienating.

O'Hagan (1994) clearly articulated that a crisis is triggered by hazardous events, which may be a single extreme episode or a series of stressful difficulties. In both instances, the person's normal coping mechanisms are disturbed, necessitating the use of emergency behaviours. If these emergency measures do not help, the person moves into the active stage of crisis, characterised by bewilderment and extreme anxiety. Workers need to take this into account when approaching any situation involving domestic violence.

- On average a woman will return to her violent partner seven times before leaving him (Cooper, 1992). Despite this, women victims of domestic violence are ten times more likely than non-battered women to report child abuse (Stark et al., 1979).
- What is clear from the available material is that the prospect of leaving an abusive relationship can be as frightening as the prospect of staying.

Browne and Herbert (1997) identified a number of reasons for remaining in the violent relationship:

- Learned helplessness.
- Negative self-concept.
- Economic hardship of leaving is too great.
- Cannot cope alone.
- Difficulties getting a job and meeting new friends.
- Children need a father.
- Divorcees are stigmatised.
- Husband will reform.

There are a number of characteristics of women who seek refuge and then return:

- Married women (four times more likely to return).
- Fewer previous separations.
- Intermittent and less severe violence.
- Little contact with the police.
- No involvement with child protection agencies.
- Unemployed or economically dependent.
- Shorter stays in refuges.
- Initial intention to return.

Implications of choosing to stay or return: living with (acceptable) risk?

It is important that we are clear about the implications of the woman taking such a decision: will this instigate child protection procedures and/or legal proceedings? Rose and Savage (1999) considered such issues in relation to child sexual abuse and the considerations are exportable to domestic violence given the high co-existence (Calder, 2003b). There are strong parallels for women whose partners are violent and/or sexually abusive. Both issues are complex and may remain unspoken for some time by all members of the family. Uncovering the whole picture involves unpacking complex layers of secrets and distorted messages. Women living in situations of violence may be immobilised through shock or fear. Remaining in a violent relationship does not mean that the care and protection of the children is not a primary concern. Pressure to leave by professionals places the onus of responsibility for the violence on the woman. If a woman is not able to leave, she faces the possibility of being labelled a bad parent and as colluding with the violence. Thus begins the 'fight' with professionals at a time when information and time to assimilate this is most needed. Women in violent relationships may be acutely aware that leaving does not mean the violence will cease. Thus they may be constantly weighing up the safety issues on a day-to-day basis. Women will be employing complex strategies to avoid violence in the home. Mental ill health, alcohol and drug misuse can be as a result of ongoing violence. Women need to know they are not being judged by workers for the actions of their partners. If we can agree that the children's protection is a shared and primary concern it is more likely that a creative solution can be found. In order for this to begin we need to believe women are not helpless victims.

They identified that it is possible for some women to continue their relationship, in some shape or form, with partners who are Schedule 1 offenders and in doing so could also remain carers of their children. In working with women whose choice conflicted with the traditional notion of a 'good mother', their own assumptions were challenged. Their belief remained that, if the 'risk' presented by the continuing relationship between the women and their partners could be managed safely for the children, then this was the best outcome for them in the longer term.

Experience has shown that, if women feel pressurised into ending their relationships, the outcomes for the children are rarely satisfactory and many continue the relationship, but in a clandestine way. The primary task for workers therefore is to be clear about their own values and judgements about women who make this decision, and develop strategies for themselves that prevent these negatively impacting on a carer.

In working with women whose choice conflicted with the traditional notion of a 'good mother', our own assumptions are often challenged. However, the belief should remain that, if the 'risk' presented by the continuing relationship between the women and their partners could be managed safely for the children, then this should be the best outcome for them in the longer term. The women who attended their group (Rose and Savage, 1999) said that they knew within the first five minutes of meeting their social worker that they were considered 'bad' parents. This then got in the way of establishing any positive working relationship. The pattern that most commonly developed was a 'fight' to maintain the positions taken in those first five minutes. For us, the starting point had to be that women make a choice, at a time when they are under great stress. This choice need not mean that the children cannot be made safe. All the women they worked with were clear that they shared the desire for their children to be safe. The most significant confusion lay in workers failing to define with the women what the risk was, or where the differing responsibilities lay for managing that. The use of the child protection and court system only served to reinforce the position of fight rather than adding clarity to the plan. The task for the worker, therefore, becomes one of establishing what is understood of the risk at each stage and considering the options available to support its effective management. This inevitably separates out different responsibilities for different strategies. For example, at the start of the process, it may be that relatively little is known about an offender's individual cycle of abuse, relationships within the family, etc., so it may be that the only safe option is for the alleged offender to leave the household. The responsibility to do this should lie primarily with the offender, rather than asking the woman to tell him to go. An agreement may then be formed about how the relationship is to be maintained for the woman in a way that is safe for the child.

As the process moved on, the task of the worker is to provide the information and support that the woman needs to make and develop an informed decision about the risk, in much the same way as workers themselves need to. It may be, therefore, that a programme of work will look at understanding the cycle of offending, defining sexual abuse, and considering the effects on the victim. In providing the information and exploring the issues in a general way, the women were quick to make the connections with their own situations and re-evaluate their position. Having achieved this, the task then changes to considering practical, emotional and cognitive ways that the woman can manage the risk. Alongside this, there has to be an acknowledgement of the enormity of the task and an identification both of what the women can and cannot be responsible for, and what support may be available. For example, it may be acknowledged that, in continuing a relationship, the child may need someone outside the family who is established as an alternative safe adult as well as their mum.

For some of the women, a major change occurred when they were able to let go of the need to be responsible for changing their partner's behaviour. Their role then changed to expecting to be informed and involved in any on-going treatment programmes. The final, and additional, task for the worker is to assess whether the suggested management of the risk is safe for the children. If it isn't, where this process has been followed, it should be relatively easy to be clear about why not. Overall, the worker needs to ensure that they work at the pace of the woman and slow down the demands they make on her to make final choices about her future. Alongside this, we should avoid making assumptions about the women themselves or their capacity to change.

If the mother does wish to return to the abuser, we need to agree a plan of action with her including:

- Curling up into a ball to protect the abdomen and the head when the violence is taking place.
- Remove any potential weapons from the home.
- Shout and scream loudly and continuously while being hit.
- Teach the children to dial 999 if they feel unsafe.

- Encourage her to plan ahead for what she will do the next time the violence erupts.

Assessment areas

- Workers need to identify clearly the range of abusive behaviour perceived by the mother within the adult relationship (physical, sexual, psychological, spiritual, emotional and the range and frequency of threats made to her or the children).
- Did it ever escalate in seriousness and frequency? The best predictor of future violence is a history of violence.
- Establish: did he ever tell you that if you left him he would make sure you were never with anyone else?
- Did he ever threaten to kill you?
- Does he own a gun?
- Does he feel comfortable about using a gun?
- Has he used a gun before in any way?
- Has he ever threatened you with a gun or other weapon before?
- How impulsive is he?
- In the relationship did he act without thinking through the consequences?
- Was he predictable or unpredictable in his behaviour?
- Does he have a history of depression – sadness, feelings of worthlessness and depression when combined with a history of abusive behaviour can increase the risk of future violence?
- What does your partner feel he has to lose if he hurts you now? The less he has to lose, the greater the personal risk to the mother and the children.
- What would you do if he found you?
- What is your safety (and escape) plan?
- Did he ever treat you as his property?
- Did he act as though he owned you?
- Has he told you he has changed? In what way? Has anyone evidenced these claims? (Dugan and Hock, 2000).
- We need to find out why she feels she must stay in the relationship.
- We need to elicit clues as to why she may go back and consider offering some support to address her needs and her vulnerability.
- We need to consider what she has done to protect herself and the child to date.
- Ask about the positive qualities of the relationship.
- Search for and identify the woman's strengths.

There is an emerging link between domestic violence and animal abuse. Ascione conducted some research in Utah with 101 women in five shelters in Utah who owned a pet in the last year and 120 pet-owning women from the community who were not experiencing domestic violence. He found that 54% of the women in shelters reported that their partner had hurt or killed a pet compared with 5% of the other women. Many women may thus delay fleeing an abusive relationship for fear of what might happen to their pets if they leave them. For a detailed discussion of the research on animal abuse and interpersonal violence, the reader is referred to Lockwood and Ascione (1998).

Arkow (2001) reported that in 2000 the Society for the Prevention of Cruelty to Animals (SPCA) surveyed a group of women in Ontario women's shelters. Some 44% had pets abused or killed by their partners, 42% had pets threatened by their partners, and 43% reported that concerns over the safety of their pets prevented them from leaving sooner. Workers thus need to screen for this co-existence and may do so by asking a series of questions:

- Do you currently have a pet?
- Has your partner ever hurt or killed one of your pets?
- Has your partner ever threatened to hurt or kill one of your pets?
- Has any member of your family ever hurt or killed one of your pets?
- Did concern over your pet's welfare keep you from leaving the abuser sooner?

The Battered Partner Shelter Survey (Ascione and Weber, 1997) was developed specifically for assessing animal abuse in domestic violence situations, and thus might potentially be administered to a mother when in a safe placement. It is reproduced as Figure 5.6.

Once a response to the mother's immediate needs have been made, it is important to make an assessment of safety. Conducting a safety assessment may help her think through her situation and make decisions about what she needs to do. A full safety assessment should consider:

- The history of abuse of the woman and her children, considering any escalation in frequency, intensity or severity.
- Whether the abuser is making verbal threats, being physically violent, threatening to harm or abduct the children, physically harming the children, frightening or threatening friends or neighbours, or presenting as frequently intoxicated and more abusive in this state.
- The woman's current fear of her situation and her beliefs about her immediate danger.
- Self-harm or suicide threats or attempt by the woman.
- The woman's attempts to get help during the last twelve months.
- The availability of emotional support and practical support from friends and family (Scottish Executive, 2003).

The child

Introductory comments

Children's contact and experience of violence towards their mothers can take a range of forms. They may witness or overhear violence; intervene to protect their mother, either directly, risking assault to themselves, or indirectly by seeking help from a friend, relative or neighbour or contacting an agency for help. They may be encouraged to support and/or participate in the abuse and degradation of their mother. Children may be directly abused either in a situation where the man openly and deliberately rules the household, terrorising everyone, or secretly and separately from the abuse of their mother. Research suggests that domestic violence is the most common context for child abuse, and that the violent male is the most typical child abuser. Unfortunately child protection systems target women, not men, and often concentrate on the woman's ability to parent and protect, rather than focusing on the impact of the man's behaviour on his victims.

Aims of the intervention

Intervention needs to ensure that we provide services for children which meet their individually assessed needs. We need to assume that they may have been directly abused as well as living with the domestic violence. We need to help them start to come to terms with their experiences of domestic violence and to enable them to overcome any practical or emotional difficulties they have developed. Workers need to advise children who disclose that the violence is not their fault; that it is right to seek help for the problem; and that they are not responsible for stopping the violence.

Figure 5.6: Battered Partner Shelter Survey (BPSS)/Pet Maltreatment Survey
F. R. Ascione & C. Weber © 1995

**BATTERED PARTNER SHELTER SURVEY
(BPSS)/PET MALTREATMENT SURVEY**
F. R. Ascione & C. Weber © 1995

Participant Code: _____

DEMOGRAPHIC INFORMATION

1. Age _____   2. Marital Status _____
                                    (married, divorced, single)

3. Children living with you now (*if any*):
                     Boys   *Girls*
Ages: _____   _____
             _____   _____
             _____   _____
             _____   _____

4. Education (last grade of school completed)   Partner _____
    (e.g., 11 – junior in high school, 13 – one year of college   Self _____

5. Employment (job title or description)
    (e.g., homemaker, unemployed, mechanic, teacher, . . .)
    Partner _____
    Self _____

6. Ethnic group (self)
    Caucasian _____   Hispanic _____   Asian _____
    Native American _____   Black American _____   Other (specify) _____

PETS IN THE HOME

7. Do you now have a pet animal or animals?
    No _____   Yes _____
    If Yes, kind(s) Dog _____   Cat _____   Bird _____   Other (specify) _____

8. Have you had a pet animal or animals *in the past 12 months*?
    No _____   Yes _____
    If Yes, kind(s) Dog _____   Cat _____   Bird _____   Other (specify) _____

9. Do your pets receive *regular* veterinary care?   No _____   Yes _____

10. Have your pets ever received *emergency* veterinary care?   No _____   Yes _____

11. Do your pets have most of their vaccinations?   No _____   Yes _____

12. How many pets have you had in the last 5 years _____

WHAT HAPPENED TO THE PETS

13. Has *your partner* helped care for your pets?
    No _____   Yes _____
    Please describe the type of care provided

14. Has your *partner* ever *THREATENED* to hurt or kill one of your pets?
    No _____   Yes _____
    PLEASE DESCRIBE THE INCIDENT(S) IN AS MUCH DETAIL AS POSSIBLE:

Figure 5.6: *Continued*

15. How did you feel after the pet was THREATENED?
    _____ Numb, I was extremely upset but felt nothing.
    _____ Terrible, I felt very upset.
    _____ Mildly upset.
    _____ It didn't bother me at all.

16. Were you relieved that the pet was being threatened and not you?
    No _____   Yes _____

17. Has *your partner* ever ACTUALLY HURT or KILLED one of your pets?
    No _____   Yes _____
    PLEASE DESCRIBE THE INCIDENT(S) IN AS MUCH DETAIL AS YOU ARE ABLE:

18. How did you feel after the pet was hurt or killed?
    _____ Numb, I was extremely upset but felt nothing.
    _____ Terrible, I felt very upset.
    _____ Mildly upset.
    _____ It didn't bother me at all.

19. Were you relieved that the pet was being threatened and not you?
    No _____   Yes _____

20. How close were you to the pet that was abused or threatened?
    _____ Not at all close
    _____ Liked but not very close
    _____ Very close; source of comfort and friendship

21. Did anyone call the police of humane society (or animal control) to report the animal abuse?
    No _____   Yes _____
    If yes, who made the call? _____
    Who was called? Police _____   Humane Society or Animal Control _____
    What was their response? _____

22. Have *you* ever hurt or killed one of your pets?
    No _____   Yes _____
    PLEASE DESCRIBE THE INCIDENT(S) IN AS MUCH DETAIL AS POSSIBLE:

If your *children* are all either younger than 5 or older than 17,
OR
if you have children between 5 and 17, but no child participating in the study, please complete the next four
questions (#23, 24, 25, and 26)
If not applicable, skip questions #23, 24, 25, and 26; continue with #27.

23. Do your children help care for your pets?
    No _____   Yes _____
    Please describe the type of care given.

24. Have any of your children ever *OBSERVED* pet abuse in the home?
    No _____   Yes _____

Figure 5.6: *Continued*

25. Have any of your *children* ever hurt or killed one of your pets?
    No _____   Yes _____
    PLEASE DESCRIBE THE INCIDENT(S) IN AS MUCH DETAIL AS POSSIBLE:

    How long ago did this occur? _____
    Sex and age of the child when this happened: Boy _____   Girl _____
                                                                    _____ years old

26. What was done at the time of the incident?
    _____ Nothing
    _____ Child was reprimanded
    _____ Authorities were called
    _____ Other (please describe)

27. Did concern over your pet's welfare keep you from coming to this shelter sooner than now?
    No _____   Yes _____   Please explain:

28. During the time together with your current partner have you noticed any *change* in your partner's
    willingness to use violence against you or your children?
    _____ No, he has NEVER been violent.
    _____ No, he has ALWAYS been violent.
    _____ Yes, he has become LESS violent.
    _____ Yes, he has become MORE violent.

29. Have you noticed any *change* in your partner's willingness to threaten or abuse your pet?
    _____ No, he has NEVER threatened or hurt our pet(s).
    _____ No, he has ALWAYS threatened or hurt our pet(s).
    _____ Yes, he has become LESS threatening and abusive toward pets.
    _____ Yes, he has become MORE threatening and abusive toward pets.

30. Are there any other pet or animal-related issues you would like to describe (e.g. treatment of farm animals,
    wild animals, strays)?
    No _____   Yes _____
    PLEASE DESCRIBE THE INCIDENT(S) IN AS MUCH DETAIL AS POSSIBLE:

Workers need to deal with the immediate consequences of their intervention with children and take some time trying to observe and make sense of a range of puzzling and difficult to manage behaviour. It is important to observe and note whether the child is very passive perhaps having learned to keep quiet for self-preservation. Are they compliant to all or most of what is requested of them? Are they able to exhibit any feelings or have they become adept at suppressing them? Are they excessively independent given their age? This may reflect a degree of self-sufficiency on the part of the child or even a dissociation from what is going on around them.

Assumptions when approaching work with children

It is important to make certain assumptions when approaching any assessment work with children. These are that the child is more than the sum of their experience of domestic violence, and that the domestic violence is the problem, not the child.

We thus need to get to know children in a holistic sense. We also need to ground our work informed by knowledge about domestic violence as it affects children's lives. Part of this is an understanding that many children will struggle to talk about what they experienced at home as they see that as their daily existence. Workers need to observe and listen carefully in order to try and understand what the child inside is really feeling. Children's behaviour is the best indicator of their feelings. It is also important to see the child as an expert on their own life, capable of making choices.

Principles for working with children and young people

- Build a relationship in which the child feels respected, safe and supported.
- Acknowledge the child's need to trust an adult before expressing their fears and feelings.
- Children may not be able to express feelings; note change in behaviour as an indicator.
- Respect the child's right to privacy and confidentiality/explain any exceptions and always check information sharing.
- Make sure the child understands you.
- Ensure the child feels in control of the process.
- Reflect the child's words.
- Don't shy away from difficult issues.
- Do not minimise the abuse.
- Don't be judgmental.
- Don't be shocked or show surprise by what they are saying.
- Emphasise that it is not the victim's fault or responsibility.
- Let them know that they are not the only child who has experienced violence.
- A child may want to hear adults affirm what is right and wrong rather than providing solutions or rescuing them.
- Recognise the child's other context, school friends, neighbours, other family members, and family pets.

Responding to children: some guidelines

We need to give the child a measure of control in the interviews so we do not replicate the control of the abuser and work at their pace, often achievable through multiple interviews (Sudermann and Jaffe, 1999).

- If you feel the child may disclose ensure environment is quiet, safe, secure and private.

- Listen without judging, expressing shock or making critical comments.
- We need to assess the child on an individual basis. Observing the child's verbal and non-verbal behaviour, taking into account the child's own resilience and coping skills.
- Consider the developmental age of the child. What is appropriate for a teenager would not be appropriate for a three year old.
- Listen and advise accordingly.
- Assure confidentiality with regard to known agency procedures.
- Always believe the child, and ensure that the child's wishes and views are taken into account at all times.
- Discuss any fears the child may have around the domestic violence, and how they can deal with it.
- Emphasise that domestic violence is not the norm. It is unacceptable.
- Ensure the child knows they are not to blame for the violence.
- There is never an excuse for the violence.
- Make the child aware where the responsibility for the violence lay – with the violent partner.
- Encourage the child to communicate with the mother. (Some mothers stay living with the violence because they believe it is in the best interest of the child – however, this may not be what the child wants in reality).
- Encourage the child to break the silence and speak – possibly to members of the extended family, thus enabling them to support the child.
- Encourage any hobbies or strengths that the child may have for example; schoolwork, swimming etc in which they may find a release, thus helping to build their self-esteem, and encourage the child to be resilient.
- Encourage friendships with their peers.
- Determine what action you can take.
  - Help the child to make a 'safety plan'
  - Provide the child with clear information – e.g.: Childline, Women's Aid advice line, police, social services department.
  - With the agreement of the child (if they are of an age to understand) consider approaching the mother, discreetly, and without alerting her partner, to offer support and advice.
- Depending on what the child tells you, and your assessment of the child's needs, refer to other agencies e.g. NSPCC, domestic violence support groups, counselling services, and psychological services.

Obstacles to engagement and corrective strategies

Many children will have been instilled with a code of secrecy by the perpetrator and they may have been reprimanded for discussing 'family business' with 'outsiders' or threatened with being rejected by the family if they disclose. In trying to overcome this barrier, workers are well advised to enlist the assistance of their mother and to equip themselves with as much information as they can gather about the abuse to reassure the child that they are not 'telling' (Arroya and Eth, 1995). It is also sensible to allow the child some measure of control of the interview as otherwise we may be recreating the control they experienced from the abuser. This involves such detail as where they sit, how they want to communicate (drawing, conversation etc), and the content and order of any sessions. Do not expect spontaneous disclosure or detail from a child as they will normally need to test the worker out and determine whether they can trust them or not. They may also struggle to change their coping style instructed of them by the abuser and may worry about any consequences of disclosure for their mother. Some may be embarrassed about their family behaviour.

Assessment areas

There is no blanket approach that we can take to assess how each child will be affected, and this often leads to a great deal of confusion for professionals, particularly where children in the same family are affected in different ways, and to different degrees. However, just as with their mothers, children will often respond best to direct questions asked in a way that is most appropriate to each child's age and stage of development. In planning the assessment process with each child practitioners will need to assess and collect information on the following in order to assess the impact of domestic violence and the level of risked posed to the child.

Assessment questions

Figure 5.7 sets out a useful framework for elements of the assesment. In order to generate the necessary information the following additional questions may be useful:

● What have they experienced? In what ways has this threatened the child? We need to remember that their recollection may be affected by shock, time skew, etc., yet their subjective view of whether they thought it was life-threatening is an important cue as to how they need to be helped.
● Are they aware of any family secrets? Children may continue to withhold information to protect themselves and their parents; or alternatively they are aware of secrets held within the family and they are unaware of the detail. This can lead to them becoming anxious, confused and they may internalise the feeling that something is not right.
● Is there any evidence of dissociation?
● Is there any evidence that child abuse co-exists?
● What changes have there been, in any aspects, since the child's home circumstances changed? Is there any decrease in their behaviour problems, levels of vigilance, etc., and has there been any further details about what they may have experienced when the domestic violence was taking place.
● Establish the presence of violence in the child's life – covering access to violence on television, video, internet, school bullying etc.

When assessing the impact of the violence on the children, workers should ask the following questions (of the mother):

Physical injuries and health impact:

● What kinds of health issues does the child have?
● Medical problems due to domestic violence?
● Changes to the child's health in recent months?

Psychological and emotional impact:

● Have there been any emotional changes?
● Any withdrawal, depression, increased irritability, anxiety, and nightmares?
● Are you aware of any suicidal thoughts or acts of self-harm by the child?

Behavioural problems:

● Have your children had behaviour problems in the family, school, and peer relationships?
● Have your children used physical force or threats of physical force against you or others?
● Are the children dealing with anger in ways that disturb you?

Social problems:

● Have your children suffered social disruptions due to domestic violence; moves, changing

Figure 5.7: Assessment considerations with children (Rowsell, 2003)

Element of assessment	Considerations, benefits, potential outcomes
Assess child's level of awareness, and feelings about, violence and abuse being perpetrated upon its mother.	Will enable practitioner to identify how much the child is aware of the abuse, the level of risk that is being experienced by the child, and begin to raise issues of responsibility. Will enable practitioner to share this with mother (and perpetrator if appropriate).
What is the quality of the child's relationship with its mother?	Will enable the practitioner to gain greater insight into the impact of abuse on each child, and how this is impacting the child's relationship with its mother. Will identify key areas of concern, and present practitioner with a clear pathway in any therapeutic work to be undertaken.
What is the quality of the child's relationship with the perpetrator?	Will help the practitioner identify whether the child holds the perpetrator responsible for the abuse, whether the child is being manipulated by the perpetrator, and whether on-going contact with the child is likely to be safe or not.
What is the quality of the child's relationship with each of its siblings?	Will identify strengths and weaknesses in sibling dynamics, and identify clear areas of therapeutic work that will need to be undertaken with each child.
What role does the child play within its family, and has it been given or assumed responsibilities that are beyond its years or capabilities?	Will identify where the child is being asked to assume too much responsibility, and will assist practitioner to make judgements on how this is impacting upon the child's health and developmental needs. Will again identify how therapeutic work may be used to deconstruct unhealthy family dynamics.
Assessment of child's general health and all areas of development, including assessment of: physical health and growth and development; social skills and ability to function in different social situations; intellectual and educational development, including understanding, school attendance, performance and the way the child presents; emotional development including child's moods, confidence levels, self-esteem etc. This will need to be done by liaising with health, education and other relevant agencies.	Will enable practitioner to consider total impact, identify problem areas, and identify differences between siblings. Will also ensure that other professionals are alive to the issues and the risks, and direct resources appropriately.
What strategies does the child have in place to cope/use to cope?	Will assist to identify impact of abuse on child, and identify level of risks being taken by the child in order to cope with violence and abuse.
What support networks are in place for the child, what other significant adults are involved in the child's life?	Will identify to what degree each child has support networks, whether these are appropriate or not, whether these can be extended or tapped into by the practitioner. Will also provide practitioner with a greater picture as others may be approached and asked to assist with the assessment process.

(Rowsell, 2003)

schools, isolation from friends, loss of family members?

● Problems with social relationships with peers, family, other adults?
● Problems in learning?

Workers may ask these of the child about particular incidents:

● What happens when your mum and dad (as appropriate to the family) disagree?
● What does your dad do when he gets angry?
● Did you ever hear or see your dad hurting your mum? What did you do?
● Who do you talk to about things that make you happy?
● What kinds of things make you scared or angry?
● Do you worry about your mum and dad?
● When was the most recent incident of abuse or violence?
● Ask, if the child feels able, to give details about the incident.
● Was their mother locked in a room or prevented from leaving the house? Ask if this has ever happened before.
● Ask if alcohol or substance abuse was ever involved?
● Was any weapon used or threatened to be used? Ask if a weapon has been used or threatened before.
● Where were the child's siblings during the incident?
● Have the police ever come to their house before? And what happened?
● What do they do when the violence is happening? Do they try to intervene? What happens?
  (adapted from Mullender and Morley, 1994)
● To what extent do they blame themselves for the violence and the failure to prevent it? The way children respond to, make sense of, and assign responsibility for domestic violence is dependent upon a range of factors including:
  ○ Whether the child themselves has overheard, witnessed or been directly abused by the man.
  ○ Whether the man is encouraging the child to take his side or take part in the abuse of their mother or siblings.
  ○ The type of abuse experienced by themselves, their siblings and their mothers.
  ○ Its severity, frequency, and duration.
  ○ The quality of the child's relationship with its mother, and its siblings. (This is even

more significant where the child is being singled out, encouraged to participate in the abuse of their mother or siblings, or being overtly or covertly abused by the man directly).

○ The child's own use of positive or negative resources and coping strategies and the implications of these (e.g. some children will throw themselves into school, others will truant).
○ Whether the child is given opportunities to disclose, and is subsequently believed by those important to them.
○ How family members and significant others respond to the violence and abuse.
○ The quality of the child's support networks and those available to their mother.
○ The quality, speed and sensitivity of agency interventions (if any have occurred).
○ The level of tolerance within the child's community to domestic violence and child abuse in general.

Information from other professionals

Children who have experienced domestic violence often 'play out' aspects of their experiences given the opportunity. Small children from two (or even younger) up to five or six, who choose to play violent, destructive, frightening games, with whatever play materials are available are describing their terrifying reality. The key is to take your time in this area: watch the child play, observe their covert monitoring of all the carer says: there may and should be many clues.

Children who live with violence bring many of their fears and concerns into the classroom. They may be reflected in their behaviour, in anxiety about being separated from their mother, and in difficulties with concentration and distractibility. Many show symptoms associated with post-traumatic stress disorder. They often have a distrust of the world as they see it as being hostile and unpredictable. They may have tremendous difficulty trusting or being comforted by a teacher. They may also have problems getting on with their peers. They may be aggressive and misread social cues from others.

Peer relationships are linked to key developmental accomplishments such as psycho-social adjustment in the middle years of childhood. We need to assess what opportunities there have been for the child developing any kind of peer relationships and then whether any were successful. Were they reluctant to bring friends home because of what they might witness? Were they insular to prevent disclosing the abuse they were witnessing? Were they prevented from networking by the abuser as part of their controlling tactics? Did they have any opportunity to get involved in any sports, recreational activities or community activities?

Assessing the impact of domestic violence on children

In considering a child's exposure to violence, it is essential to understand the multiplicity of experiences and responses that are determined by the interplay of factors both within the child and in their surroundings, which include:

- **Characteristics of the violence itself:** that is, the child's relationship to the perpetrator and victim, proximity to the incident, response to the caregivers.
- **The developmental phase of the child who is exposed:** that is, the status of emotional and cognitive resources for mediating anxiety associated with objective and fantasised dangers.
- **The familial and community context of the violent incident:** that is, is the incident isolated and unusual or part of a chronic pattern of experience of daily life?
- Recognition of, and sustained responses to, the possible effects of the child's exposure to violence by family members, school personnel and community institutions.

Although there is tremendous variation among children, at the acute moment of the traumatic event, common observations have been recorded including:

- Intense longing for the presence of and concern about the safety of primary caregivers.
- Disbelief and denial of the outcome or occurrence of the event.
- Revival of memories and much talk about previous losses, injuries, fights witnessed.
- Emotional lability that can range from isolation of affects to tearfulness to rage and replaying of events with ideas that might have altered the real outcome and developing intervention fantasies.
- Attribution of blame to those not involved in the violent event (e.g. with social institutions) and attendant, at times explosive, anger.

- Revelling in the excitement of the action with bravado (e.g. talk of the types of weapons used).
- Acceptance indifference (e.g. if it happens all the time then it is no big deal).

How the child makes sense of what they witnessed and the particular meanings that emerge over time as a child begins to digest and to organise fragments of traumatic memory are embedded in a developmental framework. A child's responses to traumatic events thus reflect both the unique characteristics of the event, as well as the particular phase-specific concerns, anxieties, and fears that are stimulated and made more complicated by what the child has witnessed. Children whose development is already fragile, and who have not attained the optimal potential of each developmental phase, are at greatest risk. The essential consideration for a worker is how we assess and then balance risks and adversity with protective mechanisms and resilience to try and understand a child's response to their experiences. The following summary reports on some of the findings available to us that relate to the field of domestic violence.

Resilience

Humphreys (2001) pointed out that care is needed in not assuming how children will react to living with domestic violence. While there is an increased likelihood of problems for children living with domestic violence, not all children are negatively affected. Jaffe et al. (1990) have been careful to point out that there are children in their studies who show few negative symptoms and a higher level of compliance than those in comparative groups. A study by Hughes and Luke (1998) of 58 women and their eldest children living at a women's refuge found that 60% of children were found to be not distressed or only mildly distressed. Each situation therefore needs to be assessed individually to explore safety strategies that are in place for both women and children, the effects in all areas of the child's life, and the networks that may support children, including those at school and in the extended family.

   Wraith (1994) has noted that adults have a powerful need to deny children's hurt. By only focusing on the presenting behaviours rather than the origins of them, then we may believe that children are more resilient than they actually are.

The nature and extent of the consequences on individual children may be moderated or mediated by a variety of factors including: the age of the child; children's coping strategies and individual resiliency; gender; the nature, severity and frequency of the violence; whether the pattern of violence has ceased; attendant environmental factors, such as the mother's ability to parent, and the availability of legal and social protection are important in exacerbating or reducing effects (Hughes, 1988). Garmezy (1983) argued that the individual attributes of the child, social support somewhere within the family system and social support from figures outside the family are critical in resilience developing within children. In one investigation of protective factors positive child temperament feelings of self-worth, school competence and a positive relationship with the mother all serve to mitigate the effects of domestic violence. Grotberg (1997) suggested that children's resilience and ability to cope in the face of aversive circumstances can be encouraged by supportive interactions with adults which specifically foster autonomy, the development of personal communication skills, and a sense that they are important and will be listened to and taken seriously.

Hughes et al. (2001) argued that since few studies have specifically examined resilience in children exposed to domestic violence, we can import some of the findings from the literature on physically abused children and resilience. In doing so they identified the following:

- **Individual level:** young age e.g. under five and adolescence; birth complications, physical and mental disabilities and difficult child behaviours.
- **Interactional level:** abuse from the parent to the child.
- **Community level:** low socio-economic status, living in a single-parent household, and receiving public assistance.
- **Societal level:** approval of violence, approval of corporal punishment and unequal power distribution of power in society and in the family.

Mullender et al. (2002) identified two key issues as critical to children's ability to cope:

- **Being listened to and taken seriously as participants in the domestic violence situation:** many wanted to be told what was going on by the adults in their lives, both family members and professional helpers, rather than being kept in the dark as a way of protecting them from upsetting knowledge. People needed to explain to them in ways in which they could understand and then become involved.
- **Being able to be actively involved in finding solutions and in helping to make decisions:** children and young people wanted to talk and be listened to as well as being consulted about possible options and then having their advice considered. Most of the children and young people reported that their attempts to contribute had often gone unnoticed and McGee (2000) also found evidence of this sense of powerlessness.

Hague et al. (2002) reported on their examination of children's understandings and coping strategies with regard to domestic violence. They found that children use wide-ranging and often creative coping strategies even though the protective factors that experts have identified as being essential for positive coping are often absent in cases of domestic violence. The only protective factor which was often present was secure attachment to the mother, even though this may be conflicted. It follows therefore that coping with domestic violence may be additionally difficult when compared with other adverse situations since key protective factors are either absent or compromised.

Mullender et al. (2002) also identified two further categories of coping strategies:

- **Immediate:** how the child or young person had coped during actual incidents of violence. These included: responses or frames of mind which had helped the child or young person deal with the actual incident; strategies to achieve safety or to summon help; ways both of supporting and being supported by siblings; and means of trying to protect their mothers and intervening in the violent situation. General short-term strategies included hiding, crying, cuddling, protecting and reassuring siblings, trying to protect mothers, telling an adult, often a relative, and getting help from the police and other agencies; and
- **Longer-term:** coping with the situation both after the event and over time: either defensive or accommodating the abuse situation by adapting to what is going on; or re-framing or overcoming the abuse so that they can move forward. This often happened when they had

grown up or left the violence and they were able to see, with some distance, that the father was responsible for the violence. Longer-term ways of coping included developing safety strategies, talking to someone, seeking help from adults and professionals, finding a safe haven, supporting mothers, sticking together with and helping siblings, and trying to be actively involved in addressing the issue. Some children used creative methods of coping such as routinely finding a quiet space somewhere for themselves in order to gather their resources and calm themselves. Others turned regularly to a trusted adult for support (maybe a grandparent) without necessarily telling the person the whole story.

Eisikovits and Winstok (2001) provided us with a very useful process model whereby a child constructs and negotiates their reality as livable in a violence-ridden environment. The process described is spiral and continuous.

Recollection: negotiating what happened. This first stage begins after the violence has occurred. The family members attempt to negotiate within the boundaries of the event to determine what happened, who did what to whom etc. The purpose of this negotiation is to arrive at an agreed-on scenario of the violent event. At this stage, partners may exaggerate, dramatise, minimise, or show indifference to the event. The child who experiences the actual occurrence and the negotiation process is learning how the collective memory is negotiated and constructed as well as how they can live with the gap between what they have witnessed and what is to be remembered.

Causality: negotiating why it happened. In this stage the negotiation moves beyond the descriptive boundaries of the event. The causes attributed to it can range from accounts related to the perpetrator's mental and emotional state (e.g. my dad came home upset from work) to mystical beliefs (e.g. he is Taurus, so he is so explosive). At this stage the participants either feel satisfied with the explanation and agree on it or adjust the explanation to the event or the event to the explanation. Throughout the child learns how to attribute causality and to adjust events and causes to each other.

Moralisation: negotiating what it means. In the third stage, the child draws the moral implications of what took place. He may judge the violent event as deserved or undeserved. This moves the child's understandings of the event

beyond its boundaries and places it in the overall value and attitudinal context of the family culture as a whole. In this way, the moral lessons the child learns from the event affect, and are affected by, the normative structure of the family context.

The way that the abuse was handled when it occurred is critical in shaping the impact on the child.

Protective mechanisms

Rutter (1985) suggested that the protective factors and behaviours which contribute to coping mechanisms include positive self-esteem, personality factors (such as being easygoing and humorous), secure attachment to the primary caregiver, and the existence of networks of personal support. Hague et al. (2002) found that the victims of domestic violence rarely had access to these protective factors and relied almost exclusively on their mother. Thus, state intervention to remove the child from the mother if there is a concern about her failure to protect can have devastating consequences for the children involved.

Given the closeness to their children, mothers can have a protective influence, buffering the effects of witnessing domestic violence. Moore and Pepler (1998) found that the strongest predictor of children's adjustment was low verbal aggression from the mother to her children. Conversely, the most troubled children were those whose mothers were both depressed and aggressive towards them (Pepler and Moore, 1995). The problem is often that abused mothers may have few resources to bring to the task of parenting. Given the myriad of additional stressors it is not surprising that some mothers fall short in providing the nurturance and support necessary for the optimal development of their children.

Schools are a potentially important protective venue for children via the provision of additional emotional and educational support which buffers some of the deleterious effects of living in a high-risk home environment and they also offer an input on violence in the home that models the prevention of the origins of such behaviour. The school may also be the right place to undertake some work with young people around relationships, particularly if we want to lessen the possibility of any inter-generational violence. It is also important to impart culture and transmit key learning skills.

The longer the domestic violence goes on, the more acute the discord, the fewer mediating influences, the worse the outcomes for children.

Protective factors specifically associated with overcoming adversity for children exposed to domestic violence include those particular to the child, the parent, and the environment. One of the characteristics associated with the child that has been associated with a lower risk of negative outcome is an age older than 5 years. Parental factors found to provide a protective function for children in families with domestic violence are parental competence and the mother's mental health. Protective factors associated with the broader environmental context include the availability and strength of social support (Hughes et al., 2001).

Risks and compounding variables

Current theories related to children's adjustment difficulties focus on the interaction of risk and protective factors in relation to development. Risk factors are those which lead directly to disorder (e.g. marital conflict) whereas protective factors operate to buffer the effects of the risk variable. Risk and protective factors may reside within individuals and/or within their environments. Davies and Cummings (1994) identified multiple risks experienced by children exposed to family violence:

- Children witnessing escalating forms of aggression from their father to their mother can be traumatised e.g. many may see attempted choking.
- Witnessing persistent violence undermines children's emotional security and their capacity to meet the demands of everyday life.
- They may suffer from chronic levels of arousal and dys-regulation (leading to high levels of emotional and behavioural reactivity when the conflict arises. Pepler et al. (2000) found that exposure to verbal aggression was the strongest predictor of adjustment difficulties, perhaps as they had become sensitised to it being a precursor to more extreme forms of behaviour.
- Children may experience daily lessons in the use of aggression and learn to mirror the aggressive strategies used by their parents. This may be in the form of modelling and imitating the aggressive behaviours they observe or it may be they learn to use disruptive behaviour to distract argumentative

parents. Jaffe et al. (1990) found that children may learn that violence is an acceptable way to resolve any family conflict, that the male members can exert physical force and power in the home.

To this we can add:

- Witnessing domestic violence may destroy the belief in the victim's parent's ability to protect and make life secure for the child and may force a localising of loyalty and a premature developmental stage (Dutton, 2000).
- Children may experience torn and confused loyalties, lack of trust, unnaturally good behaviour, taking on the mother's role, guilt, isolation, shame, anger, lack of confidence and fear of a repeat or return to violence (Stark et al., 1979).
- Domestic violence frequently co-exists with physical, sexual and emotional abuse and the effects of these individually and cumulatively is devastating. Straus et al. (1980) estimated that between 40–68% of children are physically involved in the domestic violence; Truesdell et al. (1986) found that between 10–30% of girls are victims of sexual abuse at the same time that their mothers are enduring domestic violence.

These risk factors interact in a number of ways which mean that their combined effect may be many times stronger than their effect in isolation. There is an understanding from research that there is a cumulative risk – the total number of risk factors that a child has, rather than the specific risk factor – that may be the most powerful predictor of later problems. There is also very good evidence that risk status within a developmental framework has a cascading effect over time.

O'Keefe (1994) identified some vulnerability factors that exacerbated exposure to violence. They included numerous exposures, high mother–child violence, and frequent stressful life events in the child's life.

Children's sense of responsibility about the violence

It would be wrong to believe that children are merely bystanders: at an emotional level they often feel they are personally involved, either being responsible for causing the violence or having a responsibility for protecting the mother during it and assuage their father's anger. It is not uncommon for children to blame themselves for the violence or to blame themselves for not stopping it. Children under the age of eight tend to interpret events in relation to themselves and as such believe they have caused the violence (Parkinson and Humphreys, 1998). Children's sense of responsibility for causing the violence is often exacerbated by the knowledge that the event which led to the violent episode concerned them. Straus, Gelles and Steinmetz (1980) found that violence is often precipitated by arguments about the children; many children also intervene to try to protect the mother or to obtain help; even sometimes calling the ambulance or running to obtain assistance.

The ongoing work with the child: a proposed schedule

Blanchard (1999) sets out the following areas that need to be covered in our work with the young person:

- Explore (and enhance) their self-esteem.
- Explore their feelings.
- Dealing with anger.
- Getting them to tell their story: good or bad memories; time line; what are they responsible for?
- Family relationships: what do they want to inherit from both their parents? Repeat for what they would not want to inherit.
- Dealing with loss and grief.
- Coping with change.
- Making their own safety plan/net: any safety plan for the child needs to be negotiated with the mother. It is important that while the child's needs are taken into account, the mother's relationship with the child is not undermined. Safety planning is a key practical strategy that needs to be accessible, detailed and practical. Children need to know that it is neither safe nor their responsibility to intervene. Workers do need to ensure that they have access to a range of measures, including safe premises and money before committing them into the safety plan.

Review of safety planning (Rose, 2001)

Where a child is old enough they should be involved in creating a plan for their own safety (see Figures 5.8 and 5.9). The formation and review of the safety plan is an important way to

check that the woman, and where appropriate, the child, have understood what is agreed.

MacNeeley (2002) offered some useful guidance on safety planning for children. Using safety planning as a risk assessment tool involves children themselves in identifying where the risks lie in their personal communities. They can also identify what strategies they have used in the past to cope and what possible options are available for the future. She identified the following safety planning tool:

- Define areas of children's lives: identifying where they spend time (football, friends houses etc) and to map who is in their family and social circle (including how much they like being at each place).
- What typically happens in each place?
- Focus on the risk or vulnerability: on the map they have drawn.
- Define the risk, its nature and its circumstances: also identify who the risk is from.
- Identifying strategies and options: for the kinds of worrying situations they have been in or might find themselves in again.
- Specific realistic options for each child's risk area: like if they can use a mobile, and how they can identify a safe adult in particular settings. Encourage the child to talk through their risk situation and the various options they have identified.
- Learning new skills: get them to spot the nearest phone box or how a child might draw attention to themselves in a time of crisis.
- Sharing their knowledge: with their mother. If the mother does not recognise the risk to the child, then you can take her through the same process.

Special circumstances: assessing domestic violence in pregnancy

Issues raised in pregnancy

Many women are repeatedly raped by partners, and a significant number of women will become pregnant as a consequence of sexual violence. Without any doubt women will then have to engage with a whole range of difficult issues in relation to their pregnancy, and the child that they have conceived and given birth to, will be a constant reminder of their abuse. Professionals will need to find a way of creating time, and space for women to talk about their experiences

Figure 5.8: Safety plan with child (Rose, 2001)

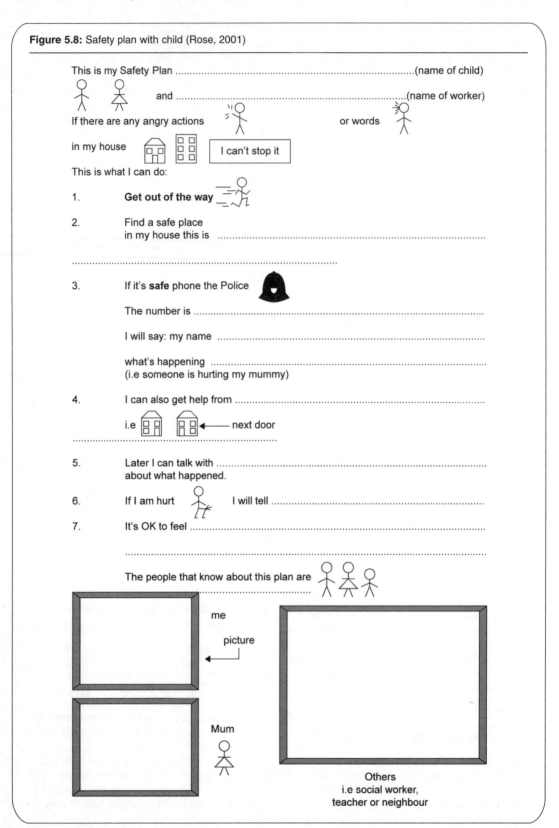

Figure 5.9: Safety plan with young people (Rose, 2001)

This plan records how to keep _____ safe.
You have the right to be safe and cared for in a safe place. ☐ agree
Violent words or actions at home are not your fault. ☐ agree
You cannot stop the violence. ☐ agree
To protect yourself you can break rules, like: say no, shout, kick and scream if you need help,
also: _____
The best thing you can do when there is violence at home is to get out of the way. ☐ agree

To be safe I can do things:
1. **Get out of the room where the violence is occurring**.
   The room/place in may house where I feel safe is _____
   There is a lock on the door.   yes ☐ no ☐
   or I could go to _____

2. The nearest phone is _____
   If it is safe I can phone 999, ask for the police. I will need to say; my name _____
   my home address _____
   what's happening ie _____

3. The people I can trust in an emergency are _____
   A code word so they know I need help is _____

4. My brothers and sisters
       have a safety plan too that I know   yes ☐ no ☐
       know my safety plan   yes ☐ no ☐

5. If we have to leave the house I would like to go to _____
   I have a bag of things that are important to me at (friends/relatives house) _____

6. If I am hurt I will tell (including phone numbers) _____
   If my Mum is hurt I will tell (including phone numbers) _____

7. I can talk about how I feel with (including phone numbers) _____
   The people that know this plan are:
       Safe carer _____
       Safe relative/friend _____
       Teacher _____
       Social worker _____
       Others _____

I can't stop the violence, I can do these things to help keep safe. ☐ agree

Signed _____ Date _____
Safe carer _____ Date _____
Worker _____ Date _____

---

of rape, and feelings towards their child, without making the assumption that she will not be able to effectively mother, or pose any greater risk.

Physical and sexual abuse during pregnancy induces stress in the pregnant women and if the abuse is severe or prolonged, maternal levels of the stress hormone cortisol are raised. This can lead to poor foetal growth which in turn can lead in subsequent development to adult diseases such as hypertension, diabetes, psychiatric disorders such as schizophrenia and depression and heart disease (Barker, 1994).

Whilst all women are vulnerable to domestic violence, being pregnant or having small children has been acknowledged as a particular risk factor (Amaro et al., 1990; Gazmararian, 1996; McFarlane et al., 1992; McFarlane et al., 1998; Noel and Yam, 1992; Parker et al., 1993). Many women report that the onset of physical violence occurs during pregnancy, or where it is already a feature that it increases in frequency and severity during this time. Some men use repeated pregnancy, as a tactic to maintain power and control. After all it is very difficult to leave the abuser if you have a number of small children. Very often the abdomen becomes the focus of physical assaults during pregnancy, and some babies are miscarried, stillborn or born disabled as a result.

We also know that the incidence of domestic violence against teenagers is higher than rates for the general community (Western Australia Health Department, 1997). The problem of young unsupported parenthood is thus compounded by the additional risks of physical and sexual abuse of both the adolescent mother and newborn child. Furthermore, we know that abuse is often initiated during a first pregnancy and this period remains a time of critical importance.

Quinlivan et al. (1999) found in a study of adolescent pregnancy:

- Victims of domestic violence were significantly less likely to plan or semi-plan their pregnancy than controls and presented later for antenatal care.
- Drug use, drinking alcohol and the use of non-prescription drugs was significantly higher among the victims of domestic violence. It could be that substance abuse was providing an escape for them from an abusive home environment.
- Victims of domestic violence reported social isolation and homelessness as well as discontinued contact from the father of their child. These factors combined with increased rates of major psychosocial disorders leaves the mother vulnerable as a new mother. Failure to adequately address major psychosocial disorders can result in increased maternal perceptions of behavioural difficulties in the newborn, disrupt parenting and infant bonding and may result in abnormalities of child development.
- Teenage mothers experiencing domestic violence had significantly higher rates of genital tract infection and Pap smear abnormalities compared to control mothers. Anaemia was also a major problem.
- They were also significantly more likely to be diagnosed with puerperal sepsis, postnatal depression and acute situational crises and poor mother-crafting skills, often in combination.

- Newborn children often had smaller head circumferences. Leading causes of neo-natal morbidity included poor weight gain, jaundice, suspected sepsis requiring treatment and irritability/possible withdrawal syndrome.

Screening for domestic violence

Pregnancy and birth are events which provide opportunities to reach isolated families who become more visible to services during this time. The antenatal period provides an opportunity for more systematic risk analysis to be undertaken and services provided. It is important therefore that direct questions (supported by women) be put to women presenting for antenatal care to reflect these statistics and to try and demonstrate concern for their health and safety. Pregnancy represents a very vulnerable time for women – sometimes just talking about such problems can institute changes. These may include:

- In the last year has anyone at home hit, kicked, punched or otherwise hurt you?
- In the last year has anyone at home often put you down, humiliated you or tried to control what you can do?
- In the last year has anyone at home threatened to hurt you?
- Would you like any help with this now?

Who can we share this information with? We have to be mindful that the mother will probably fear that an admission of family violence will result in the infant being placed away from their care and thus acts as a powerful disincentive to raise the issues.

Impact of domestic violence on the unborn baby

Babies in utero can be amazingly protected, but disasters do still occur. Domestic violence features among the causes of such poor outcomes. We often do not know how often, because more often than not, we do not ask. It is often very difficult to ask a grieving mother coming to terms with a tragedy, whether there was domestic violence in the pregnancy.

Domestic violence also impacts on obstetric outcomes in a number of insidious ways. Low birth weight (with the high additional health risks this entails), miscarriage, abortion and stillbirth are all associated with violence during pregnancy. Women who are subject to domestic violence are admitted to hospital more frequently than others during pregnancy. Webster et al. (1994) demonstrated that they were much more likely to be prescribed medication during pregnancy and the incidence of asthma and epilepsy was higher among this group. They were more likely to use tobacco, alcohol, minor tranquillisers and non-prescription pharmaceuticals which added to a tendency to present later and for less antenatal care and with it potential short and long-term health problems for the baby and themselves. The long-term health effects of violence against women can include gastrointestinal diseases, particularly irritable bowel syndrome, migraine and chronic headache, multiple somatic conditions, recurrent pelvic and abdominal pain as well as the depression and mental health problems and other mental disorders, eating disorders, substance abuse and sexual and relationship difficulties which are more commonly acknowledged (Lydiard and Falsetti, 1999).

For a core assessment schedule for unborn babies the reader is referred to Calder (2003c).

The mother–child relationship

Introductory comments

The abuse of power within families harms not just the individual women, children and young people involved, but the fabric of the mother–child relationship. Through the orchestration of power, perpetrators actively disrupt and undermine this relationship. Disconnection as we know is at the heart of trauma. Where children have lived with the violence, the tactics of violence and abuse employed by the perpetrator of that violence such as verbal abuse, criticism and putdowns commonly reported by women as some of the most damaging aspects of the abuse have been actively used to shape the young person's view of their mother, and of her capacities. We need to remember this when considering our interventions. We need to help break the secrecy about the violence in a way that allows the mother and her offspring to debrief together about the abuse they have endured and re-connect around stories of strength and survival.

Attitudes towards mothers vacillate between resentment and extreme loyalty. Some children

appreciate their mother's efforts to protect them and see the injustice of the violence meted out to their mother. Others struggle to understand why they have remained with the abuser for so long and may be angry that they did not leave them earlier. Children may be resentful of the lack of responsiveness from the mother yet there may be some limited understanding about how emotionally exhausted the mother may be. There is growing support for the view that children react more to the stress their mothers are under than to the violence itself (Thoburn et al., 1995).

While it is important not to overestimate the ability of mothers to care for their children, when they are themselves recovering from trauma, there is a very real danger in assuming that only workers represent the interests of children adequately. We need to ask what it is that women are doing to keep their children safe and healthy.

Children may look to their mothers for direction as to whether it is safe to talk to outsiders about what they have experienced within the home. This is important to unpick since mothers themselves rarely have a complete understanding about what the child knows about the violence. Jaffe et al. (1990) suggested that many mothers may not be aware of the high level of distress and disturbance which children experience as a result of witnessing domestic violence and considered this may be truly a reflection of the mother's emotional well-being and her coping levels.

Mothers who are abused are often relegated by the abusive partner to a power position equal to or less than that of the children in the family. One unfortunate outcome is that mothers often use physical discipline and other ineffective and negative parenting practices (e.g. lack of consistency, yelling or screaming) in an attempt to regain control over the child's acting-out. It follows therefore that we should explore with mothers strategies for re-establishing boundaries and limit-setting.

We need to explore with both the mother and the child how they may want to heal and gain some sense of direction and hope in their lives.

Where children are removed from home, then the mother will be more isolated and at a time when there is an increased risk for her own safety. Care has to be given to the decision to remove children from home as the end result could be that women are placed at greater risk of abuse and mothers are charged with the failure to protect her children.

Assessment questions

We need to assess whether the child is being aggressive to the mother and whether the abuser has encouraged the child to behave in this way. Bond (2002) reported that 17% of the callers to the Parentline Plus helpline reported that their child was being aggressive toward them. Workers need to identify the origins of the behaviour and approach their work with an attempt to maintain the mother and their children together even though this inverts the normal pattern of seeking to separate the abuser and the victim. Issues about anger management for the child may be appropriate and a period of respite may offer some breathing space for the necessary starting work to be undertaken.

We need to identify any negative interactions that may still exist within the family following the departure of the perpetrator and replace them with more appropriate ones.

If we know that the male child may identify with the aggressor in the abusive home, then we need to consider what evidence there is of domestic violence from the child toward their mother.

Is there any evidence of attachment problems? It is worth exploring this as we know that a child turns to the mother during periods of distress seeking soothing yet the mother may have been unavailable due to the abuse she was experiencing.

Maternal responses and traumatic impact

McIntosh (2002) argued that the absence of reflective parental thought impacts directly on the child's capacity to recover from the trauma they have experienced. When a child is not helped to deal with and integrate the impact of family violence, the overwhelming nature of events is often broken down into seemingly unconnected pieces. A child may be able to talk about what has happened but unable to describe bodily feelings or personal thoughts. As behaviour becomes severed from the emotions that drive it, so emotion becomes severed from the traumatic emotion that caused it. The meaning of the event then becomes based on disrupted patterns of processing and recall, leaving the child with impaired pathways for understanding aggressive and fearful information. In subsequent weeks, months and years, the child's real experience can break

through in disconnected expressions often marked by acute anxiety and fear. The results of 'trauma learning' are not easily distinguished (Perry and Pollard, 1998). Once established, the effects can be seen in breakthrough symptoms of chronic tension, arousal, numbing, avoidance and intrusive thoughts about the violence itself or a playing out of the unthinking state that was its context. With such un-integrated outcomes, the child is left with restrictions in their means for dealing with interpersonal conflict and intimacy.

Repairing the mother–child relationship

Mothers need reassurance that even though there was little they could have done to prevent their child's exposure to the violence, there is a lot they can do to help their child regain a sense of equilibrium following exposure to violence. Groves and Zuckerman (1997) set out the areas that need to be addressed with the mother to achieve this:

- **Help re-establish a sense of order and routine:** children have an additional need for routine and predictability after a traumatic event. Bedtime is key as it represents a time when the mother can help children anticipate what will happen each day. Any absences or separations from the mother are anxiety-provoking and thus require careful management.
- **Children need an explanation of the violent event:** linked to their developmental stage and should contain only as much information as necessary. They need to be reassured that it was not their fault and that it is OK to talk about the violence.
- **Parents need to respond to children's fears and worries honestly and with whatever reassurance is necessary:** we need to tell them what steps are being taken to try and guarantee their safety and this can be difficult when the mother does not believe that there will be no recurrence of the violence. There may be a place for religious and spiritual beliefs in instilling resilience in the children.

The child–perpetrator relationship

Introductory comments

The really competent abusers in domestic violence are very often the same competent child abusers. They are in absolute control at all times.

They know their victims well – and how to ensure they do not seek help. Their physical injuries are often controlled and never visible. Children may have been told to maintain the violence as a secret and this can have the alienating effect of preventing the child bringing friends to the home.

In the review of the literature on parenting by men who abuse women, Peled (2000) found that virtually nothing is known about abusive men's perceptions of their children or of their parenting role. Further, she found that we know very little about the issues that need to be considered when intervening in the relationships of abusive men and their children. While it has been found that concern about the impact on children is a useful motivator of men who use violence to begin to address their violence, more needs to be done to determine what should be required of men to contribute to the recovery of their children.

Assessment areas and questions

Once again, Chapter 4 addressed the impact of domestic violence on parenting. It is important however that we identify the questions that need to be asked to assess the child–perpetrator relationship. These may include:

- How does the violence affect the parenting of the perpetrator?
- Is the perpetrator able to take care of the child, to consider the child's best interests, to keep the child safe?
- Does the perpetrator support your parenting of the children?
- Does the perpetrator undermine your parenting or expect you to be the sole parent?
- Does the perpetrator use the children to control you?
- Does the perpetrator use physical force against the children?

Areas of concern regarding parenting skills of perpetrators:

- Lack of general knowledge about child development.
- Unwillingness to take part in parenting education programmes.
- Minimisation of the impact of the abuse on their children.
- Resistance to examining parenting behaviours and making changes.
- Resistance to learning and demonstrating alternative methods of conflict.

- Held beliefs about needing to be in control of their families.
- View the children's natural assertion as a threat to control.
- Tendency to blame behaviour problems of children on their mother.
- Difficulty in viewing the family through their children's eyes.

(Bell and McGovern, 2003)

We need to establish whether the young person feels responsible for the domestic violence or the failure to stop it.

We need to explore the child's feelings towards their father. Like sexual abuse victims, many love their father and simply want the abuse to stop and things to return to how they were before the violence became public. Ballard (1999) identified that many children have a range of feelings toward their father. They may hate, fear and feel revulsion for them. Conversely, they may be desperately anxious to love them, but find that such love is not reciprocated. Where it is they struggle to make sense of the affection shown on some occasions compared to the moody and violent behaviour on others.

We also need to establish whether there is evidence of child abuse and associated with this are the risks associated with ongoing contact. For details on how to assess the value and harm associated with any contact please refer to Chapter 6.

The siblings

- Are the siblings a source of support and comfort?
- Have they acted as a buffer to the impact of the domestic violence?
- Have they exacerbated the child's aggressive behaviour?
- Have they abused any built-in power differential?
- Does this mirror the use of power and aggression within the adult relationship?
- Did they act as a young carer? For which children?
- If so, what developmental opportunities were they denied? With what impact?

The community/extended family

Embeddedness of the mother within the local community is associated with lower levels of domestic violence (Cazenave and Straus, 1979).

This is associated with the belief that the sight and sound of domestic violence can often be detected by neighbours who live in close proximity. Berk et al. (1984) found that about 25% of the beatings were reported to the police by neighbours. Equally, the same percentage may be hesitant to report the same issue (Sigler, 1989).

Since many adult victims of domestic violence are isolated and unable to benefit from community connections, then it follows that children will be among the hardest to reach groups.

Questions to ask

We need to identify any supports available which can form part of the safety plan.

- To what extent are family members supportive of the child? If they leave and go to a relative, will the relative be protective/allow access?
- What level of risk does the relative occur?

- Does the relative pose any risk to the child?
- To what extent are they also traumatised, thus compounding the child's distress?
- Are there resources available to the child and the family in the community?
- Do social norms preclude open discussion about the domestic violence?

Summary

Any assessment requires we generate information in all the identified areas to test any hypotheses we have generated at the outset of the case. There are a number of different schedules for collecting information in domestic violence circumstances and the aim of this chapter was to try and organise the best of what we know, recognising that this will require constant revision and update as our knowledge base changes.

Chapter Six

Child Contact and Domestic Violence: Issues and Assessment Considerations

Custody and contact issues are a very important area within the larger domestic violence arena. The deleterious effects of growing up in a domestic violence setting can either be exacerbated or diminished by the court.
(Lemon, 2000)

Introduction

It is commonplace to find that children are caught up in the turbulence and in their parents' disputes over contact. Sometimes the contact difficulties are episodic and sometimes they have become chronically intractable.

There has been a tendency in the past for workers and the courts not to tackle allegations of domestic violence and to leave them in the background on the premise that they were matters affecting the adults and were not relevant to issues regarding the children. Indeed, the general principle that contact with the non-resident parent is in the interests of the child may sometimes have discouraged sufficient attention being paid to the negative effects on children living in a household where violence has occurred. It may not have been widely appreciated that violence to a partner involves a significant failure in parenting, failure to protect the child's carer and failure to protect the children emotionally (see Harold and Howarth, this volume).

It is important that social workers receive continued education on domestic violence and its impact on children, as well as the difficulties that occur during child visiting arrangements. Decisions around contact should be child-centred and related to the specific child in its present circumstances but acknowledging that the child's needs will alter over different stages of development.

In this chapter I will argue for a presumption of no contact between the offending parent and the child unless it is deemed to be in the child's best interests. This latter condition allows for each case to be examined and evaluated individually and on its own merits. In doing so there is also a danger of an individual assessment by a judge being subjective and reflecting gender biases (Kaye, 1996).

The legal position in the UK: the bedrock of the pro-contact culture

The Children Act itself makes no mention of domestic violence nor do any of the ten volumes of guidance notes accompanying it. Current research would indicate that this is a serious over sight if the best interests of the child are to be promoted. The Act does not require courts to consider the safety of the other party or of other children in the family and seems to make the assumption that all parents behave in a reasonable and caring manner, even at the point of separation or divorce. Indeed, the Children Act 1989 fails to recognize that male violence is a significant factor in marriage breakdown and that the violence does not always end with the end of the relationship.

Where parents do separate the Act also assumes that the children will invariably benefit from having continued, frequent and substantial contact with their fathers and yet in the context of a family subject to domestic violence, child contact provides a further opportunity for violence and repeat victimisation. Contact with fathers is seen as a right irrespective of the history of violence.

The Children Act 1989 makes the welfare of the child the paramount consideration when the court is considering an order for residence or contact. The Act also provides a checklist which the court must consider. This checklist does not refer specifically to the circumstance of domestic violence, although it does require the court to have regard to any harm which the child has suffered or is at risk of suffering. Such suffering could include the effects of witnessing domestic violence. However, research suggests that domestic violence is not generally taken into account when arrangements for children's contact with parents post-separation are made (Hester and Radford, 1995). The outcome of negotiations, which are given preference under the 'no order' principle, may compromise the safety of the woman or the children due to a belief by all parties and the professionals that the father 'must' have direct contact. There is also a requirement for a higher standard of proof to be made available to the court where the allegations become more serious.

Three kinds of contact are possible:

- **Indirect contact:** letters, cards and gifts and sometimes phone calls, but no face-to-face contact with the child.
- **Direct contact:** time spent with the non-resident parent, which may involve home visits.
- **Visiting or staying contact:** unsupervised visits or overnight stays, usually at the offender's home.

Further changes on family law procedures promote mediation and agreement and contribute to encouraging parental agreement with minimal delay. It also emphasizes looking towards the future when past harm is an important pointer of future risk (Calder, 2003). What is clear is that mediation is not appropriate in the majority of case where there has been domestic violence. The violence may undermine the voluntary nature of mediation and also create an extreme imbalance of power between bargaining parties.

The courts tend to have reference to the following principles involving contact applications:

- The welfare of the child is the paramount consideration and the court is concerned with the interests of the mother and the father in so far as they bear on the welfare of the child.
- It is almost always in the interests of the child whose parents are separated that they should always have contact with the parent and whom the child is not living.
- The court has power to enforce orders for contact which it should not hesitate to exercise where it judges that it will overall promote the welfare of the child to do so.
- Cases do unhappily arise in which a court is compelled to conclude that in existing circumstances an order for immediate direct contact should not be ordered because so to order would injure the welfare of the child.
- In cases in which for whatever reason direct contact cannot for the time being be ordered it is ordinarily highly desirable that there should be indirect contact so that the child grows up knowing of the love and interest of the absent

parent with whom in due course direct contact should be established.

(Re P contact: supervision, 1996, 2FLR314)

Throughout the 1990's domestic violence was rarely acknowledged by the courts as a cogent reason for denying contact (Humphreys and Thiara, 2002).

Busch and Robertson (2000) identified some deficits by the judiciary when considering issues of residency and contact in domestic violence cases:

- Physical violence was viewed a-contextually, without any reference to the array of power and control tactics which were being utilized by perpetrators. Single acts, such as punches or kicks, were evaluated from the viewpoint of (typically) male judges as relatively trivial. Judges ignored or failed to understand the fear and intimidation which abusers could invoke by actions which, to outsiders, might seem trivial or even loving, but which were, in fact, carefully coded messages reminding women of their vulnerability to further attack.
- There was little understanding of separation violence. Judges often assumed that women would be safe from further violence once they separated from their partners. The key issue for many judges was 'why doesn't she leave?'.
- Violence against a partner was typically regarded as irrelevant to custody or contact determinations. There was a view among many judges that one could be a violent spouse (even a spouse killer) but still be a good parent. Custody and contact decisions were frequently made as if a parent's violence was irrelevant to his ability to provide a physically and psychologically safe environment for children.
- Many women who gained protection orders found them to be ineffective ('just a piece of paper') as police inaction and judicial approaches commonly gave men who breached the orders no meaningful consequences. Discourses of judges and other practitioners all too often adopted perpetrator's justifications for violence, with the violence itself characterized as relationship based. Social, historical and cultural constructs which legitimized perpetrator violence were often unquestioned.

In the late 1990s, challenges to the presumption for contact began to be made in the context of domestic violence. In 1999, the Children Act Subcommittee of the Lord Chancellors Domestic Violence Advisory Board on Family Law issued a consultation paper on *'contact between children and violent parents: the question of parental contact in cases where there is domestic violence'*. The results of this consultation led to the adoption of new guidelines to be taken into account when considering issues of child contact where domestic violence is a concern. While the guidelines fell short of recommending a change to the Children Act 1989, they do provide a challenge to the automatic assumption that contact is in the best interests of the child.

The subsequent passage of the Adoption and Children Act (2002) requires courts to take into account the impact of domestic violence on a child when making contact orders. These changes will apply to applications for contact and residence, and also to all proceedings where the court applies the welfare checklist under the Children Act 1989. It is hoped that the presumption in future cases would be that contact with an abusive parent is going to have an adverse effect. In effect, domestic violence formally becomes a child protection issue for the first time. Unfortunately it does not embrace all those cases in private proceedings where unsupervised contact visits may be taking place. Lobbying on this latter point is ongoing.

As a measure of the lack of integrated thinking across government departments (Calder, 2003c; 2004) the recent consultation and subsequent report 'Making contact work' (Lord Chancellors Department, 2002) recommends for stronger and legally sanctioned measures for the enforcement of contact. This appears to be advocating a presumption of contact despite the evidence-base to the contrary which has increasingly indicated that contact does not always, or necessarily, equate with the welfare or best interests of children (Hester, 2002). This selective interpretation would not be tolerated by the judiciary if advocated or practiced by workers involved in cases where domestic violence was a feature.

The presumption of contact is clearly a rights-based approach to legislation and policy (Bailey-Harris et al., 1999). I think it is important to clarify this issue. It is the right of the child not the right of the parent and the right of the child is a qualified one which is subject to the child's best interests. In many situations it is right and appropriate that local authorities pursue

maintaining relationships where children are not living with their birth parents. However, a tension exists if the 'rights' of the parent are not assumed to be in accordance with the rights of the child. Where contact is contentious and subject to legal proceedings the reality is that children do not do the deciding, and it would be inappropriate therefore to suggest that the issue of contact is the right of the child, but more honestly, a right **for** the child. It is this right for the child both to embrace and reject the need for contact, which must be protected and promoted by the adults who are asked to act in loco parentis.

Of concern is the fact that the judicial statistics show that of 61,356 contact orders issued by the courts, only 518 cases resulted in the refusal of contact (Women's Aid, 2003). There is also evidence of contact orders being granted to schedule one offenders or offenders whose behaviours had caused sufficient concern for children's names to be added to the Child Protection Register.

At the present time an application by the offender for a contact order is probably the easiest way to track down and harass his victims. This arises either because the court discloses there whereabouts in the paperwork; the location of the court hearing or the address of the solicitor acting for her will give the offender some idea as to the area where she lives. If the offender frames their departure as having gone missing taking the children then the court may well instruct the police to find the child and may well order disclosure of the address to the court. Humphreys and Thiara (2002) found that 14 women in their sample (of 100) believed the child contact application of the offender was motivated by a desire to track her down. 41% said that they had been subjected to post-separation violence as a result of child contact arrangements. They also found that handover for contact at the mother's house was the most frequent arrangement followed by handover in a public place.

Many women receive contradictory messages from different parts of the system when they should be united in supporting primary and secondary victims of domestic violence. On the one hand the child protection intervention frequently states that their partner or ex-partner represents an ongoing risk to their children and that either separation must occur or be maintained to ensure the safety of the children. On the other hand, these same men apply for,

Figure 6.1: Special issues in contact disputes with allegations of domestic violence

Issue	Normal contact dispute	Contact dispute with allegations of abuse
Central issue	Promoting children's relationship with visiting parent; co-parenting	Safety for mother and children
Focus of court hearing	Reducing hostilities; setting schedule	Assessing lethality risk and level of violence; protection
Assessment issues	Children's stage of development, needs, preferences Parenting abilities	Impact of violence on mother and children; developmental needs Father's level of acceptance of responsibility Safety plan for mother and children Parenting abilities
Planning for the future	Contact schedule that meets needs of children	Consider suspended, supervised or no contact
Resources required	Mediation services Divorce counselling for parents and children Independent assessment/evaluation	Specialised services with assessment and knowledge and training about domestic violence Supervised contact centre Coordination of court and community services Well-informed lawyers, judges and relevant professionals

and are often granted contact with the additional problem that they continue to know where the mother lives.

Jaffe and Geffner (1998) produced a useful table (see Figure 6.1) to differentiate between the issues raised in normal contact disputes and disputes in situations of domestic violence that is helpful for all concerned in deciding the way forward.

Relevant statistics

The decision to separate or divorce does not free the victims of domestic violence from continued threats and abuse, particularly if contact is maintained through child visiting. Shepard (1992) found that 60% of women reported ongoing psychological abuse in the form of threats and intimidation, often involving mutual children, after legal intervention and counselling had taken place.

The 1999 Judicial Statistics for England and Wales show that 46,214 private law contact cases were heard by the courts in that year. 41,862 contact orders were granted. In only 1,752 cases (4%) was contact refused. The judicial statistics do not reflect the full scale of the problem. Due to the strong presumption of contact many women are advised by their solicitors that there is not much point contesting the case: they might as well agree to contact informally – even where they wanted to do so because they were afraid

their children would be abused, neglected or abducted (Women's Aid, 2002).

Metropolitan Police statistics show that between April 2000 and June 2001 there were 30,314 offences under the Protection from Harassment Act 1996 in London alone. The British Crime Survey 1998 found that about a third of stalking incidents were perpetrated by someone who was previously in an intimate relationship with the victim (Saunders, 2002).

Many family court judges insist that people going through custody and divorce cases are good people, but that they often behave badly because they are so stressed out by the pressures of the separation and court dispute. The reality is that nothing could be further from the truth (Zorza, 2001). Ptacek (1999) found that almost 80% of the male abusers have criminal records, 46% for violent offences and 39% have prior restraining orders entered against them and 15% for violating these orders within the first six months.

Dobson (2002) pointed to the disturbing statistic that since 1998 nine children have been killed by their fathers during contact visits; and according to a 1999 survey of 130 parents by the government's advisory board on family law, three-quarters of children who were ordered by the courts to have contact with abusive or violent parents suffered either sexual or physical abuse, emotional harm, neglect, or were abducted or involved in an abduction attempt. Currently only 12% of contact centres are able to offer the sort of high vigilance supervision required in cases of child abuse or domestic violence.

The risk of violence continues during separation and after divorce, raising concerns about safe visitation arrangements (Saunders, 1994). Minnesota Department of Corrections (1987) reported that almost half (47%) of battered women were victimised by an ex-spouse or friend, exceeding the percentage of those married to their abuser (44%). Leighton (1989) in a Canadian study found that a quarter of the women reported threats against their lives during custody visitations.

Research findings

Shepard (1992) examined some of the problems associated with child visiting in cases of domestic violence. She found the following results:

- Over one-third of the mothers reported that their former partners had used the following behaviours frequently or very frequently during the last six months: said negative things about them to the children; gave them angry stares or looks; withheld or were late with child support payments; threatened to hit or throw something at them; pushed, grabbed, or shoved them; put down their family or friends; took children places mothers felt were unsafe or harmful; threatened to get legal custody of the children; demanded to see the children without considering the schedules of others; slapped, hit, or punched them; made them do something humiliating or degrading; told them they were bad parents; threw, hit, or smashed something; physically restrained them; and physically attacked the sexual parts of their bodies. 29% reported that they had been physically forced to have sex and half were pressured to have sex they did not want.
- Over half of the mothers expressed concerns about the safety of their children. Over half of the mothers reported that in the last 6 months their partners had become drunk while caring for their children; 21% became drunk frequently or very frequently. 25% of the partners were reported to have driven recklessly when children were in their care.
- The men indicated that their partner had refused to let them see the children, criticised

them in front of the children, threatened to use the courts to limit visiting, and did not consult them about important decisions regarding the children. 9% reported that their partners had physically assaulted them when they had contact in relation to visiting.
- The presence of child adjustment problems was evident. Psychological abuse was related to child behaviour and anxiety problems more so than actual physical abuse experienced by their mothers.

Hester and Radford (1996) looked at the safety of child contact arrangements following divorce and separation where there had been a history of domestic violence to the mothers. They found that many professionals allowed contact between children and their fathers to take precedence over child welfare. They found that fathers commonly used contact with children as a route to further abuse the mother. Only 7 of the 53 mothers interviewed in England were able to arrange contact between fathers and the children which did not threaten their own safety and/or their children's well being. Most mothers initially wanted children to see their fathers for a variety of reasons; however, contact arrangements broke down due to the violence. There was no evidence to support claims made by many professionals interviewed that contact arrangements broke down mostly because mothers were 'hostile' to the idea of contact between fathers and children. Professionals' concerns to bring about agreed or mediated settlements in England left many mothers feeling they had been pushed into making unsafe agreements about child contact arrangements. They concluded that contact should not be presumed to be in the best interests of the child if there has been domestic violence to the mother. Indeed, they argued that 'contact should not be presumed to be in the best interests of the child where there has been domestic violence. The starting point should be the presumption of no contact. Where contact can be shown to genuinely benefit the child and pose no risk to the mother, it must be properly supervised, with due consideration given to safety matters'.

In 1997 a survey of 54 Women's Aid refuges found that:

- 67% reported cases of women being abused during contact handover
- 31% reported cases of children being physically or sexually abused during contact visits

- 31% reported incidents where court welfare officers had given women no choice but to have a joint meeting with their abuser to discuss contact arrangements
- 14% reported incidents where the contact order stated the address of the refuge
- 50% reported cases where the father, having been granted contact, failed to turn up, causing distress to the children.

(Women's Aid Federation, 2001)

In 1999 a survey of 130 abused parents found that 76% of the 148 children who were ordered by the courts to have contact with their estranged parent were said to have been abused as a result of this:

- 10% were said to have been sexually abused during contact
- 15% were physically assaulted
- 26% were abducted or involved in an abduction attempt
- 36% were neglected during contact
- 62% suffered emotional harm. Most of these children were under the age of 5.

(Radford, Sayer and AMICA, 1999)

Perhaps the most worrying finding in this report is that direct contact was slightly more likely to be ordered in cases where there were allegations of child abuse. This suggests that it is actually dangerous for women to mention abuse in private proceedings because usually this will be construed as vindictive or hostile behaviour. 30% of the women involved in the survey said they were told by the judge that domestic violence was not relevant. 39% were threatened with imprisonment for refusing to comply with a contact order and 25% were warned that residence might be granted to their abusive partner.

The Women's Aid Federation (2003) reported on family court practice with regard to domestic violence and child contact. They found that:

- Only 3% thought that appropriate measures are now being taken to ensure that these arrangements are safe.
- Only 6% believe that children who say they do not want contact with a violent parent are taken seriously.
- 46% of respondents knew of cases where a violent parent has been able to use contact proceedings to track down his former partner.
- 83% said that their young children were unlikely to disclose their abuse to a professional in a one-off interview.

Purpose of contact

The purpose of contact should be overt and abundantly clear and have the potential for benefiting the child in some way. The benefits of contact for the child include the importance of the father as one of the two parents, in the child's sense of identity and value, the role model provided by a father and the male contribution to parenting of children and its relevance to the child's perception of family life as an adult.

There are many different purposes of contact, including: the maintenance or reparation of beneficial relationships, the sharing of information and knowledge and the testing of reality for the child. There are fewer benefits associated with indirect contact although there are some: experience of continued interest by the absent parent, knowledge and information about the absent parent, keeping open the possibility of development of the relationship and the opportunity for reparation.

Risks and direct contact

There are a number of risks associated with direct contact. The overall risk is that of failing to meet or undermining the child's developmental needs or even causing emotional abuses and damage directly through contact as a consequence of contact. Specifically this includes: escalating the climate of conflict around the child which will undermine the child's general stability and sense of emotional well being. This can create a tug of loyalty and a sense of responsibility for the conflict in children which in turn impacts and effects the relationships of the child with both parents. There may also be direct abusive experiences, including emotional abuse by denigration of the child or the child's resident carer. There may be continuation of unhealthy relationships such as dominant or bullying relationships, those created by fear, bribes or emotional blackmail, by undermining the child's sense of stability and continuity by deliberately or inadvertently setting different moral standards or standards of behaviour, by little interest in the child himself or by under-stimulating or uninteresting contact. Unreliable contact allows children to be frequently let down and children forced to attend contact against their wishes is abusive (Butler-Sloss, Thorpe and Waller, 2000). There may be a continuing sense of fear by the child: either because the child has post-traumatic anxieties or symptoms which are re-aroused by the abuser, fear of violent parent by the child, an awareness of the continued sense of fear by their mother; as well as the negative impact on the child's own attitudes to violence, to forming parenting relationships and the role of fathers. Hester and Radford (1996) found that contact after separation put children who had witnessed violence to their mothers in the difficult position of feeling that they held the burden of responsibility to protect their parents. Hester and Radford found that the children often tried to minimize the harm or keep the peace by holding back information from the father or mother, mediating between the two and covering up or toning down the violence and threats of abuse.

Bancroft and Silverman (2002) reported a number of sources of risk to children from unsupervised contact:

- risk of continued or intensified undermining of the mother's authority and of mother–child relationships
- risk of rigid, authoritarian parenting
- risk of neglectful or irresponsible parenting
- risk of exposure to new threats or acts of violence toward the mother
- risk of psychological abuse and manipulation
- risk of physical or sexual abuse of the child by the offender
- risk of inconsistency in contact attendance
- risk of the child learning attitudes supportive of domestic violence
- risk of abduction
- risk of exposure to violence in the offender's new relationships.

Inverting legislation: the presumption of no contact: playing catch up with other countries

The presumption of no contact until deemed to be in the child's best interests is a clear and tough position statement to adopt. It flies in the face of legislation enshrined within the Children Act and also the principle that domestic violence of itself cannot constitute a bar to contact. Some see it as just one factor in the difficult and delicate balancing exercise of discretion. In such a risk balancing exercise, in cases of proven domestic violence the seriousness has to be weighed according to the risks involved and the impact on the child against any positive factors (if any). It would need to consider the ability of the

offending parent to recognize his past conduct, be aware of the need for change and make genuine efforts to do so. All these would need to be demonstrated with evidence rather than reliance on verbal assurances.

There is increasing consensus that there should be no contact unless it is proven that the contact offers something of benefit to the child and to the child's situation. Without the following it is clear that the balance of advantage and disadvantage tipping against contact:

- Some (preferably full) acknowledgement of the violence.
- Some acceptance (preferably full if appropriate i.e. the sole instigator of violence) of responsibility for that violence.
- Full acceptance of the inappropriateness of the violence particularly in respect of the domestic and parenting context and of the likely ill-effects on the child.
- A genuine interest in the child's welfare and full commitment to the child. i.e. a wish for contact in which he is not making the conditions.
- A wish to make reparation to the child and working towards the child recognising the inappropriateness of the violence and the attitude to and treatment of the mother and helping the child to develop appropriate values and attitudes.
- An expression of the regret and the showing of some understanding of the impact of their behaviour on their ex-partner in the past and currently.
- Indications that the parent seeking contact can reliably sustain contact in all senses.

(Butler-Sloss et al., 2000)

They suggested that without the first and sixth points above they could not see how the non-resident parent could fully support the child and playing a part in undoing the harm caused to the child and support the child's current situation and need to move on and develop healthily.

The offending parent clearly has to demonstrate that he is a fit parent to exercise contact, that he is not going to destabilise the family, and that he is not going to upset the children and harm them emotionally (Sterling, 2001).

Consequences of withholding contact

It is important to acknowledge that some consequences do arise of withholding direct contact. These include the deprivation of a relationship with the biological father; loss of opportunity to know that parent first-hand; loss of opportunity to know grandparents and other relatives on the father's side of the family; loss of that parent if the child has enjoyed a positive and meaningful relationship with him; the loss of opportunity for direct contact of the parent is able to provide positive and supportive contact; absence of the opportunity for any repair to the relationships or to the harm done; and a lessening of the likelihood the child being able to get in touch and of some form of meaningful relationship at a later stage (Butler-Sloss et al., 2000).

Creating a context for children's healing

Bancroft and Silverman (2002) identified several elements as being critical to the creation of a healing environment for children who have experienced domestic violence:

- a sense of physical and emotional safety in their current surroundings
- structure, limits and predictability
- a strong bond to the non-abusing parent
- not to feel responsible for taking care of the adults
- contact with the abusive parent
- a strong bond to their siblings.

Clearly the issue of promoting contact is a contentious one. They argue that few children prefer to stop all contact with their abusive fathers. Rather, they generally wish to be able to continue to express their love for their father, to have him know them, and to be able to tell him about key events in their lives. They may also want reassurance that he is not in overwhelming emotional distress. However, this contact must not interfere with their other healing needs, including the strengthening of the mother–child relationship.

Issues of supervised contact

The attractiveness of contact can be undermined by the hostility that children may see or sense between their parents, particularly at handover points. Workers also have to consider the potential for children to see supervised contact as something restrictive and regulating rather than safe.

There should be a second presumption that whenever there is to be any contact between children and the offending parent, it should be supervised in a safe environment and this of necessity precludes using relatives and friends of the offender as the supervising officer.

Sturge and Glaser (2000) identified several problems in deciding whether or not to promote supervised contact as a safe way of maintaining or forging some kind of relationship. The difficulties include:

- The quality of such experiences for a child (or parent) if this is continued over a long time. It is an abnormal situation, it is often disliked by the child both because of its artificiality and because of the restricted opportunities for interest, fun and stimulation within it; such arrangements often make the child and parent feel tense and ill at ease and may result in the child simply holding the parent responsible for having to put up with it. This may result in further alienation and no real benefit to the child.
- There is a lack of resources: good contact centres with good facilities and good supervision are scarce and by and large not available for long-term arrangements; it is expensive.
- It is unlikely to lead to improvements in a parents sensitivity or parenting skills or to lead to a situation where it becomes safe for the child to be alone with that parent.
- There are few situations where it might be considered if a time frame is set. It is only appropriate where the contact may be therapeutic or where change to the risk in the short-term is anticipated.

However, supervision of contact does have some purposes:

- Safety from physical and emotional harm.
- Checks on the fitness of the parent at the start of contact and/or the availability of a supervisor to support the child.
- To facilitate the management of contact so it is positive for the child.
- Support for the child to allow them to be more at ease and safe.

One study (Humphreys and Thiara, 2002) identified that in only a small number of cases was their one-to-one supervision which offered high vigilance. Aris et al. (2002) reported on their study into the experiences of men, women and children using contact centres and found that there is ambiguity regarding levels of vigilance required which could clearly compromise the safety of some women and children.

While contact should only be directed where it will actually benefit a child, there is a tendency toward supervised contact as a compromise ('cop out') rather than take the hard decision of terminating all contact.

Assessment considerations

Risk assessment procedures cannot guarantee the safety of contact but they can help in putting together an evaluation of the domestic violence which will help to inform professional practice. Risk assessments devised specifically for professionals working with women affected by domestic violence can provide invaluable information. They can be used to help in assessing whether contact should happen at all, the level of vigilance needed should contact be set up and in the development of safety plans for women and children . . . More detailed information on the effects of domestic violence on children needs to be gathered and presented to the courts . . .

(Radford, Sayer and AMICA, 1999: 33)

Because of the wide range of potential sources of harm to children from offenders, risk assessment is of necessity a process requiring careful investigation and evaluation. Because secrecy, denial and cover-up are all integral threads in the fabric of violence, validating a history of domestic violence requires sophisticated and sensitive interviewing skills, astute observation and multiple sources of data. Often evidence of a history of victimization is uncovered through small pieces of a larger puzzle (Jaffe et al., 2003).

The assessment should identify whether contact will be in the best interest of the child; whether this can be made safe for the child and mother; what individual work may help and support the child, the mother; what expectations are on the violent partner. The task of the social worker is to ensure that the **significance of any experience of domestic violence for the child informs any decision for contact.** Where the child is living with their mother, it is crucial that risks to the woman are also considered in any decisions about contact. Any risks will inevitably impinge either directly or indirectly on the child.

For social workers involved in this process or in assessing the risk to children in these circumstances, it is important to remain aware that the research evidence indicates that:

- There are strong links between domestic violence and child abuse.
- Domestic violence impacts on children both directly and indirectly. This impact can have longer term damaging effects.
- Violent men can use contact as a further opportunity to further abuse women and children.
- Violent and abusive men do not stop being abusive once a relationship ends.

Judicial considerations

Butler-Sloss et al. (2000) identified that at court hearing a contact application in which domestic violence allegations were raised should consider the conduct of both parties towards each other and towards the children, the effect of the violence on the children and the carer and the motivation of the parent seeking contact. The prospect of contact proceedings being motivated more by a determination to exercise power over a former partner and the children rather than by any desire for continuing contact should be explored. The impact on the mother is an important area to consider as the effects of the abuse on the mother may render her capacity to deal with the application very poorly.

Assessing risk

Saunders (1994) reminds us that we should assess the risks from the abuser and the victim in coming to a conclusion as to who is more likely to abuse their children and who may be most suited to meeting the children's needs. Factors that may affect the risk of abuse include:

- Parental separation: many men who abuse cling to the marital relationship after separation and continue to harass and physically abuse their partners. They may try to control their partner by using the children as 'spies' or he may lash out at the children if he views his partner and children as a single entity and feels vengeful. The children may also be exposed to more violence if either partner is a victim or offender in a new relationship. Some 50% of men have a chance of battering in a new relationship. Such potential for continued violence is an essential consideration when considering contact with the children.
- The witnessing of parental violence is a predictor of abusiveness in the children as they grow up, especially for males.

- When a mother learns that her ex-partner wants residence or contact with the children, her stress can become overwhelming especially since most women's goal of leaving is to protect the children (Chesler, 1987). As seen in Chapter 4, the mother's experience of domestic violence can certainly effect her ability to parent. The goal of the assessment is to determine the prognosis for recovery once she is safe from violence.

To this we can add:

- The child may be directly at risk. Men who have a history of repeated abuse of their partners generally have a poor ability to discriminate their own needs from those of their children. The risk to children of abuse is likely to increase after separation because the offender may transfer his attention from his usual target of abuse, the mother, who is now inaccessible, to the next most vulnerable targets, the children (Kaye, 1996).

In order to decide the child safety issue workers should consider:

- The nature and the seriousness of the child and/or spousal violence.
- How recently and frequently such violence had occurred.
- The likelihood of further violence.
- The physical or emotional harm caused to the child by the violence.
- The opinions of the other party as to safety.
- The wishes of the child (depending on their age and maturity).
- steps taken by the violent party to prevent further violence from occurring.

(Busche and Robertson, 2000)

Workers need to:

- Understand the nature of the abuse: has the mother being subjected to sadistic abuse which might indicate the risk of emotional harm to the child? Has the child been listened to and taken seriously? Is the child traumatised by the violence which she has witnessed previously? Is the abuser claiming this is a case of parental alienation syndrome? IS there a risk that the abuser will undermine the stability of the child by setting different moral standards?
- Get a clear picture: how many children are involved? Have they been affected by

violence? What dangers could the mother and the children face if contact is granted? Were there any independent witnesses to the violence/abuse? Has the case gone to court or has informal contact emerged? What kind of contact has been ordered or is taking place (if any)?
- Identify available evidence: ask the women if there is any evidence of the violence and help her to compile this information, including details of any independent witnesses, to give to her solicitor.
- Refer her to a solicitor with a good understanding of domestic violence, child protection and contact issues.

(Saunders, 2002)

Basic questions should be asked about domestic violence when seeking to establish the impact upon children:

- Its pattern over time, frequency, the harm resulting, any threats or attempts to kill or commit suicide etc.
- The effect of violence on the children (whether they witnessed the abuse, where they there when it happened, whether they intervened to protect the mother or were implicated in the violence by the father, whether they were also abused and neglected etc.
- The probable safety of contact arrangements: what resources exist locally to provide adequate supervision, has contact previously been safe, whether the mother and children are likely to feel secure and safe.
- The father's capacity to parent and capacity to comply with conditions attached to a contact order.
- Extra care needs to be taken in addressing the needs of younger children. Assessments need to consider the impact which a contact order for one child may have on siblings and the family as a whole.

(Radford, Sayer and AMICA, 1999)

Workers need to establish with mothers:

- What fears about contact do they hold?
- What fears do they have about the safety and welfare of the children?
- What can be done to evidence the mothers concerns and conversely what can be done to allay them?
- What level of support as regards safety in contact do mother's feel they need?

Bancroft and Silverman (2002) identified a list of tactics the offender is likely to utilise in contact disputes:

- projecting a non-abusive image
- use of his new partner as a character reference
- using the mother's anger or mistrust to discredit her
- defensive counter-accusations
- presenting himself as the party who is likely to communicate
- manipulating mediation or dispute resolution
- use of litigation as a form of abuse
- using the woman's sexual orientation against her
- using actions in one court to his advantage in another
- involving his own parents.

Each of these needs to be tested out by the workers. Workers also need to consider the following of the offender:

- What is their motivation for contact: is it a desire to promote the best interests of the child or to create an opportunity to perpetuate violence, intimidation or harassment of the resident parent?
- What is their likely behaviour during contact?
- What is the likely impact of such behaviour on the children?
- Their capacity to appreciate the effect of past and future violence on the other parent and the children.
- Their attitude towards his past violence.
- Their capacity for change and to behave appropriately.

Bancroft and Silverman (2002) set out a useful framework for considering the risk to children from the perpetrators of domestic violence. The factors for assessment include:

- The abuser's history of physical abuse toward the children.
- The abuser's history of neglectful or underinvolved parenting.
- The abuser's history of sexual abuse or boundary violations with the children.
- The abuser's level of physical danger to the partner or former partner.
- The abuser's level of psychological cruelty toward the partner or former partner and toward the children.
- The history of using the children as weapons and of undermining mother–child relationships.

- The abuser's level of willingness to risk physically or emotionally hurting the children incidental to his abuse of their mother.
- The level of coercive or manipulative control that the abuser has exercised over his partner during the relationship.
- The abuser's level of entitlement, self-centredness or selfishness.
- The abuser's substance abuse history.
- The abuser's refusal to accept the end of the relationship or to accept his former partner's decision to begin a new relationship.
- The level of risk to abduct the children.
- The abuser's level of refusal to accept responsibility for past violent or abusive actions.
- The abuser's mental health history.

If a child lives in a hyper-arousal state to survive violence they can't learn new things and separation by itself doesn't change their belief. They only have access to their catalogue of previous experiences i.e. unpredictability, threat, pain and assault. It follows therefore that if there has been no work done with the man the child the child's safe parent and their relationship, in contact it is highly likely that the child will be in hyper-arousal state and as such will therefore focus on non-verbal cues, body movement, facial expression and tone of voice.

It is important that workers:

- Give them time to talk about it.
- Emphasise that the violence is not their fault.
- Let them know that they are not the only child experiencing this.
- Make sure they understand it is not their responsibility to protect their mother/carer whilst validating the child's concern and any action they may have taken to protect their mother.
- Allow them to express their feelings about what they have witnessed.
- Find out if you can whether the child is currently in danger themselves from the perpetrator and take any steps to protect the child.
- Check with the child whether they have a safety plan and a network of adults who they trust – if not work on this with them.
- Don't minimise the violence.
- Offer them support with any difficulties in school.
- Keep the child's confidentiality unless it is necessary to tell someone for the child's safety

– always check with or inform the child about whom you are going to share information with.

● Give the child information about sources of advice and support they may want to use.

If the child's experience of their relationship with their parent or carer is abusive, we cannot assume that it is beneficial to the child. We need to consider what needs to change and *if* the relationship is without abuse is of true benefit to the child (welfare principle). We can assume therefore that there is interference with the accomplishment of normal developmental tasks. The progression of mastery of one's self environment, and relationship with others is significantly disrupted by the child's permanently altered awareness and new role vis-à-vis the perpetrator. Sgroi (1982) identified the impact of abuse on their identities and include impaired trust, poor self image, including past history, difficult adult relationships including those that have been abusive, distorted body awareness, sense of failure, limited belief in self, depression, diminished parenting skills, denial, distorted expectations of partner and children, victim empathy, poor or distorted boundary setting, anger, ability to communicate, assertiveness, impaired socialisation/social skills, poor concrete environmental support.

The development of the relationship between the perpetrator and the child is based on a distortion of thinking and action. Within the relationship there will be blurred role boundaries. There will be long-standing cognitive manipulation of the child. The child will lack conviction that what happened was wrong and was not their fault. The relationship between the child and their mother is also likely to have been distorted by the perpetrator. The child will believe in the domination and power of the perpetrator. The non-abusing carer will not have had time to unpack the overwhelming and conflicting range of emotions for herself, let alone those of her children. Siblings will have experienced distortions in their relationships with other family members (Jones and Parkinson, 1995).

We need to elicit knowledge of how the child made sense of their experiences of domestic violence, including what they understand by domestic violence, whether they view themselves as having experienced domestic violence including denial, how the child feels at the time

and now, what the child did during the violence – including any direct action i.e. phoning police, leaving home, and indirect action – telling someone, keeping out of danger: who if anyone the child feels is responsible/to blame and who helped the child/the mum.

Bala (2000) highlighted that children's wishes can be very problematic in situations of domestic violence. The child may see the abused parent as weak and ineffectual and thus wish to align themselves with the more powerful and stronger abusive parent. The latter may be very manipulative and the denigration of the other parent may influence a child's relationship with the victim of abuse. It may be psychologically difficult for an abused parent to accept a situation where children are ambivalent or express a desire to live with a parent who has been abusive. At times, the abuser may coerce or threaten the child to express views favourable to himself. Sometimes individuals who abuse their partner present very well, are highly manipulative, and are able to 'con' assessors. It follows therefore that while not determinative, a child's wishes should have less weight in cases where there has been domestic violence than in other contexts. When there has been a significant history of domestic violence and the children have become fearful of the abuser and express a desire not to see him, this should be a very persuasive factor in denying contact.

Butler-Sloss et al. (2000) identified that going against the child's wishes must involve indications that there are prospects of the child changing their view as a result of preparation work or the contact itself, there is a history of meaningful attachment and a good relationship, the non-resident parent has child-centred plans as to help the child to overcome their resistance; there are some indications of ambivalence such as an adamant statement of not wanting to see that parent accompanied by lots of positive memories and affect when talking of that parent.

Outcome measurement

There are a number of high risk factors associated with child contact which has been identified by research into domestic homicide and the experience gained from those working in supervised contact centres in the USA and Canada. These high risk factors commonly associated with domestic homicides include:

- An escalation in the severity and frequency of the violence.
- The abuser's use of, or access to, weapons.
- Sexual violence and marital rape.
- A history of either partner's drug or alcohol abuse.
- Either partner's previous threats or attempts to kill the other party in the relationship.
- The abuser's threats or attempts to kill the children.
- Threatened or attempted suicide by either partner.
- The abuser exercising control and domination over his partner (controlling most of her daily activities, ensuring that his view of 'reality' dominates, etc.).
- Obsessive jealousy.
- Violence during pregnancy.
- Violence to others outside the intimate relationship.

(Cambell et al., 1998)

Bancroft and Silverman (2002) identified 12 steps that are indispensable for the abuser to be able to become a responsible and safe parent and which can be used by workers to assess how far up the staircase they have come and what they still need to achieve before safe contact can be considered:

- They must disclose fully the history of physical and psychological abuse toward his partner and children.
- They must recognise that this behaviour is unacceptable.
- They must recognise that this behaviour was chosen.
- They must recognise and show empathy for the effects of his actions on his partner and children.
- They must identify his pattern of controlling behaviours and entitled attitudes.
- They must develop respectful behaviours and attitudes.
- They must re-evaluate his distorted image of his partner.
- They must make amends both in the short and in the long term.
- They must accept the consequences of his actions for him.
- They must commit to not repeating their abusive behaviour.
- They must accept change as a long-term (probably lifelong) process.
- They must be willing to be accountable.

Re-establishing contact following domestic violence

McIntosh (2002) explored the tensions for children as a result of court-ordered contact. If handled inappropriately it can mitigate against rather than promote recovery. She acknowledged that for some children, at the right time, with the right support, they can benefit from contact with the offender. The success hinges on the workers capacity to think about the child's experiences of contact and to facilitate therapeutic contact specific to each situation, in conjunction with the residential parent's and the visiting parent's ability to act on the needs of their child in contact. Through the child's eyes, success specifically hinges on the visiting parent's ability to show that they can think about, understand, and accept the child's experience of fear, and through this thought give evidence of a changed dynamic (p236). McIntosh went on to conduct a study involving 49 children who had experienced various levels of domestic violence and conflict. She closely observed them through their first six months of visiting at contact centres. Whilst she found that many children re-established a foundation of trust through supported, facilitated contact, she also found that some children's psychological functioning deteriorating dramatically through the course of visiting. Each of these cases was marked by the child's past experience of a direct and very frightening threat to their mother's safety and to their own, often via attempted abduction. Children as young as nine months, in this situation, displayed signs of being overwhelmed in the course of visiting, and developmental lags and behavioural problems became evident as time went by.

Planning for contact

Where contact is planned there are some basic safety measures which should *always* be in place. There are some fundamental ground-rules that need to be established and agreed with the child, the perpetrator and non-abusing carer. This may fall into a number of areas:

- The purpose of contact: is this an assessment session, is it to facilitate the child therapeutically, is it taking place because of direction from the court etc.?
- Venue: ensuring visibility and safety.

- Time and duration: is it sensitive to the needs of the child, including school commitments, tiredness, times of abuse etcetera?
- Role of the supervisor: there must be a shared understanding as to whether the supervisor is there to observe and intervene if concerns are raised or has a more proactive role in facilitating the contact. It will also be important to establish for the child whether the supervisor is neutral and therefore does not have a relationship with the child, or is their ally and clearly present to empower the child.
- Child's arrival and departure from contact: who brings and takes the child, who leaves first, greetings and goodbyes allowed particularly in relation to physical contact?
- Agreed activities during contact: contact needs to be carefully planned and should reflect the interests of the child. It should also maximise the positive aspects of the adult's parenting skills. This should be based on the acquired knowledge of what, if anything positively binds the child and adult together.
- Agreements about talking and touching: it is important to clarify whether kissing, hugging, sitting on knees etc. is alright, or not. It is also helpful if the worker establishes with the child anything that they do not wish or is inappropriate to talk or be asked about by the adult i.e. the abuse, passing messages home, providing information.
- Time alone with the child: it is crucial that everyone knows whether the child and parent are allowed to be alone together unsupervised at **anytime.** This may involve making plans for if the child needs taking to the toilet or a drink or snack making etc.
- Presents: it is not unusual for estranged parents to want to bring gifts for the child. The meaning of this for the abused child must inform any decision about it.
- Intervention: the supervisor must be clear with the child and the adult how they will intervene if they are concerned during contact and what response they expect from the parent.
- Recording: if the contact is part of an ongoing assessment, agreement must be reached about what will be recorded, how it will be recorded and where the information may be shared.
- Worries and safety plans: it is important that the child identifies to whom and how they can communicate any worries they may have during contact. In my experience it can be useful to agree an 'emergency code word' that the child chooses and can use during contact if they become anxious or need the contact to stop. It is also useful if the child has access and permission to speak with an adult not involved in supervising the contact with whom they can express any feelings they may have.
- The non-abusing carer: it is likely that the non-abusing carer will have their own feelings about the contact, and it will be important to ensure that the child understands what is to be fed back and by whom. It may also be necessary to identify what part the child wants the non-abusing carer to play after contact i.e. don't ask me any questions about it, I need time on my own, I need you to hug me etc.
- There should also be an agreement about immediate action the perpetrator should take to stop contact if they are aroused, and the process of debriefing within the context of any treatment they receive.

These and any other issues relevant for the individual situation must form the basis of a written agreement both with the child and the adult. The agreement with the child must reflect their age and understanding and can make use of pictures or diagrams where words are not understood. The starting point should be that the perpetrator has apologised to the child and that they alone are responsible for the abuse. The supervisor should feel confident that they are in control of the contact. The impact for the child needs to be evaluated and should take into account not only what happens during contact but what is said and how the child behaves and presents following contact.

Summary

Children have the capacity to recover from the effects of domestic violence once they are in a safer, more stable environment. Research also suggests that children who continue to have contact with the offender in situations of domestic violence show the greatest problems, exhibiting the most marked behavioral problems. All the research highlights that child contact arrangements provide a point of great vulnerability for both women and children and a context in which control by abusive ex-partners can continue (Humphreys and Thiarra, 2002). More detailed assessments are needed to explore whether contact is appropriate for individual children, starting from a premise of no contact. Where contact is considered in the child's best interests, we have to be creative in considering the best option for contact, and this may not always be face-to-face contact. Contact needs to be more carefully matched to the needs of the child and the abused parent to have safety. The greater the professionals' awareness and understanding of domestic violence, the greater the beneficial effect upon safety of child contact outcomes. This chapter has hopefully reviewed the legal position in relation to contact, considered the deficits through research and practice experience and begun to convert the evidence into a preliminary assessment framework.

Chapter Seven

Outcome Measurements

Overall measurement

The evaluation of the information collected should enable workers to:

- Clarify the risks; immediate and longer-term status of the adult relationship.
- Engage with the woman as to her needs and wishes in terms of the relationship including health, safety, practical issues.
- Define in more detail the needs/impact on the children.
- Produce a chronology of events.
- Assess the relationship between the children, their mother and establish if there are other safe adults in the children's lives.
- Assess the parenting capacity of the mother as well as her insight/action in relation to the impact on the children.
- Determine the health/development/ educational attainment (where appropriate)/ identity/relationships/self-care skills, emotional/behavioural/social functioning of each child.
- Establish what opportunities exist for the child to speak openly and be heard.
- Assess whether the perpetrator of the violence acknowledges their role and responsibility in the risk and their willingness to seek help.

Outcomes for the mother

This information should facilitate the worker being clear with the woman, what the perceived risks are, why, and what expectations may be placed on her to manage/minimise those risks. Alongside this should be the support that is available to the woman to maximise the positive coping strategies and minimise the negative consequences for both her and the children. This should then form the basis for the agreed safety plan. Where the worker and the woman are not in agreement as to the level of risk to the children, the worker will need to consider whether:

(a) A revised safety plan is acceptable.
(b) The risk to the children remains but can be managed.
(c) The risk requires a child protection conference/legal intervention.

Defining the changes

At each stage of assessment a safety plan should be agreed following the advice and pro-forma contained in Figures 5.5, 5.8 and 5.9. Where other professionals are involved and have a role this should also be agreed between agencies and held on file. The review of the safety plan will provide ongoing information about the risks to the woman and children and the relative success of intervention and support in keeping both safe.

On a more individual level, work should help the woman define the risk and impact for each of the children. There should be clarity as to what the woman is being asked to be responsible for (i.e. to keep the man out of the house; or ensure that the children can flee to a safe place; call the police; ensure the child receives reassurance etc.); what she cannot be responsible for (i.e. changing his violent behaviour; making the children feel differently about what they are experiencing etc); and what support is available (including friends, neighbours, relatives as well as statutory agencies). Legal sanctions may be obtained to keep an abusive partner out of the house.

If a woman has left a violent relationship and returned, it is important to understand the circumstances for this and the implicit messages this may have reinforced with the children. If leaving their partner becomes a future decision it should be informed by the previous experiences.

The needs of each of the children should be defined and what the woman is being asked to do to keep them safe. Whilst it is never the child's responsibility to protect themselves it is important that children who are old enough are enabled to participate in the safety planning for themselves. This can include, who they may go to, talk to, which room is safest during a violent attack, what position to take, who to contact and how, etc. The emotional impact of the violence should be addressed for all children. Any aims to provide therapeutic support or to achieve changes in behaviour with a child, will not succeed if the child does not feel safe at home.

In order to measure the outcomes of the safety plan for the child it will be important to liaise with other professionals. The information about the child may include:

Child's relationship with:
    mother – type of attachment
    violent partner – parenting role
    siblings
    significant safe adults.
Child's self-esteem/identity.
Child's social skills/functioning/socialisation.
    self-care skills/routines

emotional presentation
    – at home
    – at school

behaviour
    – at home
    – at school

understanding about the violence
    – frequency and form of the violence
    – length of exposure to the violence
feelings about the violence
    – likely impact – behavioural/physical/
    psychological.
Education
    – attendance/performance/potential/
    presentation.
Health
    – specific needs/growth/development.
                    (Rose, 2001)

Where the intervention with the woman looks at improving her parenting skills/self-esteem/sense of control and responsibility this can be measured through agreeing targets as to what the woman is expected to achieve i.e. all the children to be in school; attendance at the family centre; able to identify three things she's achieved for herself etc. It is important to acknowledge that whilst the woman remains in a violent relationship, many of these goals may be limited and/or undermined by the violent partner. It is important that workers identify the predisposing, precipitating and perpetrating factors that make up the risk. From this the elements requiring change can be reviewed.

MacNeely (2002) set out a useful framework (Figure 7.1) for considering the mothers understanding of the risks to her children and how the worker can then best intervene:

Other measures of movement in the mother may include:

- They are able to express their feelings regarding the violence they have experienced.
- They have developed their capacity to recognise violent behaviour and its consequences and to access support.
- Enhance their willingness to take responsibility for their own behaviour.
- Enhance their self-esteem and self-efficacy.
- Promote non-violent ways to solve problems.

Figure 7.1: Assessing a mothers understanding of the risks to her children (MacNeely, 2002)

Assessment of risk	Worker response
Mother identifies or acknowledges risk to children.	Focusing on reducing risk by drawing up a safety plan with mother, children and agencies, as appropriate.
Identified risks to children, but mother has no realistic options because of her partner's violence towards her.	Work with mother to reduce the risk of violence towards her, as part of a plan to reduce the risk to the children. Take appropriate action to protect the children if necessary.
Mother does not recognise risks to children because she is unaware of the risks to them.	Review the safety plan with her. If she then understands the risks, work with her to try and reduce them. If she doesn't acknowledge the risks, take appropriate action to protect the children.
Mother does not acknowledge the risks because she is not committed to parenting/ protecting the children.	Review the safety plan with her. Take appropriate action to protect the children.
Mother does not acknowledge the risks because she is abusing the children.	Review the safety plan with her. If she wants to reduce the risk to the children, determine what steps she needs to take. If not, take immediate action to protect the children.

(page 128)

- Improved relationships with others.
- To allow the child to gain a sense that they are regaining some control over their lives.
- To assign responsibility for the abuse with the perpetrator.
- To develop clear plans for the future safety of the child.
- Working with the parents on personal development and parenting skills.

Some questions to ask the mother to elicit whether there has been a redistribution of power and responsibility in her relationships may include:

- What has your partner/ex-partner been invited to take responsibility for as a result of the intervention?
- How has this freed you from your previous super-responsibility role?
- In what ways do you feel you have more power, or what areas of your life do you have more control over?
- How has this come about? What have been the consequences for your partner's previous role of domination and control of you and the children?
- How might your children perceive family dynamics differently from how they did before the intervention?
- How have the changes you have made influenced how the children perceive you today? (Burke, 1999).

Perpetrator's willingness to stop the abuse

Men's history of abuse is by far the strongest predictor of future domestic violence. Garner (1998) found that the partners of men with a prior criminal record of domestic violence were 30% more likely to report these men for subsequent violence. Men with a prior criminal record were 34% more likely to be re-arrested than men without a prior criminal record of domestic violence.

Indicators of change?

If the violent partner can be engaged with this is clearly the most significant area of change. There are some resources available to help men manage their violent behaviours but these are limited. If possible there should be a written agreement which is reflective of the degree of risk the man

presents i.e. to live outside the household pending further assessment; alternative courses of action he may take to avoid a violent situation; expectations following a violent episode etc.

Ultimately, the person responsible for stopping the abuse is the perpetrator. **All of the behaviour changes on the following list are necessary in order for measurable and consistent changes in abusive behaviour to occur:**

- Honesty and openness with social services and other key agencies.
- Stopping the abuse of the woman or children.
- Acknowledgement of abusive behaviour as a problem.
- Acknowledgement of the effect of abusive behaviour on children.
- Acknowledgement of his responsibility for stopping abuse.
- Co-operation with current efforts to address abusive behaviour.
- Awareness of the negative consequences of abusive behaviour for the woman, children and the abuser's physical well-being, self-image, legal status, social relationships, and employment.
- Co-operation during the interview and assessment process.
- Demonstrated commitment to safety of woman and children.
- Compliance with court orders.
- Respect for limits set by woman and/or other agencies.
- Support for parenting efforts of woman including less tendency to blame problems of children on their mother.
- Consideration of children's best interests over his parental rights.
- Successful demonstration of alternative methods of conflict resolution.
- Ability to view self through family members' eyes.

Workers need to be cautious about whether the man has changed as an inaccurate assessment will endanger women and children further. We can also utilise variations of the Duluth power and control wheel to help us consider whether there has been any changes from the originating concerns – see Figures 7.2, 7.3 and 7.4.

Maddie Bell and Joan McGovern have been developing some threshold scales in Northern Ireland designed to differentiate levels of risk within preventive domestic violence situations. This is an essential consideration for all professionals faced with an increased rate of reporting of domestic violence incidents. The current threshold scales are reproduced as Figure 7.5 and represent work in progress, but I felt it important to include them as they model how practice generates its own evidence-based solutions.

Figure 7.2: The Duluth non-violence wheel

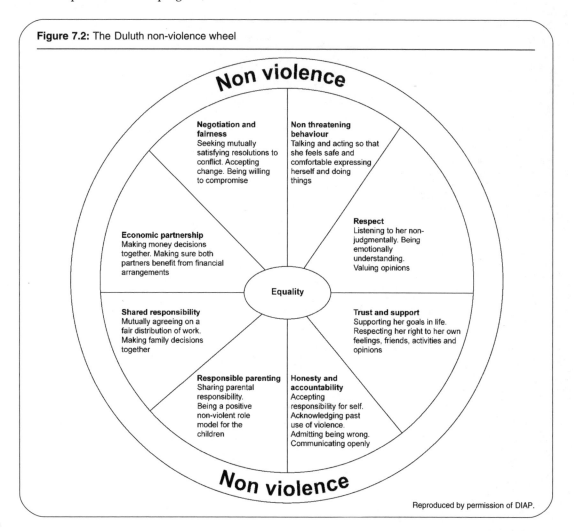

Reproduced by permission of DIAP.

Figure 7.3: The Duluth abuse of children wheel

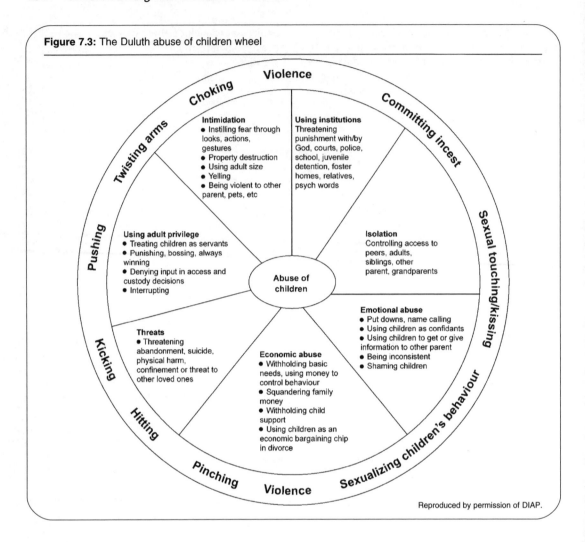

Reproduced by permission of DIAP.

Figure 7.4: The Duluth nurturing children wheel

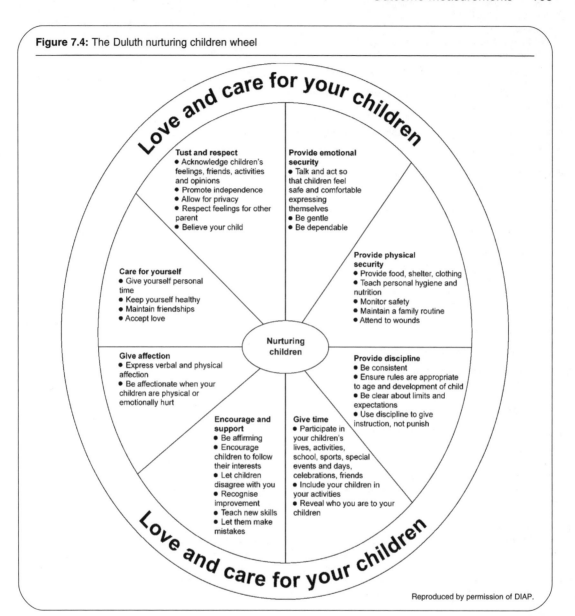

Reproduced by permission of DIAP.

Figure 7.5: Threshold scales for domestic violence risk assessment model – pilot SHSSB

Rating the Assessment: Threshold scales

The above must all be considered in each case.

- Severity of the incidences
- Pattern, frequency and duration of violence incidences
- Perpetrator's use of the children/children caught up in the abuse
- Escalation of violence and use of isolation
- Sexual violence/abuse
- Perpetrator's attitude to the abuse
- Age of perpetrator and victim

Additional Vulnerabilities:

- Age of victim
- Victim's personal vulnerabilities
- Age of perpetrator
- Age of children
- Disability Issues within family unit
- Cultural Issues within family

Factor Classification:

- Evidence of domestic violence
- Risk Factors/Potential vulnerabilities
- Protective factors

Threshold scales 1 and 2:
Scales 1 and 2 assess the severity, nature and impact of the domestic violence on the children as 'HIGH RISK' so the threshold of significant harm is reached and child protection procedures are implemented

Threshold Scales 3 and 4
Threshold scales 3 and 4 assess the domestic violence as moderate and family support is deemed the supportive intervention. These scales specifically address the 'GREY AREAS' in making an assessment of the severity, nature and impact of the domestic violence on children. Scale 3 has a specific risk factor regarding the age of children living in the family – the age of the child increases the level of risk and can raise the threshold scale for the family to scale 2

Threshold Scales 3 and 4
Using the threshold scales we are anticipating that the pilot study will 'PICK UP' on the decision-making of SSW staff who currently hold t thresholds regarding case classification/family support or child protection. There should be a clear, more consistent case classification and this will impact on current service provision.

Scales children's vulnerability and application of threshold scales
In threshold scales 1 and 2 children are at risk of significant harm. There are no upper limits on the age range except in families where there are only teenagers/young people (14 years +) and where there is evidence that the young person is using protective strategies and is not being physically/sexually abused and/or is not perpetrating abuse towards other family members.
   In threshold scale 3 children are deemed to be in need of family support interventions as some protective strategies are being used by the victim and the children However, if there are children under the age of seven in the family this could raise the threshold scale to 2 because young children are at an increased risk as they do not have safety strategies and are dependent on their mothers to protect them.

Figure 7.5: *Continued*

Any Child in family is suffering significant harm- no upper age limit

Very Severe – scale 1 – Child in family in need of protection (please tick box)

	Yes	No	Suspected
Evidence of domestic violence			
Repeated serious physical violence – life-threatening violence	☐	☐	☐
Incidents of sexual violence	☐	☐	☐
Pattern, severity, frequency of abuse/violence history	☐	☐	☐
Duration of violent incidents – i.e. hours/minutes, children exposed to traumatic events	☐	☐	☐
Substantial risk of serious physical violence in the family	☐	☐	☐
Adult requires treatment for injuries sustained	☐	☐	☐
Medical attention required but not sought	☐	☐	☐
Unexplained injuries	☐	☐	☐
Recurring or frequent requests for police intervention	☐	☐	☐
Non-molestation Order may exist or past Protection orders	☐	☐	☐
Repeated incidents of separation	☐	☐	☐
Threats of or use of weapons by one family member against another	☐	☐	☐
Abused partner believes threats and fears perpetrator	☐	☐	☐
Incidents of physical violence have occurred during pregnancy	☐	☐	☐
Substance abuse by perpetrator Substance abuse by victim	☐	☐	☐
Risk Factors/Potential Vulnerabilities:			
Absolute domination of emotional, financial and sexual spheres by one member	☐	☐	☐
Jealous/excessive possessive behaviour of perpetrator	☐	☐	☐
Other partner is submissive/worn down by abuse	☐	☐	☐
Abused partner is pregnant	☐	☐	☐
Perpetrator's lack of insight into how his abuse is impacting on partner and children	☐	☐	☐
Perpetrator's lack of empathy for abused partner and children	☐	☐	☐
Disruptive childhood experiences of perpetrator	☐	☐	☐
Disruptive childhood experiences of abused partner	☐	☐	☐
Mental Health Issues – Perpetrator	☐	☐	☐
Mental Health Issues – Abused partner	☐	☐	☐
Disability Issues within family	☐	☐	☐
Cultural Issues within family	☐	☐	☐
Age of perpetrator and abused partner	☐	☐	☐
Physical discipline of children by Perpetrator	☐	☐	☐
Abused partner uses physical discipline on children as a alternative to harsher physical abuse by perpetrator/father figure	☐	☐	☐
Aftermath of violence-reaction and impact on children	☐	☐	☐
Aftermath of violence-reaction and impact on abused partner	☐	☐	☐
Contact issues –consider risks to children	☐	☐	☐

Any child in family is at risk of significant harm – upper age limits could apply 14 years+

Severe – scale 2 – Child in family in need of protection (please tick)

	Yes	No	Suspected
Evidence of Domestic Violence:			
Incidents of physical violence in family	☐	☐	☐
Incidents of sexual violence	☐	☐	☐
Adult physically assaulted by another family member but no medical attention required	☐	☐	☐
Threats (to kill or seriously injure) abused partner	☐	☐	☐
Threats (to kill or seriously injure) Child	☐	☐	☐

Figure 7.5: *Continued*

Any child in family is at risk of significant harm – upper age limits could apply 14 years+ Continued

Severe – scale 2 – Child in family in need of protection (please tick)

	Yes	No	Suspected
Evidence of Domestic Violence:			
Recurring or frequent requests for police intervention	☐	☐	☐
Incidences of violence occur in presence of children	☐	☐	☐
History of Protection Orders/Protection order exists	☐	☐	☐
Substance abuse by perpetrator	☐	☐	☐
Substance abuse by or victim	☐	☐	☐
Risk Factors/Potential Vulnerabilities:			
Possible sexual abuse by perpetrator of family member	☐	☐	☐
Emotional and financial control maintained by perpetrator	☐	☐	☐
Imbalance of power and control	☐	☐	☐
Mental Health Issues – Perpetrator	☐	☐	☐
Mental Health Issues – abused partner	☐	☐	☐
Disability Issues within family	☐	☐	☐
Cultural Issues within family	☐	☐	☐
Age of perpetrator and partner	☐	☐	☐
Perpetrator's lack of insight into how his abuse is impacting on partner and children	☐	☐	☐
Perpetrator's lack of empathy for abused partner and children	☐	☐	☐
Physical discipline of children by Perpetrator	☐	☐	☐
Abused partner uses physical discipline on children as an alternative to harsher physical abuse by perpetrator/father figure	☐	☐	☐
Aftermath of violence-reaction and impact on children	☐	☐	☐
Aftermath of violence-reaction and impact on abused partner	☐	☐	☐
Contact issues – consider risks to children	☐	☐	☐

Any children under 7 years of age, this can raise the threshold immediately – Child is potentially at risk of significant harm.

Serious – scale 3 Child in need of supportive services (please tick)

	Yes	No	Suspected
Evidence of Domestic Violence:			
Minor incidences of physical domestic abuse	☐	☐	☐
Minor injuries received by abused partner no medical attention sought	☐	☐	☐
Violent incidences were of short duration	☐	☐	☐
Threats of harm to victim but not towards children	☐	☐	☐
Children were present in the home but did not directly witness incidents	☐	☐	☐
Children under 7 years in family	☐	☐	☐
Risk Factors/Potential Vulnerabilities:			
One family member controlled through limited access to financial resources	☐	☐	☐
Intimidation, and/or isolation	☐	☐	☐
Caregiver has experienced prior abusive relationships	☐	☐	☐
Perpetrator attempts to control partner's activities, movements and contacts with other people	☐	☐	☐
Family members put in fear by looks, actions, gestures and destruction of property	☐	☐	☐
Mental Health Issues – Perpetrator seeking appropriate help	☐	☐	☐
Mental Health Issues – Abused partner seeking appropriate help	☐	☐	☐

Figure 7.5: *Continued*

Any children under 7 years of age, this can raise the threshold immediately – Child is potentially at risk of significant harm Continued

Serious – scale 3 Child in need of supportive services (please tick)

	Yes	No	Suspected
Risk Factors/Potential Vulnerabilities:			
Threats of harm and/or pushing and shoving of one family member by perpetrator	☐	☐	☐
Disability Issues within family	☐	☐	☐
Cultural Issues within family	☐	☐	☐
Age of perpetrator/abused partner	☐	☐	☐
Protective Factors:			
Older children used protective strategies (8 years +)	☐	☐	☐
Abusive partner seeking help	☐	☐	☐
Abused partner attempts to use protective strategies	☐	☐	☐

Moderate – scale 4 Child in need of supportive services (please tick)

	Yes	No	Suspected
Evidence of Domestic Violence:			
1–3 minor incidents of physical violence which were short in duration	☐	☐	☐
Abused partner did not require medical treatment	☐	☐	☐
Risk Factors/Potential Vulnerabilities:			
Children were not drawn-in to incidences	☐	☐	☐
Violence was minor in that the mother was not prevented from seeing to the needs of her children	☐	☐	☐
Control of perpetrator is not intense	☐	☐	☐
Disability Issues – supports personnel safety for abused partner/child	☐	☐	☐
Cultural Issues – supports victim/children	☐	☐	☐
Caregiver has experienced prior abusive relationships	☐	☐	☐
Protective Factors:			
Older children used protective strategies	☐	☐	☐
Presence of children was a restraint for the perpetrator	☐	☐	☐
Abused partner sought appropriate support	☐	☐	☐
Abused partner has positive support from family/friends	☐	☐	☐
Perpetrator accepts responsibility for violence	☐	☐	☐
Abused partner appears emotionally strong (not worn-down by the abuse)	☐	☐	☐
Abused partner is willing to accept help from Social Services/other agencies	☐	☐	☐

Minimum – scale 5 family support may be required (please tick)

	Yes	No	Suspected
Verbal aggression	☐	☐	☐
Family member's activities constrained through verbal aggression	☐	☐	☐
Member may exhibit anxiety or apprehension in the presence of perpetrator	☐	☐	☐
Caregiver has experienced prior abusive relationships	☐	☐	☐

Summary

This chapter has organised some of the embryonic measurement tools when deciding how to measure the risks to the primary and secondary victims in cases of domestic violence. We need to try to utilise them as they offer us a foot into the door when trying to maintain objective assessments in a potentially emotionally charged and subjective area of child protection practice.

Chapter Eight

Where Next?

Rowsell (2004) has usefully furnished us with a framework to map the source of the problem facing victims of domestic violence with the effect of excluding them socially (see Figure 8.1) and has challenged us to move towards a model of inclusion (see Figure 8.2).

In order to establish where we are individually and organisationally she has asked us to consider our process of change (see Figure 8.3).

In order to be clear about where we need to get to she has set out some targets within the umbrella of a total community response (see Figure 8.4).

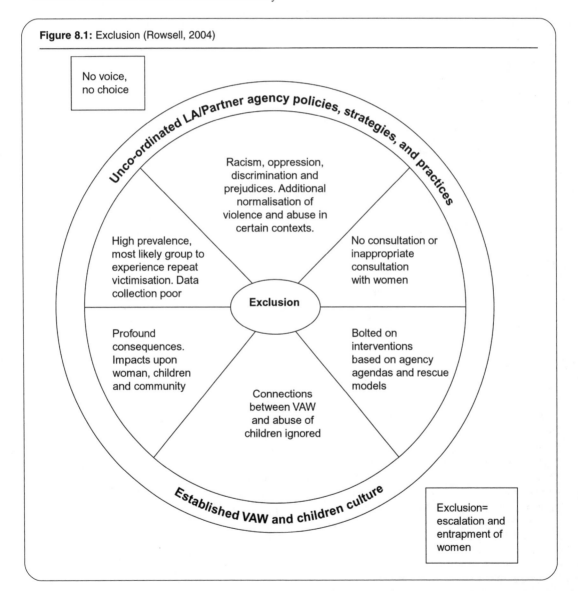

Figure 8.1: Exclusion (Rowsell, 2004)

No voice, no choice

Unco-ordinated LA/Partner agency policies, strategies, and practices

Racism, oppression, discrimination and prejudices. Additional normalisation of violence and abuse in certain contexts.

High prevalence, most likely group to experience repeat victimisation. Data collection poor

No consultation or inappropriate consultation with women

Exclusion

Profound consequences. Impacts upon woman, children and community

Bolted on interventions based on agency agendas and rescue models

Connections between VAW and abuse of children ignored

Established VAW and children culture

Exclusion= escalation and entrapment of women

Figure 8.2: Inclusion (Rowsell, 2004)

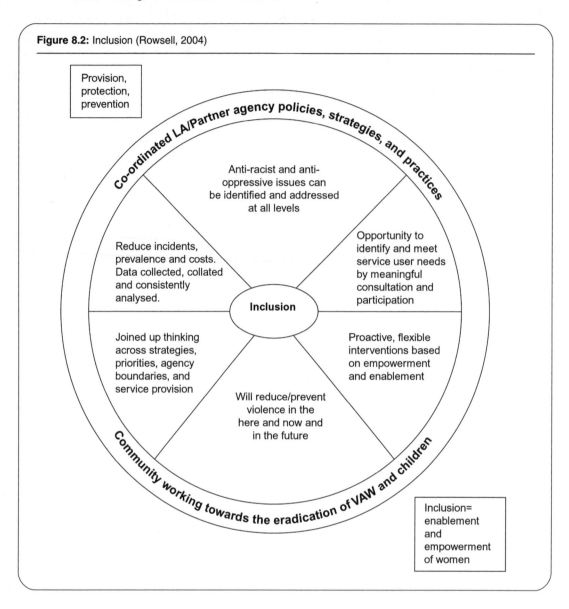

Provision, protection, prevention

Co-ordinated LA/Partner agency policies, strategies, and practices

Anti-racist and anti-oppressive issues can be identified and addressed at all levels

Reduce incidents, prevalence and costs. Data collected, collated and consistently analysed.

Opportunity to identify and meet service user needs by meaningful consultation and participation

Inclusion

Joined up thinking across strategies, priorities, agency boundaries, and service provision

Proactive, flexible interventions based on empowerment and enablement

Will reduce/prevent violence in the here and now and in the future

Community working towards the eradication of VAW and children

Inclusion= enablement and empowerment of women

In order to maximise the chances of success, we need to make and use strategic links locally, culminating in clear strategic strategies (operational and training) (see Figure 8.5) and the assessment framework set out in this book represents but one small building block in this much larger, essentially important endeavour.

I wish you well in your journey and hope this text helps to some degree improve the outcomes for women and children who have endured the multiple and deleterious effects of living with domestic violence. I would strongly recommend that you refer yourself to the detailed frameworks for engaging women in a strengths-based approach as articulated in detail in Calder, Peake and Rose (2001).

Figure 8.3: Process of change (Rowsell, 2004)

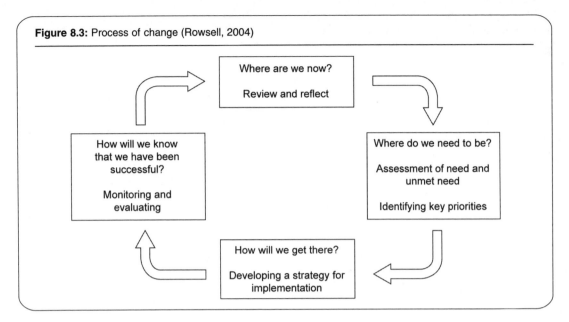

Figure 8.4: Total community response to domestic violence (Rowsell, 2004)

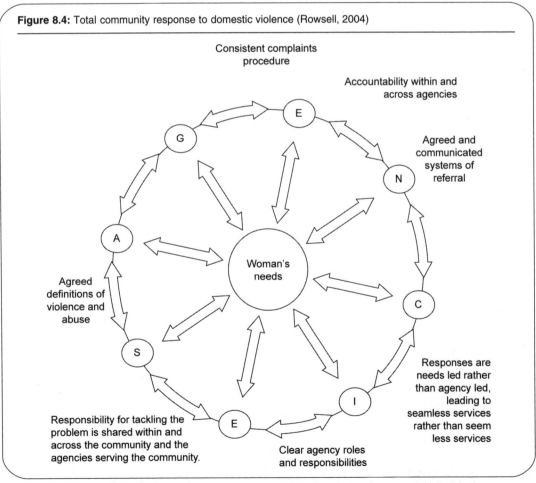

Figure 8.5: Making strategic links (Rowsell, 2004)

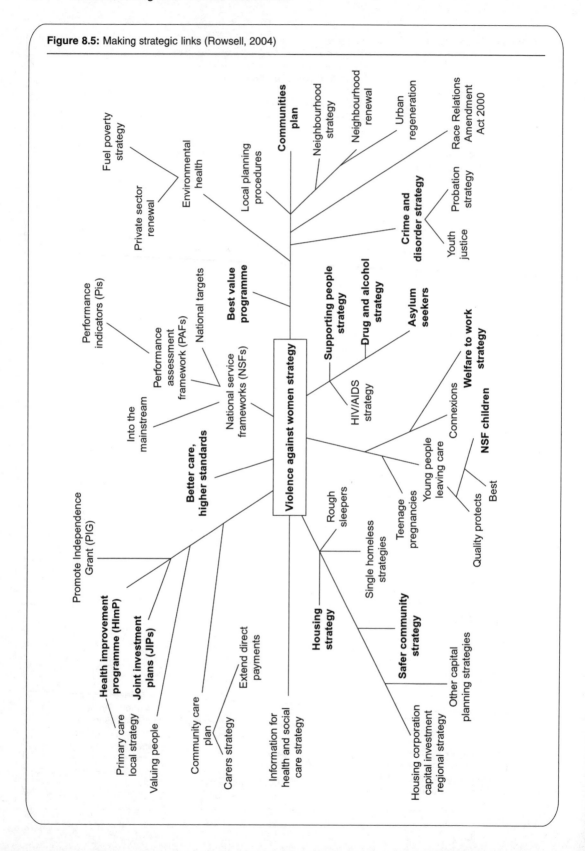

Resource list

Women's Aid
Women's Aid Federation of England
PO Box 391
Bristol BS99 7WS
Tel: 0117 944 4411 (office)
08457 023468 (helpline)

Northern Ireland Women's Aid Federation
129 University Street
Belfast BT7 1HP
Tel: 01232 249041 or 01232 249358
01232 331818 (24 hour helpline)

Welsh Women's Aid
38–48 Crwys Road
Cardiff CF24 4NN
Tel: 029 2039 0874

London Women's Aid
PO Box 14041
London E1 6NY
Tel: 0171 392 2092 (24 hours)

Refuge
2–8 Meltravers Street
London WC2R 3EE
Tel: 020 7395 7700 (office)
Fax: 020 7395 7721
24 hour national helpline: 0870 599 5443

Scottish Women's Aid
Norton Park
57 Albion Road
Edinburgh EH7 5QY
Tel: 0131 475 2372

Zero Tolerance Helpline
Tel: 0800 028 3398
0800 028 3397 (Textphone)

Republic of Ireland Nation Network of Women's
Refuges and Support Services
Tel: 003539 0279078

Domestic abuse helpline
A national helpline is available for anyone who is
experiencing domestic abuse, or knows someone
who is. Run by North Ayrshire Women's Aid, it
operates between 10 a.m. and 10 p.m., 7 days a
week and currently averages 50 calls per week.
Tel: 0800 027 1234

We're no exception
This is a campaign organisation raising
awareness about and campaigning against
violence against disabled women. They provide a
service for young people and adults aged 16–65.
They can give advice on rehabilitation services.
Tel: 0141 945 5662 (Mon–Fri 09.00–16.00)

Lesbian and gay line
Provide support, practical help, and information
on health issues, counselling and referral to
specialist agencies.
Tel: 01387 261818

Refuge for Women with Learning Difficulties
Beverley Lewis House
PO Box 7312
London E15 4TS
Tel: 0181 522 0675

Broken Rainbow. A referral service for lesbians,
gay men, bisexuals and transgender people
experiencing domestic violence.
Tel: 07812 644 914

Ethnic minority women's groups
Black Association of Women Step Out (BAWSO)
109 St Mary Street
Cardiff CF1 1DX
Tel: 01222 343154

Newham Asian Women's Project
661 Barking Road
London E13 9EX
Tel: 020 8472 0528
020 8552 5524 (advice line)

Southall Black Sisters
52 Norwood Road
Southall UB2 4DW
Tel: 020 8571 9595
Fax: 020 8574 6781

Jewish Women's Aid
PO Box 14270
London N12 8WG
Tel: 0800 591203 (freephone)
0171 486 0860 (office)

Hemat-Gryffe Women's Aid
Hemat-Gryffe Women's Aid aims to provide safe
temporary accommodation to women and their
children primarily of Asian, black and ethnic
minority background that have experienced
abuse. They provide information and support on
housing and help with arranging permanent
re-housing. They also provide information on
immigration, social security payments and other
necessary help as needed.
Open 9 a.m.–4 p.m., Mon–Fri
Tel: 0141 353 0859 (24 hour answering machine
service)

Shakti Women's Aid
Shakti provides a service for Black and Asian women and children. They can help with immigration issues and laws concerning separation and divorce, and can give advice on what benefits are available. If the woman is still with her partner, they can give practical advice.
Tel: 0131 475 2399 (09.00–17.00)

Victim support
Victim Support National Office
Cranmer House
39 Brixton Road
London SW9 6DZ
Tel: 020 7735 9166 (enquiries)

Victim Support Scotland
14 Frederick Street
Edinburgh EH2 2HB
Tel: 0131 225 7779

Victim Support Line
PO Box 11431
London SW9 62H
Tel: 0845 3030900

Advice and legal advice
NACAB (National Association of Citizens Advice Bureaux)
Middleton House
115–123 Pentonville Road
London N1 9LZ
Tel: 020 7833 2181

Rape Crisis
PO Box 69
London WC1X 9NJ
Tel: 020 7837 1600 (24 hour helpline)

Cardiff Rape Crisis Line
PO Box 338
Cardiff CF2 4XH
Tel: 029 2037 3181

Rights of Women
52–54 Featherstone Street
London EC1Y 8RT
Tel: 020 7251 6575 (office)
Tel: 020 7251 6577 (advice)

Immigration Advisory Service
Tel: 020 7378 9191
Immigration and Joint Council for Welfare of Immigrants
Tel: 020 7251 8706

Lesbian and Gay Switchboard
Tel: 020 7837 7324

Miscarriage Association
C/O Clayton Hospital
Northgate
Wakefield WF1 3JS
Tel: 01924 200799 (national helpline)

Agencies for parents and children
AMICA (Aid for Mothers Involved in Contact Action)
C/O Rights of Women
52–54 Featherstone Street
London EC1Y 8RT
Tel: 020 7251 6575

Childline
Freepost 1111
London N1 0BR
Tel: 020 7239 1000 (office)
0800 1111 (freephone helpline for children and young people)

Childline (Wales)
9th Floor
Alexander House
Alexander Road
Swansea SA1 5ED
Tel: 01792 480111 (office)
0800 1111 (freephone helpline for children and young people)

Reunite (for parents of abducted children)
International Child Abduction Centre
PO Box 24875
London E1 6FR
Tel: 020 7375 3440 (advice line)

Children 1st
Children 1st supports families under stress, protects children from harm and neglect, helps children recover from abuse and promotes children's rights and interests.
Tel: 0131 337 8539

Parentline
A confidential helpline for parents.
Tel: 0808 800 2222

Concerns about animal abuse can be reported to:

Royal Society for the Prevention of Cruelty to Animals (RSPCA)
Tel: 0870 5555 999 (24 hour line covering England and Wales)
Scottish Society for the Prevention of Cruelty to Animals (SSPCA)
Tel: 0870 7377 722

Ulster Society for the Prevention of Cruelty to Animals (USPCA)
Tel: 08000 280010 (24 hour line covering Northern Ireland)

Irish Society for the Prevention of Cruelty to Animals (ISPCA)
Tel: 003531 4977874 (covering The Republic of Ireland)

Useful websites

http://www.domesticviolencedata.org
The Domestic Violence Data source is an information co-ordinating system providing up-to-date material about domestic violence in England, Wales, Scotland, Northern Ireland and the Republic of Ireland.

Although targeted mainly at practitioners, researchers and other academics, the site is also sensitive to the needs of those who have experienced violence.

http://www.womensaid.org.uk
Website of Women's Aid, providing information and help and local refuge contact details and sources of help for women experiencing domestic violence, as well as information about domestic violence, and links to other useful websites.

http://www.homeoffice.gov.uk/domesticviolence
Sets out the Government's policy around domestic violence; lists relevant publications and provides links to other useful websites

References

Abbey A (1991) Misperceptions as an antecedent of acquaintance rape. In Parrot A and Bechofer L (Eds.) *Acquaintance rape: the hidden crime*. NY: Wiley.

Abbott JR, Johnson J, Koziol-McLain J and Lowenstein SR (1995) Domestic violence against women: incidence and prevalence in an emergency room population. *Journal of the American Medical Association*. 273 (22): 1763–7.

Abbott P and Williamson E (1999) Women, health and domestic violence. *Journal of Gender Studies*. (1): 83–102.

Abrahams C (1994) *The Hidden Victims: children and domestic violence*. London: NCH Action for Children.

Achenbach TM (1991a) *Manual for Teacher's Report Form and 1991 Profile*. Burlington: University of Vermont, Department of Psychiatry.

Achenbach TM (1991b) *Manual for the Child Behaviour Checklist 4–18 and 1991 Profile*. Burlington: University of Vermont, Department of Psychiatry.

Achenbach TM (1991c) *Manual for the Youth Self-Report and 1991 Profile*. Burlington: University of Vermont, Department of Psychiatry.

Achenbach, TM, McConaughy SH and Howell CT (1987) Child/adolescent behavioural and emotional problems: Implications of cross-informants correlations for situational specificity. *Psychological Bulletin*. 101: 213–32.

Adams D (1990) Identifying the assaultive husband in court. *Response*. 13: 13–6.

Adamson LA, and Thompson RA (1998) Coping with interparental conflict by children exposed to spouse abuse and children from non-violent homes. *Journal of Family Violence*. 13: 213–32.

Advisory Board on Family Law, Children Act Subcommittee (2002) *Making Contact Work: A Report to The Lord Chancellor on The Facilitation of Arrangements for Contact Between Children and Their Non-Residential Parents and The Enforcement of Court Orders for Contact*. London: Lord Chancellors Department.

Amaro H, Fried L, Cabral H and Zukerman B (1990) Violence During Pregnancy and Substance Use, *American Journal of Public Health*. May (80) 575–9.

Amato PR and Keith B (1991a) Consequences of parental divorce for the well-being of children: A meta analysis. *Psychological Bulletin*. 110: 26–46.

Amato PR and Keith B (1991b) Parental divorce and adult well-being – A meta analysis. *Journal of Marriage and the Family*. 53: 43–58.

American Humane Association (1994) *Child protection leader: domestic violence and child abuse*. Englewood: American Humane Association.

Angold A and Rutter M (1992) Effects of age and pubertal status on depression in a large clinical sample. *Developmental Psychopathology*. 4: 5–28.

Aris R, Harrison C and Humphreys C (2002) *Safety and Child Contact: an Analysis of The Role of Child Contact Centres in The Context of Domestic Violence and Child Welfare Concerns*. London: Lord Chancellors Department.

Arkow P (2001) Putting the link all together. *The Latham Letter*. Spring 2001, 15.

Arroya W and Eth S (1995) Assessment following violence-witnessing trauma. In Peled E, Jaffe PG and Edleson JL (Eds.) *Ending the cycle of violence: Community responses to children of battered women*. Thousand Oaks, Ca: Sage Publications.

Asbury J (1987) African-American women in violent relationships: an exploration of cultural differences. In Hampton RL (Ed.) *Violence in the black family: correlates and consequences*. Lexington, Mass: Lexington Books.

Australian National Strategy on Violence against Women (1993) Canberra, National Committee in Violence against Women.

Babcock J, Waltz J, Jacobsen N and Gottman JM (1993) *Journal of Consulting and Clinical Psychology*. 61: 40–50.

Bachman R and Pillemer KA (1992) Epidemiology and family violence involving adults. In Ammerman RT and Hersen M (Eds.) *Assessment of family violence: a clinical and legal sourcebook*. NY: John Wiley and Sons.

Bachman R and Saltzman LE (1995) *Violence against women*. Washington DC: Bureau of Justice Statistics.

Bagshaw D and Chung D (2000) *Reshaping responses to domestic violence: the needs of children and young people*. Presentation to 'The way forward: children, young people and domestic violence', Carlton Crest Hotel, Melbourne, 26–27th April.

Bailey-Harris R, Barron J and Pearce J (1999) From Utility to Rights? The Presumption of Contact in Practice. *International Journal of Law, Policy and The Family*. 111.

Bala N (2000) A differentiated legal approach to the effects of spousal abuse on children: A Canadian context. *Journal of Aggression, Maltreatment and Trauma*. 3(1): 301–28.

Ballard TJ, Saltzman LE, Gazmararian JA, Spitz AM, Lazorick S and Marks JS (1998) Violence during pregnancy: measurement issues. *American Journal of Public Health*. 88(2)

Bancroft L and Silverman JG (2002) *The Batterer as Parent: Addressing The Impact of Domestic Violence on Family Dynamics*. Thousand Oaks, CA: Sage Publications.

Bandura A (1973) *Aggression: A social-learning approach*. Englewood Cliffs, NJ: Prentice-Hall.

Bandura A (1977) *Social learning theory*. Englewood Cliffs, NJ: Prentice-Hall.

Bandura A (1986) Fearful expectations and avoidant actions as coeffects of perceived self-inefficacy. *American Psychologist*. 12: 1389–91.

Bard M (1970) Role of law enforcement in the helping system. In Monahon J (Ed.) *Community mental health and the criminal justice system*. Elmsford, NJ: Pergamon Press.

Barker BDP (1994) *Mothers, babies and disease in later life*. London: BMJ Publishing Group.

Barnett OW, Miller-Perrin CL and Perrin RD (1997) *Family violence across the life span*. Thousand Oaks, Ca: Sage Publications.

Baruch DW and Wilcox JA (1944) A study of sex differences in preschool children's adjustment coexistent with interparental tensions. *Journal of Genetic Psychology*. 64: 281–303.

Bass E and Davies L (1992) *The courage to heal: a guide for women survivors of child sexual abuse*. NY: HarperPerrenial.

Bassuck E and Rosenberg L (1988) Why does family homelessness occur? *American Journal of Public Health*. 78 (7): 783–7.

Bastian L (1995) *Criminal victimization 1993*. Washington, DC: Bureau of Justice Statistics.

Baucom DH, Epstein N, Rankin LA and Burnett CK (1996) Assessing relationship standards: The Inventory of Specific Relationship Beliefs. *Journal of Family Psychology*. 10: 209–22.

Beach SRH, Etherton J and Whitaker D (1995) Cognitive accessibility and sentiment override: Starting a revolution-comment. *Journal of Family Psychology*. 9: 19–23.

Beck AT, Steer RA, and Garbin MG (1988) Psychometric properties of the Beck Depression Inventory: Twenty-five years of evaluation. *Clinical Psychology Review*. 8: 77–100.

Beeman SK and Edleson JL (2000) Collaborating on family safety: challenges for children and women's advocates. *Journal of Aggression, Maltreatment and Trauma*. 3 (1): 345–58.

Beinvenu MJ (1970) Measurement of marital communication. *Family Coordinator*. 19: 26–31.

Bell J (2002) Violence in the home. *Community Care*. 28 November–4th December, 25.

Bell M and McGoren J (2003) *Domestic violence risk assessment model*. Northern Ireland: Barnardos.

Bell T (1979) Ongoing research. *British Journal of Projective Psychology and Personality Study*. 24.

Belsky J (1981) Early family experience: A family perspective. *Developmental Psychology*. 17: 3–23.

Belsky J (1984) The determinants of parenting: A process model. *Child Development*. 55: 83–96.

Belsky J and Rovine M (1990) Patterns of marital change across the transition to parenthood. *Journal of Marriage and the Family*. 52: 109–23.

Belsky J, Rovine M and Fish M (1989) The developing family system. In Gunnar MR and Thelen E (Eds.) The Minnesota Symposium on Child Psychology: Vol. 22. *Systems and Development*. Hillsdale, NJ: Erlbaum.

Belsky J, Youngblade L, Rovine L, and Volling B (1991) Patterns of marital change and parent–child interaction. *Journal of Marriage and the Family*. 53 (2): 487–98.

Berk RA, Berk SF, Newton PJ and Loseke DR (1984) Cops on call: summoning the police to the scene of spousal violence. *Law and Society Review*. 18: 479–98.

Berkowitz CD (1997) Failure to protect: a spectrum of culpability. *Journal of Child Sexual Abuse*. 6: 1, 81–4.

Berkowitz L (1989) Frustration-aggression hypothesis: Examination and reformulation. *Psychological Bulletin*. 106: 59–73.

Bernard J and Bernard M (1984) The abusive male seeks treatment: Jekyll and Hyde. *Family Relations*. 33: 543–47.

Bilinkoff J (1995) Empowering battered women as mothers. In Peled E, Jaffe P and Edleson J (Eds.) *Ending the cycle of violence: community responses to children of battered women*. Thousand Oaks, Sage Publications.

Binney V, Harknell G and Nixon J (1987) *Leaving violent men: a study of refuges and housing for abused women*. Leeds: Women's Aid Federation of England.

Black D and Newman M (1996) Children and domestic violence: a review. *Clinical Child Psychology and Child Psychiatry*. 1 (1): 79–88.

Blanchard A (1999) *Caring for child victims of domestic violence*. Wangara: Nandina Press.

Bograd M (1982) Battered women, cultural myths and clinical interventions: A feminist analysis. *Women and Therapy*. 1: 69–77.

Bograd M (1990) Why we need to gender to understand human violence. *Journal of Interpersonal Violence*. 5 (1): 132–5.

Bond H (2002) Parental control. *Care and Health*. 21, 14–6.

Borbowski M, Murch M and Walker V (1983) *Marital violence: the community response*. London: Tavistock Publications.

Bowen K (2000) Child abuse and domestic violence in families of children seen for suspected sexual abuse. *Clinical Pediatrics*. 39 (1): 33–40.

Bowker LH, Arbitell M and McFerron JR (1988) On the relationship between wife beating and child abuse. In Yllo K and Bogard M (Eds.) *Feminist perspectives on wife abuse*. Newbury Park, Ca: Sage Publications.

Bowlby J (1958) The nature of the child's tie to the mother. *International psychoanalysis*. 39: 350–73.

Bowlby J (1973) *Attachment and loss: Vol. 2. Loss*. NewYork: Basic Books.

Bowlby J (1979) *The making and breaking of affectional bonds*. London: Tavistock.

Bowlby J (1980) *Attachment and loss Vol 3. Loss: Sadness and depression*. New York: Basic Books.

Bradbury TN and Fincham FD (1992) Attributions and behaviour in marital interaction. *Journal of Personality and Social Psychology*. 63: 613–28.

Bradbury TN and Fincham FD (1990) Attributions in marriage: review and citique. *Psychological Bulletin*. 107: 3–33.

Brand PA and Kidd AH (1986) Frequency of physical aggression in heterosexual and female homosexual dyads. *Psychological Reports*. 59: 1307–13.

British Crime Survey (1996) London: Home Office.

British Crime Survey: England and Wales (2000) London: Home Office.

Brody GH, Arias I and Fincham FD (1996) Linking marital and child attributions to family processes and parent–child relationships. *Journal of Family Psychology*. 10: 408–21.

Brody GH, Pellegrini AD and Sigel IE (1986) Marital quality and mother–child and father–child interactions with school-aged children. *Developmental Psychology*. 22: 291–6.

Bronfenbrenner U (1979) *The ecology of human development*. Cambridge: Harvard University Press.

Brown Y (1991) *Child protection workers knowledge of domestic violence*. Unpublished Honors thesis, Monash University.

Browne A (1987) *When battered women kill*. NY: The Free Press.

Browne A and Dutton DG (1990) Escape from violence: risks and alternatives for abused women: what do we currently know? In Roesch R, Dutton DG and Sacco VF (Eds.) *Family violence: perspectives on treatment, research and policy*. Burnaby, British

Columbia: British Columbia Institute on Family Violence.

Browne K and Herbert M (1997) *Preventing family violence*. Chichester: John Wiley and Sons.

Browne KD (1989) Family violence: spouse and elder abuse. In Howells K and Hollin C (Eds.) *Clinical approaches to domestic violence*. Chichester: John Wiley and Sons.

Browne KD (1993) Violence in the family and its links to child abuse. *Bailliere's Clinical Paediatrics*. 1 (1): 149–64.

Buehler C (1995) Divorce law in the United States. *Marriage and Family Review*. 21: 99–120.

Bumpass LL and Sweet JA (1989) National estimates of cohabitation. *Demography*. 26: No. 4, 615–25.

Burke C (1999) Redressing the balance: child protection intervention in the context of domestic violence. In Breckenbridge J and Laing L (Eds.) *Challenging silence: innovative responses to sexual and domestic violence*. Sydney: Allen and Unwin.

Burman B, Margolin G and John R (1993) America's angriest home videos: Behavioral contingencies observed in home reenactments of marital conflict. *Journal of Consulting and Clinical Psychology*. 61: 28–39.

Busche R and Robertson N (2000) Innovative approaches to child custody and domestic violence in New Zealand: the effects of law reform on the discourses of battering. *Journal of Aggression, Maltreatment and Trauma*. 3 (1): 269–99.

Buss A and Durkee A (1957) An inventory for assessing different kinds of hostility. *Journal of Consulting Psychology*. 21: 343–9.

Butler-Sloss E, Thorpe P and Waller I (2000) *Re L; Re V; Re M and Re H (Contact: Domestic Violence) Court of Appeal*, 19th June 2000, 2 FLR 334.

Buvinic M, Morrison AR and Shifter M (1999) Violence in the Americas: a framework for action. In Morrison AR and Biehl ML (Eds.) *Too close to home: domestic violence in the Americas*. Washington, DC: American Psychological Association.

Buzawa E and Buzawa C (Eds.) (1996) *Do arrests and restraining orders work?* Thousand Oaks, CA: Sage Publications.

Caesar PL and Hamberger LK (Eds.) (1989) *Treating men who batter: theory, practice and programs*. NY: Springer Publishing Company.

Calder MC (1990) Child Protection: Core groups: Participation not partnership. *Child Abuse Review*. 4 (2): 12–3.

Calder MC (1991) Child Protection: Core Groups: Beneficial or Bureaucratic? *Child Abuse Review*. 5 (2): 26–9.

Calder MC (1992) *Towards an ecological formulation of system maltreatment: identifying the casualties*.

Unpublished MA dissertation, University of Lancaster.

Calder MC (1999) Towards anti-oppressive practice with ethnic minority groups. In Calder MC and Horwath J (Eds.) *Working for children on the child protection register: An inter-agency practice guide.* Aldershot: Ashgate.

Calder MC (1999b) A conceptual framework for managing young people who sexually abuse: towards a consortium approach. In Calder MC (Ed.) *Working with young people who sexually abuse: New pieces of the jigsaw puzzle.* Dorset: Russell House Publishing.

Calder MC (1999c) *Assessing risk in adult males who sexually abuse children: A practitioners guide.* Dorset: Russell House Publishing.

Calder MC (2000) *A complete guide to sexual abuse assessments.* Dorset: Russell House Publishing.

Calder MC (2001) *Juveniles and children who sexually abuse: frameworks for assessment.* 2nd edn Dorset: Russell House Publishing.

Calder MC (2002) *Children affected by domestic violence: generating a framework for effective inter-agency responses.* Presentation to a Nexus conference 'Not in front of children: responding to conflict at all ends of the spectrum', TUC Congress Centre, London, 27th June.

Calder MC (2003) The Assessment Framework: A critique and reformulation. In Calder MC and Hackett S (Eds.) *Assessment in child care: using and developing frameworks for practice.* Dorset: Russell House Publishing.

Calder MC (2003b) Child sexual abuse and domestic violence: parallel considerations to inform professional responses. *Seen and Heard.* 12 (4):

Calder MC (2003c) *From Clarity Comes Chaos: The Impact of Government Frameworks for Young People Who Sexually Abuse.* Keynote Presentation to Durham ACPC Conference, Durham, 13th June 2003.

Calder MC (2003d) Unborn children: A framework for assessment and intervention. In Calder MC and Hackett S (Eds.) *Assessment in childcare: Using and developing frameworks for practice.* Dorset: Russell House Publishing.

Calder MC (2004) The Integrated Children's System: Out of The Frying Pan and Into The Fire? *Child Care in Practice* (In Press)

Calder MC, Peake A and Rose K (2001) *Mothers of sexually abused children: A framework for assessment, understanding and support.* Dorset: Russell House Publishing.

Calder MC and Waters J (1991) *Child abuse or child protection: What's in a name?* Paper presented to a one day conference on child abuse for the Association of Psychological Therapies, University of York, 18 June.

Cambell A (1993) *Out of control: men, women and aggression.* London: Pandora.

Cambell J (1998) *Empowering survivors of abuse: health care for battered women and their children.* Thousand Oaks, CA: Sage Publications.

Cambell JC (1986) Nursing assessment of risk of homicide with battered women. *Advances in Nursing Science.* 8 (4): 36–51.

Campbell JC (1992) If I can't have you, No one can: power and control in homicide of female partners. In Radford J and Russell D (Eds.) *Femicide: the politics of women killing.* NY: Twayne Publishers.

Cambell JC and Alford P (1989) The dark consequences of marital rape. *American Journal of Nursing.* 89: 946–9.

Cambell JC and Lewandowski LA (1997) Mental and physical health effects of intimate partner violence on women and children. *Psychiatric Clinic of North America.* 20: 353–74.

Cambell JC and Soeken KL (1999) Women's responses to battering over time: an analysis of change. *Journal of Interpersonal Violence.* 14 (1): 21–40.

Cambell J, Soeken K, McFarlane J and Parker B (1998) Risk Factors for Femicide Among Pregnant and Non-Pregnant Battered Women. in Cambell J (Ed.) *Empowering Survivors of Abuse: Health Care for Battered Women and Their Children.* Thousand Oaks, CA: Sage Publications.

Cammaert L (1988) Non-offending mothers: A new conceptualisation. In Walker LE (Ed.) *Handbook on sexual abuse of children: Assessment and treatment issues.* 309–25. NY: Springer.

Campbell JC, Miller P, Cardwell MM and Belknap RA (1994) Relationship Status of Battered Women Over Time. *Journal of Family Violence.* (9) 99–111.

Caplan P (1985) The scapegoating of mothers: A call for change. *American Journal of Orthopsychiatry.* 56: 610–3.

Carlson BE (1984) Causes and maintenance of domestic violence: an ecological analysis. *Social Service Review.* 58: 569–87.

Carlson BE (1984b) Children's observation of interparental violence. In Roberts AR (Ed.) *Battered women and their families.* NY: Springer.

Carlson BE (1990) Adolescent observers of marital violence. *Journal of Family Violence.* 5: 285–99.

Carlson BE (1991) Domestic violence. In Gitterman A (Ed.) *Handbook of social work practice with vulnerable populations.* NY: Columbia University Press.

Carlson BE (1991b) Outcomes of physical abuse and observation of marital violence among adolescents in placement. *Journal of Interpersonal Violence.* 6: 526–34.

Carlson BE (1997) Mental retardation and domestic violence: an ecological approach to intervention. *Social Work*. 42 (1): 79–89.

Carmen E (1981) Violence against wives: treatment dilemmas for clinicians and victims. International *Journal of Family Psychiatry*. 2: 353–67.

Cazenave NA and Straus MA (1979) Race, class, network embeddedness and family violence: a search for potent support systems. *Journal of Comparative Family Studies*. 10: 281–99.

Chesler P (1987) *Mothers on Trial: The Battle for Children and Custody*. Seattle: Seal Press.

Choice P and Lamke LK (1997) A conceptual approach to understanding abused women's stay/leave decisions. *Journal of Family Issues*. 18 (3): 290–314.

Christensen A (1988) Dysfunctional interaction patterns in couples. In Noller P and Fitzpatrick MA (Eds.) *Perspectives on marital interaction*. Philadelphia: Multilingual Matters.

Cleaver H et al. (1999) *Children's needs-parenting capacity: the impact of parental mental illness, problem alcohol and drug use and domestic violence on children's development*. London: TSO.

Coleman FL (1997) Stalking behaviour and the cycle of domestic violence, *Journal of Interpersonal Violence*. 12 (3): 420–32.

Coley SM and Beckett JO (1988) Black battered women: A review of empirical literature. *Journal of Counselling Development*. 66: 266–70.

Compas B (1987) Coping with stress during childhood and adolescence. *Psychological Bulletin*. 101 (3): 393–403.

Compas BE, Phares V, Banez GA and Howell DC (1991) Correlates of internalising and externalising behavior problems: Perceived competence, causal attributions, and parental symptoms. *Journal of Abnormal Child Psychology*. 19: 197–218.

Conger KJ and Conger RD (1995) Differential parenting and change in sibling differences in delinquency. *Journal of Family Psychology*. 8, 287–302.

Conger RD, Conger KJ, Elder GH, Lorenz FO, Simons RL and Whitbeck LB (1992) Linking economic hardship to marital quality and instability. *Journal of Marriage and The Family*. 52: 643–56.

Conger RD, Conger KJ, Elder GH, Lorenz F, Simons R and Whitbeck L (1993) Family economic stress and adjustment of early adolescent girls. *Developmental Psychology*. 29. 2: 206–19.

Conger RD, Conger KJ and Matthews LS (1999) Pathways of economic influence on adolescent adjustment. *American Journal of Community Psychology*. 27: 519–41.

Conger KJ, Conger RD and Scaramella LV (1997) Parents, siblings, psychological control, and adolescent adjustment. *Journal of Adolescent Research*. 12 (1): 113–38.

Conger RD and Elder GH (1994) *Families in troubled times: Adapting to change in rural America*. New York: De Gruyter.

Conte J and Schuerman J (1987) The effects of sexual abuse on children: a multidimensional view. *Journal of Interpersonal Violence*. 2: 380–90.

Cooper C (1992) Beating the crime. *Community Care*, 10th September 1992, 12–3.

Counts DA, Brown JK and Cambell JC (Eds.) (1992) *Sanctions and sanctuary: cultural perspectives on the beating of wives*. Boulder, Colorado: Westview Press.

Crawford M and Gartner R (1992) *Women killing: intimate femicide in Ontario 1974–1990*. Toronto, ON: Women We Honor Action Committee.

Crick NR and Dodge KA (1994) A review and reformulation of social information-processing mechanisms in children's social adjustment. *Psychological Bulletin*. 115: 74–101.

Crick NR and Dodge KA (1996) Social information processing mechanisms in reactive and proactive aggression. *Child Development*. 67: 993–1002.

Crockenberg S (1985) Toddlers reactions to maternal anger. *Merrill Palmer Quarterly*. 31: 361–73.

Crokenberg S and Forgays DK (1996) The role of emotion in children's understanding and emotional reactions to marital conflict. *Merrill Palmer Quarterly*. 42: 22–47.

Cromwell NA and Burgess AW (Eds.) (1996) *Understanding violence against women*. Washington, DC: National Academy Press.

Culross PL (1999) Health care system responses to children exposed to domestic violence. *Future Child*. 9 (3): 111–21.

Cummings EM (1998) Children exposed to marital conflict and violence: Conceptual and thoeretical directions. In G. W. Holden, R. Geffner (Ed.) *Children exposed to marital violence: Theory, research and applied issues*. Washington, DC: American Psychological Association.

Cummings EM (1994) Marital conflict and children's functioning. *Social Development*. 3: 16–36.

Cummings EM, Ballard M, El-Sheikh M and Lake M (1991) Responses of children and adolescents to interadult anger as a function of gender, age, and mode of expression. *Merrill-Palmer Quarterly*. 37: 543–60.

Cummings EM and Cummings JS (1988) A process-orientated approach to children's coping with adults' angry behavior. *Developmental Review*. 3: 296–321.

Cummings EM and Davies PT (1994) Maternal Depression and child development. *Journal of Child Psychology and Psychiatry and Allied Disciplines*. 35, 73–112.

Cummings EM and Davies PT (1994) *Children and marital conflict: The impact of family dispute and resolution.* New York: Guildford Press.

Cummings EM and Davies PT (1996) Emotional security as a regulatory process in normal development and the development of psychopathology. *Development and Psychopathology*. 8: 123–39.

Cummings EM, Davies PT and Campbell SB (2000) *Developmental Psychopathology and Family Process: Theory, Research, and Clinical Implications.* New York: The Guilford Press.

Cummings EM, Davies PT and Simpson KS (1994) Marital conflict, gender, and children's appraisals and coping efficacy as mediators of child adjustment. *Journal of Family Psychology*. 8: 141–9.

Cummings EM, Goeke-Morey MC, and Papp LM (2003) Children's reponses to everyday marital conflict tactics in the home. *Child Development*. 74: 1918–29.

Cummings EM, Lannotti RJ and Zahn-Waxler C (1989) Aggression between peers in early childhood: Individual continuity and developmental change. *Child Development*. 60: 887–95.

Cummings JS, Pelligrini DS, Notarius CI and Cummings EM (1989) Children's responses to angry adult behaviour as a function of marital distress and a history of inter-parent hostility. *Child Development*. 60: 1035–43.

Cummings EM, Vogel D, Cummings JS and El-Sheikh M (1989) Children's responses to different forms of aggression of anger between adults. *Child Development*. 60: 1392–404.

Cummings EM, Zahn-Waxler C and Radke-Yarrow M (1981) Young children's responses to expressions of anger and affection by others in the family. *Child Development*. 52: 1274–82.

Cutrona CE and Suhr JA (1994) Social support communication in the context of the marriage: An analysis of couple's supportive interactions. In Burleson BB, Albrecht TL and Sarason IG (Eds.) *Communication of social support: Messages, relationships and community.* Thousand Oaks, CA: Sage.

Dadds MR, Atkinson E, Turner C, Blums GJ and Lendich B (1999) Family conflict and child adjustment: Evidence for a cognitive contextual model of intergenerational transmission. *Journal of Family Psychology*. 13, 194–208.

Dallos R and McLaughlin E (1993) *Social problems and the family.* London: Sage Publications.

Dalrmpyle J and Burke B (1995) *Anti-oppressive practice: social care and the law.* Buckingham: Open University Press.

Daly M, Singh LS and Wilson M (1993) Children fathered by previous partners: a risk factor for violence against women. *Canadian Journal of Public Health*. 84: 209–10.

Davidson T (1977) Wifebeating: a recurring phenomenon throughout history. In Roy M (Ed.) *Battered women.* NY: Van Nostrand Reinhold.

Davies L and Krane J (1996) Shaking the legacy of mother-blaming: no easy task for child welfare. *Journal of Progressive Human Services*. 7: 2, 3–22.

Davies PT and Cummings EM (1994) Marital conflict and child adjustment: An emotional security hypothesis. *Psychological Bulletin*. 116: 387–411.

Davies PT and Cummings EM (1995) Children's emotions as organisers of their reactions to interadult anger: A functionalist perspective. *Developmental Psycholgy*. 31: 677–84.

Davies PT and Cummings EM (1998) Exploring children's emotional security as a mediator of the link between marital relations and child adjustment. *Child Development*. 69: 124–39.

Davies PT, Forman E and Stephens K (2000) *Strategies for testing the emotional security hypothesis: New methodological advances.* Paper presented at the Biennial Meeting of the Society for Research on Adolescence. Chicago, Illinois.

Davies PT, Harold GT, Goeke-Morey MC and Cummings EM (2002) Child Emotional Security and Interparental conflict. *Monographs of the Society for Research in Child Development.*, 270: 67, 3.

Davies PT, Myers RL and Cummings EM (1996) Responses of children and adolescents to marital conflict scenarios as a function of the emotionality of conflict endings, *Merrill-Palmer Quarterly*. 42: 1–21.

Davies PT, Myers RL, Cummings EM and Heindel S (1999) Adult conflict history and children's subsequent responses to conflict: An experimental test. *Journal of Family Psychology*. 13: 610–28.

Davies PT and Windle M (1997) Gender-specific pathways between maternal depressive symptoms, family discord, and adolescent adjustment. *Developmental Psychology*. 33: 657–68.

Davis LV (1987) Battered women: the transformation of a social problem. *Social Work*. 32: 306–11.

D'Ercole E and Struening E (1990) Victimisation among homeless: implications for service delivery. *Journal of Community Psychology*. 18 (2): 141–52.

DeVoe ER and Smith EL (2002) The impact of domestic violence in urban pre-school children. *Journal of Interpersonal Violence*. 17 (10): 1075–101.

Dobash RE (1977) *The Relationship Between Violence Directed at Women and Violence Directed at Children Within the Family Setting.* Appendix 38, Parliamentary Select Committee on Violence in the Family, London, HMSO.

Dobash RE and Dobash RP (1980) *Violence against wives.* London: Open Books.

Dobash RE and Dobash RP (1992) *Women, violence and social change.* London: Routledge.

Dobash RP, Dobash RE, Wilson M and Daly M (1996) The myth of sexual symmetry in marital violence. *Social Problems.* 39 (1): 71–91.

Dobash RE, Dobash RP and Cavanagh K (1985) *The Contact between Battered Women and Social and Medical Agencies,* in Pahl J (Ed.) *Private Violence and Public Policy: The Needs of Battered Women and the Response of the Public Services.* London, Routledge and Kegan Paul.

Dobson A (2002) Domestic violence. *Care and Health.* 15, July, 18–19.

Dodge KA (1986) A social information processing model of social competence in children. In Perlmutter M (Ed.) *Minnesota Symposium on Child Psychology (Vol. 18)* Hillsdale, NJ: Erlbaum.

Dodge KA (1980) Social cognition and children's aggressive behavior. *Child Development.* 51: 162–70.

Dodge KA (1983) Behavioral antecedents of peer social status. *Child Development.* 54: 1386–99.

Dodge KA (1993) Social-cognitive mechanisms in the development of conduct disorder and depression. *Annual Review of Psychology.* 44, 559–84.

Dodge KA, Murphy RR and Buchsbaum K (1984) The assessment of intention-cue detection skills in children: Implications for developmental psychopatholgy. *Child Development.* 55, 163–73.

Dodge KA, Pettit GS and Bates GE (1995) Effects of physical maltreatment on the development of peer relations. *Development and Psychopathology.* 6 (1): 43–55.

Dodge KA and Somberg DR (1987) Hostile attributional biases among aggressive boys are exacerbated under conditions of threats to the self. *Child Development.* 58: 213–24.

Doherty WJ (1981a) Cognitive process in intimate conflict 2: Efficacy and learned helplessness. *American Journal of Family Therapy.* 9: 35–44.

Doherty WJ (1981b) Cognitive process in intimate conflict 1: Extending attribution theory. *American Journal of Family Therapy.* 9: 3–13.

DoH (1995) *Child Protection: Messages from Research.* London: HMSO.

DoH (1999) *Working Together to Safeguard Children: A guide to inter-agency working to safeguard and promote the welfare of children.* London: HMSO.

DoH (2000) *A framework for assessing children and families.* London: HMSO.

Downey G and Coyne JC (1990) Children of depressed parents: an integrative review. *Psychological Bulletin.* 108: 50–76.

Downs A (1972) Up and down with ecology and the 'issue-attention' cycle. *Public Interest.* 32: 38–50.

Driver E (1989) Introduction. In Driver E and Droisen A (Eds.) *Child sexual abuse: feminist perspectives.* Basingstoke: Macmillan.

Dube SR, Anda RF, Felitti VJ, Edwards VJ and Williamson DF (2002) Exposure to abuse, neglect, and household dysfunction among adults who witnessed intimate partner violence as children: Implications for health and social services. *Violence and Victims.* 17 (1): 3–17.

Dugan MK and Hock RR (2000) *It's my life now: starting after an abusive relationship or domestic violence.* NY: Routledge.

Dunn J and Munn P (1985) Becoming a family member: Family conflict and the development of understanding in the second year. *Child Development.* 56: 480–92.

Dutton DG (1985) An ecologically nested theory of male violence towards intimates. *International Journal of Women's Studies.* 8 (4): 404–13.

Dutton DG (1988) *The domestic assault on women: psychological and criminal justice perspectives.* Toronto, ON: Allyn and Bacon.

Dutton DG (2000) Witnessing parental violence as a traumatic experience shaping the abusive personality. *Journal of Aggression, Maltreatment and Trauma.* 3 (1): 59–67.

Dutton DG and Browning JJ (1988) Concerns for power, fear of intimacy and aversive stimuli for wife assault. In Hotaling G, Finkelhor D, Kirkpatrick JT and Straus MA (Eds.) *Family abuse and its consequences: new directions in research.* Newbury Park: Sage.

Easterbrooks MA, Ballard M and Cummings EM (1994) Individual differences in preschoolers' physiological and verbal responses to videotaped angry interactions. *Journal of Abnormal Child Psychology.* 22: 303–20.

Easterbrooks MA, Cummings EM and Emde RN (1994) Young children's response to constructive marital disputes. *Journal of Family Psychology.* 8, 160–9.

Easterbrooks MA and Emde RN (1988) Marital and parent–child relationships: The role of affect in the family system. In Hinde RA and Stephenson-Hinde J (Eds.) *Relationships within families: Mutual influences.* New York: Oxford University Press.

Eberly M and Montemayor R (1998) Doing good deeds: An examination of adolescent prosocial behavior in the context of parent-adolescent relationships. *Journal of Adolescent Research.* 13, 403–32.

Echlin C and Osthoff B (2000) Child protection workers and battered women's advocates working together to end violence against women and children. *Journal of Aggression, Maltreatment and Trauma.* 3 (1): 207–19.

Edleson JL (1999) Children's witnessing of adult domestic violence. *Journal of Interpersonal Violence.* 14 (8): 839–70.

Edleson JL (1999b) The overlap between child maltreatment and woman battering. *Violence against Women.* 5: 134–54.

Edleson JL and Tolman RM (1992) *Intervention for men who batter.* Newbury Park, Ca: Sage Publications.

Edleson JL, Mbilinyi LF, Beeman SK and Hagemesiter AK (2003) How children are involved in adult domestic violence. *Journal of Interpersonal Violence.* 18 (1): 18–32.

Eidelson RJ and Epstein N (1982) Cognition and relationship maladjustment: Development of a measure of dysfunctional relationship beliefs. *Journal of Consulting and Clinical Psychology.* 50: 715–84.

Eisikovits Z and Winstok Z (2001) Researching children's experience of interparental violence: toward a multi-dimensional conceptualization. In Graham-Bermann SA and Edleson JL (Eds.) *Domestic violence in the lives of children.* Washington DC: American Psychological Association.

Elicker J, Englund M and Soufre AL (1992) Predicting peer competence and peer relationships in childhood from early parent-child relationships. In Parke RD and Ladd GW (Eds.) *Family-peer relationships: Models of linkage.* 77–106.

El-Shiekh M and Cummings EM (1995) Children's responses to angry adult behavior as a function of experimentally manipulated exposure to resolved and unresolved conflict. *Social Development.* 4: 75–91.

Emery RE (1982) The Children's Perception Questionnaire (CPQ). In Touliatos J, Perlmutter BF and Straus MA (Eds.) *Handbook of Family Measurement Techniques.* Sage.

Emery RE (1982b) Interparental conflict and the children of discord and divorce. *Psychological Bulletin.* 92: 310–30.

Emery RE, Fincham FD and Cummings EM (1992) Parenting in context: Systemic thinking about parental conflict and its influence on children. *Journal of Consulting and Clinical Psychology.* 60: 909–12.

Emery RE and O'Leary KD (1982) Children's perceptions of marital discord and behaviour problems of boys and girls. *Journal of Abnormal Child Psychology.* 10 (1): 11–24.

Engfer A (1988) The interrelatedness of marriage and the mother–child relationship. In Hinde RA and Stephenson-Hinde J (Eds.) *Relationships within families.* Oxford, England: Clarendon Press.

Erel O and Burman B (1995) Interrelatedness of marital relations and parent–child relations: A meta-analytic review. *Psychological Bulletin.* 118 (1): 108–32.

Everitt A and Hardiker P (1996) *Evaluating for good practice.* London: Macmillan.

Fall KA, Howard S and Ford JE (1999) *Alternatives to domestic violence: A homework manual for battering intervention groups.* Philadelphia: Accelerated Development.

Fantuzzo JW, Boruch R, Beriana A, Atkins M and Marcus S (1997) Domestic violence and children: Prevalence and risk in five major cities. *Journal of the American Academy of Child and Adolescent Psychiatry.* 36, 116–22.

Fantuzzo JW and Lindquist UC (1989) The effects of observing conjugal violence on children: A review and analysis of research methodology. *Journal of Family Violence.* 4: 77–94.

Fantuzzo JW, DePaola LM, Lambert L, Martino T, Anderson G and Sutton S (1991) Effects of inter-parental violence on the adjustments and competencies of young children. *Journal of Consulting and Clinical Psychology.* 59: 258–65.

Fantuzzo JW, Mohr WK and Noone MJ (2000) Making the invisible victims of violence against women visible through University/community partnerships. *Journal of Aggression, Maltreatment and Trauma.* 3 (1): 9–23.

Farmer E (1993) The impact of child protection interventions: the experiences of parents and children. In Waterhouse L (Ed.) *Child abuse and child abuser.* London: Jessica Kingsley.

Farmer E and Owen M (1995) *Child protection practice: private risks and public remedies.* London: HMSO.

Farmer E and Owen M (1998) Gender and the child protection process. *British Journal of Social Work.* 28 (4): 545–64.

Farrington DP (2000) Adolescent violence: Findings and implications from the Cambridge study. In Boswell G (Ed.) *Violent Children and adolescents: Asking the question why?* 19–35.

Fauber RL, Forehand R, Thomas AM and Wierson M (1990) A mediational model of the impact of marital conflict on adolescent adjustment in intact and divorced families: The role of disrupted parenting. *Child Development.* 61: 1112–23.

Fauber RL and Long N (1991) Children in context: The role of the family in child psychotherapy. *Journal of Consulting and Clinical Psychology*. 59: 813–20.

Faulk M (1974) Men who assault their wives. *Medicine, Science and the Law*. 14: 180–3.

Fernandez M (1997) Domestic violence by extended family members in India. *Journal of Interpersonal Violence*. 12 (3): 433–55.

Ferraro KJ and Johnson JM (1983) How women experience battering: the process of victimization. *Social Problems*. 30 (3): 325–39.

Fincham FD (1994) Understanding the association between marital conflict and child adjustment: Overview. *Journal of Family Psychology*. 2: 123–7.

Fincham FD (1998) Child development and marital relations. *Child Development*. 69: 543–574.

Fincham FD, Beach SR, Arias I and Brody GH (1998) Children's attributions in the family: The children's relationship attribution measure. *Journal of Family Psychology*. 12: 481–93.

Fincham FD, Beach SR, Harold GT and Osborne LN (1997) Marital satisfaction and depression: Different causal relationships for men and women? *Psychological Science*. 8 (5): 351–7.

Fincham FD and Bradbury TN (1992) Assessing attributions in marriage: The Relationship Attribution Measure. *Journal of Personality and Social Psychology*. 62: 457–68.

Fincham FD, Harold GT and Gano-Phillips S (2000) The longitudinal association between attributions and marital satisfaction: Direction of effects and role of efficacy expectations. *Journal of Family Psychology*. 14: 267–85.

Fincham FD and Linfield K (1997) A new look at marital quality: Can spouses be positive and negative about their marriage? *Journal of Family Psychology*. 11: 489–502.

Finn J (1985) The stresses and coping behaviours of battered women. *Social Casework*. 66: 341–9.

Folkman S and Lazarus RS (1980) An analysis of coping in a middle aged community sample. *Journal of Health and Social Behavior*. 21, 219–39.

Follingstad DR, Rutledge BJ, Berg ES, Hause ES and Polek DS (1990) The role of emotional abuse in physically abusive relationships. *Journal of Family Violence*. 5 (2): 107–20.

Forehand R, Neighbors R, Devine D and Armistead L (1994) Interparental conflict and parental divorce – The individual, relative and interactive effects on adolescents across 4 years. *Family Relations*. 43: 387–93.

Forehand R and Wierson M (1993) The role of developmental factors in planning behavioural interventions for children: Disruptive behavior as an example. *Behavior Therapy*. 24: 117–41.

Foster LA, Mann Veale C and Ingram Fogel C (1989) Factors present when battered women kill. *Issues in Mental Health Nursing*. 10: 373–84.

Foxcroft DR and Lowe G (1991) Adolescent drinking behavior and family socialization factors: A meta-analysis. *Journal of Adolescence*. 14: 255–73.

Foxcroft DR and Lowe G (1995) Adolescent drinking, smoking and other substance use involvement: Links with perceived family-life. *Journal of Adolescence*. 18, 159–77.

Foxcroft DR and Lowe G (1997) Adolescents' alcohol use and misuse: The socializing influence of perceived family life. *Drugs, Education Prevention Policy*. 4, 215–29.

Frude N (1980) Child abuse as aggression. In Frude N (Ed.) *Psychological approaches to child abuse*. London: Batsford, 136–50.

Frude N (1989) The physical abuse of children. In Howells K and Hollin C (Eds.) *Clinical approaches to violence*. Chichester: John Wiley and Sons.

Frude N (1991) *Understanding family problems: a psychological approach*. Chichester: John Wiley and Sons.

Frude N (1994) Marital violence: an interactional perspective. In Archer J (Ed.) *Male violence*. London: Routledge.

Fuhrman W and Buhrmester D (1985) Children's perceptions of the qualities of sibling relationships. *Child Development*. 56: 448–61.

Furstenberg FF and Cherlin AJ (1991) *Divided families: What happens to children when parents part*. Cambridge, MA: Harvard University Press.

Gable S, Belsky J and Crnic K (1992) Marriage, parenting, and child development: Progress and prospects. *Journal of Family Psychology*. 5: 276–94.

Ganley AL (1989) Integrating feminist and social learning analyses of aggression: creating multiple models for intervention with men who batter. In Caesar PL and Hamberger LK (Eds.) *Treating men who batter: theory, practice and programs*. NY: Springer Publishing Company.

Ganley AL and Schechter S (1996) *Domestic violence: A national curriculum for children's protective services*. San Francisco: Family Violence Prevention Fund.

Garbarino J (1977) The human ecology of child maltreatment: A conceptual model for research. *Journal of Marriage and the Family*. 39: 721–735.

Garmezy N (1983) Stressors in childhood. In Garmezy N and Rutter M (Eds.) *Stress, coping, and development of children*. NY: McGraw Hill.

Garner J (1998) *What are the lessons of the police arrest studies?* Paper presentation at Program Evaluation and Family Violence Research: An International conference. Durham, New Hampshire.

Gassner S and Murray EJ (1969) Dominance and conflict in the interaction between parents of normal and neurotic children. *Journal of Abnormal Psychology*. 74, 33–41.

Gayford JJ (1975) Wife battering: a preliminary survey of 100 cases. *British Medical Journal*. 25 (1): 94–7.

Gayle C (2002) Working with mothers and children. In Saunders H and Humphreys C (Eds.) *Safe and sound: a resource manual for working with children who have experienced domestic violence*. Bristol: Women's Aid Federation of England.

Gazmararian JA (1996) Prevalence of violence amongst pregnant women. *Journal of the American Medical Association*. 275: 24, 1915–20.

Ge XJ, Conger RD, Lorenz FO, Shanahan M and Elder GH (1995) Mutual influences in parent and adolescent psychological distress. *Developmental Psychology*. 31: 406–19.

Ge XJ, Conger RD, Lorenz FO and Simons RL (1994) Parents stressful life events and adolescent depressed mood. *Journal of Health and Social Behaviour*. 35, 1: 28–44.

Gelles RJ (1972) *The violent home: a study of physical aggression between husbands and wives*. Beverley Hills, Ca: Sage Publications.

Gelles RJ (1987) *The violent home* 2nd edn, California: Sage Publications.

Gelles RJ and Cornell C (1985) *Family violence: intimate violence in families*. Beverley Hills, Ca: Sage Publications.

Gelles RJ and Straus MA (1988) *Intimate violence: the definitive study of the causes and consequences of abuse in the American family*. NY: Simon and Schuster.

Giacoletti AM (1990) *Children's responses to parent and stranger discord*. Unpublished Master's thesis, West Virginia University, Morganstown.

Gibbons J, Conroy S and Bell C (1995) *Operating the child protection system*. London: HMSO.

Gil D (1970) *Violence against children*. Cambridge, Mass: Harvard University Press.

Giles-Sims J (1983) *Wife-beating: a systems theory approach*. NY: Guilford.

Giles-Sims SJ (1985) A longitudinal study of battered children of battered wives. *Family Relations*. 2: 205–10.

Glass DD (1995) *All my fault: why women don't leave abusive men*. London: Virago Books.

Glendinning A, Shucksmith J and Hendry L (1997) Family life and smoking in adolescence. *Social Science & Medicine*. 44: 93–101.

Goddard C (1981) *Child abuse: a hospital study*. Department of Social Work: University of Monash, Melbourne.

Goddard C and Hillier PC (1993) Child sexual abuse: assault in a violent context. *Australian Journal of Social Issues*. 28 (1): 20–33.

Goddard E (1992) Why children start smoking. *British Journal of Addiction*. 87, 17–8.

Goeke-Morey M and Cummings EM (2000) *Exploring the distinction between constructive and destructive marital conflict behaviors from adolescents' perspective*. Paper presented at the Biennial Meeting of the Society for Research on Adolescence. Chicago, Illinois.

Goldberg WA and Easterbrooks MA (1984) Role of marital quality in toddler development. *Developmental Psychology*. 20: 504–14.

Goldner V et al. (1994) Love and violence: gender paradoxes in volatile attachments. *Family Process*. 29 (4): 343–64.

Gondolf EW (1998) Do batterer programs work? A 15-month follow-up of multi-site evaluation. *Domestic Violence Report*. 3: 65–79.

Gondolf EW (2000) *Batterer intervention systems: issues, outcomes and recommendations*. Thousand Oaks, CA: Sage Publications.

Gondolf E and Fisher E (1988) *Battered women as survivors: an alternative to treating learned helplessness*. Lexington, Mass: Lexington Books.

Gondolf E and Russell D (1986) The case against anger control programs for batterers. *Response*. 9: 3, 2–5.

Gottman JM (1994) *Why marriages succeed or fail*. NY: Simon and Schuster.

Gottman JM (1979) *Marital Interaction: Experimental investigations*. New York: Academic Press.

Gottman JM, Kahen V and Goldstein D (1996) The Rapid Couples Interaction Scoring System (RCISS) In Gottman JM (Ed.) *What predicts divorce? The measures*. Mahwah, NJ: Erlbaum.

Gottman JM and Katz LF (1989) Effects of marital dsicord on young children's peer interaction and health. *Developmental Psychology*. 25: 373–81.

Gottman JM, McCoy K, Coan J and Collier H (1996) The Specific Affect Coding System (SPAFF) In Gottman JM (Ed.) *What predicts divorce? The measures*. Mahwah, NJ: Erlbaum.

Graham-Bermann SA and Levendosky AA (1998a) The social functioning of pre-school aged children whose mothers are emotionally and physically abused. *Journal of Emotional Abuse*. 1, 59–84.

Graham DLR and Rawlings EI (1991) Bonding with abusive dating partners: dynamics of the Stockholm Syndrome. In Levy B (Ed.) *Dating violence: young women in danger*. Seattle: Seal Press.

Greenblat CS (1983) A hit is a hit is a hit . . . or is it? In Finkelhor D, Gelles RJ, Hotaling G and Straus

M (Eds.) *The dark side of families*. Beverley Hills, Ca: Sage Publications.

Griffing S, Ragin DF, Sage RE, Madry L, Bingham LE and Primm BJ (2002) Domestic violence survivors' self-identified reasons for returning to abusive relationships. *Journal of Interpersonal Violence*. 17 (3): 306–19.

Grotberg E (1997) The international resilience project. In John M (Ed.) *A charge against society: the child's right to protection*. London: Jessica Kingsley.

Groves BM (1999) Mental health services for children who witness domestic violence. *Future Child*. 9 (3): 122–32.

Groves BM and Zuckerman B (1997) Interventions with parents and caregivers of children who are exposed to domestic violence. In Osofsky JD (Ed.) *Children in a violent society*. NY: The Guilford Press.

Grusec JE (1992) Social learning theory and developmental psychology: The legacies of Robert Sears and Albert Bandura. *Developmental Psychology*. 28(5): 776–86.

Grych JH (1998) Children's appraisals of interparental conflict: Situational and contextual influences. *Journal of Family Psychology*. 12, 437–53.

Grych JH and Cardoza-Fernandes S (2001) Understanding the impact of interparental conflict on children: The role of social cognitive processes. In Grych JH and Fincham F (Eds.) *Child Development and Interparental Conflict*. 157–87.

Grych JH and Fincham FD (1990) Marital conflict and children's adjustment: A cognitive-contextual framework. *Psychological Bulletin*. 108 (2): 267–90.

Grych JH, Fincham FD, Jouriles EN and McDonald R (2000) Interparental conflict and child adjustment: Testing the mediational role of appraisals in the cognitive contextual framework. *Child Development*. 71, 1648–61.

Grych JH, Harold GT and Miles CJ (2003) A prospective investigation of appraisals as mediators of the link between interparental conflict and child adjustment. *Child Development*. 74, 1176–93.

Grych JH and Fincham FD (1993) Children's appraisals of marital conflict: Initial investigations of the cognitive-contextual framework. *Child Development*. 64: 215–30.

Grych JH, Seid M and Fincham FD (1992) Assessing marital conflict from the child's perspective: The Children's Perception of Interparental Conflict Scale. *Child Development*. 63: 558–72.

Hackett S (2000) Sexual aggression, diversity and the challenge of anti-oppressive practice. *The Journal of Sexual Aggression*. 5: 1, 4–20.

Hague G, Mullender A, Kelly L, Iman U and Malos E (2002) How do children understand and cope with domestic violence? *Practice*. 14 (1): 17–26.

Hamberger LK and Hastings JE (1986) Characteristics of spouse abusers: predictors of treatment acceptance. *Journal of Interpersonal Violence*. 1 (3): 363–73.

Hammen C, Burge D and Adrian C (1991) Timing of mother and child depression in a longitudinal study of children at risk. *Journal of Consulting and Clinical Psychology*. 59: 341–5.

Hanson RK, Cadsky O, Harris A and Lalonde C (1997) Correlates of battering among 997 men: family history, adjustment and attitudinal differences. *Violence and Victims*. 12 (3): 191–208.

Harold GT (1999) *'Anger is in the eye of the beholder': The role of children's perceptions of parental behaviour*. Paper presented at the Society for Research in Child Development, Alberquerque, New Mexico.

Harold GT and Conger RD (1997) Marital conflict and adolescent distress: The role of adolescent awareness. *Child Development*. 68 (2): 333–50.

Harold GT, Fincham FD, Osborne LN and Conger RD (1997) Mom and Dad are at it again: Adolescent perceptions of marital conflict and adolescent psychological distress. *Developmental Psychology*. 33, 2: 333–50.

Harold GT, Pryor J and Reynolds J (2001) *Not in front of the children? How conflict between parents affects children*. London: One Plus One Marriage and Partner Research.

Harold GT and Shelton KH (2000) *Marital conflict and adolescent adjustment: The role of emotional and parent–child attachment security*. Paper presented at the Biennial Meeting of the Society for Research on Adolescence. Chicago, Illinois.

Harold GT, Shelton KH, Goeke-Morey MC and Cummings EM (2002) Relations between interparental conflict, child emotional security, and adjustment in the context of cognitive appraisals. In Davies, Harold, Goeke-Morey and Cummings, *Child Emotional Security and Interparental Conflict*. Monographs of the Society for Research in Child Development. 270: 67, 3.

Harold GT, Shelton HH, Goeke-Morey MC and Cummings EM (2004) Child emotional security about family relationships and child adjustment. *Social Developments*. 13: 350–76.

Harold GT, Shelton KH, Goeke-Morey MC and Cummings EM (in press) Marital conflict, child emotional security about family relationships and child adjustment. *Social Development*.

Harris Hendricks J, Black D and Kaplan T (1993) *When father kills mother: guiding children through trauma and grief*. London: Routledge.

Hart B (1986) Lesbian battering: an examination. In Lobel K (Ed.) *Naming the violence: speaking out about lesbian battering*. Seattle, WA: Seal.

Hart B, Stuehling J, Reese M and Stubbing E (1990) *Confronting domestic violence: effective police responses*. Pennsylvania: Pennsylvania Coalition against Domestic Violence.

Hart SD, Dutton DG and Newlove T (1993) The prevalence of personality disorder among wife assaulters. *Journal of Personality Disorders*. 7 (4): 328–40.

Healey K, Smith C and O'Sullivan C (1998) *Batterer intervention: program approaches and criminal justice strategies*. Washingon, DC: National Institute of Justice.

Heath I (2003) The presentation and diagnosis of domestic violence. In Amiel S and Heath I (Eds.) *Family violence in primary care*. Oxford: Oxford University Press.

Heery G (2001) *Preventing violence in relationships: A programme for men who feel they have a problem with the use of controlling and violent behaviour*. London: Jessica Kingsley.

Hendricks-Matthews M (1982) The battered woman: Is she ready for help? *Social Casework*. 63: 131–7.

Henwood M (2000) *Domestic violence: a resource manual for health care professionals*. London: DoH.

Herman JL (1992) *Trauma and recovery: the aftermath of violence: from domestic violence to political terror*. NY: Basic Books.

Hess PM, Foloron G and Jefferson AB (1992) Effectiveness of family reunification services: an innovative evaluative model. *Social Work*. 31: 304–11.

Hester M (2002) One Step Forward and Three Steps Back? Children, Abuse and Parental Contact in Denmark. *Child and Family Law Quarterly*. 14(3): 267–79.

Hester M and Radford L (1995) The Impact of The Children Act. In Hester M et al. (Eds.) *Women, Violence and Male Power*. Milton Keynes: Open University Press.

Hester M and Radford C (1996) *Domestic violence and child contact arrangements in England and Denmark*. London: Policy Press.

Hester M, Pearson C and Harwin N (2000) *Making an impact: children and domestic violence*. London: Jessica Kingsley.

Hetherington EM (1989) Coping with family transitions: Winners, Losers, and Survivors. *Child Development*. 60: 1–14.

Hetherington EM, Cox M and Cox R (1982) Effects of divorce on parents and children. In Lamb ME (Ed.) Non-traditional families: *Parenting and child development*. Hillsdale, NJ: Lawrence Erlbaum Associates, Inc.

Heyman RE, Weiss RL and Eddy JM (1995) Marital Interaction Coding System: revision and empirical evaluation. *Behavioral Research and Therapy*. 33: 737–46.

Hilberman E and Munson K (1977–8) Sixty battered women. *Victimology*. 2: 460–70.

Hilbert JC and Hilbert HC (1984) Battered women leaving shelter. *Journal of Applied Social Sciences*. 8: 291–7.

HMSO (1993) *British Crime Statistics England and Wales, 1992*. London: The Home Office, Research, Development and Statistics Directorate.

HMSO (1998) *Criminal Statistics England and Wales, 1997*. London: The Home Office, Research, Development and Statistics Directorate.

Hoff LA (1990) *Battered Women as Survivors*. London, Routledge.

Holden GW (1998) Introduction: The development of research into another consequence of family violence. In Holden GW Geffner R and Jouriles EN (Eds.) *Children exposed to marital violence: Theory, research and applied issues*. 1–20.

Holden GW and Ritchie KL (1991) Linking extreme marital discord, child rearing, and child behaviour problems: evidence from battered women. *Child Development*. 62: 311–27.

Holden GW, Stein JD, Ritchie KL, Harris SD and Jouriles EN (1998) Parenting behaviours and beliefs of battered women. In Holden GW, Geffner R and Jouriles EN (Eds.) *Children exposed to marital violence: theory, research, and applied issues*. Washington, DC: American Psychological Association.

Home Office (1996) *British Crime Survey*. London, Home Office.

Home Office (1999) *Domestic violence: findings from a new British Crime Survey self-completions questionnaire*. London: Home Office Research Studies.

Home Office (2000) *Domestic violence: revised circular to the police*. HOC 19/2000. Available from www.homeoffice.gov.uk/circulars/2000/hoc1900.htm

Home Office (2000b) *Domestic violence: break the chain. Multi-agency guidance for addressing domestic violence*. Available from: www.homeoffice.gov.uk/domesticviolence/mag.htm

Home Office and Cabinet Office (1999) *Living without fear: an integrated approach to tackling violence against women*. London: TSO

Hooper CA (1992) Child sexual abuse and the regulation of women. In Smart C (Ed.) *Regulating womanhood*. London: Routledge.

Hops H, Sherman L and Biglan A (1990) Maternal depression, marital discord and children's behavior: A developmental perspective. In Patterson GR (Ed.) *Depression and aggression in family interaction: Advances in family research.* 185–208.

Horwath J and Calder MC (1999) The background and current context of post-registration practice. In Calder MC and Horwath J (Eds.) *Working for children on the child protection register: An inter-agency practice guide.* Aldershot: Arena.

Hotaling GT and Sugarman DB (1986) An analysis of risk markers in husband to wife violence: the current state of knowledge. *Violence and Victims.* 1: 101–24.

Howe D (1995) *Attachment Theory for Social Work Practice.* MacMillan Press Ltd.

Howell M and Pugliesi K (1988) Husbands who harm: predicting spousal violence by men. *Journal of Family Violence.* 3 (1): 15–27.

Howes P and Markman HJ (1989) Marital quality and child functioning: A longitudinal investigation. *Child Development.* 60: 1044–51.

Hughes H (1992) Impact of spouse abuse on children of battered women. *Violence Update.* 1: 9–11.

Hughes H and Fantuzzo J (1994) Family violence: child victims. In Hersen M, Ammerman R and Sisson L (Eds.) *Handbook of aggressive and destructive behaviour in psychiatric patients.* NY: Plenum.

Hughes HM, Graham-Bermann SA and Gruber G (2001) Resilience in children exposed to domestic violence. In Graham-Bermann SA and Edleson JL (Eds.) *Domestic violence in the lives of children.* Washington DC: American Psychological Association.

Hughes HM (1988) Psychological and behavioural correlates of family violence in child witnesses and victims. *American Journal of Orthopsychiatry.* 58: 77–90.

Hughes HM and Luke DA (1998) Heterogeneity in adjustment in children of battered women. In Holden GW, Geffner RA and Jouriles EN (Eds.) *Children exposed to marital violence: theory, research and applied issues.* Washington, DC: American Psychological Association.

Humphreys C (1997) *Case planning issues where domestic violence occurs in the context of child protection.* Report to Coventry Social Services Child Protection Unit.

Humphreys C (2000) *Social work, domestic violence and child protection.* Bristol: Policy Press.

Humphreys C (2001) The impact of domestic violence on children. In Foley P, Roche J and Tucker S (Eds.) *Children in society: contemporary theory, policy and practice.* Basingstoke: Palgrave.

Humphreys C and Mullender A (2002) *Children and domestic violence: a research overview of the impact on children.* Totnes: Research in Practice.

Humphreys C and Thiara R (2002) *Routes to Safety: Protection Issues Facing Abused Women and Children and The Role of Outreach Services.* Bristol: Women's Aid Federation.

Humphreys C, Hester M, Hague G, Mullender A, Abrahams H and Lowe P (2000) *From good intentions to good practice: mapping services working with families where there is domestic violence.* Bristol: The Policy Press.

Huth-Bocks AC, Levendosky AA and Semel MA (2001) The direct and indirect effects of domestic violence on young children's intellectual functioning. *Journal of Family Violence.* 16 (3): 269–90.

Island D and Letellier P (1991) *Men who beat the men who love them.* Binghampton, NY: Harington Park Press.

Jaffe PG and Geffner R (1998) Child Custody Disputes and Domestic Violence: Critical Issues for Mental Health, Social Service and Legal Professionals. In Holden GW, Geffner R and Jouriles EN (Eds.) *Children Exposed to Marital Violence: Theory, Research and Applied Issues.* Washington, DC: American Psychological Association, 371–99.

Jaffe PG, Lemon NKD and Poisson SE (2003) *Child Custody and Domestic Violence: A Call for Safety and Accountability.* Thousand Oaks, Ca: Sage Publications.

Jaffe P, Wolfe D and Wilson SK (1990) *Children of battered women.* Newbury Park, Ca: Sage Publications.

James G (1994) *Study of working together.* Part 8 reports. London: DoH.

James K (1999) Truth or fiction: men as victims of domestic violence? In Breckenbridge J and Laing L (Eds.) *Challenging silence: innovative responses to sexual and domestic violence.* Sydney: Allen and Unwin.

Johnson N (1995) Domestic violence: an overview. In Kingston P and Penhale B (Eds.) *Family violence and the caring professionals.* London: Macmillan.

Johnson PL and O'Leary KD (1987) Parental behaviour patterns and conduct disorders in girls. *Journal of Abnormal Child Psychology.* 15: 573–81.

Johnston J and Cambell L (1993) A clinical typology of interpersonal violence in disputed custody disputes. *American Journal of Orthopsychiatry.* 63: 190–9.

Jones D and Sieg A (1988) Child sexual abuse allegations in custody or visitation cases. In Nicholson E (Ed.) *Sexual abuse allegations in custody and visitation cases.* Washington, DC: American Bar Association.

Jones E and Parkinson P (1995) Child sexual abuse, access and the wishes of children. *International Journal of Law and the Family.* 9: 54–5.

Jones LP, Gross E and Becker I (2002) The characteristics of domestic violence in a child protective service caseload. *Families in Society*. 83 (4): 405–15.

Jouriles EN, Barling J and O'Leary KD (1987) Predicting child behaviour problems in maritally violent families. *Journal of Abnormal Child Psychology*. 15, 165–73.

Jouriles EN, Norwood WD, McDonald R, Vincent JP and Mahoney A (1996) Physical violence and other forms of marital aggression: Links with children's behavior problems. *Journal of Family Psychology*. 10: 223–34.

Jouriles EN, Pfiffner LJ and O'Leary SG (1988) Marital conflict, parenting, and toddler conduct problems. *Journal of Abnormal Child Psychology*. 12: 605–20.

Jukes AE (1999) *Men who batter women*. London: Routledge.

Julian D, Markman HJ and Lindahl KM (1989) A comparison of a global and a microanalytic coding system: Implications for future trends in studying interactions. *Behavioral Assessment*. 11: 81–100.

Justice B and Justice R (1976) *The Broken Taboo*. NY: Human Sciences Press.

Kahen V, Katz LF and Gottman JM (1994) Linkages between parent–child interactions and conversations of friends. *Social Development*. 3: 238–54.

Kantor GK and Straus RJ (1986) The 'drunken bum' theory of wife beating. *Social Problems*. 34: 213–30.

Katz LF and Gottman JM (1994) Patterns of marital interaction and children's emotional development. In Parke RD and Kellam SG (Eds.) *Exploring Family Relationships With Other Social Contexts*. Hillsdale, NJ: Erlbaum.

Kaye M (1996) Domestic violence residence and contact. *Child and Family Law Quarterly*. 8 (4): 285–96.

Kazdin AE (1995) Child, parent, and family dysfunction as predictors of outcome in cognitive-behavioural treatment of antisocial children. *Behaviour research and Therapy*. 33 (3): 271–81.

Kelly L (1988) *Surviving Sexual Violence*. Cambridge: Policy Press.

Kelly L (1989) *Surviving sexual violence*. Cambridge: Polity Press.

Kelly L (1994) The interconnectedness of domestic violence and child abuse: challenges for research, policy and practice. In Mullender A and Morley R (Eds.) *Children living with domestic violence: putting men's abuse of women on the child care agenda*. London: Whiting and Birch.

Kelly L (1996) When women protection is the best kind of child protection: children, domestic violence and child abuse. *Administration*. 44 (2): 118–35.

Kelly L and Radford J (1991) Nothing really happened: the invalidation of women's experiences of sexual violence. *Critical Social Policy*. 30: 39–53.

Kelly L, Burton S and Regan L (1996) Beyond Victim or Survivor: Sexual Violence, Identity, and Feminist Theory and Practice. in, Adkins L and Merchant V (Eds.) *Sexualising the Social Power and the Organisation of Sexuality*. London: Macmillan.

Kendall S (Ed.) (2001) *Understanding domestic violence: A training pack for community practitioners*. London: CPHVA.

Kerig PK (1998a) Moderators and mediators of the effects of interparental conflict on children's adjustment. *Journal of Abnormal Family Psychology*. 26, 199–212.

Kerig PK (1998b) Gender and appraisals as mediators of adjustment in children exposed to interparental violence. *Journal of Family Violence*.13, 345–63.

Kerig PK, Cowan PA and Cowan CP (1993) Marital quality and gender differences in parent–child interaction. *Developmental Psychology*. 29, 6: 931–9.

Kerns KA (1994) A longitudinal examination of links between mother–child attachment and children's friendships in early childhood. *Journal of Social and Personal Relations*. 11: 379–81.

Kerns KA, Klepac L and Cole AK (1996) Peer relationships and preadolescent's' perceptions of security in the mother–child relationship. *Developmental Psychology*. 32: 457–66.

Khan M (2000) Domestic violence against women and girls. *Innocenti Digest*. 6: 1–22.

Kilpatrick DG, Edmunds CN and Seymour AK (1992) *Rape in America: A report to the Nation*. Arlington, VA: National Victim Center.

Kincaid P (1985) *The omitted reality: husband–wife violence in Ontario and policy implications for education*. Concord, Ontario: Belsten Publications.

Kirkwood C (1993) *Leaving abusive partners*. London: Sage.

Kitzmann KM (2000) Effects of marital conflict on subsequent triadic family interactions and parenting. *Developmental Psychology*. 36: 3–13.

Knickman JR and Weitzman BC (1989) *A study of homeless families in New York city*. NY: Human Resources Administration, Health Research Program, New York University.

Koenen KC, Moffit TE, Caspi A, Taylor A and Purcell S (2003) Domestic violence is associated with environmental suppression of IQ in young children. *Developmental Psychopatholgy*. 15, 297–311.

Koss MP and Gaines JA (1993) The prediction of sexual aggression by alcohol use. *Journal of Interpersonal Violence.* 8: 94–106.

Kovacs M (1981) Rating scales to assess depression in school-aged children. *Acta paedopsychiatrica.* 46: 305–15.

Koverola C (1995) Posttraumatic stress disorder. In Ammerman RT and Hersen M (Eds.) *Handbook of child behavior therapy in the psychiatric setting.* NY: Wiley.

Kyriacou DN, Deirdre A, Taliaferro E, Stone S, Tubb T, Linden J (1999) Risk factors for injury to women from domestic violence. *New England Journal of Medicine.* 341: 1892–8.

Ladd GW (1992) Developing social competence in adolescence: Gullotta TP, Adams GR and Motnemayor R. *Journal of Social and Personal Relations.* 9: 158–9.

LaFreniere PJ and Sroufe LA (1985) Profiles of peer competence in the preschool: Interrelations between measures, influence of social ecology, and relation to attachment history. *Developmental Psychology.* 21: 56–69.

Lebowitz L, Harvey MR and Herman JL (1993) A step-by-step dimension model of recovery from sexual trauma. *Journal of Interpersonal Violence.* 8 (3): 378–91.

Leighton B (1989) *Spousal abuse in metropolitan Toronto: research report on the response of the criminal justice system.* Ottawa: Solicitor General of Canada.

Lemon NKD (2000) Custody and visitation trends in the United States in domestic violence cases. *Journal of Aggression, Maltreatment and Trauma.* 3 (1): 329–43.

Levendosky AA and Graham-Bermann SA (2000) Trauma and parenting in battered women: an addition to an ecological model of parenting. *Journal of Aggression, Maltreatment and Trauma.* 3 (1): 25–35.

Levendosky AA, Lynch SM and Graham-Bermann SA (2000b) Mothers' perceptions of the impact of woman abuse on their parenting. *Violence against Women.* 6 (3): 247–71.

Liebermann M, Doyle A-B and Markiewicz D (1999) Developmental patterns in security of attachment to mother and father in late childhood and early adolescence: Associations with peer relations. *Child Development.* 70: 1, 202–13.

Lifton RJ (1961) *Thought reform and the psychology of totalism: a study of brainwashing in China.* NY: WW Norton.

Lloyd SA (1990) Conflict types and strategies in violent marriages. *Journal of Family Violence.* 5: 269–84.

Locke HJ and Wallace KM (1959) Short marital adjustment prediction tests: Their reliability and validity. *Marriage and Family Living.* 21: 251–5.

Lockhart LL, White BW, Causby V and Isaac A (1994) Letting out the secret: violence in lesbian relationships. *Journal of Interpersonal Violence.* 9 (4): 469–92.

Lockwood R and Ascione FR (Eds.) (1998) *Cruelty to animals and interpersonal violence: readings in research and application.* West Lafayette: Purdue University Press.

Loeber R and Dishion TJ (1984) Boys who fight at home and school: Family conditions influencing cross-setting consistency. *Journal of Consulting and Clinical Psychology.* 52: 759–68.

Loeber R and Hay D (1997) Key issues in the development of aggression and violence from childhood to early adulthood. *Annual Review of Psychology.* 48: 371–410.

Low SM, Monarch ND, Hartman S and Markman H (2002) Recent therapeutic advances in the prevention of domestic violence. In Schewe PA (Ed.) *Preventing violence in relationships: interventions across the lifespan.* Washington, DC: American Psychological Association.

Lydiard RB and Falsetti SA (1999) Experience with anxiety and depression treatment studies. *American Journal of Medicine.* 107.

Lynch CG and Norris T (1977–78) Services for battered women: looking for a perspective. *Victimology.* 2: 553–62.

Macleod M and Saraga M (1988) Challenging the orthodoxy: towards a feminist theory of practice. *Feminist Review.* 28: 16–55.

MacNeely F (2002) Safety planning for children. In Saunders H and Humphreys C (Eds.) *Safe and sound: a resource manual for working with children who have experienced domestic violence.* Bristol: Women's Aid Federation of England.

Magen RH (1999) In the best interest of battered women: re-conceptualising allegations of failure to protect. *Child Maltreatment.* 4 (2): 127–35.

Magen RH, Conroy K and Tufo AD (2000) Domestic violence in child welfare preventative services: results from an intake screening questionnaire. *Children and Youth Services Review.* 22 (3/4): 251–74.

Magen RH, Conroy K, Hess PM, Panciera and Simon BL (2001) Identifying domestic violence in child abuse and neglect investigations. *Journal of Interpersonal Violence.* 16 (6): 580–601.

Mama A (1996) *The hidden struggle: statutory and voluntary sector responses to violence against black women in the home.* London: Whiting and Birch.

Margolies PJ and Weintraub S (1977) The revised 56-item CRPBI as a research instrument: Reliability and factor structure. *Journal of Clinical Psychology.* 33: 472–6.

Margolin G, John R and O'Brien M (1989) Home observations of married couples re-enacting naturalistic conflicts. *Behavioural Assessment*. 11: 101–18.

Marriage and Divorce Statistics. Office of Population Census Survey. London, HMSO.

Martin AJ, Berenson KB, Griffing S, Sage RE, Madry L, Bingham LE and Primm BJ (2000) The process of leaving an abusive relationship. *Journal of Family Violence*. 15 (2): 109–22.

McCloskey LA and Lichter E (2003) The contribution of marital violence to adolescent aggression across different relationships. *Journal of Interpersonal Violence*. 18, 390–412.

McCloskey LA and Stuewig J (2001) The quality of peer relationships among children exposed to family violence. *Development and Psychopathology*. 13, 83–96.

McFarlane J, Parker B, Soeken K and Bullock L (1992) Assessing for Abuse During Pregnancy: Severity and Frequency of Injuries and Associated Entry into Pre-Natal Care. *Journal of the American Medical Association*. 267, 3176–8.

McFarlane J, Parker B, Soeken K, Silva C and Reel S (1998) Safety Behaviours of Abused Women after an Intervention During Pregnancy. *JOGNN*. 27 (1) 64–9.

McGee C (1996) *Children's and Mother's Experiences of Child Protection Following Domestic Violence*. London: NSPCC.

McGee C (2000) *Childhood experiences of domestic violence*. London: Jessica Kingsley.

McGee RA and Wolfe DA (1991) Psychological maltreatment: toward an operational definition. *Development and Psychopathology*. 3: 3–18.

McGibbon A and Kelly L (1989) *Abuse in the home: advice and information*. London: London Borough of Hammersmith and Fulham.

McHale JP (1994) *Co-parenting and family level dynamics*. Colloquium presented at the University of Illinois, Champaign, Illinois.

McHugh J and Hewitt L (1998) When partnership is difficult: working with abused mothers of abused children. *Australian Social Work*. 51 (1): 39–45.

McIntosh JE (2002) Thought in the face of violence: a child's need. *Child Abuse and Neglect*. 26: 229–41.

McKay M (1994) The link between domestic violence and child abuse: assessment and treatment considerations. *Child Welfare*. 73: 1, 29–39.

McKibben L, De Vos E and Newberger E (1991) Victimisation of mothers of abused children: a controlled study. In Hampton RL (Ed.) *Black family violence*. Lexington, Mass: Lexington Books.

McLaughlin IG, Leonard KE and Senchak M (1992) Prevalence and distribution of premarital aggression among couples applying for a marriage licence. *Journal of Family Violence*. 7: 309–19.

McLeod M and Saraga E (1988) Challenging the orthodoxy: toward a feminist perspective theory and practice. *Feminist Review*. 28: 16–55.

Melby JN and Conger RD (1997) Parental behaviors and adolescent academic performance: A longitudinal analysis. *Journal of Research on Adolescence*. 6, 113–37.

Melby JN, Conger RD, Conger KJ and Lorenz FO (1993) Effects of parental behavior on tobacco use by young male adolescents. *Journal of Marriage and the Family*. 55: 439–54.

Meredith WH, Abbot DA and Adams SL (1986) Family violence: its relation to marital and parental satisfaction and family strengths. *Journal of Family Violence*. 1: 299–305.

Meyer H (1992) The billion dollar epidemic. *American Medical News*. January 6th.

Miller BD (1992) Wife-beating in India: variations on a theme. In Counts DA, Brown JK and Cambell JC (Eds.) *Sanctions and sanctuary: cultural perspectives on the beatings of wives*. Boulder, CO: Westview.

Minnuchinn P (1988) Relationships within the family: A systems perspective on development. In Hinde RA and Stevenson Hinde J (Eds.) *Relationships within families: Mutual influences*. Oxford: Clarendon.

Mirrlees-Black C (1995) *Estimating the Extent of Domestic Violence: Findings from the 1992 British Crime Survey*. London: Home Office Research and Planning Unit.

Mirrlees-Black C (1999) *Domestic violence: findings from a new British Crime Survey self-completion questionnaire*. London: Home Office.

Montemayor R (1983) Parents and adolescents in conflict: All families some of the time and some families most of the time. *Journal of Early Adolescence*. 3: 83–103.

Mooney J (1993) *The hidden figure: domestic violence in North London*. London: Middlesex University.

Moore T and Pepler D (1998) Correlates of adjustment in children at risk. In Holden G, Geffner R and Jourilles E (Eds.) *Children exposed to marital violence*. Washington DC: Psychological Association.

Moos RH and Moos BS (1981) *Family Environment Scale: Manual*. Palo Alto, CA: Consulting Psychologists Press.

Morgan DR (1998) *Domestic violence: a health care issue?* London: British Medical Association.

Morrison T (1996) Partnership and collaboration: rhetoric and reality. *Child Abuse and Neglect*. 20 (2): 127–40.

Motz A (2001) *The psychology of female violence: crimes against the body.* Hove, East Sussex: Brunner-Routledge.

Mullender A (1996) *Rethinking domestic violence: the social work and probation response.* London: Routledge.

Mullender A (1997) Domestic violence and social work. *Critical Social Policy.* 17 (1): 53–78.

Mullender A (2000) *Reducing domestic violence . . . what works? Meeting the needs of children.* London: Policing and Reducing Crime Unit.

Mullender A, Hague G, Imam U, Kelly L, Malos E and Regan L (2002) *Children's perspectives on domestic violence.* London: Sage Publications.

Mullender A, Kelly L, Hague G, Malos E and Imam U (2000) *Children's Needs, Coping Strategies and Understanding of Woman Abuse.* Economic and Social Research Council.

Mullender A and Morley R (Eds.) (1994) *Children living with domestic violence: putting men's abuse of women on the child care agenda.* London: Whiting and Birch.

Mullins A (1997) *Making a Difference: Working with Women and Children Experiencing Domestic Violence.* London: NCH.

National Research Council (1996) *Understanding violence against women.* Washington, DC: National Academy Press.

NCH (1994) *The hidden victims: children and domestic violence.* London: NCH.

Neighbors BD, Forehand R and Bau J (1997) Interparental conflict and relations with parents as predictors of young adult functioning. *Development and Psychopathology.* 9: 169–87.

Noel NL and Yam M (1992) Domestic violence: the pregnant battered woman. *Women's Health.* 27 871–84.

Norton R (1983) Measuring marital quality: A critical look at the dependent variable. *Journal of Marriage and the Family.* 45: 141–51.

Notarius CI and Markman HJ (1981) The Couples Interaction Scoring System. In Filsinger EE and Lewis RA (Eds.) *Assessing marriage.* Beverly Hills, CA: Sage.

NTV (1995) *Stopping men's violence in the family: a manual for running men's groups,* Volume 1. Context and Standards, Melbourne.

O'Brien J (1971) Violence in divorce-prone families. *Journal of Marriage and the Family.* 33: 692–8.

O'Brien M, John RS, Margolin G and Eral O (1994) Reliability and diagnostic efficacy of parents' reports regarding children's exposure to marital aggression. *Violence and Victims.* 9: 45–62.

O'Brien M, Margolin G and John RS (1995) Relation among marital conflict, child coping, and child adjustment. *Journal of Child Clinical Psychology.* 24: 346–61.

O'Hagan K (1994) Crisis intervention: changing perspectives. In Harvey C and Philpot T (Eds.) *Practicing social work.* London: Routledge.

O'Hara M (1992) Domestic violence and child abuse: making the links. *Childright.* 88: 4–5.

O'Hara M (1994) Child deaths in the context of domestic violence: implications for professional practice. In Mullender A and Morley R (Eds.) *Children living with domestic violence: putting men's abuse of women on the child care agenda.* London: Whiting and Birch.

O'Keefe (1994) Adjustment of children from martially violent homes. *Families in Society.* 75: 403–15.

O'Keefe M (1996) The differential effects of family violence on adolescent adjustment. *Child and Adolescent Social Work Journal.* 13: 51–68.

O'Leary KD (1984) Marital discord and children: Problems, strategies, methodologies and results. In Doyle A, Gold D and Moskowitz DS (Eds.) *Children in families under stress.* San Francisco: Jossey-Bass.

O'Leary KD (1999) Developmental and affective issues in assessing and treating partner aggression. *Clinical Psychology: Science and Practice.* 6: 400–14.

O'Leary KD, Barling J, Arias I, Rosenbaum A, Malone J and Tyree A. (1989) Prevalence and stability of physical aggression between spouse: A longitudinal analysis. *Journal of Consulting and Clinical Psychology.* 57, 263–8.

O'Leary KD and Emery RE (1984) Marital discord and child behaviour problems. In Levine MD and Satz P (Eds.) *Developmental variation and dysfunction.* New York: Academic Press.

Okun L (1988) Termination or resumption of cohabitation in women battering relationships. In Hotaling G, Finkelhor D, Kirkpatrick JT and Straus MA (Eds.) *Coping with family violence: research and policy perspectives.* Beverley Hills, Ca: Sage Publications.

Ontario Ministry of Community and Social Services (2001) *Woman abuse: increasing safety for abused women and their children.* Ontario: Ontario Ministry of Community and Social Services.

Osborne LN and Fincham FD (1996) Marital conflict, parent–child relations and child relations: Does gender matter. *Merill Palmer Quarterly.* 42: 48–75.

Osofsky JD (1995) The effects of exposure to violence on young children. *American Psychologist.* 50: 782–8.

Osofsky JD (1999) The impact of violence on children. *Future Child.* 9 (3): 33–49.

Owen MT and Cox MJ (1997) Marital conflict and the development of infant: parent attachment relationships. *Journal of Family Psychology.* 11: 152–64.

Pagelow MD (1984) *Family Violence.* NY: Praeger.

Pahl J (1995) Health professionals and violence against women. In Kingston P and Penhale B (Eds.) *Family violence and the caring professionals.* Basingstoke: Macmillan.

Paley BP, Conger RD and Harold GT (2000) The role of parental affect and adolescent cognitive representations of parent–child relations in the development of adolescent social functioning. *Journal of Marriage and the Family.*

Parke RD, Burks VM, Carson JL, Neville B and Boyum LA (1994) Family-peer relationship: A tripartite model. In Parke RD and Kellam SG (Eds.) *Exploring family relationships with other social contexts. Family research consortium: Advances in family research.* 115–45.

Parke RD, Cassidy J, Burks VM, Carson JL and Boyum L (1992) Familial contribution to peer competence amongst young children: The role of interactive and affective processes. In Parke RD and Ladd GW (Eds.) *Family-peer relationships: Models of linkage.* Hillsdale, NJ: Erlbaum.

Parker JG and Asher ST (1987) Peer relations and later personal adjustment: Are low-accepted children at risk? *Psychological Bulletin.* 102, 357–89.

Parker B, McFarlane J, Soeken K, Torres S and Campbell D (1993*) Physical and Emotional Abuse during Pregnancy: A Comparison of Adult and Teenage Women,* in, *Nursing Research.* (May/June) 24 173–8.

Parkinson P and Humphreys C (1998) Children who witness domestic violence: the implications for child protection. *Child and Family Law Quarterly.* 10 (2): 147–59.

Patterson GR (1982) *Coercive Family Process.* Eugene, OR: Castalia.

Patterson GR, Reid JB and Dishion TJ (1992) *Antisocial boys.* Eugene, OR: Castilia.

Peled E (2000) Parenting by men who abuse women: issues and dilemmas. *British Journal of Social Work.* 30 (1): 25–36.

Peled E, Eisikovits Z, Enosh G and Winstok Z (2000) Choice and empowerment for battered women who stay: toward a constructivist model. *Social Work.* 45 (1): 9–25.

Peled E, Jaffe PG and Edleson JL (1995) *Ending the cycle of violence: community responses to children of battered women.* Thousand Oaks, Ca: Sage Publications.

Pence E and Paymar M (1986) *Power and control: tactics of men who batter: an educational curriculum.*

Duluth, Minnesota: Minnesota Program Development.

Pepler DJ, Catallo R and Moore TE (2000) Consider the children: research informing interventions for children exposed to domestic violence. *Journal of Aggression, Maltreatment and Trauma.* 3 (1): 37–57.

Pepler DJ and Moore T (1995) *Mothers' depression and aggression and the behaviour problems of children in families at risk.* Paper presented at the Biennial meeting of the Society for Research in Child Development, Indianapolis, April.

Perry BD and Pollard RD (1998) Homeostasis, stress, change and adaptation: a neuro-developmental view of childhood trauma. *Child and Adolescent Psychiatric Clinics in North America.* 7 (1): 33–51.

Peterson JL and Zill N (1986) Marital disruption, parent-child relationships, and behavior problems in children. *Journal of Marriage and the Family.* 48, 295–307.

Peterson RP, Basta SM and Dykstra TA (1993) Mothers of molested children: some comparisons of personality characteristics. *Child Abuse and Neglect.* 17: 409–18.

Pettit GS, Harrist AW, Bates JE and Dodge KE (1991) Family-interaction, social cognition and childrens subsequent relations with peers at kindergarten. *Journal of Social and Personal Relationships.* 8, 383–402.

Phillipson J (1992) *Practicing equality: women, men and social work.* London: CCETSW.

Plichta SB (1996) Violence and abuse: implications for women's health. In Falik MM and Collins KS (Eds.) *Women's Health.* Baltimore: The John Hopkins University Press.

Plotnikoff J and Woolfson R (1998) *Policing domestic violence.* London: Home Office Policing and Reducing Crime Unit.

Porter B and O'Leary KD (1980) Marital discord and childhood behaviour problems. *Journal of Abnormal Child Psychology.* 8: 287–95.

Powis B (2002) *Offenders' risk of serious harm: a review of the literature.* London: Home Office Research, Development and Statistics Directorate.

Preston-Shoot M (1995) Assessing anti-oppressive practice. *Social Work Education.* 14: 2, 11–29.

Prinz RJ, Foster Sl, Kent RN and O'Leary KD (1979) Multivariate assessment of conflict in distressed and non-distressed mother adolescent dyads. *Journal of Applied Behaviour Analysis.* 12: 691–700.

Pryke J and Thomas M (1998) *Domestic violence and social work.* Ashgate: Arena.

Ptacek J (1999) *Battered women in the courtroom.* Boston: Mass: Northeastern University Press.

Putallaz M (1987) Maternal behavior and children's sociometric status. *Child Development.* 58: 324–40.

Quinlivan JA, Peterson RW and Gurrin LC (1999) Adolescent pregnancy: psychopathology missed. *Australian and New Zealand Journal of Psychiatry.* 33: 864–8.

Rabenstein S and Lehmann P (2000) Mothers and children together: a family group treatment approach. *Journal of Aggression, Maltreatment and Trauma.* 3 (1): 185–205.

Radford L and Hester M (2001) Overcoming mother blaming? Future directions for research on mothering and domestic violence. In Graham-Bermann SA and Edleson JL (Eds.) *Domestic violence in the lives of children.* Washington DC: American Psychological Association.

Radford L, Sayer, S and AMICA (1999) *Unreasonable fears? Child contact in the context of domestic violence: a survey of mother's perceptions of harm.* Women's Aid Federation of England.

Radloff LS (1977) The CES-D Scale: A self-report depression scale for research in the general population. *Applied Psychological Measurement and Research.* 1: 385–401.

Reder P and Duncan S (1999) *Lost innocents: a follow-up study of fatal child abuse.* London: Routedge.

Reder P et al. (1993) *Beyond blame: child abuse tragedies revisited.* Routledge.

Reid WJ and Crissafulli A (1990) Marital discord and child behaviour problems: A meta-analysis. *Journal of Abnormal Child Psychology.* 18: 105–17.

Renzetti C (1992) *Violent betrayal: partner abuse in lesbian relationships.* Newbury Park, Ca: Sage Publications.

Reynolds CR and Richmond BO (1978) What I think and feel: A revised measure of children's anxiety. *Journal of Abnormal Child Psychology.* 6: 271–80.

Rice F, Harold GT and Thapar A (2002) Assessing the effects of age, sex and shared environment on the genetic aetiology of depression in childhood and adolescence. *Journal of Child Psychology and Psychiatry.* 43, 1039–51.

Rice KG (1990) Attachment in adolescence: A narrative and meta-analytic review. *Journal of Youth and Adolescence.* 19, 5: 511–38.

Roberts AR (1987) Psychosocial characteristics of batterers. *Journal of Family Violence.* 2: 81–94.

Rodgers K (1994) Wife assault: the findings of a national study. *Juristat.* 14: 9.

Rose K (2001) *Domestic violence and child protection: Practice guidance for social services.* Salford ACPC.

Rose K and Savage A (1999) Safe Caring. In Wheal A (Ed.) *The RHP Companion to Foster Care.* Lyme Regis: Russell House Publishing.

Rosenbaum A and O'Leary KD (1981) The unintended victims of marital violence. *American Journal of Orthopsychiatry.* 51: 692–9.

Ross VM (1977) Rape as a social problem. *Social problems.* 25: 75–89.

Rossman B (1994) Children in violent families: current diagnostic and treatment considerations. *Family Violence and Sexual Assault Bulletin.* 10 (3–4): 29–34.

Rossman BB and Rosenberg MS (1992) Family stress and functioning in children: The moderating effects of children's beliefs about their control over parental conflict. *Journal of Child Psychology and Psychiatry.* 4: 699–715.

Rothery M, Tutty L and Weaver G (1999) Tough choices: women, abusive partners and the ecology of decision-making. *Canadian Journal of Community Mental Health.* 18 (1): 5–18.

Rounsaville BJ (1978) Theories in marital violence: evidence from a study of battered women. *Victimology.* 3: 11–31.

Rowsell C (2000) *Closed Eyes, Covered Ears, Silenced Women, Inevitable Consequences? Women on Probation and their Experiences of Violence and Abuse,* unpublished Masters research thesis, Leeds Metropolitan University.

Rowsell C (2001) Presentation to Relate national conference, 3rd April.

Rowsell C (2003) Domestic violence and children: making a difference in a meaningful way for women and children. In Calder MC and Hackett S (Eds.) *Assessment in child care: using and developing frameworks for practice.* Lyme Regis: Russell House Publishing.

Rowsell C (2004) *Supporting people:* paper presented to Salford Domestic Violence Policy and Strategy Group, 26th January.

Roy M (1982) *The abusive partner.* NY: Van Nostrand Reinhold.

Roy M (1988) *Children in the crossfire: violence in the home – how does it affect our children?* Deerfield Beach, Fl: Health Communications Inc.

Russell A and Finnie V (1990) Pre-school children's social status and maternal instructions to assist group entry. *Developmental Psychology.* 26: 603–11.

Rutter M (1985) Resilience in the face of adversity: protective factors and resistance to psychiatric disorder. *British Journal of Psychiatry.* 147: 598–611.

Rutter M and Quinton D (1984) Parental psychiatric disorder: Effects on children. *Psychological Medicine.* 14: 853–80.

Sale AU (2001) Nowhere to go. *Community Care.* 19–25 July, 22–3.

Sato RA and Heiby EM (1992) Correlates of depressive symptoms among battered women. *Journal of Family Violence.* 7: 229–45.

Saunders A (1994) Children in women's refuges: a retrospective study. In Mullender A and Morley R

(Eds.) *Children living with domestic violence.* London: Whiting and Birch.

Saunders A, Epstein C, Keep G and Debbonaire (1995) *It hurts me too: children's experiences of domestic violence and refuge life.* Bristol: WAFE, NISW and Childline.

Saunders DG (1988) Wife abuse, husband abuse or mutual combat? In Yllo K and Bograd M (Eds.) *Feminist perspectives on wife abuse.* Beverley Hills, Ca: Sage Publications.

Saunders DG (1982) Counselling the violent husband. In Keller PA and Ritt LG (Eds.) *Innovations in clinical practice: A sourcebook.* Sarasota, FL: Professional Resource Exchange.

Saunders DG (1994) Child custody decisions in families experiencing woman abuse. *Social Work.* 39: 51–9.

Saunders DG (1995) A typology of men who batter: three types derived from cluster analyses. *American Journal of Orthopsychiatry.* 62: 264–75.

Saunders H (2002) Responding to Child Contact Problems. in Saunders H and Humphreys C (Eds.) *Safe and Sound: A Resource Manual for Working With Children Who Have Experienced Domestic Violence.* Bristol: Women's Aid Federation of England, 129–32.

Schechter S and Gray LT (1988) A framework for understanding and empowering battered women. In Straus MA (Ed.) *Abuse and victimization across the lifespan.* Baltimore: John Hopkins University Press.

Schechter S and Edleson J (1994) *In the best interests of women and children: a call for collaboration between child welfare and domestic violence constituencies.* Paper presented at the conference on domestic violence and child welfare. Wingspread, Racine: June 8–10th.

Schumm WR and Bagarozzi DA (1989) The Conflict Tactics Scales. *American Journal of Family Therapy.* 17: 165–8.

Schumm WR, Paff-Bergen LA, Hatch RC, Obiorah FC, Copeland JM, Meens LD and Bugaighis MA (1986) Concurrent and discriminate validity of the Kansas Marital Satisfaction scale. *Journal of Marriage and the Family.* 48: 381–7.

Scottish Executive (2003) *Responding to domestic violence; guidelines for health care workers in NHS Scotland.* Edinburgh: TSO.

Scott KL and Wolfe DA (2000) What works in the treatment of batterers. In Kluger MP, Alexander G and Curtis PA (Eds.) *What works in child welfare.* Washington, DC: CWLA Press.

Scott P (1977) Assessing dangerousness in criminals. *British Journal of Psychiatry.* 131: 127–42.

Scott-Gliba E, Minne C and Mezey G (1995) The psychological, behavioural and emotional impact of surviving an abusive relationship. *Journal of Forensic Psychiatry.* 6(2): 343–358.

Scourfield JB (1995) *Changing men: UK agencies working with men who are violent towards their women partners.* Monograph 141. Norwich: University of East Anglia.

Secretary of State for the Home Department (2003) *Safety and justice: the government's proposals on domestic violence.* London: TSO.

Sgroi S (Ed.) (1982) *Handbook of Clinical Intervention in Child Sexual Abuse.* Lexington Books, D.C. Heath and Co.

Shankleman J, Brooks R and Webb E (2000) *Children resident in domestic violence refuges in Cardiff: a health needs and health care needs assessment.*

Shaw E, Bouris A and Pye S (1999) A comprehensive approach: the family safety model with domestic violence. In Breckenbridge J and Laing L (Eds.) *Challenging silence: innovative responses to sexual and domestic violence.* Sydney: Allen and Unwin, 238–55.

Shaw DS, Emery RE and Tuer MD (1993) Parental functioning and children's adjustment in families of divorce: A prospective study. *Journal of Abnormal Child Psychology.* 21(1): 119–34.

Shepard M (1992) Child visiting and domestic abuse. *Child Welfare.* 74 (4): 357–65.

Shepard M (1992b) Predicting batterer recidivism five years after community intervention. *Journal of Family Violence.* 7: 167–78.

Shulman S, Elicker J and Soufre AL (1994) Stages of friendship growth in preadolescence as related to attachment history. *Journal of Social and Personal Relationships.* 11, 341–61.

Siddiqui H (2003) Asian and Ethnic minority women's groups. In Amiel S and Heath I (Eds.) *Family violence in primary care.* Oxford: Oxford University Press.

Sigler RT (1989) *Domestic violence in context: an assessment of community attitudes.* Lexington, MA: Lexington Books.

Sillars AL (1982) *Verbal tactics coding scheme: Coding manual.* Unpublished manuscript, Ohio State University.

Sillars AL, Coletti SF, Parry D and Rogers MA (1982) Coding verbal tactics: Non-verbal and perceptual correlates of the 'avoidance-distributive-integrative' distinction. *Human Communication Research.* 9: 83–95.

Simons RL (1996) *Understanding differences between divorced and intact families: Stress, interaction and child outcome.* Understanding Families. Sage Publications: New York.

Simons RL, Whitbeck LB, Conger RD and Conger KJ (1991) Parenting factors, social skills, and value commitments as precursors to school failure, involvement with deviant peers, and delinquent behavior. *Journal of Youth and Adolescence.* 20: 645–64.

Sinclair D (1985) *Understanding wife assault: a training manual for counsellors.* Toronto: Ontario.

Singer MI, Miller DB, Guo S, Slovak K and Frierson T (1998) *The Mental Consequences of children's exposure to violence.* Clevand, OH: Case Western Reserve University.

Skinner M L, Elder GH and Conger RD (1992) Linking economic hardship to adolescent aggression. *Journal of Youth and Adolescence.* 21, 259–76.

Snyder DK (1979) Mulitdimensional assessment of marital satisfaction. *Journal of Marriage and the Family.* 41: 813–23.

Snyder DK (1981) *Marital Satisfaction Inventory.* Los Angeles: Western Psychological Association.

Spanier GB (1976) Measuring dyadic adjustment: New scales for assessing the quality of marriage and similar dyads. *Journal of Marriage and the Family.* 42: 825–39.

Sroufe LA (1983) *Infant-caregiver attachment and patterns of adaptation in pre-school: The roots of maladaptation and competence.* Minnesota Symposia on Child Psychology, 16, 41–83.

Stanko EA, Crisp D, Hale C and Lucraft H (1998) *Counting the costs: estimating the impact of domestic violence in the London Borough of Hackney.* London: Crime Concern.

Stanley C and Goddard C (1997) Failures in child protection. *Child Abuse Review.* 6 (1): 46–54.

Stanley JP (1991) *Child abuse and other family violence.* Unpublished Masters Thesis, Department of Social Work, Monash University, Melbourne.

Stark E (1984) *The battering syndrome: social knowledge, social therapy and abuse of women.* Binghampton, NY: State University of New York.

Stark E and Flitcraft A (1985) *Women battering, child abuse and social heredity: what is the relationship?* In Johnson NK (Ed.) *Marital violence.* London: Routledge and Kegan Paul.

Stark E and Flitcraft A (1988) Women and children at risk: a feminist perspective on child abuse. *International Journal of Health Studies.* 18 (1): 97–119.

Stark E and Flitcraft A (1996) *Women at risk: domestic violence and women's health.* Thousand Oaks, CA: Sage Publications.

Stark E, Flitcraft A and Frazier W (1979) Medicine and patriarchal violence: the social construction of a private event. *International Journal of Health Studies.* 9: 461–93.

Statistics Canada (1994) *Family violence in Canada.* Ottawa: Ministry of Industry, Science and Technology.

Steinmetz SK (1980) Violence prone families. *Annals of the New York Academy of Sciences.* 347: 251–5.

Stephens N, McDonald R and Jouriles EN (2000) Helping children who reside as shelters for battered women: lessons learned. *Journal of Aggression, Maltreatment and Trauma.* 3 (1): 147–60.

Sterling V (2001) Effect of Domestic Violence on Contact. *Justice of The Peace.* 165: 599–602.

Sternberg KJ, Lamb ME and Dawad-Noursi S (1998) Using multiple informants to understand domestic violence and its effects. In Holden GW, Geffner RA and Jouriles EN (Eds.) *Children exposed to marital violence: theory, research, and applied issues.* Washington DC: American Psychological Association.

Sternberg KJ, Lamb ME, Greenbaum C, Cichetti D, Dawud S, Cortes RM and Lorey F (1993) Effects of domestic violence on children's behaviour problems and depression. *Developmental Psychology.* 29: 44–52.

Stratton P, Munton T, Hanks HG, Heard D and Davidson C (1988) *Leeds Attributional Coding System Manual.* Leeds, Great Britain: Leeds Family Therapy and Research Center.

Straus MA (1974) Leveling, civility and violence in the family. *Journal of Marriage and the Family.* 36: 13–29.

Straus MA (1979) Measuring intrafamily conflict and violence: The Conflict Tactics Scales. *Journal of Marriage and the Family.* 41: 75–88.

Straus MA (1992) *Children as witnesses to marital violence.* Report of the 23rd Ross Roundtable. Columbus, OH: Ross Laboratories.

Straus MA (1990) The Conflict tactics scale and its critics: An evaluation and new data on validity and reliability. In Straus MA and Gelled RJ (Eds.) *Physical violence in American families: Risk factors and adaptations to violence in 8,145 families.* New Brunswick, NJ: Transaction.

Straus MA and Gelles RJ (1986) Societal change and change in family violence 1975–85. *Journal of Marriage and the Family.* 48: 465–79.

Straus MA and Gelles RJ (1990) *Physical violence in American Families.* New Brunswick, NJ: Transaction Publishers.

Straus MA, Gelles RJ and Steinmetz S (1980) *Behind closed doors: violence in the American family.* NY: Anchor Books.

Straus MA, Hamby SL, Boney-McCoy S and Sugarman DB (1996) The Revised Conflict Tactics Scale (CTS2) *Journal of Family Issues.* 17: 283–316.

Strube MJ and Barbour LS (1984) Factors related to the decision to leave an abusive relationship. *Journal of Marriage and the Family.* 46: 837–44.

Sturge C and Glaser D (2000) Contact and Domestic Violence: The Experts' Court Report. *Family Law.* September 2000, 615–28.

Sudermann M and Jaffe PG (1999) Child witnesses of domestic violence. In Ammerman RT and Hersen M (Eds.) *Assessment of family violence: a clinical and legal sourcebook.* Chichester: John Wiley.

Sugarman D and Hotaling G (1989) Dating violence: prevalence, context and risk markers. In Pirog-Good MA and Stets JE (Eds.) *Violence in dating relationships: emerging issues.* NY: Praeger.

Sugg NK and Inui T (1992) Primary care physicians' response to domestic violence: Opening Pandora's box. *Journal of the American Medical Association.* 267: 3157–60.

Szinovacz ME (1983) Using couple data as a methodological tool: the case of marital violence. *Journal of Marriage and the Family.* 45: 633–44.

Sykes D and Symons-Moulton B (1990) *A handbook for the prevention of family violence.* Hamilton, Ontario: Seldon Printing Ltd.

Tara-Chand A (1988) *Violence against women by known men.* Training pack: Leeds Inter-agency project.

Telch CF and Lindquist CU (1984) Violent versus non-violent couples: a comparison of patterns. *Psychotherapy.* 21 (2): 242–8.

Thaper A, Harold GT and McGuffin P (1998) Life events and depressive symptoms: A multivariate genetic analysis. *Journal of Child Psychology and Psychiatry.*

Thoburn J, Lewis A and Shemmings D (1995) *Paternalism or Partnership? Family Involvement in the child protection process.* London: HMSO.

Thompson N (1996) *People skills.* London: Macmillan.

Thornberry TP, Freeman-Gallant A, Lizotte AJ, Krohn MD and Smith CA (2003) Linked lives: the intergenerational transmission of antisocial behavior. *Journal of Abnormal Child Psychology.* 31, 171–84.

Tomison A (2000) *Exploring family violence: links between child maltreatment and domestic violence.* Melbourne: Australian Institute of Family Studies.

Torres S (1987) Hispanic-American battered women: why consider cultural differences? *Response.* 10: 20–21.

Towle C (1931) The evaluation and management of marital status in foster homes. *American Orthopsychiatry.* 1, 271–84.

Trimpey ML (1989) Self-esteem and anxiety: key issues in an abused woman's support group. *Journal of Family Violence.* 10: 297–308.

Truesdell D, McNeil J and Deschner J (1986) Incidence of wife abuse in incestuous families. *Social Work.* 32: 138–40.

Tucker JS, Ellickson PL, Klein DJ (2002) Five year prospective study of risk factors for daily smoking in adolescence among early non-smokers and experimenters. *Journal of Applied Social Psychology.* 32, 1588–603.

Vaughan G (2000) Violence, sexuality and gay male domestic violence. In Buckley K and Head P (Eds.) *Myths, risks and sexuality.* Dorset: Russell House Publishing.

Vogel EF and Bell NW (1960) The emotionally disturbed child as a family scapegoat. In Bell NW and Vogel EF (Eds.) *A modern introduction to the family.* New York: Free Press.

Walby S and Myhill A (2000) *Reducing domestic violence: what works? Assessing and managing the risk of domestic violence.* London: Home Office.

Waldo M (1987) Also victims: understanding and treating men arrested for spouse abuse. *Journal of Counseling and Development.* 65: 385–8.

Walker LE (1979) *The battered woman.* NY: Harper and Row.

Walker LE (1983) The battered woman syndrome study. In Finkelhor D (Ed.) *The dark side of families.* California: Sage Publications.

Walker LE (1989) *The battered woman syndrome.* New York: Springer Press.

Waters E and Cummings EM (2000) A secure base from which to explore close relationships. *Child Development.* 71,164–72.

Webster J, Sweett S and Stolz TA (1994) Domestic violence in pregnancy: a prevalence study. *Medical Journal of Australia.* 16.

Weidman A (1986) Family therapy with violent couples. *Social Casework.* 4: 211–8.

Wellard S (2003) Victims on the margins. *Community Care.* 6–12 March, 32.

Western Australia Health Department (1997) *Midwives Notification database.* Western Australia Health Department.

White JW and Koss MP (1993) Adolescent sexual aggression within heterosexual relationships. In Barbaree HE et al (Eds.) op cit.

Widom CS (1989) Does violence beget violence? A critical examination of the literature. *Psychological Bulletin.* 106: 3–28.

Widom CS (1989b) *The intergenerational transmission of violence.* NY: Harry Frank Guggenheim Foundation.

Wierson R, Forehand M and McCombs A (1988) The relationship of early adolescent functioning to parent-reported and adolescent-perceived interparental conflict. *Journal of Abnormal Child Psychology.* 16, 707–18.

Williams OJ, Boggess JL and Carter J (2001) Fatherhood and domestic violence. In

Graham-Bermann SA and Edleson JL (Eds.) *Domestic violence in the lives of children*. Washington DC: American Psychological Association.

Wilson M and Daly M (1987) Risk of maltreatment of children living with step-parents. In Gelles RJ and Lancaster JB (Eds.) *Child abuse and neglect: biosocial dimensions*. NY: Aldine de Gruyter.

Winchester R (2002) Common assault. *Community Care*. 14–20th November, 24–6.

Wolf S (1984) *A multi-factor model of deviant sexuality*. Paper at 3rd International conference on victimology. Lisbon, Portugal, November 1984.

Wolfe DA, Jaffe P, Wilson SK and Zak L (1985) Children of battered women: the relation of child behaviour to family violence and maternal stress. *Journal of Consulting and Clinical Psychology*. 53: 657–65.

Women's Aid (1997) *Women's Aid annual report 1996–7*. Bristol: Women's Aid.

Women's Aid Federation (2001) *Briefing on Child Contact and Domestic Violence. http:// www.womensaid.org.uk* dated 11.10.02

Women's Aid Federation (2003) *Failure to Protect? Domestic Violence and The Experiences of Abused Women and Family Courts – Executive Summary. http://www.womensaid.org.uk* dated 24.11.03.

Wood J, Foy DW, Layne C, Pynoos R and James CB (2002) An examination of the relationships between violence exposure, post-traumatic stress symptomatolgy, and delinquent activity: an 'ecopathological' model of delinquent behaviour among incarcerated adolescents. *Journal of Aggression, Maltreatment and Trauma*. 6 (1): 127–47.

Wraith R (1994) The impact of major events on children. In Watts R and Horne D (Eds.) *Coping with trauma*. Bowen Hills, Queensland: Academic Press.

Yearnshire S (1997) Analysis of cohort. In Bewley S, Friend J and Mezey G (Eds.) *Violence against women*. London: RCOG.

Yllo K and Straus MA (1981) Interpersonal violence among married and cohabiting couples. *Family Relations*. 30: 339–47.

Zorza J (1996) Battered women behave like other threatened victims. *Domestic Violence Report*. 1 (6):

Zorza J (2001) Batterer manipulation and retaliation: denial and complicity in the family courts. *Feminista!* 4 (7): 1–17.